W9-AMN-597

rman Press Agency

Brandt with Günter Guillaume the improbable masterspy and Brandt's nemesis.

Opposite top: 1966—Chancellor-designate Kiesinger and Mayor Brandt meet to work out coalition cabinet.

Opposite middle: 1969—British Prime Minister Harold Wilson, Israeli Prime Minister Golda Meir and Foreign Minister Brandt at the International Congress of Socialist Parties in Eastbourne, England.

Opposite bottom: 1969—Brandt and author, Viola Drath, conferring on his campaign train during the political duel with Chancellor Kiesinger over Party leadership.

Top: 1961—West Berlin Mayor Brandt and Chancellor Adenauer in Berlin.
Bottom: 1963—Mayor Brandt greets President Kennedy on his arrival in Berlin.

United Press International

United Press International

ess and Information Office of the German Republic

German Picture Agency

1970—Chancellor Brandt kneeling at the monument to Warsaw's former ghetto.

Opposite top: 1974—Chancellor Brandt meets with Henry Kissinger in Bonn.

Opposite bottom: 1974—Brandt resigns. Shown here conferring hastily with successor Helmut Schmidt.

German Press Agency

Deutsche Presse Agentur GmbH, Frankfurt/Main

United Press International

United Press International

United Press International

ashington Journal

nited Press International

Brandt with American Presidents

Horstmüller

Bippa/Rota

United Press International

Opposite top: Chancellor Brandt socializes with opera star, Anneliesse Rothenberger, and Mexican Olympic champion, Joseph Neckermann, at a fund-raising "Sports Ball" in 1971.

Opposite middle: Brandt jokes with British TV star Una Stubbs and pop star Cliff Richards (left) during reception at 10 Downing Street.

Opposite bottom: Brandt at White House reception with President and Mrs. Nixon and singing stars, "The Carpenters."

Chancellor Brandt and Soviet Party Chief Leonid Brezhnev during 1971 conference on European Security.

rman Picture Agency

The Many Faces of Willy Brandt

Author's photo

German Information Center

German Information Center

United Press Internatio

man Information Center

erman Press Agency

German Information Center

German Press Agency

Chancellor Brandt and his Norwegian-born wife, Rut, socializing and at home.

United Press International

Simon

German Press Agency

WILLY BRANDT

PRISONER OF HIS PAST

WILLY BRANDT

PRISONER OF HIS PAST

Viola Herms Drath

Chilton Book Company Radnor, Pennsylvania

Published in Radnor, Pennsylvania, by Chilton Book Company
and simultaneously in Don Mills, Ontario, Canada,
by Thomas Nelson & Sons, Ltd.

Designed by Adrianne Onderdonk Dudden

Manufactured in the United States of America

Library of Congress Cataloging in Publication Data

Drath, Viola Herms.
Willy Brandt, prisoner of his past.

Bibliography: p.
Includes index.
1. Brandt, Willy, 1913– 2. Guillaume, Günter, 1926– 3. Germany, West—Politics and government. I. Title.
DD259.7.B7D7 943.087'092'4 75–24964
ISBN 0–8019–6196–3

1 2 3 4 5 6 7 8 9 0 4 3 2 1 0 9 8 7 6 5

Foreword

Willy Brandt has been a notable figure in the political centers of Europe for a quarter of a century. During this time he has become a persuasive advocate of ideas widely acceptable to leaders in capitals as far apart as Washington and Moscow. His resignation as Chancellor of Germany in 1974 does not mean he has no future. Head of the German Socialist Party, and better known to millions as the Mayor of Berlin, Brandt's quick reaction to revelations of scandal and political error has left him with the opportunity to create a new position for himself. Whether he will succeed in achieving this urgent goal cannot be predicted, but he has an important place among the leaders of a changing Europe. He could add a new cohesion among European nations, with Germany still in a major role.

Viola Herms Drath's book, *Willy Brandt,* develops a serious analytical account of the period preceding Brandt's resignation. She also devotes careful attention to the months following May, 1974. She defines the moods and describes the life of a man who has, according to Drath, turned to some extent in the direction of his radical past.

His early years, with a career begun in circumstances far from auspicious, were followed by struggles which widened his perspective. However, his revolutionary activities in Germany, Norway, Sweden, and Spain were somewhat eccentric and did not show promise of an emerging statesman. As Mayor of Berlin he accomodated himself to a considerable degree to the moderate socialism of a capitalist era. He controlled his earlier rebellious characteristics sufficiently so that they were not offensive to the anticommunist, capitalistic-orientated leaders of Washington, London, Brussels, and Paris. So much was this the case that I questioned some of my German socialist friends—including Frau Hannah Reuter, Frau Annedore Leber, Gunther Klein, and Fritz Erler—as to the seriousness of his party ideology.

In the early 1950s, when I was concerned in a responsible way with the reconstruction of Berlin, I knew the history of his past political activities in Norway. I also knew that some of his Socialist rivals did not think him worthy of the tradition or the mantle of his sponsor and teacher, the late Ernst Reuter, former Mayor of Berlin.

Brandt's radical ideas, or any reservations he had about the profit system, in no way interfered with our work together on the restoration of Berlin's industrial capacity. The funds that went into Berlin to conquer unemployment and to restore the operations of its metal, electrical, garment, and other major industries were spent according to familiar capitalist principles, and Marxist-Leninist ideas did not influence our planning together. His dealings with conservative Washington showed pragmatism on his part, but not hypocrisy.

When I sponsored his first trip to the United States as Mayor of Berlin in 1957, and the granting of an honorary degree at the University of Pennsylvania that year, I did not think of Willy as a leftist politician so much as a German patriot. In describing his character and political position to my brother, the late John Foster Dulles, before their first meeting, I could sincerely praise Brandt's contribution to Berlin's recovery and the wholehearted manner in which Brandt and our AID officers had collaborated in building up the city's productive potential. I remember well our conversation in the office of the Secretary of State, when Foster jokingly said that Brandt had infiltrated the American government by winning my confidence.

Portions of this book are very stimulating and provocative; they should lead the reader to serious thoughts, not only to Brandt's role in German politics, but to his future in Europe. If he can keep his charm and persuasiveness and conquer his moody lapses into discouragement, that future could become constructive and creative. His success, if it is within his grasp, calls for serious and continuing effort.

During the years I knew Brandt best, the Germans in Bonn, Berlin, or Munich gave little impression of being greatly concerned over his life as a "swinger." It was known that he had times of overindulgence and a reoccurence of these tendencies could hamper his usefulness and age him prematurely. This possiblity cannot be completely dismissed, but Mrs. Drath is more convinced than I am that these periods of erratic behavior are worth the reader's attention.

In any case he contributed substantially in two major respects. He contributed to the unity of the SPD which was threatened by division as the older leaders disappeared and some of the younger politicians thrashed about seeking the proper course for the future. He also took courageous steps, "little steps," toward normalization of East-West relations in his *Ost-Politik* which did not betray relations with the West. Thus he merited the Nobel Peace Prize.

Brandt is still well liked in Germany and abroad, and his experience should make it possible for him to hold a strong position. There are only a few strong men in Germany, in the democracies, or, for that matter, in the Communist world.

The gap between the Mayor and Chancellor Adenauer was unbridgeable. But in practical matters neither man undermined the policies which made Bonn and Berlin strong. Brandt's relations with Helmut Schmidt, the present Chancellor of Germany, with Herbert Wehner, and with the leading socialists as described by the author correspond to my own. Mrs. Drath's views of Konrad Adenauer do not. Nor do I concur in a suggestion I found in the early part of the text that Brandt was the first German to create good relations between the Federal Republic and the United States. Relations with the former mayors of Berlin, and with Adenauer, Erhard, Kiesinger, even the volatile Franz Joseph Strauss, were cordial and constructive in Washington as well as in Germany. There was a rich heritage there for Brandt to exploit. I agree with her that Brandt has not shown himself to be a creative politician, but he made good use of opportunities others created for him.

In giving these impressions, I recognize some gaps in my knowledge as to the direction and intentions of the SPD and of the young socialists who are trying to dominate the party. Mrs. Drath's text will assist the reader in forming his own opinion about Brandt and the current political condition of Germany. Such information is important to an intelligent outlook on the future of Germany in Europe.

It is essential for young American politicians to understand the significance of these events and of present day Germany to the United States.

There is rich fare and serious analysis in this study of a man who has shown political skill and strength for a number of years, and may again, in Germany and in Europe.

Eleanor Lansing Dulles
May 30, 1975

Contents

Introduction

These multiple reflections—focusing on different facets of Brandt's life and character—hopefully form a mosaic of psychological insights and political data that comprise what one might call an impressionistic portrait. Purposefully ignoring the traditional concepts of biography, this approach yields yet another reward: It tends to illuminate the broad canvas of Brandt's unique human and political environment.

Above all, the Nobel Prize laureate emerges as a lifelong professional party functionary, a product and a creature of his party that has no counterpart in America's mobile democratic political system. His cumbersome rise through the ranks of the tightly structured Social Democrat party hierarchy that makes and breaks its politicians with its absolute control over fifty percent of the nominations for parliament and high offices, and has nearly absolute say in decisions concerning the other half, has no parallel in this country, except, perhaps, in the hierarchic structure of the labor unions with their strict concepts of disciplined solidarity.

The long exhausting march into triumphal power and glory, marked as it is by character-leveling detours and conscious cultivation of a widely visible style—in the manner of Jack Kennedy, after whom Brandt modeled himself for a while—proved to be the relentless journey into the inescapable isolation of a lonely man burnt out and prematurely gone soft and morose.

Contrary to his detractors, there is nothing reprehensible about Brandt's—by any voter's standard—untidy past. Quite the contrary, the politician's long and thorny, meandering road to the top, replete with detours into political radicalism and human blunders, suggests an unchallengeable Socialist constancy and an admirable commitment to social justice.

The sum of our actions that constitute our lives has a way of subtly imprisoning from time to time the most alert among us in the psychological and intellectual patterns set in the past. Instead of freeing Brandt from the complexes accumulated since his early "not easy" childhood that made him the classical outsider of society, regardless of its political stripe or ideological color, by squarely facing up to them, his advisers helped to entrap him in legends, myths and existential inconsistencies. In screening from public view the less endearing episodes of their hero's past, which was to become burdensome only because of these efforts, they created a superman image no politician could have lived up to.

Working in Washington as a foreign correspondent during Watergate and its aftermath was not without beneficial results. The elimination of any traces of power worship, which had revealed itself as pesky sand in the mechanism of democracy, guaranteed a workmanlike approach to politicians and politics. The heightened sense of the general confusion between media visibility and leadership, mainly foisted on the public via instant communication, stifled all temptation to draw easy parallels between Richard Nixon's crisis-ridden struggle from oblivion to his moment in history and the erratic and phenomenal climb and fall of Willy Brandt.

Unlike the poor, psychologically insecure boy from Whittier, the poor, insecure boy from Lübeck, who confessed to not being "a saint," was no crook. His weaknesses, and he indulged in many, counted perhaps among his most lovable assets. The German media certainly knew much more about them than it felt obliged to report. In the desire to enshrine their Willy Brandts, JFKs, LBJs and FDRs, together with other collectors of the female vote, in the traditional fragmented images of neutered, saintly leaders, the media's contribution fully matched the chauvinist attitude of male historians. In bypassing the temptation of a hasty, historical assessment of the Brandt era, with its solid tension-reducing accomplishments in foreign affairs and its ambitious program of inner reforms that provided the country with social impulses whose reverberations were heard and felt even abroad, a close look is taken at the magic Brandt personality.

Cutting through the self-serving Brandt cult with the help of his peers, his friends, his women and his opponents, it became possible to scrutinize the many sentimental legends that have always surrounded this fascinating, scandal-prone political figure. Instinctively aware that legends create insuperable distances between individuals, Brandt rarely tried to discourage them. As a person, Brandt preferred to remain an enigma. Neither his drinking companions nor his female friends pretend to "know" him. None of his numerous political friends have ever gotten close to him.

That the politician who managed to capture the imagination of the world for a brief moment, and even changed it, could be tripped up by a treacherous man named Guillaume, was neither a ludicrous accident nor the result of a sinister plot. Brandt's fall started long before the day the East German spy entered the chancellor's office.

If politics is indeed, as Max Weber has it, a slow drilling of hardwood boards with passion and a sense of measure, then the aging politician may possibly have sacrificed on his uneven way up, one of the main ingredients, tenaciousness.

It is in this human context, in measuring the politician by his own yardstick, that Willy Brandt, whose character became his fate, bears all the earmarks of a tragic figure.

V.H.D.
Washington, August 1975

List of Abbreviations

APO Extraparliamentary opposition. *Ausserparlamentarische Opposition*
BfV Federal Bureau for the Protection of the Constitution (German FBI). *Bundesamt für Verfassungsschutz*
BND Federal Intelligence Service (German CIA) *Bundesnachrichtendienst*
CARE Cooperative for American Relief Everywhere
CDU Christian Democratic Union. *Christlich Demokratische Union*
CIA Central Intelligence Agency (U.S.)
CSCE Conference on Security and Cooperation in Europe
CSU Christian Social Union. *Christlich Soziale Union*
DDR (East) German Democratic Republic. *Deutsche Demokratische Republik*
DKP German Communist Party. *Deutsche Kommunistische Partei*
EEC European Economic Community (Common Market)
EFTA European Free Trade Association
FDP Free Democratic Party *Freie Demokratische Partei*
FRG Federal Republic of Germany. *Bundesrepublik Deutschland*
GDR German Democratic Republic. *Deutsche Demokratische Republik*
Juso Young Socialist (SPD member under 35). *Jungsozialist*
KPD Communist Party of Germany. *Kommunistische Partei Deutschlands*
MfS Ministry of State Security, German Democratic Republic
NAP Norwegian Labor Party
NATO North Atlantic Treaty Organization
OSS Office of Strategic Services (U.S. Precursor of CIA)
POUM United Marxist Labor Party. *Partido Obrero de Unificación Marxista*
PSP Socialist Party of Portugal. *Partido Socialistica Portugues*
SAJ Socialist Workers' Youth. *Sozialistische Arbeiterjugend*
SAP Socialist Workers' Party of Germany. *Sozialistiche Arbeiterpartei Deutschlands*

SDS Socialist German Students' League. *Sozialistischer Deutscher Studentenbund*

SED Socialist Unity Party of Germany (GDR). *Sozialistische Einheitspartei Deutschlands*

SJV Socialist Youth League. *Socialistischer Jugendverband*

SPD Social Democratic Party of Germany. *Sozialdemokratische Partei Deutschlands*

SPÖ Socialist Party of Austria. *Sozialistische Partei Österreichs*

WILLY BRANDT

PRISONER OF HIS PAST

rtr 1

- - b l i t z *' *' *' *' *' *'

bonn -- inoffiziell ; b r a n d t zurueckgetreten
reuter hz/gba 0100 no 7/6/74

1
The Resignation

It is difficult to speak the truth, even though there is only one; for it is alive and therefore has an ever-changing face.

Franz Kafka

It was about 9 P.M. when a drawn, weary Willy Brandt reached for his black, felt-tipped pen to put his signature on the fateful document that brought an end to his reign as Germany's federal chancellor.

The long day of hectic debates by the coalition's leaders had been thoroughly exhausting.

His talk with the federal prosecutor, Siegfried Buback, about the investigation into the Guillaume spy case had proven disheartening. The situation was unchanged.

There was good reason to assume his private life would be dredged up by the opposition press in connection with the Guillaume affair.

Notwithstanding Foreign Minister Scheel's contention that his resignation would have the impact of a "medium earthquake" in foreign affairs, the chancellor, after a series of stormy sessions, had reluctantly come to the realization that few of his trusted political friends and colleagues were particularly eager to block his final exit.

To his official letter of resignation, Brandt attached a private note to outgoing President Gustav Heinemann, who was on a farewell visit to Hamburg:

> It has not been easy for me to write this letter which Horst Grabert is bringing you. But upon mature consideration I had no other choice. Everything has been carefully discussed with Schmidt, Wehner,

> Kühn, Börner, as well as with Scheel and other friends. I will stay in politics, but I must get rid of my present burden. Please, don't be angry, try to understand. . . .

Brandt slumped deep into his chair in front of his ornate baroque desk—it had been Adenauer's—and took a long breath. He did not speak. The skin of his ruggedly handsome face, with the comfortable lived-in look, was flushed. While his closest aides and coworkers were abjectly busying themselves cleaning out drawers in the spacious offices of the Palais Schaumburg to keep from falling apart, Chief of Staff Horst Grabert, acting as the chancellor's courier, was taking off on his mission to Hamburg. Grabert's military aircraft hit Hamburg's busy runway around 11 P.M. Before midnight, President Heinemann accepted the resignation of his friend—without comment. His attempt earlier that week to dissuade Brandt from his "all-round satisfactory solution" was in vain.

Meanwhile, Brandt's crew assembled for the last time in the chancellor's imposing office. Drawing on his legendary willpower, Brandt tried to cheer them up. As they filled their glasses with a robust Mosel wine, the chancellor's attempts at banter and kidding took on an almost eerie quality. "Brandt was so tense and so gay at the same time," one of the participants observed, "that it worried one."

Brandt's tired, unseeing eyes glided over the precious Tintoretto above the moss green settee. The next and fifth chancellor of the Federal Republic would have no taste for such splendor. Within ten days, the palatial atmosphere was replaced by a more masculine, contemporary look induced by black leather, sleek lines, and polished wood. Two exquisite Chagalls, an oil portrait of the Social Democratic party's founder, August Bebel, and a couple of floral pieces by Paula Modersohn were to add a nuance of managerial luxury.

It was after 11 P.M. when Brandt found the strength to face the final farewell. One of the younger secretaries stifled a sob as he made the solemn round of last handshakes. His face an impenetrable mask, he slowly descended the curving marble staircase. For a second he became aware of the painting of Konrad Adenauer in the hall, a startlingly roguish likeness of his favorite adversary, executed by a Kokoschka student in the master's broad colorful brushwork. As Brandt approached the door his features arranged themselves automatically into a ghostly smile—one of his more recent trademarks—for the benefit of the invalid doorman in his glass box.

A few minutes later, an elated Horst Ehmke, Minister of Research, Technology, Post and Communication, returned to the Palais Schaumburg from a television appearance. Brandt's ambitious former chief of staff, responsible for hiring the spy Guillaume, had just told the Germans that there was no reason for him to resign.

Nonplussed over the devastating news of Brandt's letter of resignation, Ehmke started to worry about his mentor. They should not have let Brandt go off by himself in that ultimate state of depression.

—BLITZ

—UNOFFICIAL: BRANDT RESIGNED

REUTER HZ/GBA 0100 5/7/74

"Impossible," gasped the young night editor of one of Bonn's newspapers as the incredible message emerged on the teletype.

"He's finally lost his guts," mumbled an older colleague, shaking his head.

Actually, the sensational news broke ten minutes earlier on the North German radio network. Phones immediately became hopelessly jammed with calls from an unbelieving public.

Within the half hour, the ringing abruptly stopped. The federal press office had issued the official announcement. The speaker, reading from a letter addressed to President Heinemann, tried to keep a steady voice:

". . . I take the political responsibility for negligence in connection with the spy affair Guillaume and declare my resignation from the office of Federal Chancellor."

The resignation of Willy Brandt became effective immediately and his deputy, the amiable Foreign Minister Walter Scheel, took office until a successor could be elected.

The momentous news hit Bonn like lightning. Suddenly the whole complex of high-rise press buildings along Tulpenfeld were ablaze. Hundreds of teletypes started clattering in the night. Thousands of typewriters competed in their tough race for time. Corridors echoed hurried steps and hysterical voices. Elevators passed in a state of perpetual motion.

Bonn's Watergate

Insiders, who had speculated all along about a "bomb," phoned each other out of bed. Now the postponement of the urgent budget debate in Parliament, Scheel's cancelled trip to Brussels, and the continuous meetings of party bigwigs began to make sense. One member of the opposition party had already summed it up in a radio interview: Brandt had "accepted the consequences out of sheer desperation."

But for the time being, the majority of the people seemed to prefer the stab-in-the-back theory: The Nobel Peace Prize winner betrayed and felled by a villainous East German spy was a more compelling, a more Teutonic version.

In Bonn's picturesque market square, flanked by the magnificent baroque facade of the gilt-trimmed, pastel pink stucco city hall, a sizeable crowd gathered during the suspenseful evening hours. As they had been two years before, when Brandt was facing a vote of no confidence in Parliament, the leftist Socialist student organizations were at hand with their demands on behalf of the working class. Among the smiling Willy posters, the Communist newspaper *Red Flag* is distributed with provocative diligence. "Aren't they the same young radicals who are responsible for Willy's troubles?" challenges the owner of a nearby bar angrily. Restlessly, the SPD's Young Socialists rotate about their attractive neo-Marxist leaders. However, neither Heidemarie Wieczorek-Zeul nor Wolfgang Roth are in the mood for rousing protests.

At midnight, a subdued crowd of SPD faithfuls, old and young, carrying flaming torches and hurricane lights, lined up in front of Willy Brandt's official villa on Venusberg, Bonn's most exclusive and expensive residential section.

The elegant, fourteen-room white house, No. 12 Kiefernweg, lies in darkness. Only Huszar, the Brandts' enormous white Hungarian sheepdog, seems to be awake. Some of the party leader's fervent admirers break out in the rhythmic chant: *Willy Brandt, bleib im Amt* (stay in office). But a party official curbs their enthusiasm. "Willy has lived through one of the hardest days of his whole life. Let us give him rest now," he urges. The crowd obeys. They stand in silent solidarity. The solemn tribute to their fallen leader was a touching if impotent gesture.

As the stunning reports from Bonn travel around the world, the high drama enacted along the banks of the placid Rhine was nearly played out. For a few historic moments the provincial capital had indeed become what many self-important German politicians would like to take for granted: the focus, or, better yet, the navel of the world. Soon the laudatory comments from the world's fellow leaders come pouring in. Somehow they never quite understood how the erosion of Brandt's popularity—demonstrated amply by the substantial loss of votes during a number of regional elections—could have occurred so soon after his landslide election victory in 1972. Once more, Brandt was celebrated as a man of vision, a statesman of stature, the good and decent citizen of the "other Germany" who singlehandedly had effected the reconciliation and normalization of relations with the FRG's Eastern neighbors.

There is exuberant praise for the dyed-in-the-wool Democratic Socialist who had dared to ask for "more democracy," the Nobel Peace Prize laureate who had tirelessly worked for peace and the peaceful integration of West Germany into the international framework of the superpowers' détente. No matter whether his famed Ostpolitik [Germany's policy toward the East] proves to be temporary or permanent, a success or a failure, the underlying motivation helped the restoration of trust and moral credit in a progressive democratic society such as the Federal Republic of Germany had not quite experienced before.

Jens Otto Krag, ex–prime minister of Denmark, who has known Brandt since 1947 and who nominated him for the Nobel Peace Prize, rates Ostpolitik "as a necessary part of détente." Krag contends that "European affairs were in a bad state," with Europeans still hating the Germans, before the advent of Brandt's reconciliation policy. Besides, Ostpolitik had defused the explosive Berlin situation.

"Considering the limitations a person in high office faces, most of us find that we have a very narrow field to work in," Krag, Head of the Delegation of the Commission of the European Communities, told me in a conversation in his Washington office during the spring of 1975. "Brandt's contribution was made in three areas. Firstly, he established the SPD as a viable alternative in democratic Germany. Secondly, he initiated an East–West policy that certainly is here to stay. By keeping the lines open to the United States and using his connections in Europe's Northern countries, Brandt neatly fitted his policy into the Western cooperative effort. Thirdly, he contributed greatly to the reduction of anti-German sentiment. If the Danes, who have shared boundaries with the Germans for centuries, have changed from their very anti-German attitude, it is because of Brandt and his shift in policies. Both played a big part in their decision to come into the Common Market."

Fervent anti-Nazi Willy Brandt symbolized and projected the moral fortitude necessary to come to terms with Germany's bitter heritage of World War II as he determinedly set out to heal the wounds in the East. This, and his distaste for military power politics, had greatly contributed to the new wave of sincere esteem and respect the country was enjoying abroad.

Among the well-wishers, anguished voices can be distinguished. Sweden's Socialist premier, Olof Palme, angrily accuses the East Germans of "blatant ignobleness," blaming the Communist leaders for manipulating the chancellor's fall. The East Germans in turn blamed the inner conflicts in Brandt's administration for the crisis —"not the blown-up espionage affair."

Jean Lecanuet, chairman of France's Democratic Centrist party, for once agrees with Palme. "What we experience in Germany today is proof that a socialist party at an opportune moment inevitably falls victim to communism," he warns. Budapest newspapers, on the other hand, see Brandt as victim of a right-wing smear campaign. TASS, the Soviet Union's news agency, devotes a mere six lines to Brandt's resignation.

Commentators determined to interpret the events in Bonn in a wider international context are not in short supply. After all, the spring of 1974 had seen a long succession of Western governments in a continuous state of crisis. Only in France has the change of administration been triggered by natural causes, the death of President Georges Pompidou. Was there a linkage, a chain reaction between the difficulties the English, Belgian, Italian, Icelandic, and Canadian—not to speak of the American and Greek—governments were experiencing? Or the capitulation of Golda Meir in Israel?

Could it be, as the elaborate sociopolitical studies of the advocates of Marxist dialectical materialism contend, that western capitalism was indeed doomed to crack up on its built-in contradictions? For the time being, analysis of the various causes for elements of instability in the democracies suggests multiple conclusions.

The lid is kept on

"All historic experience affirms that one would not attain the possible, if in this world the impossible would not be reached for again and again," Max Weber wrote. Did Willy Brandt reach for the impossible? Or did he stumble into the snares and pitfalls embedded in his own character?

The chancellor's hurried and totally unexpected resignation had all the makings of a major scandal. Laced with a genuine East German spy at his elbow—no doubt controlled by KGB spymasters in the Kremlin and under quiet observation by the CIA—a generous dose of sex, political blackmail, party intrigue, and any number of speculations about the "real" reasons for the fall, it could have equaled Washington's Watergate or London's celebrated Profumo affair. In Bonn the lid was kept on. German investigative reporting is largely left to the lowly tabloids. The dignified gentlemen of the press frown on peeping through keyholes. They prefer chiseling away at personalities with finely crafted editorials. For all the public chastizing and shouting there is a private give-and-take relationship between the power and the press which neither is quite prepared to jeopardize.

During a media conference in Bitburg, the danger of a "unionized databank of good behaviour" for journalists was one of the topics under discussion. Of all the media, the public radio and TV networks, which are subject to varying degrees of governmental control, displayed the least inclination to practice the "adversary advocacy" so cherished by the American media.

Although Bonn had been filled with the wildest rumors after the arrest of Brandt's personal aide, charged with being a spy from East Berlin, nobody imagined the true dimensions of the incident or its impact on Bonn's political landscape.

The spy who came from East Berlin

Stocky, humble, middlebrow Günter Guillaume, Brandt's ever-present personal aide and shadow, in charge of liaison between the chancellor and the Social Democrats' headquarters, was arrested on April 24, 1974, on his return from a vacation in southern France. In the hope of a quick exchange for West German political prisoners, he promptly revealed his identity. His name was Günter Karl Heinz Guillaume, born in 1927 in Berlin, an officer in East Germany's People's Army and an espionage agent for the German Democratic Republic's Ministry of State Security (MfS).

With his wife Christel, who was also in the service of the Ministry of State Security, he had come to West Germany in 1956 in the guise of a refugee who had left the "Soviet zone" because life there did not correspond to his "ideals of freedom." As a trusted aide to the chancellor, who—according to the press—on occasion supplied his boss with his slippers and female companions, he was in an excellent spot to acquire knowledge of state secrets.

The incomprehensible thing was that Guillaume had come under suspicion of being an agent during a routine security check of top government officials at the time he was hired in January 1970 in the chancellory's economic policy planning department. Although the personnel council advised the chancellor's chief of staff, Horst Ehmke, against hiring Guillaume because his lack of qualification could lead to the accusation that he was selected for the job purely on the basis of his party connections . . . although Berlin's chief of police informed Bonn of the "suspicion of agent's activities" in West Berlin, dating back to a report by the investigative committee of the "Free Jurists" in 1955 . . . although General Gerhard Wessel, head of the Federal Intelligence Service (BND, the German CIA) advised against Guillaume's employment in the chancellor's office on principle, while suggesting to Ehmke a personal interview with the subject . . . although Egon Bahr, state secretary in the chancellor's office and chief negotiator of the East treaties, told Ehmke "even if you have a positive impression [of Guillaume] a certain security risk remains" —the investigation by the Federal Bureau for the Protection of the Constitution (BfV, the German FBI) was soon suspended.

Undoubtedly the findings of the Free Jurists would have been taken less lightly had the organization been noted for leftist leanings instead of its right-wing position. Brandt and his circle were so conditioned to ignoring the statements of right-wing groups that the Free Jurists' charges were dismissed from sheer habit.

The obliging functionary advanced rapidly in the citadel of power. In Febuary 1973 he was promoted right into the chancellor's office. Presumably he and his boss would have remained there for years to come had it not been for a suspicious investigator at the BfV who became increasingly disturbed by the fact that he came across the name Guillaume in three different espionage cases. The last case, involving an East German informer couple named Sieberg, prompted him to report his suspicion to his superior in April 1973. As executive secretary of the SPD's Frankfurt subdistrict, Guillaume had hired the German Democratic Republic (GDR) agent, Ingeborg Sieberg, as secretary for the party's press office in 1965. The investigation of contacts and comparison of dates led to the top secret recommendation that the Guillaumes be put under observation.

Some eleven months before the spy's apprehension, the president of BfV informed his chief, Minister of the Interior Hans-Dietrich Genscher, of the grave but unsubstantiated accusations against the chancellor's aide. Genscher, in turn, saw "no way out of informing Chancellor Brandt." On May 30, 1973, Brandt was briefed in strictest confidence. But because of the "vagueness" of the charges and an apparent lack of hard evidence, Guillaume was left in his delicate position. Secretly, in the hope of uncovering a spy ring and other contacts, the BfV launched an all-out investigation. Only Brandt's top officials were appraised of the preventive measures, one of which was to keep top secret documents away from Guillaume.

"Had I known at that time what the BfV people already knew then, Guillaume would not have stayed in my immediate surroundings," Brandt told friends after the catastrophe. According to other sources, however, the East German MfS supposedly tipped off the West German security people about Guillaume by accident. This leads to speculation about the timing and the nature of the alleged blunder.

Actually, French sources claim that the Service de Documentation Exterieure et de Contre-Espionnage was onto Guillaume since December 1973 when an employee of the state bank fled East Germany and revealed the existence of the spy's special account fattened by monthly deposits of his officer's salary. Supposedly the list of such special secret accounts totals some 5000.

Never had a spy come so close to the inner sanctum of power. During the Four Power Agreement negotiations on Berlin, the Allies were often stupefied by the detailed advance knowledge the Soviet negotiators had of their overall planning. It seemed as though they were playing with marked cards. Guillaume, of course, was also privy to the secret preparations for the sensitive renunciation-of-force treaties with Moscow and Warsaw.

There still is no way of assessing even roughly the political and strategic advantages the officials of the German Democratic Republic might have extracted from their listening post at the source during the difficult talks about the Basic Treaty, conducted by Brandt's special minister Egon Bahr. Guillaume knew precisely how flexible or inflexible Bonn's position was on the points under discussion. He knew the soft spots, the logistics, and the strength of psychological resistance.

An enlightening comment is found in the attempt of Erich Honecker, first secretary of East Germany's Socialist Unity (Communist) party, to justify intelligence work in Bonn even during accelerated negotiations. On the twentieth birthday of the Ministry of State Security, in February 1970, at the Friedrichstadt Palace in East Berlin, he explained:

> In the old days, the imperialists could scheme and plot behind the scenes. They could talk peace in public while actually preparing for war. Today, these security agencies of ours are helping to expose the mystery of what causes war. Their courageous efforts are making us familiar with West German revanchist plans so that the public may be alerted. Here our comrades in the state security services are making a true contribution to peace.

Profile of the Improbable Masterspy

Guillaume had no higher education. The report of the investigative Commission for the Examination of Security Questions, issued November 1974, shows that his father, a musician, committed suicide in 1948. His mother, who had been a hairdresser, had remarried. Now retired from a job as a postal clerk, she lives in East Berlin. Young Guillaume was trained as a photographer.

Rumor has it that he learned his trade from no other than Hitler's court photographer and personal friend, Heinrich Hoffmann, an acquaintance of his father's, who allegedly urged him to become a member of the Nazi party on Hitler's fifty-fifth birthday, April 20, 1944. Thanks to influential Hoffmann, so the story goes, the lad escaped military service. He nevertheless emerged from a British prisoner-of-war camp at the end of the war.

An avid collector of Hoffmann's photos of Nazi luminaries, he tried to sell his treasures to the Soviets. Instead of offering cold cash, they promoted occasional assignments for him in Soviet-controlled newspapers. Officially he was a free-lance photographer until he landed a job as photo editor at the Communist publishing house *Volk und Wissen,* which had served as a front and a platform for a number of GDR spies before they were sent off on assignments in the West.

What the spymasters who trained Guillaume as an informer at the MfS intelligence center in Potsdam-Eiche must have liked best about their student was that he appeared average in every respect. A perfect John Doe, he was equipped with a natural camouflage that predestined him to go unnoticed in his espionage activities.

To this day, Brandt cannot imagine that the lowbrow "bore" was capable of scheming to manipulate his way into the chancellor's office. He and his circle are convinced that Günter Guillaume's arrival at the topmost spot was nothing but "sheer accident." In their opinion, the flap was entirely due to lack of exact coordination and cooperation between the BND and the BfV, as well as other bureaucratic idiosyncrasies.

The Guillaumes had settled in Frankfurt. They ran a typing service that also handled mimeographing and photocopying, and they helped Christel's mother with her coffee shop. Guillaume worked in a construction office and on production in a textbook publishing house. As a photojournalist, he prepared election campaign material for the SPD Hesse–South district and contributed regularly to its monthly publication.

He had joined the party in November 1957. He was willing to work at licking envelopes and other boring tasks. Becoming known for his reliability and organizing proficiency, he also left the impression of really being down on communism. In 1964, his loyal eagerness was rewarded with the executive secretary's job for the subdistrict. His wife served as secretary. Four years later, the new party functionary had risen to the post of executive secretary to the SPD municipal assembly caucus in Frankfurt, much to his own surprise, he admitted during his trial.

Meanwhile, his first important contact was established. Georg Leber, Minister of Traffic, member of the SPD presidium, ex-chief of the construction workers' union and of working-class background, took a liking to the conscientious, self-educated party worker. He let him organize his campaign in 1969. Through Leber, Guillaume met another important member of the party, Dr. Herbert Ehrenberg. The ambitious, fast-talking economist was slated for a top position in the SPD chancellor's office. Before long, Ehrenberg found a desk in his department at the Palais Schaumberg for the handy functionary from Frankfurt.

The fact that Guillaume's cover was finally blown was "due to the special prudence of some of the BfV officials," the investigating commission's report stated. The commission was uncommonly critical of the highhanded manner in which Ehmke and his officials dismissed the warning signals that reached them in December 1969. Because of "time pressure," officials in the chancellor's office "obviously underestimated the significance of the security checkup." The commission also noted that the "personal involvement of the chief of staff [Ehmke] in the examining process did not affect it favorably."

The forty-six-year-old Guillaume kept a well-informed mistress or two, usually the secretary of a high official or minister dealing with East-West affairs. His favorite courier was his wife, Christel. Top secret material was handcarried by her to Amsterdam or East Berlin.

While Bonn government sources, after his exposure, tried vainly to belittle Guillaume's role in the chancellor's office as that of an insignificant employee, the boulevard press was having a heyday. In its fattest headlines readers were informed of the escalating scandal: for instance, thanks to Guillaume's treachery, at least twenty-four West German agents had been arrested in East Germany by the secret service. The clever spy allegedly stole the list of Bonn's hundred top agents right from under the nose of the Federal Republic's security guards. On May 3, *Bild* came up with an even bigger and more intriguing heading: *Bahr's Secretary Mistress of Spy.* Egon Bahr, of course, was chief treaty negotiator.

Passing the buck

Brandt's coalition government found itself face to face with a crisis it could ill afford. Implementing its first impulse to hush up the whole unsavory affair, Research and Postal Minister Horst Ehmke demanded an end to all public discussion of the spy case for reasons of national security. The career-conscious former law professor had good cause for concern. As Brandt's former chief of staff he bore the responsibility for hiring Guillaume, on Leber's and Ehrenberg's recommendations as a hard-working party member.

Ehmke did not believe in having his brilliant career stifled by a mere spy. He neatly passed the buck to Günther Nollau, head of the BfV, which is under the jurisdiction of Interior Minister Hans-Dietrich Genscher. But Genscher, prospective chairman of the Free Democrats, did not feel responsible either. The charges and countercharges flying between the two politicians created a climate of hostility that put a severe strain on the coalition.

When he learned that neither of his ministers was willing to assume responsibility for the disastrous Guillaume affair, Brandt retreated into one of his frequent brooding spells. He took it as a personal offense that Honecker and especially East Germany's Premier Stoph, with whom he had met in Erfurt and Kassel, would plant a spy in his office. He had extended hope and goodwill and they had in effect whipped him with the olive branch.

Why Honecker's "diplomatic precautions" were so incomprehensible to Brandt is not altogether clear. As a refugee from Norway he had been fully exposed to the intrigue-filled hothouse atmosphere of Communist and Allied espionage and Nazi counterespionage in Stockholm during the war years, when the Scandinavian capital was the unchallenged world center of organized conspiracies, agents provocateur, and simple information-gathering activities.

Chancellor Brandt's last ordeal was only beginning. Soon he would have different and even graver reasons for despair.

Once under arrest, Guillaume kept silent. The red-faced criminal investigators were forced to respect his honor as an officer in the People's Army. By tracing his steps, however, they soon struck gold. Undeniable evidence existed that the master spy, theoretically under observation since May 29, 1973, by the BfV, nevertheless had managed to get access to top secret NATO documents, including communications from President Nixon, during Brandt's annual vacation.

"There are times when one is spared nothing," a bitter Brandt told the Bundestag on April 26, 1974. Denouncing the manner in which the "SED state" had demonstrated its hostility toward the SPD chairman he assured his audience that Guillaume's activities did not entail working with secret records. The press soon found out that Brandt was wrong.

In his diary notes of that day, Brandt offered the following explanation of the incident: "I thought of his normal work in the chancellor's office—when I made my remarks before the Bundestag I was not conscious of the special case, when during the summer vacation in Norway in 1973 secret teletypes indeed passed through his hands."

Before suspicions were aroused, Guillaume had been scheduled to accompany the chancellor and his family to their Norwegian summer retreat near Hamar. Nollau and his boss, Minister Genscher, thought it best not to change these arrangements for fear the spy might learn about his having been discovered and their efforts to trap him. By agreeing to this cat-and-mouse game, Brandt virtually became his own counterspy.

As a precautionary measure, it was planned to route all top secret messages through the German embassy in Oslo, which would then transmit the decoded messages directly to the chancellor. The elaborate communications center at a nearby youth hostel would be used for press information only. There was, however, a flaw in the plan. Brandt's chief assistant, Reinhard Wilke, also going on vacation, neglected to inform his deputy of these arrangements. He later stated that he did not think this necessary since Guillaume was covered by Nollau's security people. Incredibly, Guillaume was not under observation during this trip. The security agents in Brandt's entourage were not informed of Guillaume's role either. The secret messages went to the youth hostel center after all and were decoded on the spot. The absurd scene when security men hand them to the eagerly waiting Guillaume for delivery to Brandt was worthy of the best of Laurel and Hardy flicks.

The Chancellor's compromising appointment book

There are other tragicomic aspects to this curious spy scandal. In order to find out which important conversations the spy might have overheard and reported to his East German masters, the chancellor's appointment book was carefully scrutinized, the visitor list checked and rechecked. The log, it was noted, contains a number of extraordinarily long, drawn-out interviews with lady journalists and female workers during campaign trips. The startling details of the activities in the chancellor's elegantly appointed railway salon car were filled in during the interrogation of his own security bodyguards. The tiny

German capital's best kept secret, known to Bonn's journalists all along, was suddenly in the open. Brandt, the idolized father figure of the last elections, the peacemaker ennobled by the Nobel Prize, was also a ladies' man.

"I am not a saint on a pedestal," was his sheepish defense at a Berlin conference after the storm. Anyone in close contact with Willy had to become aware, sooner or later, of his love for whiskey and women. More than once, reference to these weaknesses was made with profound contempt by Herbert Wehner, the Social Democratic party's puritanical strong man.

Despite his sixty-one years, thinning hair and increasing bulk, the introverted Brandt, who could be the loneliest man in a crowd at formal receptions and banquets, was still attractive to women, especially those turned on by power or the promise of masculine prowess. There were distinct vibrations of vitality and virility about him which voters and women alike found hard to resist. By nature introspective, with a certain propensity toward the mystic, uptight over a bundle of insecurities acquired in childhood and youth, and mistrustful of his fellow men because of his colorful life's experience, he found the company of women stimulating and relaxing at the same time. "Women give one courage," he once observed.

As one gets to know Brandt, one finds that his many references to his "friends" are but a subconscious cover for an utter lack of intimates. He has associates, drinking companions, and esteemed colleagues, but no friends. "I never had anyone who was really close to me," he once confided. Conditioned by a lonely boyhood, he finds it difficult to open up to other people, to share his feelings, and to exchange reserve for trust.

A man trapped by the deeply ingrained psychological makeup formed of the anxieties an outsider of bourgeois society learns to suffer and bear—which in turn account for inscrutable emotional complexities, intense moodiness, and the most perplexing mixture of stubborn consistency and tractability—Brandt grew up as a virtual exile in Lübeck long before he ever went into exile in Norway. Considered a loner by his mother and in his own party, the statesman who had liberated his countrymen by compelling them to come to terms with the trauma of their past never quite managed to crash the human alienation barrier that kept him prisoner of his own past.

Through proper bureaucratic channels, the criminal investigator's explosive disclosures about Brandt's love life made their way to the Department of Justice, the Minister of the Interior and, not surprisingly, to key members of the opposition. On the evening of April 30, Justice Minister Gerhard Jahn dutifully placed a phone call to Hamburg's luxurious Atlantic Hotel to inform his chief of the unforeseen turn of events. Brandt, in town to address a traditional May Day labor union rally of 30,000, was severely disturbed. When Genscher awakened him the following morning with even more of the sordid details, he immediately understood the proportions of his embarrassing dilemma.

Brandt's private life and background have always been shrouded in a veil of mystery. He has done little to illuminate the grey areas of that background. After all, legends—and he was by now a living legend—are nourished by speculation, not by precise data. Even the origins of his Ostpolitik, for the most part negotiated in secret, remain opaque. Although this is disputed by SPD officials, the first feelers he extended toward the Eastern bloc with the help of Italian Communists back in 1967 were virtually undercover jobs, concealed even from Chancellor Kiesinger.

In dazed depression, Brandt follows through with the scheduled trip to the island of Helgoland. His wardrobe, blue pants with an ill-matching grey jacket, betrays his state of mind as well as the absence of Guillaume, who would not have tolerated such a costume. The absent aide is very much on Brandt's mind. To one of the reporters he confides that he did not even especially care for Guillaume. The man struck him as not particularly bright, at best limited, without the keen intelligence of his predecessors. Brandt seems to have considerable difficulty in picturing Guillaume's humble talents as the routine cover of a skilled espionage agent. As an escape from the overpowering gloom he stays up late that night, linking arms with Helgoland's Social Democrats, drinking, and singing chanteys. But there are moments when he can no longer contain his disgust. "Shitty life," he curses.

Between toughing it out and resignation

During the next tortured days, when Brandt alternately worried that he might have been "too credulous," and fumed against the people in the GDR who had paid him back in the worst way for his honest efforts to reduce the tensions between the two German states, he was torn between fits of defeatist self-pity and fighting outrage.

Militantly assuring an audience in Wilhelmshaven that he will not stop exercising his right to pursue the "necessary brand of politics because somebody has put a louse in my fur" on May 2, his spirits are down the next day. The result of a quick poll did not lift the general gloom: 63 percent of the persons asked thought much damage was done by the GDR spy; 47 percent thought the persons responsible should resign.

Back in Bonn on May 3, during a luncheon at the Palais Schaumberg with his most intimate advisors, Brandt drops the first ominous hint of the possibility of his resignation. Minister Egon Bahr, his aides Reinhard Wilke and Wolf-Dietrich Schilling, Horst Grabert, and his two press officers are not sure what to make of his veiled allusions, although it was becoming apparent that the chief was looking for a quick way to head off the escalating scandal.

Between talks with Portugal's Socialist leader Mario Soares about the fall of Salazar's half-century old authoritarian regime and discussions of the 1975 budget, Brandt surprises Helmut Schmidt with the offhand remark that he should "count on the chancellorship suddenly coming his way."

In a telephone conversation, Brandt shares his thoughts on resignation with President Heinemann. Heinemann advises him to sleep on it. But there is no more rest. Franz Josef Strauss, the indestructible and vociferous chairman of the Bavarian Christian Social Union is shooting his famous irony-drenched arrows.

It was Strauss—also known as a man with an extraordinary fondness for the girls—who, when Brandt's railroad car gallantry surfaced in the press later in May, was to comment in mock admiration: "Respect, respect!" It came as a severe shock to Brandt and his almost archaic, nineteenth-century sense of dignity that he had become the target of the most squalid jokes. While the smiling Willy liked to laugh, especially at his own unsophisticated humor, he could never bear to be the object of ridicule.

That evening, Brandt huddles once more with his friends. Egon Bahr, often cited as the architect of Brandt's Ostpolitik, and Günter Gaus, former editor of the opinion-molding *Spiegel* and first West German diplomatic representative to East Germany, together with

Holger Börner, SPD executive secretary, and Karl Ravens, parliamentary state secretary, are not in an enviable position. They discuss a drastic reshuffling of the cabinet and decide that such an alternative would work only if the party were not on a losing streak. In the end these men are obliged to concede that they have run out of options. The stagnating reforms, the energy crisis, and Wehner's showy attacks from Moscow on the chancellor's indecisiveness were unlikely to be cancelled out by neutralizing the powerful Wehner or the recalcitrant Schmidt, who had openly downgraded Brandt during the spring election campaign. It would be impossible to fire Ehmke as the party responsible for hiring the spy without also ousting Hans-Dietrich Genscher and BfV president Günther Nollau for their inglorious parts in handling the spy affair. Nollau was Wehner's untouchable intimate; Minister of the Interior Genscher was slated to be chairman of the Free Democratic party (FDP). If he were jettisoned, it would have meant the end of the coalition.

All of them were well aware of Professor Dahrendorf's remarks that there was no compelling need to keep the fortunes of his small Free Democratic party tied to those of Brandt's downward spiralling Social Democratic party. The independent Dahrendorf, known to say what others think, coolly pointed out to the coalition partners that the SPD's unchecked inflation and narrowly ideologized economic policy was driving a substantial part of the voters into the arms of the conservative opposition. The FDP had been highly critical of SPD reforms, especially after the party's reversals at recent elections.

"I could well imagine the FDP in the opposition," the professor concluded, adding diffidently that it would, of course, tolerate a Social Democratic minority government.

This came as a low blow. Chancellor Brandt and his friends remembered only too well the FDP's part in the toppling of Ludwig Erhard and his government in 1966. The versatile FDP had simply pulled out of the coalition with the Christian Democratic Union and its Bavarian sister party, the Christian Social Union (CDU/CSU), leaving the government to its instant collapse. Brandt and his top advisers agreed: a defection of the FDP must be avoided at all costs. The weakened SPD could hardly survive such a break.

WEHNER'S VERDICT

Brandt's next conversation partner is undoubtedly the most forceful one. Herbert Wehner, the Social Democrats' powerful mastermind, chief strategist, evil genius, prima donna, old-time comrade-in-arms and antagonist, is not in a cheerful mood. Wehner, of course, had known about Brandt's dalliances for a long time. With a vast private intelligence network at his disposal, a useful hobby apparently carried over from his training in Moscow's Comintern many decades ago, there was no way of estimating the many facts and secrets this determined man might have stored away in his mistrusting mind. The grim-looking party functionary, who has never quite outlived the stigma of his Communist past, came right to the point. Instead of luxuriating in his outrageous sarcasms as usual, he examines the alternatives: Brandt could stay in office and remain party chairman; he could give up the chancellorship or both offices. Thanks to Nollau, Wehner was fully familiar with the contents of the depositions witnesses had given to criminal investigators. Brandt, in a sense, was Wehner's discovery. He had actively promoted and supported his candidacy for chancellor since 1960, had "built him up," as Brandt's detractors maintain.

Wehner paints the bleakest of prospects. The opposition press would make the most of calumny and slander, he warns. Brandt's escapades would be linked to the lurid stories about the sex life of the porno-loving spy. Brandt's playmates would be all over the front pages. Guillaume might even have taken compromising photos. They could turn up anytime anywhere. After cracking the morality whip for the sake of the party and the survival of the coalition, he falls silent. There is no doubt where he stands.

Brandt could not count on Wehner to help him out of this crisis.

In the guest house of the Social Democrats' Friedrich Ebert Foundation in Bad Münstereifel, a number of party and labor union leaders are waiting for Willy Brandt that Saturday. The scheduled topic for discussion: inflation and the instability of the mark.

But soon a more urgent matter takes precedence. The heated dispute over the mismanagement of the Guillaume affair by the government reveals that few of the union leaders present are averse to Brandt's resignation.

When Brandt talks of his "almost firm" decision to resign late that night, the comrades Börner and Ravens try to talk him out of it. "They apparently assume that the increasing adversities since the beginning of the past year have broken my spirit," Brandt writes in his diary on the fateful weekend of May 4–5, 1974. "I will not completely exclude this. Who is able to come up with a full accounting of himself? At any rate I cannot deny, next to mistakes, conditional weaknesses."

Brandt is much too formal a person to entrust his innermost thoughts and motivations for firming up his decisions to a diary, especially one designed to go public.

The historic event takes place on Sunday afternoon in the innermost circle of party leaders and confidants. Only Schmidt, party deputy chairman, finance minister, and nominated heir, argues strenuously for toughing it out. At least Brandt should hold off until Monday, when President Heinemann and the FDP leadership could be consulted and informed. Schmidt, whose eye has been on the chancellorship for a long time, definitely does not want to make history as a chancellor killer.

"At least remain as party chairman," he pleads when the die is cast. "Only you are able to care for the party, I cannot do that."

For a moment Willy Brandt stares at the dapper, pipe-puffing Schmidt in utter amazement. He remembers with great clarity Schmidt's scathing remarks, just a couple of months ago, about the desolate condition of the party because of Brandt's "slovenly" leadership.

Like the stunned bystanders at the scene of an accident, different participants remember different things. Wehner maintains that it was not Schmidt but he who objected to Brandt's resignation. But Brandt distinctly remembers Wehner's stony silence.

"Perhaps he was struck silent with consternation," he told me during his visit to Washington eleven months after the enactment of the drama, his voice tingling with cynicism. Contrary to the others, he does not remember the chairmanship of the party as a subject under discussion.

When Venusberg neighbor Walter Scheel strolls over to No. 12 Kiefernweg that Sunday evening, Brandt has already drafted his letter of resignation to President Heinemann. Scheel, who reads it, advises against such a drastic step. Worried about the fate of the coalition, the pragmatic chairman of the FDP tries to convince his colleague not to resign because of the Guillaume trifle.

"We'll sit this one out on one side of our behind," he says comfortingly. Concerned about his upcoming election as president, he does not relish anybody rocking the boat at this crucial juncture in his career. In this day and age, nobody thinks twice about a politician's sex life, he asserts.

Scheel, the urbane Rhinelander, nevertheless managed to turn a deaf ear to hints of his own renunciation of the presidency for Willy Brandt's sake. In his luckier and more powerful days, Brandt had turned down the office which under present circumstances would have provided a face-saving retreat.

The intelligence agencies' snafu

Brandt is in a stupor. The unrelenting pressure of the last six days had taken its toll. The chain of disappointments, human and professional, filled him with disgust and a profound despair. The people who had not let him down could be counted on the fingers of one hand. Worst of all, the whole mess was not altogether the result of his own misjudgments. Yet it was conceivable that he was subject to blackmail, and not only by Guillaume. Of course, he maintained, he had "nothing to hide" when he insisted that he too had a "right for protection of his personal sphere." He would never again be able to talk to Stoph, Honecker, or any other representative of East German officialdom with the same candor, the same lack of restraint.

The idea of his own security people, those in charge of his protection, spying on him was infuriating.

"They were unable to catch a spy, but they were quite able to spy on my private life and embellish it," he angrily charged later. Sharing the incriminating data with members of the opposition party constituted for Brandt the ultimate insult. Genscher had given him bad advice by proposing to keep Guillaume on his staff for observation. The public would have its doubts about a chancellor's double duty as counteragent.

"My reaction was wrong," he admitted in an interview with *Stern* magazine. "For that, I have to take responsibility."

It was, of course, well known that the three rival security agencies built up during twenty years of Christian Democratic and Christian

Social Union reign, were well stocked with members of the opposition and their sympathizers. Had Brandt's former chief of staff's attempt at a shake-up of key personnel backfired? Had the agencies taken their revenge on the Social Democratic chancellor for Ehmke's zealous housecleaning in 1970? The answer to these questions is no.

Second man in the *Bundesnachrichtendienst* (BND), once known as the famed Gehlen organization, was Dieter Bloetz, a Social Democrat. The BfV's Nollau was Wehner's friend and protégé. The head of the Federal Criminal Bureau was a long-time party member.

Who had betrayed whom?

Willy Brandt's concern was not prompted by incipient paranoia. The public statement by opposition leader Karl Carstens to the effect that the leadership of the CDU/CSU probably had better information on the Guillaume case than the administration, nourished further suspicions in Bonn. On the basis of "reliable information," Strauss was the first politician to accuse Brandt of lying to parliament by declaring Guillaume had no access to top secret information. Strauss knew better: "All coded and uncoded messages sent to Norway were initialed by Guillaume."

In his eloquent denial of a secret feedback to the CDU/CSU, Strauss initially contradicted himself by maintaining that Ehmke was only "believed" to have rendered the agencies free of CDU/CSU influence.

Had there indeed been interplay between the security agencies and the opposition? Carstens subtly shifts ground. In his opinion, the entire responsibility rests with the person who hired Guillaume despite the cautioning of the BND.

"Since Minister Ehmke was chief of staff in the chancellor's office at that time, he indubitably is responsible," he charges. "Mr. Ehmke has violated the time proven principles of personnel policy. This caused very serious disadvantages for the Federal Republic."

By putting party politics before professional and security requirements in hiring Guillaume, Ehmke was negligent in his duties. Carstens demands his resignation.

The chancellor does not see it that way. Ehmke had tendered his resignation at one time, but Brandt's sense of fairness would not tolerate this course of action while Genscher remained in office. And Genscher—a heavy-set man of imposing girth with a grim determination to occupy Scheel's chair in the Foreign office—will not budge without pressure and, for the sake of the coalition, pressure could not be applied.

Everybody had passed the buck and the buck stopped at the top. Brandt felt emotionally drained after he had made the historic decision. Or had he made it?

THE DRAMA'S FINAL ACT

Willy Brandt's reputation was not built on his decisiveness. Monday, May 6, is a day just about everybody in Brandt's inner circle would like to erase from the calendar. During the vicious haggling over top cabinet posts, prestige and power, Churchill's observation about democracy being the worst form of government except for all others becomes a genuine experience.

In the endless sessions of the coalition's top officials, a committee of six, Brandt pursues two objectives: a smooth transition of government into the hands of Schmidt and the continued chairmanship of the Social Democrat party for himself. Passing second thoughts about retaining the chancellorship are brutally dispelled by a prodigious lack of encouragement. While Brandt's party chairmanship is not in jeopardy at the moment, he is not unaware of Wehner's random remarks about his excellent qualifications for other situations: the chairmanship of the Socialist Internationale, the position of Minister of European Affairs, or the Secretary-General's chair at the United Nations. Neither has he forgotten Schmidt's biting criticism that the party was on the verge of disintegration under Chancellor Brandt. He will not be eased out.

Settling on the efficient Schmidt as successor causes no problems. Schmidt has no rival. But the wrangling and jockeying for advantageous positions by the coalition partners tends to turn into a series of filibusters and shouting matches. Schmidt's opinion of Genscher, his vice president and foreign minister designate, a politician without experience in foreign affairs or the command of a single foreign language, is well known. Yet even the dynamic Schmidt, the "Mr. Can Do," with a justified reputation for bending things to his will, is unable to convince Scheel to stay on with the new team. Scheel, who would be acting chancellor until Schmidt's official election by the Federal Assembly, a mere formality since the SPD/FDP coalition had the majority vote, prefers the ceremonial role of president.

Schmidt, with his keen respect for power, cannot understand why.

In the end, arguments are resolved by compromise for the sake of solidarity. The automatic political process with its businesslike routine has calmed the emotions and taken the edge off the crisis.

In the evening Scheel, as acting chancellor, conducts his first meeting with the parliamentary floor leaders. His announcement of the premature end of the Brandt era comes as shocking but not entirely unexpected news.

The next morning in Bonn is as bleak and grey as the outlook for the Social Democrats. The general temper in the Bundeshaus—a confusing labyrinth of a former teachers' college, serving as a house of parliament since 1949—resembles that of the stock market on the day a new bottom is reached. The worried politicians who hurry from committee meetings to TV interviews and from the hot floodlights back into heated conferences, hardly notice the misty, penetrating rain.

At 9 A.M. sharp, the dispirited members of Brandt's cabinet assemble for the last time around the oval table with its unique centerpiece: a four-faced clock, a gift from Adenauer, who had been an avid antique clock collector. Brandt is not present. Schmidt is still in Hamburg with President Heinemann. Genscher and Ehmke try to avoid each other's eyes. The other thirteen cabinet members—two are at a European Economic Community (EEC) meeting in Brussels —seem to have nothing to say to each other. After Scheel reads Brandt's thank-you note in a barely audible, tense voice, the certificates of dismissal are distributed. They are dated Tuesday, May 7.

The hastily called special session of the SPD representatives is in Herbert Wehner's charge. He tries to piece together the hectic events of the past seventy-two hours. While alleviating the fears of a split in the coalition, he agitatedly warns of an anticipated smear campaign against the person of Willy Brandt by the opposition. In his many battles as politician and provocateur, Wehner has learned that a brazen all-out attack is the best defense. His overall strategy is dependent upon a deliberate linkage and mixup of true accusations and false allegations. With some adroitness, both the true and the false can be dismissed as a pack of vicious lies and victory is virtually snatched from the jaws of defeat.

A thundering wave of applause cuts Wehner off in midsentence. Brandt, held up at the door by photographers and well-wishers, slowly makes his way to the speaker's table where a bouquet of fifty red roses, wrapped in cellophane, awaits him. It is Wehner's gift. Two hundred and thirty representatives rise for a standing ovation. Wehner can barely make himself heard when he shouts his tribute into the microphone at the top of his voice: "We feel sorrow about the events, respect for the decision, love for the person and the politics of Willy Brandt.

"This is not the end," he maintains somewhat more militantly, "but a singularly difficult situation which we must weather together."

In contrast to Wehner, Brandt appears almost calm. His serenity has the disquieting attributes of a trance. The automatic smile, which reduces his eyes to mere slits, disappears when he starts to speak in a controlled voice.

"Now is not the time for lament. Now is time for working and fighting." He mentions the "treachery of a presumed loyal co-worker" and adds enigmatically that he will not have "his personal and political integrity destroyed." The elections in Lower Saxony are near. They deserve undivided attention. He tells his comrades, "I will concentrate on that." He leaves no doubt of his intention to remain the party's chairman. "Nobody must believe that I have left our cause in the lurch."

It is a moving appeal. Egon Bahr, who has nervously drummed the table with his fingers, can no longer contain his mounting grief. As he stares determinedly into space, his eyes fill with tears that spill over and run down his pale broad cheeks. He is not the only one who is deeply moved. Annemarie Renger, Bundestag President, and Hans-Jochen Vogel, Minister for Housing and Urban Affairs, reach for their handkerchiefs.

After Schmidt's nomination, Brandt silently shakes hands with those next to him. Without a word he makes his exit, followed by the press, cameras and old faithfuls.

The curious in front of the Bundeshaus look in vain for his big black official limousine. Party Chairman Brandt gets into a wine-colored Mercedes.

Chipping away at the halo

To a degree, Wehner's apprehensions are justified. Brandt's frantically hurried resignation begins to look like a flight from office; a

Houdini-like disappearing act from a situation that has become too hot to handle. Past speculations concerning possible blackmail by the spy who knew too much take on realistic dimensions. The wrecking crew that had chipped away at the Nobel Peace Prize winner's halo all along, begins vigorously hacking to bits its last remnants. The reverence and courtesies accorded the federal chancellor are not extended to citizen Brandt, not even by the liberal press. Brandt's noble explanation that as head of the administration he had taken full responsibility for the blunders of his officials "out of respect for the unwritten laws of democracy" begins to look like a shoddy coverup.

In the following days, exposés of the events in Hamar and Brandt's active love life, pieced together from leaks provided by opposition politicians, blossom on newsstands from Munich to Hamburg. Under provocative headlines such as: "Brandt Blackmailed—Spy Wanted to Compromise Chancellor—Opposition Wants to Know Whole Truth—300,000 Marks Hush Money for a Woman?—The Truth in Installments—Shock for East and West," names, dates, and pictures splash across the pages of the anti-SPD boulevard press, including the resurrection of a lurid account of one of Brandt's old hushed-up love affairs. Back in the 1950s, Susanne Sievers had told all in a book which inconveniently appeared in print during Brandt's first campaign for chancellor in 1961.

Brandt found Sievers' account of his past so damaging to his reputation and campaign that he sought an injunction against distribution of the book. The court ruled its removal from the market because it contained facsimile copies of Brandt's handwritten love letters. This clearly constituted an invasion of privacy. Thanks to the new scandal, the Sievers memoirs became a collector's item selling for 300–500 marks.

Bild, owned by one of Brandt's most relentless foes, Axel Caesar Springer, lord and master of West Germany's biggest and richest newspaper chain, is only partially right with its contention that Sievers received 300,000 marks in "hush money" from government funds. Actually, an approximate sum was paid to her only in recent years as severance pay for her dismissal from the Federal Intelligence Agency in 1969, due to Ehmke's famous "house cleaning." Sievers, imprisoned by the East Germans in 1952, allegedly as a spy for the SPD's CIA-connected Ostbüro, and after her return, living under the protection of Brandt's political opponents in the orbit of the then

Defense Minister, Franz Josef Strauss, certainly was a woman with a notorious past.

These "bed stories," as the Germans call them, played down by the better papers, amounted only to a titillating sideshow.

Much more damaging to Brandt's reputation for openness and decency were the revelations in the press that he had lied to the Bundestag on April 26 about Guillaume's access to top secret documents. Brandt is forced to admit publicly on TV what he had strenuously denied before: Yes, "secret documents did pass through the spy's hands" during that summer in Norway and, well, his "private life" had played a part in his decision to resign.

All might have been forgiven had he not added, with an air of self-righteousness, that it is "grotesque to think a German federal chancellor subject to blackmail. At any rate, I am not." It was a little like Nixon saying, "I am not a crook."

The possibility of blackmail could scarcely be excluded as a factor as soon as Guillaume had become privy to the chancellor's secrets. From that moment on, the danger that the incriminating information could be used by the spy's masters to exert pressure on Brandt became a political reality. Was there another plausible explanation for the conspicuous rashness of Brandt's exit other than fear of exposure, the public asked? Why was it necessary to dispatch Grabert to Hamburg late at night? Why was there no time to await Heinemann's return to Bonn? Representative Reddemann of the CDU/CSU suspects Brandt had reason to fear disclosures of such gravity that only instant resignation could avert them.

Since Brandt failed to clear the air on blackmail, none of the rumors was laid to rest. They enhanced the myth around Brandt and his fall and, like any exciting spy story, animated the fantasy of a good many Germans. Was this the act of East Germany's hardline builder of the Berlin wall, Communist party chief Honecker, after he had extracted what he had wanted from the Federal Chancellor: full recognition of the German Democratic Republic under international law? Had this been accomplished with the blessings of Wehner for reasons of his own? Wehner had unexpectedly visited Honecker the day after Genscher had informed Brandt of the mounting suspicions against Guillaume. Immediately after Guillaume's arrest, he had demanded a full Bundestag investigation of the spy affair. Such an investigation, speculates Karl-Heinz Janssen in the liberal *Zeit,* "had to be—as things stood—directed against the chancellor also."

Or was the rug pulled out by Washington, prompted by the rising anti-Americanism in Germany, perhaps, and the fear that Brandt, hooked on Ostpolitik, made a less desirable partner? Henry Kissinger, who had not bothered to inform Brandt of his dramatic actions, was outraged when Bonn blocked shipment of American arms and matériel from West Germany during the Middle East crisis of October 1973.

Brandt, on the other hand, saw an attempt to involve the Federal Republic when arms were loaded onto Israeli ships flying the Israeli flag in German harbors. He and his government, pledged to neutrality by a resolution, legacy of previous administrations, to refrain from delivering arms into "tension zones," had little choice but to object to what could have been construed as an act of provocation.

Skeptics like Dean Acheson, who reasoned that the net effect of Brandt's Ostpolitik, meant to change the status quo in Europe, was actually stabilizing it by consolidating and securing Moscow's western frontiers, advised the department as early as 1971 to "cool off" Brandt. The former Secretary of State insisted on slowing down Bonn's "mad race to Moscow" and attuning it to the global pattern and pace of détente. Nixon's Secretary of State, Henry Kissinger, made a point of fully supporting Ostpolitik. But his sarcastic complaints, made in private, and occasional loud laments over Bonn's lack of consultation and cooperation became frequent enough to set in motion an endless string of assurances by state department spokesmen that all was well and friction between Washington and Bonn a figment of journalistic imagination.

Bonn's seasoned ambassador to Washington, Berndt von Staden, was puzzled by what had happened to U.S.–German relations after the Yom Kippur war. Diplomatically, he tried to pass off the testy "rhetorical escalation" as symptoms of the U.S. Secretary of State's "weariness."

Concerned about the bluntness of American criticism of Bonn, Klaus Engelen, Washington correspondent of the *Handelsblatt,* commented in New York's prestigious German-Jewish paper *Der Aufbau* on November 26, 1973: "Despite all efforts on both sides of the Atlantic to paper over the official American disappointment at the lack of cooperation of the Europeans, especially the 'declaration of neutrality' issued by Bonn's Foreign Office, with regard to the crisis in the Mideast, the waves have not calmed down. Extraordinarily pointed official statements have already triggered a public echo in America that increases the worries of the West German diplomatic representatives in Washington." Engelen goes on to explain that President Nixon's statement, Europe would have been freezing this winter had it not been for America's intervention in the Mideast, and Kissinger's expression of "disgust" with the European partners accurately mirrored Washington's mood.

President Nixon's furious assault on the Atlantic Alliance partners from Chicago in March 1974, when he charged the internally divided Europeans with trying to "gang up against the United States," upheld these disturbing conclusions. Referring to Nixon's "blunt warning" that US security support cannot be separated from allied political and economic cooperation, news analyst Murrey Marder reported on an "impending Europe–US crisis" in the *Washington Post* on March 17, 1974.

While Nixon's ire was aroused by the spectacular collision with the recalcitrant French during the thirteen-nation energy conference and their subsequent initiatives for a direct political-economic arrangement between the Common Market countries and twenty Arab nations—unanimously approved by the EEC membership—it was no secret that Bonn's knee-jerk reaction and its stubborn silence during this vital dispute angered Washington even more.

That Germany's chancellor refused to rush to the support of his country's nuclear protectors and personal political benefactors was regarded by Kissinger as an affront of such magnitude that in a moment of deep frustration he let off steam at a meeting with congressional wives by sarcastically questioning the "legitimacy" of certain European governments.

The revealing remark was quickly passed off as a "gaffe" by Marder and official Washington. But insiders who had come to appreciate the professor's steel-trap mind knew that the diplomatic mastermind was not given to slips of the tongue, Freudian or otherwise.

Were the same forces that determined the destabilization of Allende's political experiment in Chile out to neutralize the German chancellor whose unruly junior party leaders—from their point of view—kept confusing socialism with democracy? Had Brandt, known and observed by the OSS (precursor of the CIA) since his days in exile in Stockholm, indeed played with fire?

Was Brandt's downfall due to "inflation, leftist radicalism, dilettantish handling of German and foreign policy" and only triggered by the Guillaume affair, as the CDU/CSU charged? Or was Bonn's Watergate simply the result of a stupid breakdown of coordination between the bureaucracies of its intelligence organizations, as Brandt and his friends preferred to think?

Amidst all these lingering questions, only one certainty delineated itself: the trial of Günter Guillaume for high treason, freighted down with "national security" accents from the beginning, would not provide the answers.

In the end, the tragedy of the fall of the peace chancellor who resolutely set out to forge reconcilation between East and West and a better quality life—a slogan borrowed from the Americans—for his countrymen, had fizzled out in a tear-jerking melodrama.

A sad joke made its rounds in Bonn in those dark days. Question: Who would be the best successor for Chancellor Brandt? Answer: Guillaume. He knows his work best.

2
Ascent to the Summit

The Guillaume affair had been a welcome gift from heaven for the opposition. "Just now, when Willy Brandt was becoming a help to us, he up and resigns," grumbled one of the CDU/CSU leaders. While halfheartedly praising the smooth transition of power as brilliant political strategy, they would have preferred to kick the vulnerable Brandt around for a while. With one bold masterstroke, the SPD had wiped its own slate clean. If Helmut Schmidt, the all-round political pro and pragmatist, were to make mistakes, they certainly would not be of the Brandt variety.

Schmidt had been an appealing politician for some time. When Brandt received his Nobel Peace Prize toward the end of 1971, Schmidt was well ahead of the chancellor in the popularity polls.

Actually, Schmidt did not exaggerate in maintaining that he was taking on a "thankless job in a pretty shitty situation." It is not easy to follow an idol, even a fallen one. From a proud 45.9 percent of the votes in 1972, the party's biggest victory in its history, the popularity of the SPD had sagged to around 30 percent by April 1974, according to the most trusted and friendly opinion polls. Such a low reminded the party's managers of the dark 1950s, when Adenauer's CDU/CSU reigned supreme. Clearly, Brandt's vote-getting magic had all but evaporated. The rapid erosion of public confidence in the chancellor's and the party's capabilities to cope with an 8–10 percent inflation, rising unemployment, growing leftist influence within the party, and the sobering disenchantment with Ostpolitik were reflected in a dramatic loss of votes averaging from 9.5–13 percent in five regional elections between Hamburg and North Hesse. The fact that the heaviest defeats were suffered in the cities among blue- and white-collar workers, a traditional SPD stronghold, and even among the young, added to the panic in the ranks of the party's strategists. The important sociological "middle" had to be retrieved.

Luckily for the Social Democrats, the CDU/CSU was in no position to take advantage of their weakness. The opposition had neither a comprehensive program of alternatives nor the politicians to challenge the floundering Brandt administration. The much heralded eclipse of Rainer Barzel as chancellor candidate—after his ill-timed vote of no confidence failed to unseat Mr. Brandt in 1972—by uncharismatic Helmut Kohl and Karl Carstens did not solve the Christian Democrats' leadership problem.

What made the voters turn their backs on the celebrated peace chancellor, after their unprecedented support a mere fifteen months earlier? Their beloved Willy had promised to create a "modern" Germany with bold social reforms, better relations with their neighbors in the East, and progress toward a United Europe.

What had gone wrong? What were the more obvious characteristics of the Brandt years?

"A great man is not great because his personal qualities leave an individualistic imprint on great historic events but because of the possession of qualities that most enable him to serve the great social needs of his time which have grown out of the influence of general or specific causes," observed the nineteenth-century writer, George Plechanov, founder of Russian social democracy and pathfinder for materialistic Marxism.

Willy Brandt, the poor, fatherless boy from Lübeck, certainly left an imprint. His concept of détente between West Germany and her neighbors to the East made Ostpolitik a household word around the world. His acknowledgment of Germany's historic guilt had brought its redemption in the form of the Nobel Peace Prize. "During the whole of the postwar period, the unresolved Germany question has constituted a latent danger to the peace," the Nobel committee pointed out. When Federal Chancellor Brandt was granted the award "on behalf of the German people" it was not only understood as personal "encouragement for his political endeavours but as international recognition of Germany's will for peace."

To be sure, Moscow expected a positive effect. The prize was bound to create a better climate for the acceptance of its conditions by the resisting opposition. Nevertheless, the honor gave Brandt the stature of an international statesman, comparable to that of Adenauer and Bismarck—or of Gustav Stresemann, his critics charged bitterly. The unfortunate Stresemann, who served as chancellor and foreign minister from 1923 to 1929, had received the Nobel Prize only about three years before the worldwide economic crisis began to undermine the Weimar Republic, preparing the way for Hitler.

Had Willy Brandt served the social needs of his time?

Had the Germans not wanted a change of direction after twenty years of conservative Christian Democratic government? Had they not wanted to revive the stagnating circulation between East and West? Had they not wanted more democracy, more social and economic justice? Was it not time for the enactment of those great reforms that would change the fabric of the whole of society?

The chancellor—who declared in his first address to the nation in 1969 that only now had Hitler actually lost the war, that only now democracy was given a real chance—had set high moral standards and lofty political goals for himself and his government. Brandt and his party did not merely claim to be better equipped to meet present and future challenges but proclaimed that they, and they alone, could handle them. As the true representatives of the working classes they were the emissaries of the future, they argued, and therefore their's was the party of the time by historical necessity.

Adenauer's terse, often self-deprecating brand of modesty, epitomized by his offhand remark, "What do I care about the gibberish of yesterday?" (he meant his own) was not Brandt's style.

Walther Leisler Kiep, one of the CDU's foreign experts, held the moral component in Brandt's foreign policy directly responsible for the logical and highly regrettable development that anybody who was critical of it, last but not least the opposition, was relegated to the "camp of those of bad or evil will because they were against a good cause" or put down as "indecent opponents of peace" and "enemies of democracy."

Nothing is more perilous in politics than to raise hopes and make claims which, in the end, must remain unfulfilled. Had Brandt, who shared John F. Kennedy's great gift for the power of projection, raised hopes and expectations too high? Had he, like the luckless Lyndon B. Johnson, harvested a similar unrest and uneasiness, the "poison of insecurity" as Schmidt put it, after euphoria turned to disillusionment and dissent?

The CDU/CSU had contented itself with the improvement and adjustment of legislation in concert with the changing needs and attitudes of the times. While the Christian Democrats seemed to have been unable to keep step, Brandt and his comrades were leaping ahead of common consensus.

THE TROUBLE WITH REFORMS

Many of the progressive inner reforms envisioned by the Social Democrats, such as the compromise tax "reform," improved health care, and an astonishing maze of improved social benefits from birth to grave, were in reality adjustments or minireforms. They did not appreciably change society, but they constituted solid social achievements. There was only one problem: The government never quite succeeded in informing the public about the wide scope of its work. Other, more avant-garde ventures were only partially realized or not at all. Among them were codetermination and profit sharing for the workers; reform of the antiquated, inflexible university structure, designed to guarantee "equal opportunity"; the enactment of laws for the protection of the environment; and the land use reform, proposed to curb burgeoning speculation and profiteering from land sales.

The most daring and significant reform plans of Brandt's era, codetermination and profit sharing, had run into demonstrative trouble with the more conservative coalition partners in the FDP. Without much ado, profit sharing was put on ice for tactical reasons. Codetermination, one of the foremost governmental instruments for blunting the contrast between capital and labor and the reduction of social tension in the process of economic "democratization" of industry, encountered rough sailing in the Bundestag. By 1975, equal codetermination of the workers in big companies, successfully launched twenty years back in the coal and steel industry, existed in four watered-down varieties.

Brandt firmly believes that "without the system of codetermination and the implicit coresponsibility of employees and their unions," the steady growth of Germany's economy, its stability, its comparatively low rate of inflation (the lowest in the Western world in 1975), and the high degree of social tranquility would not have been possible. "When the American Chamber of Commerce in Germany intervened against the extension of codetermination a couple of months ago," Brandt told his student audience at Vanderbilt University in March 1975, "I was not only disturbed by this intervention in our domestic affairs. I also understood it as something that could have an adverse effect on the companies in question."

Eschewing the notion that such "democratic" controls of business and industry are only to be considered in the context of social democratic dogma, Brandt called them "a suitable way to defend, secure and strengthen the freedom of our modern world."

Most reforms cost money, much money, except for the liberalized divorce and pornography laws and the decriminalization of abortion, of course. On the other hand, they had brought the vocal intellectual community into the Brandt camp.

A runaway inflation was bound to dry up most of the funds earmarked for these great reform packages not blocked by the opposition as "dangerously socialistic," or by differences of opinion between the coalition partners or heated arguments between the party's left and right wings.

There was a curious lack of economic analysis as to the feasibility of the various projects in terms of marks and pfennigs. Worst of all, the reforms had taken on the semblance of a crusade. Instead of being part of an adjustable party platform, they unexpectedly emerged as a form of ideology for the New Left.

Drift to the left?

"The SPD cannot escape from the idea that 'socialism' had somehow to do with progress and humanity in the sense that it is the antithesis of capitalism. This polarized, black-and-white, good-and-evil idea is fallacious, as the SPD leadership came to realize at an early stage—

namely 1955–1965. For more than ten years, the SPD wisely avoided use of the word 'socialism' and members of the party even avoided calling each other 'comrade'," Hans Heigert commented in the prestigious SPD-supportive *Süddeutsche Zeitung* in November 1974. Heigert wondered if the party had not succumbed to an illusion by giving in to the pull of the New Left since 1967, which had rendered it more "socialist, militant and agitational."

Anyone who talks to intelligent young people today, Heigert observed, quickly learns that they are sick of the "gobbledegook of conflict strategies, emancipatory reform processes, new socialization structures, and the like."

Actually, much of this development had to do with Brandt's past as a radical Socialist. Brandt, as he once said, was born into socialism. Like many of his deeply committed comrades, he was fighting the Nazis at home and closing ranks with the Communists and any other anti-Fascist groups in the resistance in exile. Like many of these brave men, he was driven by the historical necessities of his past and as time marched on, he became a captive of the thought that political evil was to be found on the right. No matter how many disappointments and letdowns he suffered at the hands of the Communists, he would always remember Moscow as the staunch defender of peace against the Fascist aggressor and would give its most bizarre actions the benefit of the doubt.

In turn, suspicions were aroused among the bourgeoisie, who began to fear that "more democracy" in reality meant a socialism similar to that practiced in Communist countries. The concept of redistribution of wealth, interpreted rightly or wrongly by conservatives as an attack on private property and a prelude to a socialization of the whole economy, had a destabilizing effect on the middle class and industrial leaders alike. The public, already worried about the effect of inflation on dwindling savings and job security, showed little interest in costly reforms, especially those that were advocated by the New Left, which had taken a strictly anticapitalistic and therefore anti-American stance. This insecurity, based as it was on socioeconomic grievances, resulted in considerable political damage: loss of confidence in the ability of the SPD to run a government that knows how to tackle day-to-day problems.

Curiously enough, the Germans had never had it so good. They were better housed, educated, fed, clothed, vacationed, welfared, and pensioned than ever before. No one questioned by the pollsters felt specifically deprived. But all thought of themselves as exceptions. All "knew" people were out of work. All "knew" for a fact that people invested in "real values." All suffered from an acute case of existential anxiety, nourished by the unforgotten German nightmare of the 1920s with its recession and apocalyptic aftermath.

Brandt, immersed in Ostpolitik, did little to dispel the burghers' fears and confusion. "He [Brandt] stimulated or departed—he did not make order, but let things go," charged the *Welt,* one of Brandt's severest critics.

By the time the administration had ensconced its reform policies as a permanent fixture in the party's long-range program, it was dealt a mortal blow by the ensuing energy crisis. An outside force had confronted the industrial societies with a new reality: the power of raw material control and its byproducts—inflation, decline of industrial growth, unemployment. Brandt, who had developed a taste for vacations in foreign lands, had not bothered to hurry back from an admirer's luxurious estate in Southern France at the time of the Middle East crisis. His friends were frantic. Neither was a statement from Bonn forthcoming when the shortage of oil and gasoline became acute. Brandt simply did not know what to say to the public, they confided.

Brandt, of course, offered a different explanation. Secure in the knowledge that the draft of an energy bill was ready for introduction in the Bundestag—it was passed in a record-breaking three days—he tried to play down the crisis by considering neither a price freeze nor other drastic measures except for a regulation, soon lifted, that restricted Sunday driving. Because they did not dare risk talking themselves into a deeper crisis, the government, for its part, "did not consciously dramatize," he wrote in *Beyond the Day.*

"The people have the feeling that Bonn is in a deep slumber; I can only hope it is a therapeutic one," Jochen Steffen, one of the SPD's more outspoken leftist leaders commented.

The public became uncomfortably aware that its chancellor might have misjudged the importance of the crisis. Its deduction that the adept politician who had introduced so many fascinating impulses into Germany's political landscape seemed unable to act under pressure was not easily countered.

From the beginning, Brandt had remained—like Adenauer,

Kennedy and many another government leader—his own foreign minister. The pursuit of Ostpolitik consumed his time and energies. Economic policies were left to the devices of his ministers, Schiller, Möller and Schmidt, who followed each other in rapid succession. When Brandt finally—in a forced show of decisiveness—took a stand against the wage hike demands of the members of the striking public services, the transportation and traffic workers' union, because he and his economists thought them inflationary, he suffered a most humiliating defeat at the hands of his party comrade, union leader Heinz Kluncker. Kluncker pressed for and got his 12-percent wage increase. Brandt, no longer having the stamina and stomach for a prolonged test of strength, threatened to resign.

"One will have to ponder how long one can still be available," he sulked. Like all empty threats it sounded pompous.

OSTPOLITIK IS EXPENSIVE

Only after his Ostpolitik, with its spectacular summits, conferences and treaty ceremonies, was concluded did the "chancellor of the inner reforms," as he had billed himself in 1969, remember his promises. In his address to the nation in 1974, the great visions of cooperation among peoples and bridgebuilding between East and West had given way to pronouncements of "higher incomes."

Meanwhile, in Washington as well as in Bonn, the first bloom was off the relaxation of tension euphoria. Ostpolitik or détente had become a matter of money, of dollars and marks. Just how much was it worth in Soviet trade, politicians on the Potomac and on the Rhine were asking.

The cooling political atmosphere was not reflected on the economic balance sheets. Bonn's answer was that business with the Soviets, replete with half a dozen billion-mark projects, some even involving welcome cash instead of long-range credits, had quintupled since 1971. Encouraged by the success of the previous deal for pipe at a cost of 1.2 billion marks in exchange for Siberian natural gas worth about 4 billion, Krupp had sent out a thousand engineers to study the feasibility of four atomic power plants of the fast breeder type.

The answer to the wary question of how much the normalization of relations between East and West Germany was worth in terms of credits without interest, blueprinted as "swing agreement" by Chancellor Kiesinger in 1966, obviously depended on the price tag one was willing to attach to the efforts to resolve the humanitarian problems and adjustments between the two German peoples. These improvements, for the most part intangibles of highly charged emotional content, manifested themselves in better phone connections—for the first time in nineteen years West Berliners could phone East Berliners directly—improved postal and traffic arrangements, the building of an additional Autobahn, the exchange of permanent missions and newspaper correspondents, as well as more liberal visiting rights. In 1973, some 2.2 million West Germans visited the GDR, a million more than in 1971 before the Traffic Treaty was signed.

The Quadripartite Berlin Agreement finally opened the door to East Berlin and the GDR for West Berliners who had generally been barred entry—with the exception of specially negotiated holidays—to East Berlin for five years and to the GDR since 1953. Citizens of the GDR were at long last allowed to visit relatives in West Germany on "urgent family business" even if they did not qualify as pensioners or complete invalids. While an estimated eight million West Germans visited East Germany between 1972 and 1975, five million East Germans went west to have a look at capitalism in action.

According to GDR officials, the experience of observing the enormous economic insecurity the individual suffers in the materialistic West caused an unforeseen alienation that was reflected in lowered travel statistics—on both sides. West German officials have different explanations for this phenomenon: harassment of GDR citizens who want to visit the Federal Republic, and the hiking of the minimum daily amount of currency a West German traveler is obliged to exchange.

If the treaties had improved relations, why did the GDR and Moscow object to the establishment of a Federal Environmental Protection Agency in West Berlin? Why was traffic blocked time and again on the access routes to West Berlin? Reports of renewed shootings painfully reminded the West Germans of the continued existence of the monstrous wall with its barbed wire, armed East German guards, and the death strip—stretching for hundreds of miles through the countryside—where ninety-eight Germans had been shot down. The deaths of five people from gunshot wounds during an attempt to escape across the wall in the normalized atmosphere of 1973, and the draconian judgment in East Berlin in 1975, when two West Germans were sentenced to life in prison for helping GDR citizens escape to the West, made the public acutely aware of the meaning in Brandt's sober prediction of a long and stony road ahead.

"After many years of nonrelations and hostility, the people and those in government in the two German States will have to acquire experience and learn to deal with each other. We shall not be spared difficulties and frictions," the Peace Chancellor said in his policy statement of 1973.

German feelings of neighborliness became somewhat strained when Poland presented, along with its signature on the German-Polish Treaty, its reparations bill: compensation for Nazi crimes, a demand not made on the GDR and considered settled by the London agreements after the war, as well as cheap credits in the billions. This occurred just after Poland had legally swallowed the giant chunk of 40,000 square miles of erstwhile German territory east of the Oder-Neisse line, including Silesia, East Prussia, and Pomerania. Open friction between the governments in 1975 was caused by the fact that Polish Communist party chief Gierek had failed to stand behind the verbal promise of his foreign minister to permit 50,000 Germans to emigrate in 1974. The opposition was quick to point out that long before anybody ever heard of rapprochement, 100,000 Germans had been traded for shipments of wheat in 1957.

The Germans suddenly wanted to know how the low two percent interest rate on the 700 million mark loan granted to Yugoslavia affected their pocketbooks.

Resentment and frustration were fanned anew by meticulously researched and documented reports—allegedly suppressed by the Brandt administration, and released for the first time by the federal archives of Coblence in 1975—that 600,000 German civilian expellees perished in the camps and prisons of East bloc countries at the end of the war.

The longest debate

Many a supporter of détente and Ostpolitik began to wonder if it had become a one-way street. Among them was the liberal Leisler Kiep, one of the four CDU leaders who had actually voted for the important Treaty on the Basis of Relations between the Federal Republic of Germany and the German Democratic Republic that provided a modus vivendi for a coexistence of the two German states. Kiep, referring to a pattern of concessions made by the Brandt government and not necessarily honored with reciprocal actions, feared "that the instrument of the treaties—partially because of the inherent shortcomings—begins to rust" in the government's hands.

It should be noted that 80 percent of the public had favored the SPD's Ostpolitik, among them every third CDU voter. Political scientists are agreed that the memorable SPD landslide victory in 1972 had to be interpreted as an approval of Ostpolitik that amounted to a ratification by the population of the treaties in question and a rejection of the negative CDU/CSU attitude, with its unfortunate tendency to revive a latent anticommunism. Since then, the argument that Ostpolitik has wrought more formalization than normalization in the relationship between East and West has become one of the standard clichés among the skeptics.

Obviously there had been a great, perhaps even tragic, misunderstanding of the quality of détente. Whereas the Soviet-directed kind, Westpolitik, allowed for a limited expedient economic arrangement which in no way seemed to alter their inherently antagonistic ideological view of the Western political systems, the Western kind, specifically that of Bonn and Washington, was based on continuous extension of goodwill, of cooperation instead of confrontation on all fronts, in spirit and practice.

Willy Brandt was not perturbed when he spoke of coexistence as a "hard ordeal" in March 1975:

> Meanwhile we find ourselves in the period of relaxation of tension. Nobody knows with complete certainty whether it will be successful, but nobody knows a reasonable alternative. Relaxation of tension promises a constructive dialogue for the time which is needed to build a lasting peace. It promises that confrontation will diminish and be replaced by cooperation, especially in the economic and scientific spheres.

The opposition, in its refusal to ratify the East treaties, had warned that few tangible benefits would result from hurriedly drawn, ambiguously formulated agreements. However, the Christian Democrats had tried and failed since Adenauer's days to implement a solution that would deter the Soviets from cementing the status quo in Europe. And their constant denouncement, "Ostpolitik, yes—but not this way," was hardly an alternative. With the implementation of his Ostpolitik, Brandt had accepted the political reality of the status quo as the basis for a development that was supposed to surmount and change it. As a believer in the changeability of the human condition rather than that of man, he had expressed a willingness to live with two Germanys, two different states, two different political and social systems which might or might not merge into one nation in future times.

Machiavelli, that sly old hand at statecraft, believed that the politician who adapts his policy to the times prospers and "likewise, that the one whose policy clashes with the demands of the times does not." Brandt's Ostpolitik was attuned to the times.

In contrast to previous CDU/CSU governments which had tried to overcome the division of Europe by overcoming the division of Germany—seeing German reunification as the forerunner of a rapprochement between East and West Europe—Brandt hitched his political fortunes to the glittering stars of Washington-Moscow détente. The only chance to resolve the German Question was seen within the international framework of an all-European peace arrangement, the SPD-FDP coalition argued. Henceforth, the term reunification was dropped from the political vocabulary in favor of "national unity."

In a similar concept, rooted however in the dogmatic anti-Communist 1950s and in response to American suggestions in the 1960s to formulate a German policy, Franz Josef Strauss had advocated the "Europeanization of the German Question." But it was strictly based on West European integration and had failed to take into account the new political climate.

As Machiavelli recommended, Brandt pursued Ostpolitik impetuously rather than in a circumspect manner. Yet there would have been less dispute in the Bundestag and less criticism in the sobering afterglow of these history-making events had Brandt and his minister Egon Bahr conducted their negotiations in a less ardent and frenzied but more circumspect and transparent manner. Bahr, like Henry Kissinger, preferred a highly secret diplomacy with heavy emphasis on the purchase of cooperation at a dollar-mark price.

Adenauer, on the other hand, who stubbornly and quite secretly pursued his own brand of Ostpolitik, as we learn from state papers released to the public domain after his death, used to admonish his less patient critics: Patience remains the strongest weapon of the vanquished.

Only history will tell, of course, whether Brandt had shown sufficient patience. Whether his Ostpolitik remained a political beau geste, or whether it marked the beginning of a reconciliation, such as had been achieved with Bonn's neighbors in the West by Konrad Adenauer, depends largely on the character of the change of Soviet policy: whether its cooperation was tactical or strategic, a temporary device or a long range aim.

Laying the groundwork

The complex interdependent network of multilateral and bilateral treaties that provided the foundation for Ostpolitik was created during the first hundred days of the Brandt era. Like Kissinger, Brandt and Bahr believed in political momentum. The ink was hardly dry on the new cabinet's appointment commissions when the nonproliferation treaty was signed. Meanwhile Chancellor Brandt made his strong appeal during the Hague summit of the European Economic Community on December 1, 1969, for the strengthening and unifying of West Europe's voice by expanding the community of six to include Great Britain, Ireland and Denmark. He also urged the linking of the unaligned European Free Trade Association (EFTA) countries, notably Austria, Switzerland and Sweden, to the community.

"Without England, and the other states that are ready to join, Europe cannot become what it is supposed to be and what it can be," Brandt said. He underlined at the same time, for the benefit of France—a traditional opponent of Britain's membership—that EEC expansion was the best balancing device against the Federal Republic's economic overweight.

While special emissary Bahr was dispatched on his urgent mission to Moscow to talk about the renunciation of the use of force, something all previous governments were agreed upon, State Secretary Georg Ferdinand Duckwitz was on his way to Warsaw with an affirmation that the Oder-Neisse line was Poland's border and that Bonn intended to honor the "territorial integrity of the European states and their sovereignty."

At the same time, Brandt notified GDR Minister President Willi

Stoph, in his policy statement, that he was ready to recognize the "historic reality" twenty-five years after the end of the war and willing to negotiate about regular neighborly relations between the "two German states in Germany" in the context of a German contribution to the international transition from confrontation to cooperation.

Thus the grand stage of history was set for the entrance of Willy Brandt and his Ostpolitik.

THE TREATIES

Only after priming the pump at Moscow and Warsaw with a substantial display of goodwill—writing off the German Eastern provinces by recognizing the "territorial integrity of all states in Europe in their present borders"—was the reluctant GDR to be approached. On the other hand, Bonn first had to safeguard its position in West Berlin. This had to be accomplished before the GDR's chief aim of attaining international recognition in the eyes of Bonn was realized.

Therefore, West Berlin's freedom, security and unlimited access, as well as its economic, financial, political and legal linkage with the Federal Republic—including representation of West Berlin's interests in international affairs—had to be guaranteed by the Four Powers, together with their military protection of the city, before the ratification of the Moscow and Warsaw treaties. For once, the government and the opposition were in agreement: The ratification of these treaties was dependent upon a satisfactory solution for West Berlin.

While the opposition found plenty of fault with the Four Power agreement on Berlin for its failure to incorporate West Berlin into the Federal Republic, the fear held by opposition leader Rainer Barzel that West Berlin would become "a third Germany" was unjustified.

"The Soviets too are interested in a useful Berlin solution," Brandt assured the skeptics. Moscow knew very well that "Berlin is the eye of the needle through which not only the German-Soviet treaty must go but everything connected with the conference on security for Europe, also." A European security conference, frowned upon in Washington as an instrument to nail down the status quo, had been a pet project of the Kremlin's strategists for two decades.

The years 1970 and 1971 marked a stunning sequence of triumphs for Chancellor Brandt, rated as major historical breakthroughs on the long concession-skimming road to reconciliation. It was a period of new outlooks, bold initiatives, and hope-inspiring foreign policy conclusions that resembled the dazzling years before Henry Kissinger's ingenious, breathtaking balancing acts, for which he also was rewarded by the Nobel Peace Prize committee, came tumbling down.

It was impossible to imagine that the ceremonial signing of the Moscow Treaty in August 1970, with all its televised solemnity and austere Kremlin pomp, could be paled by anything. The occasion was heightened in significance by the fact that Brandt was the first German chancellor to visit the Soviet capital since Adenauer's pilgrimage there on behalf of the release of German prisoners-of-war in 1955, and crowned by Brandt's spectacular journey to Oreanda the following year for sixteen hours of informal shirt-sleeved intimacy with Brezhnev in his dacha.

The communiqué issued by Brandt and Brezhnev promised at least the dawning of a new era, if not a new millennium. The relations between Bonn and Moscow would be based on "new foundations." Bonn and East Berlin were to become members of the United Nations, a goal that was to be "promoted in a suitable manner" by Bonn and Moscow. Furthermore, the two leaders were agreed on a balanced reduction of forces, the speedy calling of a European conference on security and cooperation, and expanded bilateral trade agreements.

Nothing, one was sure, could overshadow the intense tension that characterized the emotional content of the Warsaw Treaty with all its inherent moral aspects of man's inhumanity to man. These were dramatically brought to consciousness by a simple moving gesture of atonement: Brandt's kneeling in the streets of Warsaw's old Jewish ghetto, before a Polish monument memorializing the 500,000 Jews slaughtered by the Nazis during World War II.

"The Treaty of Warsaw is intended to draw a line under the sufferings and sacrifices of an evil past. It is intended to build a bridge between the two states and their peoples. It is to open up the way for separated families to reunite and to make frontiers less divisive than hitherto. . . . Nobody has compelled us to see it this way; we have come of age. . . ." Reminding his countrymen that the treaty does not "surrender anything that was not gambled away a long time ago . . . by a criminal regime, by National Socialism," Brandt also assured them that "we do not mean to recognize injustice or acts of violence. It does not mean that we subsequently legitimize expulsion."

Next to the signing of the Traffic Treaty, the first and only major treaty negotiated by the Brandt administration that found approval with the opposition, the year 1971 was highlighted by the bestowal of the most prestigious international awards. In January, *Time* magazine turned to Brandt, the statesman, who "already stands as a great innovator of his time" for its Man of the Year, because he was the "first West German politician willing to accept the full consequences of defeat in World War II" and shaped events rather than reacted to them in his "bold approach to the Soviet Union and the East bloc." Appropriately, that glorious year when all seemed to fall into place for Brandt closed with the announcement that he was the unanimous choice from among 39 candidates as the recipient of the Nobel Peace Prize.

Critical remarks by opposition leaders, who regarded the prize—bestowed for good intentions rather than achievements and announced in the midst of the heated Ostpolitik controversy, undoubtedly the longest and most embittered fight the Bundeshaus had seen—as a direct intervention in German domestic politics, were drowned in German pride. Former FDP chairman Erich Mende's cynical comment, "One can see that the Socialist International is functioning," was contradicted by barrels of congratulatory telegrams from all over the world and a spontaneous torchlight procession that spread its enthusiastic glow well beyond the confines of Bonn's Venusberg.

Meeting in Erfurt

And yet, incredible as it sounds, all those stirring events seemed anticlimactic in a sense, compared to the most difficult, most phenomenal and hope filled history-making *Realpolitik* happening of them all: the German summit at Erfurt on March 19, 1970. The sight of the two German Willys, East Germany's Minister President Willi Stoph and West Germany's Willy Brandt, cosily chatting away in Erfurt's festively bedecked Hotel Erfurter Hof was like a dream come true for Germans on both sides of the ideological border. If anything rekindled hope for the light of German unity at the end of the tunnel of twenty-five years' separation, it was the vision of the two heads of state, side by side, exchanging optimistic comments.

"We Germans do everything so thoroughly," Brandt said. "If both sides would give a little, we certainly could get a few things going." For Willi Stoph, the "meeting was a turning point." For the first time, Brandt's talk of a change from a "regulated next to each other" to a "peaceful with each other" assumed a reality.

To the realities of the day which had "enriched" Brandt also belonged the GDR demand for reparation of 100 billion marks for the loss of manpower to the West before Berlin's wall was erected. Brandt's reply that this was not Bonn's fault but the consequence of the Socialist Unity Party's (SED) social system brought to mind that Stoph had ruled out the concept of national unity from the beginning. SED chairman Ulbricht had stressed before the meeting that the absence of a common national future was an historic reality. "The German Democratic Republic is a Socialist German nation-state; the West German Federal Republic is a capitalistic NATO state. . . . National unity cannot exist between the Krupps and the Krauses [the German Johnsons], between billionaires and multimillionaires and the working people."

The GDR, with its seventeen million people, was finally on the verge of being recognized by Bonn as a state under international law (vis-à-vis other countries). After being ignored and downgraded by the FRG's now abandoned claim of being Germany's sole representative, never before had the GDR been so close to Bonn and yet so separate. Ironically, only the official acknowledgment of separateness, only the complete break with traditional postwar policy, had cleared the hurdles that led to Erfurt and the cheers of thousands of East Germans assembled at the railroad station and in front of the hotel to catch a glimpse of the other Willy. As the "Willy" shouts built to a rousing crescendo, Brandt asked Stoph, who walked beside him, "Which Willy do they mean? The one with the *i* or the one with the *y?*"

Even before the excited crowd had gathered under Brandt's hotel window, the answer was clear. When he finally appeared at the open window the "Federal Chancellor obviously experienced difficulty in controlling his own emotions," Ulrich Kempski of the *Süddeutsche Zeitung* observed. "Timidly smiling he nods a greeting with his head;

alternately calming down the enthusiasm seconds later, with an almost imploring gesture of his spread out, turned down hands."

Notwithstanding Communist rhetoric, Erfurt proved beyond the shadow of a doubt that national feelings were anything but forgotten or dead, and that the "special character" Bonn had ascribed to the relationship of the two states was not just another of its legalistic tricks to downgrade the GDR, as some of its leaders charged, but rooted in a reality not subject to official decrees.

The dialogue that began in Erfurt was followed up in the much more uncompromising atmosphere of the second summit at Kassel, where unyielding Stoph was deliberately playing for "a pause for reflection" in awaiting the outcome of the German-Soviet negotiations. In the course of two years and some seventy meetings, Bonn's State Secretary in the Federal Chancellory, Egon Bahr, and the GDR's State Secretary to the Council of Ministers, Michael Kohl, diligently and with much adroitness worked out treaties on transit, traffic, and most importantly, the Basic Treaty, prerequisite for both states to become eligible for UN membership, designed to prevent "further alienation, reduce tensions and strengthen the people's feeling of belonging together."

The Basic Treaty would never have been concluded had the negotiators tried to resolve their differing views on the basic issues of self-determination, "special" relations between the two Germanys, the question of nation, and other points of disparity. Despite the built-in dissent, frowned upon by the opposition who rejected the treaty as a "source of friction," it withstood the test of constitutionality in the Federal Constitutional Court in a suit brought by CSU-controlled Bavaria.

"We have organized the modus vivendi and will have to learn the coexistence," Chancellor Brandt commented on November 7, 1972, with an eye firmly fixed on the elections on November 19.

Ultimately, the policy vigorously launched anew by Brandt—Ostpolitik existed before and continues after him—imparted itself as a syndrome of a novel German self-confidence and European self-awareness in the face of Washington's precarious engrossment in Indochina. Its ups and downs, determined by the general global climate of détente and its refractions on the German scene, became Brandt's destiny, severely influencing his extraordinary rise and to a large extent his abrupt fall, when the piper had to be paid and euphoria turned into a hangover.

3

An Idol Falls

By April 1972, the SPD had not only suffered a decisive defeat in the elections of Baden-Württemberg but saw its thin majority in the Bundestag crumbling away. As the emotional Ostpolitik controversy in the Bundestag raged on, some members of the FDP and SPD felt obliged to express their misgivings about the "sell-out of German interests," recognition of the inviolability of the Eastern boundaries, the international upgrading of the GDR, the affirmation of the status quo, and other by-products of Brandt's "opportunistic" Ostpolitik, by switching to the opposition party.

Some concurred with Rainer Barzel's rigorously moralistic statement, "Rivalry cannot be confederated and freedom and dictatorship do not mix." Others remembered the solemn SPD pledges, during its cold war spells in the 1960s, that it would not recognize the Oder-Neisse line, and felt misled. Actually, under the leadership of Kurt Schumacher, the SPD was the first German party to take that position.

Herbert Wehner had repeatedly voiced thoughts similar to those heard at the party's convention in Dortmund in 1966: "The unilateral separation of territories belonging to Germany in 1937 has not created new justice but new injustice. Social democracy does not recognize them." At a meeting of expellees from Silesia in 1963, Brandt advocated the "passionate" pursuit of reunification. "Breslau, Oppeln, Gleiwitz, Hirschberg, Glogau, Grünberg; these are not just names, they are living memories rooted in the souls of generations and incessantly arousing our conscience. Abandonment is treachery; who would want to deny that! The right to one's homeland [*Heimat*] cannot be gambled away for a dish of lentils. . . ."

Times had changed. *Realpolitik* was in, illusions were out. This did not mean, of course, that Brandt and his negotiator did not foster a few illusions of their own. It was no secret that the crucial term "modus vivendi" had a different and quite final ring in Eastern capitals. While Bonn took the edge of permanence from the treaties by implying a temporary arrangement open to change at some future time, East German officials regard the treaties as final because no time limit was attached to the modus vivendi stage.

Otto Winzer, the GDR foreign minister, made abundantly clear what the treaties meant to his government at the twenty-eighth session of the United Nations General Assembly. "It is equally important that the inviolability, now and in the future, of the frontier between the GDR and the FRG and the obligation of both states to fully respect each other's territorial integrity have been affirmed by international law. The Treaty has no time limit. It contains nothing that could question the finality of the agreed provisions or give them a provisional character, the character of a so-called modus vivendi."

Rainer Barzel seized the first potentially opportune moment to topple the weakened SPD-FDP coalition by introducing a vote of no confidence in the Bundestag on April 27, 1972. He had miscalculated by two votes. One of them belonged to controversial Julius Steiner, a member of the Christian Democratic Union, who claimed to have accepted a bribe of 50,000 marks for his vote for Brandt. However, the coalition's triumph was short-lived. The next day it was stalemated in a tie of votes over the federal budget. The result was that new elections became a necessity.

The political deadlock forced both government and opposition to hammer out a compromise resolution in the Bundestag concerning the Moscow and Warsaw treaties. As long as Brandt's government was assured of a majority in the Bundestag, little effort was expended in seeking advice and consent from the opposition or trying to change its negative attitude. Wehner's curt rebuff, the government was not dependent on the opposition, strengthened the strategy of confrontation pursued by Kurt Georg Kiesinger and Franz Josef Strauss. Reduced from its customary role as pacemaker in foreign affairs to mere bystander, the CDU/CSU had assumed an ambivalent posture not without the indomitable hope that any political mileage resulting from an unrelenting stance could assist in the preparation of its comeback. Actually, the CDU/CSU's lack of approval turned out to be an enormous asset for Brandt's negotiating position. It strengthened his hand immeasurably.

For the government, the compromise resolution that specified, among other points, the right to self-determination for all Germans —an item relegated to an accompanying letter when the negotiators failed to place it in the text of the treaties—presented a means of safeguarding the ratification of the important treaties. For the opposition, it was a bid for legal and political improvements. In its insistence on precise language, it clashed notably with the essential intentions of the Soviets, who purposely sought to leave the text open to variant interpretations.

The right of self-determination, for example, takes on a markedly different connotation in socialistic societies. It is tied to class concepts and the principle of internationalism because of the existence of the Brezhnev doctrine. While Bonn interpreted the Russian term *njerushimyi,* used in reference to the frontiers in question as "inviolable," the Soviets attached the firmer meaning "immovable" to it.

The CDU's Ostpolitik Slalom

After all this input and the objective improvements effected by Barzel, who had hurried to Moscow for talks with Kosygin and Foreign Minister Gromyko at Christmas, 1971, the CDU was expected to ratify the Moscow and Warsaw treaties. Subsequently, the executive committee had laid to rest its original reservations and ascertained that the treaties served to establish a modus vivendi, freedom of movement of people, ideas, and information, neither cancelling out a future peace treaty nor creating a legal basis for the frontiers existing today nor prejudicing the restoration of national unity. Surprisingly, that was not the case. Instead the CDU, possibly influenced by the uncompromising "No" of the CSU and the fear of a split, abstained from voting.

Christian Hacke finds the "slalom of CDU arguments from the *yes* of the executive committee to the abstaining vote on the Moscow-Warsaw Treaties, the *yes* on the Traffic Treaty to the *no* on the Basic Treaty," hard to understand.

The young CDU analyst contends that the credibility of the

CDU/CSU argumentation on foreign politics suffered a severe setback in the course of the events. "The traditional credit enjoyed by the CDU/CSU in foreign affairs in the widest of circles after Konrad Adenauer showed a diminishing tendency in the middle sixties, especially in the sphere of East and German politics. And since 1969, it was reduced to the same degree as the underlying 'as if character' of the oppositional argumentation became evident."

Former CDU/CSU Foreign Minister Gerhard Schröder, on the other hand, who had a part in shaping Ostpolitik in the Adenauer and Erhard administrations and recommended support of the Moscow and Warsaw treaties after the union dealt with them, offered a different opinion at the CSU party convention in Munich in November 1972: "Brandt once more has taken the easy route. Relaxation of tension is not sought by the removal of the causes of the tension but through one-sided recognizing, giving up and giving away."

The old-school diplomat firmly stuck by the provisional policies insisted upon and firmly set down by Truman and Churchill in Potsdam during the summer of 1945. Exercised over Stalin's fait accompli in Poland, which put him in command of half the country —the Poles were to be compensated with Germany's Eastern provinces—they fervently fought Stalin's demand for recognition of this, from their point of view, entirely undesirable territorial arrangement which left the West without a proper bulwark in the East. In reaching their objective of avoiding discussions of permanent boundaries and keeping open territorial questions, they nimbly postponed all decisions and insisted that the provisional character of the joint declaration be maintained until a "full peace conference." They fought as valiantly as deceptively. Truman's briefing book leaves no doubt of his conclusion that it would "be desirable to avoid" such a peace conference.

Kiep, perhaps the CDU's most liberal and independent spokesman, points to the fact that a "just and lasting peace order in Europe" held top priority in Kiesinger's coalition government. The chief interest of Brandt's policy is defined by Kiep in a letter to me in November 1974 as, "Not only geared to a long-term perspective, but to the direct claim that the borders, if one recognizes them, simultaneously must become more permeable. The question of whether the East and Germany policies of Willy Brandt brought as much rapprochement, that is permeability of the borders, as it effected recognition of the status quo for the East, unfortunately has to be answered with 'no,' because the treaty partners in the East, especially the GDR, have not fully lived up to their promises and contractual duties until now. But legal titles alone constitute no political reality . . . ."

Emphasizing that relaxation of tension is far from having become something "tangible," Kiep notes that Brandt was "not able to comply fully with this requirement." Neither the hopeful change through rapprochement nor normalization has yet materialized. "Despite this, Willy Brandt was awarded the Nobel Peace Prize."

"It is the risk of this policy that the credit extended in good faith could have been in vain," Kiep writes. "With his politics toward the East, Brandt made advance payments on a peace in the East whose returns will only show up in the interplay of European and world politics during the next years."

As a politician who all along has stressed the necessity of an active Ostpolitik because of the new relations between Moscow and Washington, Kiep nevertheless is regretfully critical of the methods practiced by Brandt as "hasty and jumpy, too yielding" and "partially dilettantish. . . . The hastiness in the procedure of negotiations on the German side has possibly prevented better results. The tempo in *Ostpolitik* and the reserve in *Westpolitik* made it clear at the same time that Willy Brandt had shifted the priorities of German foreign politics."

The question as to whether Brandt has hurt détente with his "almost unconditional desire" for it is answered by Kiep with an affirmative: "I believe yes, because his will for a renewal of the Federal Republic's environment in foreign affairs was subjected to the relativity of his wishful thinking. Here the youthful dream of young Willy Brandt, the international Socialist, that accompanied him to present days breaks through once more. This is not to say that Brandt has underestimated the Soviet Union and the idea of communism premeditatedly." Aware that the consciousness of a politician is also influenced by his fantasy and dreams, Kiep deduces that these components might have played an "overproportional part."

"No damage done"—voice from Washington

A casually optimistic assessment is offered by one of the State Department's most durable consultants and Germany experts: Eleanor Lansing Dulles, the surviving sister of John Foster and Allen. While the scholarly Dulles indicates that "no damage was done" by Ostpolitik, she shows concern over the inherent "danger of damage." Stressing that Adenauer steered precisely the right course with his Westpolitik, she adjudges Ostpolitik a risky business. "I am all for taking certain risks, but one must be conscious of the fact that one is taking them," she told me in a conversation in February 1975.

"America was not in favor of recognizing East Germany." Dulles' assertion sharply contradicts the contention held in some West German political circles and by political science professor Peter Christian Ludz, occasional adviser to Brandt as well as Schmidt, that the Social Democrats' Ostpolitik was pushed to the limits by Washington's advocates of détente.

"In order to avoid Soviet miscalculations, one must never relax. If you do, they get confused. Only the West's will to resist will stifle Moscow's encroachment. Cooperation, yes; trust, no," she resolutely warns, peering at her visitor through thick-lensed glasses. Analyzing the developments, she sees no substantial difference between Brandt and Bahr's Ostpolitik and Wehner's controversial Rapacki-inspired Germany plan, abandoned and buried without much ado in 1960.

The iron-grey-haired diplomat objects strenuously to the idea that her book, *The Wall is Not Forever,* is overoptimistic. The title, she insists, merely reflects reality. "The Berlin Wall already is full of mansized holes. It has been punctured by traffic, telephone lines and millions of people crossing back and forth," she ably defends her point of view. With regard to reunification of Germany, Dulles is somewhat more guarded in her prognosis. "Of course, the Soviets would have to change. No, so long as the Warsaw Pact exists it is hardly possible. Yet it certainly can be envisioned in the framework of a United Europe . . . probably not in this century!"

To be sure, it is easier for an American diplomat to take the long view.

Had Brandt shown sufficient patience, as Konrad Adenauer demanded?

Had he displayed the tenacity Max Weber ascribed to the greats of history?

Had he drilled at the famous hard boards, which symbolize politics for Weber, strongly and slowly enough, with equal amounts of passion and judiciousness?

Perhaps the general attitude of the German people was summed up most accurately by historian Golo Mann, son of Thomas Mann and determined supporter of Brandt's East treaties, when he wrote:

> Regarded by themselves, they were absolutely necessary, were realistic wisdom. One cannot live with neighbors forever and ever without recognizing their state boundaries or, especially, their existence. The treaties also served the securing of peace. Brandt hoped for more, a peace union, and more freedom in the states of the Russian empire, and more. He did not want to see what he, however, knew: that he was dealing in the Kremlin with cunning imperialists, for whom he came along at the right time and who would drop him, if they no longer needed him. His own disappointment now and the disappointment of many of his voters could have been avoided, if it had been defined in advance what was to be expected of the treaties in our time, and what not.

Mann was greatly distressed by yet another aspect. He had assumed that the settlement of the East treaties would be followed by an active West Europe policy. For that reason, the revelation of a previous case study in which the dissembling of the two military blocks, NATO and Warsaw Pact, was anticipated by Egon Bahr, came as a severe shock.

"Did one know in Bonn precisely and clearly what one wanted?" he questions. Had he known of Bahr's "historically unspeakably ignorant project," had he known about this "Boy Scout plan," he would have been still more cautious with his approval of the East treaties, Mann avowed. "Moscow's wish is the disintegration of the Atlantic Alliance, yet the Russian Eastern empire cannot be dissolved."

Still the historian does not hesitate to rank Brandt, after Adenauer, as one of the more important federal chancellors of the last twenty-five years. One of the major differences? Adenauer surrounded himself with able men.

THE COMPANY HE KEEPS

Machiavelli profoundly observed that the "first impression one gets of a ruler and of his brains is from seeing the men he has around him.

When they are competent and faithful, one can always consider him wise, as he has been able to recognize their ability and keep them faithful. But when they are the reverse, one can always form an unfavorable opinion of him, because the first mistake that he makes is making this choice."

Brandt's distinct lack of instinctive judgment in the appraisal of character was one of his chief handicaps. Suspicious of everyone, especially new faces, he entrusted himself to people sharp or flexible enough to dress up negative or unflattering information as palatable news. Although Brandt seldom shied away from a debate or argument, he hated criticism, even of others. He had a way of "tolerating" critical comment and complaint with a deliberately hurt and distracted air that made the conversation partner want to stop in midsentence.

The consequences became more and more apparent over the years. As the dynamic activists and independent thinkers withdrew from his official and private circle, yesmen and clever courtiers out to brighten their own reputations in the service of the fatherland were allowed to play top roles.

Instead of using the precious time after his memorable victory in 1972 to push for a definite strategy for implementing long-neglected reforms by weeding out the incompetent members of his cabinet and administration, Brandt busied himself with appearances at ceremonial functions. Finance Minister Schmidt, number one on the government's team, was furious that Brandt permitted the SPD's small coalition partner to get away with five cabinet posts. In his opinion, three would have been plenty for the Free Democrats who had provided a scant 8.4 percent of the votes. Nor was he the only politician irritated by Brandt's disconcerting tractability. After the FDP had captured the important and highly visible Foreign Office in addition to the ministries of Interior, Economics, Agriculture, and Press and Information, it was almost impossible to convince the public of the merits of SPD leadership. Furthermore, Schmidt was critical of the chancellor for disregarding the people's need for economic and social security, his inattentiveness to the party's relations with church and middle class, and the unchecked drift from the middle-of-the-road into the leftist camp.

Schmidt was adamant: the SPD's vociferous Young Socialists

scare away the voters with their socialistic concepts, among them price and investment controls, the conversion of private banks into public institutions, and the Federal Republic's exit from NATO.

In Lübeck, a number of prominent long-time Social Democrats, some of them Brandt's friends from childhood and youth, have turned their backs on the party because of the prevalence of leftist ideas.

"Herr Brandt does not do anything about it," complained 58-year-old Maria Krüger, who had known Brandt since she was fifteen.

"What happens now may endanger our nation. This time I voted CDU," Senator Werner Lewerenz, 62, proclaimed in *Quick* magazine.

Lübeck, a traditionally SPD-oriented city, voted CDU.

Once and for all, Schmidt demanded a clear statement from the party's chairman: Is the party to remain the broadly based Social Democratic "people's party" it professed to be since the inception of the Godesberg Program in 1959, or is it actually shifting ground by adopting a purely Socialist doctrine that proposes to overcome the inherent contradictions of capitalism by means of nationalization or socialization?

Brandt had little trouble in dismissing Schmidt's stern critique as that of a political rival. But when one of his favorite people, the handsome and aristocratic Klaus von Dohnanyi, in particularly good graces with pretty Mrs. Brandt, chastized him in an interview, he was unforgiving. Promoted by Brandt from the ranks of the party to Minister of Education and Science, Dohnanyi recommended, for the lightening of the burden of the chancellor, the creation of a sort of subchancellor's position for interior affairs. Dohnanyi was henceforth persona non grata at the chancellory.

However, Brandt's most deadly critic was Herbert Wehner, totally devoted party factotum and its undisputed master. The man who gave the signal to build Brandt up when the Social Democrats needed him and the man who blew the whistle on him when he failed to remain a credit to the party. Wehner had kept a watchful eye on his protégé. He had seen—as others had—a subtle change in Brandt after the elections of 1972. "The responsibility for the demolition of the politician Brandt lies with his own comrades rather than with the opposition," *Spiegel* magazine commented in May 1974.

THE STATESMAN

Perhaps the origin of the change goes back to an even earlier date. Shortly after Brandt had been honored with the Nobel Prize he made a telling remark about the manner and deliverance of his future speeches. They would have to be slightly more imbued with a "father-of-the-country touch," he contended half jokingly.

Once the peace chancellor had decided on his role as statesman, he filled it to perfection. His speeches became flabby philosophical state-of-the-world messages. They exuded a missionary quality that sounded new to enchanted vintage Brandt fans who still had the chilling cold war speeches of Berlin's mayor ringing in their ears. His sentences, once a hard staccato of simple phrases hammered down in a rousing, slightly breathless voice, now flowed along in intricate structural patterns.

Brandt had discovered his considerable talent for speechmaking in his high school days in Lübeck. He had always been blessed with a strong, resonant voice and a commanding stage presence that projected easily across the footlights. His superb memory enabled him to memorize his material after the briefest of readings. His tall, stately figure and the rugged, nonintellectual face, that could have belonged to a sailor, sea captain, or farmer, coordinated comfortably with the deep husky voice and its well-modulated cadences of sincerity.

Brandt was one of those politicians who could read from the phone book and make it sound like a program. Had he not made a career of politics he could have had a chance as an orator, a Billy Graham, or a notable actor.

As he became accustomed to the role of the detached statesman, he developed a profound sense of dignity. Brandt was rarely seen without a large entourage. His frequent outings, replete with motorcycle escorts, police cars and ceremonious black limousines, began to reflect an ostentatiousness questionable for a Social Democrat, especially one who accents the term "Socialist."

The fact that the annual personal allowance fund for Brandt and his chief of staff was twice as large (340,000 marks) as that of Christian Democratic chancellors Ludwig Erhard and Kurt Kiesinger (170,000 marks), was not lost on the taxpayers. They resented it when their well-to-do chancellor, whose income reportedly approximated 300,000 marks a year from government sources alone, struck the grand gesture of donating 25,000 marks to the bomb-damaged Lübeck cathedral, since that money actually came out of a state slush fund. They also resented his rejection as too small the swimming pool at Palais Schaumburg used by previous chancellors. Brandt had it filled in at the taxpayers' expense, while demanding a 160,000 mark enclosure hall for his swimming pool at Venusberg. And they definitely felt ripped off when Brandt's ghostwriter friend successfully hustled a sinecure at 15,000 marks a month, when their chancellor's salary was only 12,251 marks. It was noted with distress that Brandt increased the personnel in the chancellor's office from 261 to 435, and the number of costly state secretaries to 45 from the 30 of Kiesinger's time.

Like many another statesman, Brandt also wanted to immortalize his administration by extravagant building ventures. Despite his speeches about saving government money, a new 110 million mark chancellory and new presidential and parliamentary buildings were approved. The new Ministry of Justice cost 2.7 million marks in annual maintenance alone, compared with 400,000 marks for the old offices. Then there was the startling increase of government personnel. At the ministry of Housing and Urban Planning, salaries shot up from 8 million to 42 million marks! Brandt and his Social Democrats were big spenders.

THE *Gottvater* ROLE

As Brandt concentrated on cultivating his new image, he was bound to lose contact with his party comrades. Kurt Mattick, Berlin representative, was not the only member of the SPD old guard who had not been able to talk to "Willy" in years.

"Of course, standing above the daily events is to Brandt's liking, as is the role of the statesman who has accomplished his historic achievement with his Ostpolitik," one of the chancellor's advisers confided to the press. There were plenty of applauding enthusiasts ever ready to enshrine the peace chancellor in his political glory. This wave of veneration, originally fanned by famed intellectuals and celebrated writers such as Günter Grass, Heinrich Böll, and others, was foreshadowed by a climactic article in which Brandt was apostrophized as "Godhead." The piece was written by Hans Apel, who was to become Schmidt's minister of finance, and appeared in the SPD theoretical organ, *Neue Gesellschaft (New Society).*

Although Apel negated the possibility that Ostpolitik could lead to the ideological obfuscation of social democracy and communism, he nevertheless expected an intensive ideological and political debate between Communists and free Socialists. In the course of this discussion, the writer indulged in extravagant praise for the party's top leadership in a comparison of its hierarchy with the holy Trinity.

> Willy Brandt as Godhead, last resort of appeal, benevolent—sometimes too benevolent (had he only the anger of Jehovah, the God of the Jews)—and full of understanding. Herbert Wehner, the Spirit of the SPD and, we know from the Bible, that the outpouring of the Holy Spirit was not always a calm and peaceful or just process. Helmut Schmidt, however, poses some difficulties in this analogy because he certainly will not be "crucified," and yet he plays his earthly and often wondrous part of solidarity despite all his wilfulness. . . .

It would seem to be to Brandt's credit that he warned Apel against making use of this comparison—had it not been for the wrong reason. Brandt was not offended by its grotesque bad taste but feared "the possibility" that it could be "misunderstood" by the opposition, Apel reported in his *Diary of a Parliamentarian.*

That the thoroughly distressing and offensive personal cult was still very much alive shortly before Brandt's resignation can be determined from an entry in his political diary on April 7, 1974:

> Ehmke during a meeting in Hesse: "Whosoever attacks Brandt, attacks the party itself. Brandt is the embodiment of the party." Now, I have never quite claimed this for myself. But I will be glad to be the embodiment of the will for the solidarity of a combined effort as long as my strength lasts.

Ehmke's exhortation reminds one of the time when France's Sun King, Louis XIV, and other European monarchs could grandly proclaim: L'état c'est mois!

Brandt seemed to have lost all feeling for the totalitarian overtones of Ehmke's absurd statement. Instead of taking Ehmke to task in his book, Brandt self-indulgently clucked about some modification that amounted to an exercise in semantics.

The courtiers who had attached themselves to the benevolent chancellor formed an ever tightening circle around their sole source of wealth and glory. Like Nixon's palace guard, they jealously guarded their master from free-thinking spirits and independent outsiders whose intelligence, ideas and personalities might diminish their own influence. Consequently, they tried to outdo each other in building up a vainglorious image of their hero until he became a sort of national monument. In the end, their stranglehold isolated him not only from government officials and clear-eyed party leaders but from his more objective friends. Even Günter Grass, a faithful admirer who had actively supported Brandt in several election campaigns, complained of the chancellor's inaccessibility.

Wehner's shock waves from Moscow

As Brandt's remoteness progressed to the point where self-satisfaction clouded his sense of perspective, Herbert Wehner decided to bring him back to reality with a kind of shock treatment. The devastating public scolding in September 1973 was timed for high drama, since it came all the way from Moscow, where Wehner and other parliamentarians were on their first well-publicized state visit. The "Number One" has become "sluggish," he is "entranced—carried away," he likes to bathe "lukewarm" these days "as in a tub full of foam," and "what is lacking in the government is a head," Wehner intimated to members of the press.

His acid sarcasm at once opened the floodgates of pent-up discontent. Suddenly it was open season on Brandt. The SPD-supportive *Spiegel* devoted a full issue to the "crumbling monument." Augstein's editorial suggested that the weak chancellor had lost control as leader of his government.

In the absence of Brandt's initiative, energetic Helmut Schmidt seized the opportunity for short-circuiting the decision-making process. As minister of finance he could easily deal with the upcoming issues and projects, by way of approval or disapproval, on strictly budgetary terms.

The comment that Brandt was a mere figurehead, better suited for the ceremonial president's post, was a standard conclusion drawn by editorial writers of differing political shadings at that time. Even the liberal pro-Brandt *Zeit* expressed disappointment in Brandt's leadership and doubts that he would be the right man in times of crisis.

Wehner and Schmidt had made several attempts to interest Brandt in the presidency, which was to be vacated by Gustav Heinemann in 1974. Like Adenauer before him, Brandt indignantly scorned the face-saving solution. Had he in his past days of triumph actually believed the complimentary salutations of the fickle press, the mass adulations, and the flatteries of his courtiers?

In his boundless contempt, Wehner took to referring to Brandt as "Hindenburg," the notoriously weak and slightly senile chancellor who was a pushover for the feisty Hitler. As soon as Brandt finished another of his many innocuous "statesmanlike" appearances, the crafty Wehner sent him congratulatory cables for his "high class observations on our political situation."

When Wehner dared to poke fun at Brandt, once again the signal was understood by everyone. Overnight, the Nobel Prize winner became a figure of ridicule. Comedians, imitating lofty Brandt spouting banalities, blossomed forth in cabarets and on TV shows. In one instance, the chancellor's raspy voice was heard over a telephone placed on a black, red, and gold cushion emitting an endless patter of commonplace rhetoric. Brandt jokes, sometimes just warmed-over Hitler jokes, mushroomed in bars and offices.

Some of them reflected an unusual degree of public frustration:

Herbert Wehner phones Mr. Meyer: "You have won second prize in our contest. Eight days in Bonn and as an extra bonus, you will shake hands with the chancellor." Meyer, in disgust: "What do you mean? I will not shake his hand. I will kick him in the behind." Wehner: "You are not allowed to do that, that is the first prize."

Or: "Have you heard yet, helicopters are dropping hay over the Federal Republic." "Why?" "For the dumb oxen who voted for Willy Brandt."

Or, in a less vicious vein: A tourist comes to Bonn and asks: "Where is Willy Brandt's office?" Answer: "Precisely in the middle between Misfortune [*Pech*] and Delusion [*Wahn*]." *Pech* is a suburb of Bonn, *Wahn* is the name of its airport.

In learned articles, the country's top psychologists explained that jokes serve as ventilators for repressed feelings, especially feelings of disappointment. Clearly, all the monument building and hero worship, in an age when neither the star system nor eternal values could survive, had created a backlash of public resentment. The art of debunking is the people's time-proven mode of liberating themselves from the elevated custodians of newly constricting credos.

And a dressing down from Gunter Grass

Under these severe attacks, Brandt retreated even further into his statesman role, brandishing it like a shield in one last grandstand against intrigue, ideological shadow boxing, and uncontrollable international developments, before giving way to the impulses of fatalism which were to lead to resignation.

Seldom was Brandt more hurt and offended than by the reproaches of Günter Grass. The novelist, known throughout the world for his bestselling *Tin Drum,* maintained that the social-liberal government had not kept its promise of balancing power with moral forces. Grass, who proudly celebrated his friendship with the chancellor in his *Diary of a Snail,* was not willing to compromise his humanistic ideals of freedom, free speech and self-determination in the name of Ostpolitik or détente. He openly criticized the Soviet leaders for their inhumane treatment of Sakharov, Solzhenitsyn, Galytch, Maksimov, and other dissenters. Gloomily he warned of the illusion of improved relations between Bonn and Moscow at the expense of the persecuted intellectuals.

When Brandt's government withdrew its invitation to the novelist to go to Moscow as an official visitor, Grass heatedly accused Bonn of pussyfooting around the real issues. He was disappointed with the interpretation of the politics of détente according to tricky Metternich-inspired guidelines. The election victory had seduced the SPD into a paralyzing self-indulgence. Bonn had fallen into a lethargic pace that stifled the will to continue with its reform work. Too many successes and honors had carried Willy Brandt away into a sphere that cartoonists like to locate way above the clouds, he charged uncharitably.

No wonder Brandt, chafing under these affronts, thought and talked more frequently of resignation.

"I don't want to go on—he says this often. But one must not take it seriously," Klaus Schütz, Brandt's handpicked successor as mayor of Berlin, contended. Conrad Ahlers, Brandt's first press secretary, however, revealed how the chancellor had considered resignation in the summer of 1972 during the fierce confrontations of political rivals Helmut Schmidt and economics minister Karl Schiller, which led to Schiller's premature departure.

To many people, Brandt's resignation talk seemed like the coquettish pose of an extremely thin-skinned politician. But this was not necessarily so. The idea of resignation, perhaps rooted in a sense of fairness as well as awe for the burdensome responsibility of the high office, occupied his mind also in the absence of crisis.

Had Brandt contracted a condition the Germans call *Amtsmüdigkeit?*—in plain English: the higher bureaucrat's complaint of office fatigue. In a long conversation with the chancellor at Blair House in the spring of 1973, I certainly detected some of the symptoms.

GUEST OF HONOR AT THE WHITE HOUSE

Brandt had come to Washington on a state visit that May. Nixon's well-promoted "year of Europe" had failed to pull together the faltering Atlantic Alliance. Kissinger's ill-fated "Declaration of Principles," designed to revitalize and redefine its future purpose, was interpreted by the touchy Europeans as economic blackmail, an attempt to hike up their part of burden-sharing. Nor were the quarreling Europeans prepared to respond with "one voice" as Washington expected. In a hasty effort to stitch together what had been neglected by the Nixon administration over the years because of Vietnam, Watergate, China, Soviet rapprochement and other preoccupations, the European leaders were summoned to the White House one by one.

Only French President Pompidou held out for a meeting in Reykjavik, thus obliging Nixon to come halfway.

It was not a spirited evening at the White House. The state dinner guests, and the more sprightly after-dinner crowd invited for coffee, entertainment and dancing, were all in a more or less dejected mood. The President's dramatic address to the nation on TV the night before (April 30), with the announcement that Haldeman and Ehrlichman had been thrown overboard the Watergate-wrecked ship of state, had not produced the hoped-for results. The polls showed that only 50 percent of Americans believed Nixon had nothing to do with the coverup. The prospect of the upcoming senate hearings was anything but cheering to pale Pat, or to Richard Nixon who was flashing phony smiles and pumping hands with desultory determination.

Only the ebullient Henry Kissinger was his usual unrepressed self. One could hear his heavy German accent booming all over the Green Room, a cluster of ladies of all ages gathered about him. Where the quick-witted Kissinger was, there was laughter. The little, burly charmer even managed to turn rejections into laughing matters. I had asked him for an interview for the German paper I represented. Since Kissinger seemed dubious, I tried to reassure him of a more complimentary treatment than that accorded him by Oriana Fallaci, the mischievous Italian journalist. Kissinger, obviously remembering Fallaci's unkind portrayal of his huge ego, cringed:

"O my dear! Never again with ladies. They are much too clever for me!" he cried out.

Willy Brandt, the guest of honor, stood quite apart and alone in a corner of the crowded room. He looked sunburned and robust, a man in his prime, appearing younger than his nearly sixty years despite a slight portliness. He had put on weight since I had last seen him in Bonn the fall before. No ladies crowded about him. With his usual distracted air, he listened to a general who, with his taciturn wife, stood at arm's length. Our laughter attracted Brandt's attention. As he glanced in our direction he gave me a silent save-me-from-this-boredom look.

"They tell me nothing"—chat at Blair House

When our conversation was cut short by the beginning of the evening's entertainment, Brandt decided we should continue our talk over a nightcap at Blair House after the party. A notorious night owl, he was familiar with the Nixon custom of retiring guests long before midnight.

Blair House, the President's official guest house for foreign dignitaries, conveniently located across the street from the White House, is a little jewel. Its exquisite, carefully chosen antique furnishings, fine porcelains and rare fabrics generate a warm, homelike atmosphere. In the downstairs drawing room, a handful of German officials, Foreign Minister Walter Scheel and Ambassador Berndt von Staden among them, reviewed next day's heavy schedule. Brandt was not in the group. His aide—not the sinister Guillaume but pleasant Wolf-Dietrich Schilling—asked me to join the chancellor who was working on his National Press Club speech in the upstairs study.

Brandt was sitting behind the large desk in the center of the room. The speech on the necessity of the Atlantic partnership was too long, he feared. He was not sure whether or not he should make reference to Watergate. At that time, the scandal had not had much impact on the German press. After some deliberation—the matter was left to Brandt's instinct for the mood of the Press Club audience—his royally paid ghostwriter collected the manuscript for duplication. With a show of nonchalant servility, the courtier made his way to the door. But not without casting a disapproving glance in my direction. He made no pretense of hiding his dislike for potentially bothersome outsiders.

After Brandt had poured the Burgundy, he settled back in one of the linen-covered easy chairs, comfortably stretching his long legs in front of him. He had given up hard liquor a long time ago. As a result of a recent serious but unpublicized operation—the removal of a growth, fortunately benign, on his vocal chords—he was forced to give up his beloved cigarillos, too. He seemed utterly serene and at peace with himself as we scanned Eisenhower's amateurish paintings along the walls. Ike's colorful art had no particularly commendable features.

"I promise you, I will never make paintings like that when I am out of office," he laughed.

"Are you speaking about retirement?" The thought struck me as odd.

"If one has gone through a precarious operation like I have, one thinks of many things," he replied enigmatically. He was deadly serious when he explained at some length the benefits of the government's generous pension program, in his case cumulative since his days as mayor of Berlin.

"At any rate, my friends will not have to go around with a hat collecting money in my old age," he joked. The thought of leaving office and power behind him seemed to hold no dread. On the contrary, he would be free to write, travel and make a few speeches. He would be freed from the harassment of the press, disenchantment with people and, most important, the miserable isolation that was slowly engulfing him.

"But isn't it up to you to break that isolation?"

"That is not so easy. I am surrounded by people putting up walls around me. I am no longer in touch . . . they tell me nothing," he complained helplessly. His unconcealed dispiritedness certainly seemed symptomatic of an oncoming case of office fatigue.

Nobody had told him that of the twenty-five members of the German press corps in Washington only five had been invited to next day's reception in his honor at the German embassy. No politician in his right mind relishes insulting twenty journalists over invitations to a party.

"Do you understand now what I am talking about?" Brandt moaned. "But you'll see, I will fix this. I promise you, we will have all twenty-five journalists."

He did. But when the courtiers in charge of public relations found out who had interfered with their initial arrangements, they descended on the troublemaker with the tongue-lashing fury of Shakespearean witches.

When I mentioned this strange conversation to Egon Bahr after the resignation, Bahr confessed that his long-time friend and boss—since mayoral days in Berlin—had never talked to him about pensions and encroaching isolation. Bahr evidently had not spotted signs of *Amtsmüdigkeit.*

Brandt is a very complex man, with many facets to his character. It is probably an impossible endeavor to fit these facets into a meaningful composite. Can it, perchance, be sensed intuitively, divined?

It took Georg Meistermann, an abstract German painter of note, three years to come up with a controversial Brandt portrait entitled "Colored sketches for a biography of the Federal Chancellor 1969–73." Brandt looked always different to him, Meistermann marveled. Among thousands of available photos, perhaps ten yielded similar likenesses. After a succession of frustrating starts, Meistermann suddenly intuitively understood and captured the multilayered Brandt personality by means of a series of color sketches.

One of Brandt's debunkers once wrote that he strikes one as a person who carries a deep unspeakable secret around with him. What kind of secret? Something of a nature that could be used by the crafty Guillaume? Or was it just the secret sadness that befalls us when we realize the schism between our achievements and our goals.

Was the impression based on Brandt's unfortunate habit of averting his gaze when he spoke to people and before TV cameras? His difficulty with looking directly into a person's eyes had become more noticeable during those days of extreme stress.

Willy Brandt has gone through a number of clearly contradictory phases in his difficult and complicated life. Each time, a more enigmatic personality seemed to emerge. Yet, at the same time one is baffled by the singular consistency of a socialist-humanist leitmotiv meandering in and out of vision.

Was he overrated, as some of his contemporaries suggested before and after the fall? In the neutral *Neue Zürcher Zeitung*, Switzerland's most distinguished newspaper, Fred Luchsinger had judged some time ago that Brandt was a "procrastinator" and the "most overrated and misjudged European politician of recent years."

In the only interview Brandt gave directly following his resignation, he allowed that his new role as fulltime chairman of the Social Democratic Party of Germany probably demanded a "new style," Ulrich Kemski, top correspondent for the *Süddeutsche Zeitung* in Munich reported.

As with the Kennedys, style has always been extraordinarily important to the Federal Chancellor.

What will the next Willy Brandt be like?

4
The Assessment

The prominent politicians making this assessment of Willy Brandt and the Brandt era—among them two European chancellors—were carefully chosen because of their reputations of fairness and balanced judgment. The verbal expedition in search of the multifaceted Brandt personality would have been ill-served by the distorted views of confirmed and undaunted Brandt fans or fanatical detractors and Brandt haters. Love and hate blur the vision and becloud the mind.

If there was one unexpected problem encountered in these interviews, which were conducted in the summer of 1974, it was that of keeping the politicians on track. Most wanted to expound on their own policies rather than dwell on Brandt. Given the unsuppressable penchant of politicians for hearing themselves talk, one still wonders about the impact of a chancellor, on the verge of becoming a nonperson, so shortly after his spectacular exit. Unless, of course, Bonn still was in a state of shock.

Brandt Era Like Euphoric Mini-Trip—
Kurt Georg Kiesinger

At seventy, the tall, lean Kurt Georg Kiesinger is every inch the distinguished exchancellor of the Grand Coalition (CDU/CSU and

SPD, 1966–69). Impeccably dressed, his silvery hair neatly groomed, he emanates the serenity, expansive kindness and generosity of the elder statesman who finds himself beyond the desperate struggle for daily headlines.

As befits a former chancellor and CDU party chairman, Kiesinger commands the biggest and most beautiful office in *Lange Eugen,* the drab skyscraper where other members of parliament are crowded into dinky offices which they must share with their office staff consisting of one and only one secretarial assistant. Suite 1717 on the top floor is equipped with an anteroom for legislative staffers and two of the prettiest and friendliest secretaries one could hope to find in all of Bonn. Aside from these attractions, it boasts a truly breathtaking view of the winding Rhine with its imposing flow of weathered barges and glittering white steamers, its sleek bridges shooting across the wavy surface to tree-lined banks. Among the trees one can see the moldy decay of magnificent Victorian manor houses and the topsy-turvy chaos of the industrial parks of yesteryear against the velvety green silhouette of the gently stretching Siebengebirge hills.

All this natural beauty is not lost on Kiesinger, a lawyer by profession, known as a lover of nature and nature poetry and an occasional poet. Because of his poetic, sometimes highly literary nineteenth-century vocabulary, the press called him King Silvertongue during the hectic elections of 1969 when the grandfatherly aesthete was campaigning against barnstorming, plain-talking Brandt.

Although he has been out of office for years, the handsome, sociable Christian Democrat is still much in demand. Kiesinger, always one of the most accessible of politicians, is in a buoyant mood. He has just returned from a visit to Iran and is in the process of supervising the packaging of a number of cases of wine from his region in appreciation of the Shah's hospitality.

At a state dinner given by Chancellor Schmidt the evening before, he had found an enchanting, highly intelligent and dynamic dinner partner in Madame Broz.

"I suspect Madame runs the country—at least partially—with Tito being eighty-three," he volunteers. Not without pride, Kiesinger alludes to the fact that it was his government that reestablished diplomatic relations with Yugoslavia against the protests of the conservatives in his own party, who tried to uphold the Hallstein doctrine which denied official relations with countries recognizing the German Democratic Republic.

Kiesinger is delighted to explain to me, a familiar visitor from Washington with whom he has had many an exchange over the course of recent years, the political situation climaxed by Brandt's spectacular fall.

On Foreign Affairs

"Brandt's politics aroused that sort of intoxicating expectation that must be followed by a *katzenjammer*—a big hangover, a moderating process, if you will. It is useful to keep in mind, however, that long before the spy affair, the SPD's popularity had declined by 10 percent compared with the results of the last federal elections. I had hoped that the FDP would disappear from the political scene in some of the states."

The CDU/CSU has never quite forgiven the Free Democrats for their defection to the SPD in 1969.

"Since there was an euphoric expectation, a high, and not just in foreign politics, the public expected much more than was to come. In reality, the Four Power Berlin Agreement was the only substantive result of Brandt's Ostpolitik. The few instances of human easements and relief negotiated on paper are in fact destroyed in practice. For example, now East German doctors can no longer travel to West Germany because they have been classified as carriers of state secrets. The East German population is openly cautioned not to issue invitations. Their government cannot afford even this minute degree of permeation." It is perhaps typical of this politician and his quest for the golden middle—exemplified by the politics of coalition, of harmonizing and synthesizing different views—that the fall of his antagonist rouses charitable feelings rather than vindictiveness.

"Nikita Khrushchev's Berlin ultimatum of November 27, 1958, has demoralized the West," he remarked matter-of-factly, referring to the Soviets' demand that West Berlin be severed from the Federal Republic, and their massive threat to cut off all Allied transports to West Berlin if it was not transformed into a "free city" within six months.

"I most assuredly would have negotiated the East treaties in a much tougher and more cautious manner. Now we will have to live with them." (The East treaties were not ratified by the CDU/CSU.) "Open-end modus vivendi resolutions like that are always dangerous because the Soviets regard them as final documents. Treaties with open dissent are harmful inasmuch as they breed conflicts. Egon Bahr's assessment of the situation of the West was wrong. I would have held out two or three years longer in order to frame something one is able to live with. Détente, after all, is a condition where one is opponent and partner at the same time. It is a compulsory partnership for peace, as it were."

His eyes fixed on the distant, misty horizon of the Rhine Valley, he continues, "Golo Mann, who has favored Ostpolitik for years, sees himself defeated in his expectations. His deliberations, like those of many another sympathizer, went along these lines: if Brandt aligns himself with the East's status quo, then the prospects of European unity will be promoted by necessity. Of course, we know that the will to unification has always been revived in the face of danger. This policy of détente, on the other hand, had a devastating effect on Western cooperation. Therefore, the European situation today looks more desolate than ever. Brandt's politics has decisively contributed to a weakening of the European community."

Kiesinger's analysis was free of passion. He had warned years ago that Brandt's Ostpolitik would lead to nothing. In the heat of the election of 1969 he angrily dismissed SPD recognition of the GDR as an "out-and-out capitulation." If there is reprimand for his old political foe, it is expressed indirectly these days. For example, he emphasizes that as chancellor he tried to stay discreetly in the background in foreign politics, especially in European affairs, "because leftover resentments against Germans were still widely perceivable reactions." Unfortunately, the charming exchancellor faced a personal problem that never touched his highly visible foreign minister, Brandt the emigrant. Kiesinger had joined the Nazi party by the time he became an official in Hitler's foreign office during the war years from 1940–1945. Understandably, when he advanced to the highest political office not everybody was ready to forget and forgive his Nazi past as a youthful conformist aberration.

On Inflation

Kiesinger's assessment of domestic policies is no less tempered. "Brandt emerged with the thesis: Only now will we have a modern Germany, only now will we realize a democracy. Helmut Schmidt happens to be a trifle more modest. He talks of holding the line on government spending, like Erhard and me before him. Our inflation of 8 percent is relatively low compared to Japan's 25 or America's 11 percent. But our labor unions think they have to ask for a 15 percent wage hike—they settled for 12 percent—to catch up with inflation and progressive taxation. Behind the fear of inflation is that of a paralyzing stagflation. Presently, our unemployment figures are not alarming, but our experts anticipate 3 percent. Such a figure is enough to incite unrest among our workers—we have between 4 and 5 million foreign workers and their families in our country—who prefer price stability over pay raises." Kiesinger feels that he successfully dealt with a recession and a $4 billion budget deficit when he took over in 1966; nevertheless he admits: "It is easier to fight a recession than a stagflation."

On Brandt's Style

"After Brandt received the Nobel Peace Prize he behaved like a high priest. Schmidt is a very capable man. Efficiency aside, he is much better in sensing and meeting the demands of a modern style. Our youth is much more willing to accept his impudent pizazz than the father figure and hero worship that was popular in the 1960s."

On Elections

"Like people everywhere in the world, our voters will make their primitive decision: they will vote their pocketbooks. If they are doing well, they will not change horses. If they hurt financially, they will vote for a change. Actually the SPD vote-getting record of 1972 (up from 224 parliamentary seats in 1969 to 230) was not impressive. But the Social Democrats know how to make much ado about little. Fewer and fewer voters come out to listen to the politician in the market square, unless he bears a prominent name. For that reason, political personalities, including me, are still in demand to attract audiences.

"Today we are baffled by an incalculable elasticity of the voting pattern. In Neustadt, a small town in Hesse, for example, the voting picture of 29 percent for the CDU/CSU and 51 percent for the SPD was completely turned around. Thanks to the general sobering process, the CDU was able to attract a substantial part of the youngest voters to whom ideologies are as suspect as ideologists. As I predicted earlier, the reaction against the rebels who began to crowd the political scene in 1968 has become noticeable. I was putting my hopes on this new generation all along. It is a fresh and energetic generation that comes into its own now. One of our columnists wrote quite recently that Kiesinger has his ear near the grass roots. A number of professors confirm my views; they find the new students entirely different. While this can hardly be chalked up as an achievement for the CDU as opposition, it certainly can be attributed to the ideologization on the part of the Jusos."

On Nostalgia for The Grand Coalition

"After the Brandt-fog lifted, one observed a distinct nostalgia for the Grand Coalition and a sudden recognition of its accomplishments. These days, many of the letters of my constituents begin with 'If you were still chancellor much would be different. . . .' " On his seventieth birthday, Kiesinger received a lengthy telegram of congratulations from Chancellor Schmidt, in which the SPD leader made reference to the achievements and the resolved tasks of the Grand Coalition as well as its necessity in 1966.

Another gift Kiesinger seems to treasure is the book, *Problems of the Third World,* with its laudatory inscription by Hans-Jürgen Wischnewski, the SPD's choice for Minister of Development Aid in 1966–68. To have an SPD functionary freely rhapsodize about the "good old coalition days" must please Kiesinger immensely, because it was the SPD that bestowed on him the biting label, "walking mediation committee" during the bitter election battle. Today, that uncomplimentary label for an overly conciliatory chancellor must have a pleasant ring to a party whose internal strife and leadership problems endanger its cohesion.

On The Brave New World

"The Brandt years resemble a euphoric mini-high. Now that our heads are clear once more, we can foresee future turbulences of a severity seldom experienced in this world. I am pessimistic concerning the future. The oil crisis was but the first warning signal. How to solve this? A greater and greater part of the affluence of this world, a profit of $80 billion to be precise, must and will turn up as investment in the West. How will this be handled? What changes will this bring about? Are these changes compatible with our means of democracy? Zero economic growth—a brave, new, optimistic concept, a solution for many a pressing problem, but at the same time a germinal factor for another problem: unemployment. Environmental and population control require a solidarity that eventually should cancel out the most blatant disparities.

"Up to now we abided by the motto: Every man for himself. Still, no matter how we look at it, no matter if the context is currency reform or agricultural production, our fate is interdependency. It is our most essential, our most vital task to accept and come to terms with this reality. Entirely new ground has to be broken. Most importantly, we must make an intelligent and energetic break for solidarity. If I were younger I would devote all my energies to this challenge."

On His Memoirs

Kiesinger lacks neither the enthusiasm of youth nor its imagination. Above all, he can still empathize. It is not easy to keep the exchancellor on the subject of Brandt once he starts on the path of his fascinating reminiscences. It is as though one is living history when Kiesinger evokes his quarrels with Charles de Gaulle about a united Europe under French stewardship and possible Soviet support, or the banter-like talks with Kennedy on the atomic test ban treaty—Kiesinger was the last German official to visit JFK—or the testy arguments with Lyndon Johnson, when the German vented his anger about "atomic complicity." There is a reason for the past occupying his mind as much as the future: Kiesinger is in the process of writing his memoirs. Unlike Brandt, who felt compelled to rush out a self-serving apologia in the first heat of defeat (*Beyond the Day,* published in the fall of 1974) Kiesinger is taking his time. In his stories of powerful men and the unhealthy relationship some had with power as well as the misfortunes they brought about—even for themselves —one can look forward to an amusing and detached account of the last several decades.

On Brandt's Unwanted "Sozi" Bloc

"The SPD is in a real crisis. Neo-Marxist forces are exerting their very strong influence. These Marxist Social Democrats are incurable dreamers with missionary tendencies. Brandt's 'Sozi' [Socialist] bloc is not wanted. Brandt may be a man of goodwill, but the Soviets will not tolerate this. Bahr's concept of change through rapproachement, initiated against Wehner's better judgment, is suicidal politics. The Guillaume affair did not just happen before the regional elections," he adds ominously, as his eyes wander in the direction of the discreetly opening door. Dr. Reinhard Schmoeckel, Kiesinger's personal aide, regrets to interrupt but Mr. George McGhee, former U.S. Ambassador to Bonn, has arrived for his appointment.

"Do come again before you leave Bonn," Mr. Kiesinger urges with his most engaging smile. He appreciates a good listener as much as any politician who excels as a raconteur.

European Detente Built on Brandt's Initiative—
Bruno Kreisky

"Willy Brandt and I met in exile at an international Socialists' study group in Stockholm in 1940. I had emigrated to Sweden late in 1938. Brandt had just fled there from Norway after it was occupied by German troops. He was honorary executive secretary of this group attempting to work out a blueprint for peace. Europe after the war was our subject. We also discussed the cooperation of socialists in an international context, economic planning after the war, and the establishment of a 'Socialist International'."

Dr. Bruno Kreisky, chancellor of Austria since 1970, chairman of the Socialist Party of Austria (SPÖ) since 1967, and chairman of the Socialist International, of which Willy Brandt is vice-chairman, settles back in his huge, brown leather club chair next to an impressive phone table with a most intricate push button system, rivaling a regular switchboard.

"The Myrdals belonged to this group as well as Socialists from eleven European countries. The fact that Brandt—as a German—was able to hold this collection of Hungarians, Poles, Spaniards, Scandinavians and other nationals together attests to his diplomatic skills, his tact and extraordinary negotiating abilities."

Kreisky, born in Vienna in 1911, is a short and lively man, with curly blondish hair and a full, fleshy face with mobile features. The intellectual's inclination for understatement is enhanced by a convivial openness. In his well-cut grey suit, Kreisky reminds one of the dapper literati who used to enliven the famous Vienna cafes with their civilized discussions. Yet under all that outgoing Viennese *Gemütlichkeit,* one senses a will of steel. His ballroom-sized office, a warm composition of muted shades of leather and wood panelling, at once comfortable and matter-of-fact, reflects the personality of its inhabitant.

"Our contacts were rather loose in those days. Brandt was calm and patient. He has always spoken with the same hoarse voice. I don't think he has changed much. It is hard to tell, because we change too. We like to laugh together; we also know how to be silent together."

"You really enjoy each other's company?"

"It is the old relationship of two Socialists. Our personal relationship . . . our friendship has grown more solid since both of us became chancellors. In addition, we share the same Scandinavian experience. Both of us are caught up in this cultural atmosphere. Our wives are Scandinavians."

Kreisky's wife, Vera, is a native of Stockholm. The first Mrs. Brandt is Norwegian, as is the second. Here the comparison ends. Mrs. Kreisky is the highly educated daughter of a well-to-do industrialist. Small-town girl Rut Brandt, a chauffeur's daughter, has no formal education.

Similar Careers

Indeed, no other politician's career resembles that of Willy Brandt more closely than Bruno Kreisky's. At the same time no two backgrounds could be more dissimilar. Each became chairman of his party, then foreign minister of his country, and finally, chancellor. Both joined radical socialist organizations in their high school years. Kreisky became a member of the Socialist Workers' Youth (SAJ), Brandt, of the Socialist Workers' Party of Germany (SAP).

In accordance with his proletarian childhood milieu, Brandt comprehended the socialist's ABCs, taught him at the knee of his Marx-indoctrinated truckdriver grandfather, as a class struggle filled with resentment against the Haves. On the other hand, young compassionate Kreisky, son of a wealthy, cultured Jewish textile mill owner in whose home intellectuals of all persuasions—including Arthur Schnitzler—gathered for an exchange of ideas, came to socialism via the humanist route: He simply wanted to better the circumstances of the working class.

Both Brandt and Kreisky rose quickly through the ranks to chairmanship of their respective organizations. Both became impassioned Nazi fighters. Both escaped from their homeland and spent their formative years in Scandinavia. Kreisky, arrested as leader of the Revolutionary Socialist Youth in 1935, was sentenced to one year in jail for treason by the Dollfuss regime and jailed again by the Gestapo after Austria's annexation by Hitler in 1938, narrowly escaping Nazi concentration camps by his emigration. Brandt's principal reason for leaving his country was the prospect of a job with the SAP in Oslo and, to be sure, escape from Nazism and the oppressing stigma of illegitimacy that clouded his life in Lübeck.

Both future chancellors engaged in journalistic activities. Kreisky soon found employment as an economic researcher for a Swedish co-op. Brandt, however, remained the dutiful party functionary, carrying out occasional conspiratorial missions. Brandt left his real name, Herbert Frahm, and German citizenship behind. Kreisky remained Kreisky and Austrian.

Contrary to rumors, Willy Brandt did not consult his old friend about his resignation.

"The resignation came as a surprise to all his friends," Kreisky explained. "I never would have expected that. I was shocked, because the relaxation of tension in Europe is built on Brandt's initiative. It is almost grotesque—on the edges of Europe there are fires everywhere, yet in the core all is stabile. Austria certainly has been one of the beneficiaries of the relaxation of tension. For me that means the establishment of a pacifying balance, not a military balance."

Kreisky pauses a moment before continuing.

"Schmidt is an immensely efficient chancellor, but Brandt symbolized a moral category, and that is a category one cannot relinquish in politics. The prestige of Brandt is high in the world of politics. He was an integrating factor in European affairs. I, for one, know very well that there would not have been a solution for the European outsiders of the European Economic Community—and there are quite a few nations—without the active participation of Willy Brandt."

"What do you mean by Brandt's moral function?"

"He has demonstrated the courage for realistic politics. People are ambivalent. They all want realistic politics, but they don't want to be torn from their hopes and dreams. Brandt has enhanced the German reputation in other countries. The historical significance of the Brandt years for the German people cannot be discerned today. One can sense it and perhaps recognize that he was the first German chancellor of whom the world was not afraid. Adenauer's achievements were great, because he tried to restore Germany to its useful function. But with Brandt, the word chancellor—immediately the name of Bismarck, the iron chancellor, flashes through one's mind —no longer carries the connotation of fear."

Pioneer in Détente

"You have been a pioneer in the preparation of a climate for détente. Didn't you do some of the initial mediating between Khrushchev, Adenauer, and Brandt? After all, it was Adenauer who remarked to Chancellor Raab that he would not mind having 'your Kreisky' as a foreign minister." Adenauer, anxious to keep up contacts with the Soviets in one form or another, thought Kreisky "the most suitable" person to do so. For it was Kreisky who successfully negotiated the Austrian State Treaty of 1955 that freed his country of Soviet occupation and reinstated its national independence.

Kreisky has an excellent memory. "Adenauer and I talked about East-West relations several times a year. I was involved in two abortive missions, in 1959 and 1960. Both times I was approached by the Soviets."

After Khrushchev's Berlin ultimatum, Kreisky, in an article published early in 1959, had advocated a "special status" solution for all of Berlin (East and West) under the control of UN police forces assembled primarily from the four big powers.

Assuming that the article was inspired by and serving as a test balloon for Brandt, Berlin's Governing Mayor, the Soviet ambassador in Vienna advised Kreisky that Khrushchev was interested in a private meeting with Brandt. Kreisky managed to deliver the important message in person during Brandt's stopover on a return flight from New Delhi. Brandt, who had asked Kreisky repeatedly for his help in establishing direct contact with the Soviets, accepted the offer. But nothing happened. Neither Kreisky nor Adenauer, who was fully briefed on this development, could understand why Brandt backed away from his initial decision.

Kreisky's second effort to pass on a six-page note on Berlin from Soviet Foreign Minister Gromyko during Khrushchev's visit in Vienna ended even more disastrously. On vacation in Scandinavia, Brandt turned the matter over to Egon Bahr. News leaks developed, followed by distorted newspaper headlines.

———

"What do you expect of party chairman Willy Brandt?"

"As party chairman, Brandt will inevitably have to step into the background—into the shadow of Helmut Schmidt. Brandt as a nonpolitical human being in a nonpolitical situation is unimaginable for me. It would be difficult to accept such a fact. But the world has a short memory."

"Brandt seems to think of European integration on a Socialist basis," I suggested.

"First of all, the Socialist movement in Europe needs a strong theoretical foundation. Keep in mind, we are talking about the conservation of the West, the Occident. If Brandt wants to take on this task, the theoretical aspects need to be transposed into political forms and workable guides to action. Altogether untried things, new concepts, have to be submitted. This cannot be accomplished in an ivory tower of theory.

"We seem to be further away from European integration than a few years ago. Without it, however, there seems to be no way of stabilizing its economy.

"Europe may not be unitable—one has to gather it together. As a concept, the integration of Europe can be related to the idea of social democracy—both have supranational premises. On this basis one can easily talk to England's Prime Minister Harold Wilson, for example. To date, the left wing Labourites traditionally have been against European integration because it used to be the preserve of Conservative politics. Therefore, the international cooperation of the labor unions is going to advance European integration more than anything else. An approach along those lines seems promising. Certainly the Italians are ready for it."

Third Phase

"Should not the Social Democrats rather harness their energies to solve their domestic reform quarrels and ideological issues before expanding into the politics of European integration?"

"Social democracy is only at the beginning of its historical development. It is now in its third phase: democratization on all social levels, the flooding of all areas with the ideas of democracy. In its first phase we have seen the creation of proletarian consciousness and political democracy, and in its second phase the welfare state. But one has to keep in mind that a state can develop social reforms only up to the point where they can be financed. We had our arguments with the Communists, and we had to draw a sharp line between us again and again. In my opinion, it is the task of the Social Democrats to work out a valid alternative to communism. If social democracies represent and maintain the idea of a permanent democratization of our societies then they will become an alternative to conservatism as well as to communism."

When Kreisky talks of the integration of democratic Europe, he thinks in terms of 300 million people with equal social legislation, European development aid, and progressive cultural integration. Although he hopes for an intensified economic cooperation with the Communist East and an all-European traffic system, he has no illusions about rapprochement leading to a convergence of the two economic systems: the West's social democracy and the East's communistic dictatorship.

"If it is Brandt's firm conviction to realize a social democracy, it is unthinkable that he bypasses the exertion of influence on heavy industry," Kreisky interjects. An integrated Europe offers, in his view, a new means of dealing with the uncontrollable, multinational corporations by way of devising a multinational strategy for their regulation.

"I hope you are going to talk to Palme on this subject." Kreisky and Palme have written extensively on democratization and European integration.

While the Austrian chancellor finds praise for Brandt's "autonomous attitude" toward America in the matter of arms shipments from German soil during the Middle East crisis, he seems worried about the many facets of the SPD radical left wing.

"There is too much dogma and, perhaps, a conduct one can no longer describe as social democratic. Brandt is a valuable human being with a distinct bent for self-criticism. But self-criticism can be destructive. In this position one has to wrestle with one's conscience almost every hour. Is what one has done really right? Political instinct is not everything—emotions and facts have to be kept in proper balance. No, I did not sense any office fatigue in Brandt, but it is possible that he was overcome by a physical matter."

The espionage activities of the East do not shock the sophisticated Austrian. At least, he sees no reason for polemics against the Communists on that account. He is convinced that the Western powers also have their agents stashed away in high places.

Kreisky had met with Brandt in Salzburg in the spring of 1974 to discuss a book project on the future of socialism in Europe.

"Brandt possesses a tremendous sense of dignity," he observes with an amused smile. "I don't like it if a lot of fuss is made over me. We Austrians are casual people. This probably has to do with the mixture of the people. We have Hungarians, Czechs, Germans, Jews, Bohemians, people from the Balkans, and from who knows where."

Kreisky's Simplicity

The Austrian chancellor travels without entourage; sometimes a secretary accompanies him. He has been seen in the center of one of Vienna's crowded railroad stations, waiting for a red cap.

I am reminded of Kreisky's impressive simplicity on my way out, when I hurry through the mirrored anteroom, where the sole ornament is the large painting of the signing of the State Treaty at Belvedere Castle, and down the wide, carpetless marble staircase to the grand entrance of the ancient palace—which made its last sensational headlines in 1934 when Chancellor Engelbert Dollfuss was assassinated there by the Nazis.

The lone policeman on duty in front of the grey facade salutes casually as I pass. There are no barriers, no fences, no roaming groups of policemen with walkie-talkie sets. This certainly is not Bonn.

On the other hand, neither is there a trace of busty Empress Maria Theresa nor the wily Metternich. Even Vienna, eternal city of grand palaces and parks that the Hapsburgs loved and built so well, is not the same. Unattractive, inelegant tourists push down the *Kärntnerstrasse,* crowding each other at the torn-up, dust-and-noise-filled end where the shrouded cathedral stands barricaded into oblivion in the name of progress, called the subway. Cameras slung over slouching shoulders, they patiently stand in line to see the famed Lippizaners and their fancy saddles, emblazoned with gold heraldry, and trot down the narrow lanes with the memorable facades that convey so well the legendary Viennese spirit of yesterday—that unlikely combination of stern dignity and playful frivolity nowadays diminished by commercialism.

"Genuine Sacher Torte," the obtrusive sign screams for customers at the side entrance of the historic Sacher Hotel, fabled inn and playground of the old empire's nobility and notorious. Not even this venerated hallmark of a graceful past has been able to withstand the ineffable transition from pomp to vulgarity.

The People Have Been Deluded—

Richard von Weizsäcker

Dr. Richard von Weizsäcker, the CDU's respected but defeated choice as candidate for the office of President of the Federal Republic, was born in Stuttgart in 1920. He is a lawyer by profession and has studied jurisprudence at the universities of Oxford, Grenoble and Göttingen. A leader who distinguished himself as a member of the Evangelical Council and as President of the German Evangelical Church Convention (1964 to 1970), he is one of the most scholarly and influential newcomers to the Bundestag since 1969.

Since suave, soft-spoken, quietly persuasive von Weizsäcker had to catch a train back to Worms that afternoon, he was pressed for time when I spoke to him. Hence, we met briefly in a corner of the big lobby of the Bundestag while the debate on tax reform proceeded in the plenum. Because of the time element, he spoke rapidly in an intense, uninterrupted stream-of-consciousness style. With his head bent forward, his arms resting on his knees, and his eyes fixed on an unidentifiable spot on the floor, he presented the essence of concentration.

No, he is not disappointed by Brandt's Ostpolitik—because he had no illusions about it. Yes, he was in agreement with the attempt to normalize relations with Germany's Eastern neighbors. His quarrel was never *if* Ostpolitik, but *how?*

". . . the probability of a German government exerting influence on global East-West developments was always overrated. The promotion of détente by the West under American leadership as such, has been supported by German governments before Brandt and will be supported by governments after Schmidt.

". . . however, the Brandt government has managed to establish the notion—amongst our own people, above all—that there was a continuing cold war, and peace and cooperation were only pursued since the Brandt government moved in on Bonn. This is an illusion that was bound to lead to grave disappointments. Now, as before, the Russians are arming—more and faster than all the Western countries together. They transpose military potential into political influence.

". . . their aim, clearly, is the prevention of the union of Western Europe as well as an economic and scientific cooperation with Western Europe based on a gradual political extension of their own sphere of influence in the West.

". . . that is to say, they neither want to attack nor destroy us. What they want is our scientific and economic potential. This policy and an ongoing test of power politics with the West has been continued regardless of the age of détente. What has not happened is an expected conversion to peaceful cooperation and communication.

". . . I have nothing against Brandt. He has been sold to the people as the great peacemaker. Yet nothing has changed in the Russian point of view. Our people have been deluded and disappointed. To be sure, the CDU has not conducted a faultless Ostpolitik—our security oriented thinking has been mired in immobility. The Grand Coalition found a useful foundation for a middle-of-the-road approach between the points of danger—not by pinning extravagant expectations on the Soviet Union, and not by hurried actions.

". . . in my judgment the treaty with Poland has been a bitter experience, but an inevitable one. I never thought the Moscow Treaty ready for signature, even though its goal—renunciation of force—merited it. I certainly think of the Basic Treaty with the German Democratic Republic as the worst of them. The questions in need of regulation could have been easily regulated without benefit of a state treaty. In its preamble we are right away confronted with the statement that the partners of this treaty could not come to an agreement. What kind of a treaty is this, I ask you? International recognition of the GDR was no longer delayable. I am aware of that.

"... it appears that German foreign policy is in conflict with itself. On the one hand, our aim is national unity. On the other, we let ourselves be praised by our Western Allies for declaring the German question as settled and finished. It is highly contradictory when the government insists that the question of our national unity remains open and at the same time an exchange of ambassadors with the GDR is consummated.

". . . there has been no cooperation between government and opposition. Consultations on Ostpolitik in the interest of finding mutually acceptable ways of handling matters of vital national importance were not desired by the SPD, especially not by Mr. Wehner. The SPD obviously wanted to use Ostpolitik as a tool for domestic advantage. Egon Bahr made Ostpolitik, Herbert Wehner made domestic politics. Factual problems and concrete issues were subordinated to this purpose. Bahr's activist German politics, no doubt, sprang from a condition requiring urgent exigency, but genuine need does not necessarily bring about change. . . ."

Richard von Weizsäcker's low voice is drowned out by the insistent ringing of the parliamentary bell. It is time to vote.

I ask one last question: How does he assess Brandt's policy for Europe?

For a moment, the CDU politician stares at me in mock consternation.

"I am stunned that you ask about that. I was under the impression that the SPD has stuck to a low profile, a retardatory policy on that subject. Or could it be that the prospect of a socialist Europe has provided Brandt with a new impetus?"

Von Weizsäcker looks quite worried as he hastens back into the crowded assembly hall.

Brandt Has Brought the Federal Republic Out of Its "I" Position—

Kurt Mattick

With his white hair and a touch of the inimitable Berlin dialect, Kurt Mattick comes on as a kindly, sharp-eyed and incorruptible gentleman, philosopher, party functionary. In the course of his long political career, the five-term veteran of the Bundestag has acquired many time-consuming responsibilities. As former chairman of Berlin's Social Democrats and longtime member of Berlin's legislature, he rates as one of the most experienced and reliable SPD politicians. Busy as he is, he sets no time limit for our talk about the "Brandt impact." When we meet in his spacious office in Bonn's Bundeshaus, he asks his secretary to hold all phone calls. Mattick is the only politician I talked to who showed surprise at the absence of a tape recorder. Generally speaking, tape-recorded interviews do not rank high on the popularity list of Bonn politicians.

Mattick, one of Brandt's oldest friends and party associates, is a genuine Berliner with all the proverbial character traits: unconventional outspokenness and a keen sense of reality. Born in 1908 and starting out in life with an elementary school diploma and a mechanic's certificate, he has never learned to mince words. As a member of the metal workers' union, young Mattick came in contact with Nazi resistance groups and took part in their activities. His political apprenticeship as personal assistant to Professor Dr. Otto Suhr, who became Berlin's mayor in 1955, started in 1946 and could not have been more expert.

With his disarming honesty, Mattick can be relied upon to tell it like it is. He comes right to the point.

"Of course, there has been a sobering process after Willy Brandt's resignation," he readily admits. Then he qualifies: "Where it was necessary. In fact, the shock was great. In Belgrade, for example, people cried in the streets."

Mattick raises his eyebrows in slight disdain.

"These are the people who measure politics by the politicians. They think if Brandt goes, so does his politics." Like all Berliners, Mattick is blessed with a rare urbanity. He is not easily impressed and respects nothing.

"Brandt has been exhausted for a long time. After all, Guillaume was just the drop that caused the kettle to spill over. Brandt was pumped dry and empty. He never was a morning person. He was used to a more bohemian lifestyle. The change of pace, the conditioning it took to go to an office morning after morning was against his very nature. He no longer could choose his working hours. His high office needed him in the mornings, not evenings. I am sure that the diseases Willy suffered in recent years were merely symptoms of stress and exhaustion. It suited him to say: 'I cannot go on anymore'."

Having known Brandt since before 1948, he has seen him develop as a man and politician and has watched his first successes and missteps.

"Brandt is ingenious as a politician insofar as analysis is concerned. But when it comes to the selection and contact with people, everything seems to go wrong for him. He was in trouble this way in Berlin as well as in Bonn." If Mattick acts like a forbearing parent registering disappointment with a gifted but slightly wayward child, it is not without reason. It was his recommendation that prompted Kurt Schumacher, the SPD's highly respected party chairman, to entrust the unknown Brandt with liaison between Berlin's SPD and the Allied occupation forces stationed there. Schumacher had asked Mattick, SPD secretary in Berlin's city council since 1946, and Franz Neumann, the Social Democrats' Berlin party chairman, to take a look at "the young man" from Norway. Neumann, sensing a competitor, wanted to turn Brandt down but Mattick approved.

Unflappable Willy

"Willy was an unflappable foreign minister. He displayed the necessary sobriety and a sense of urgency. But as chancellor he assembled men around him who were not knowledgeable. Egon Bahr was a sort of mystic, a brooding personality, and this was disastrous in view of the fact that Willy had the same qualities. His speechwriter, Klaus Harpprecht, had no depth whatsoever. Brandt became isolated. I did not have a good talk with him in years. He was walled off by a handful of intellectuals. And to top it all, Klaus Schütz [Berlin's mayor and a former Brandt assistant] and Harpprecht talked him into adopting an American politician's style."

Mattick is not the only party official who has seen disturbing changes in Willy Brandt. "In Berlin he still knew how to fight. Today I am not sure that he can handle the personal cult that has grown around him. This hurts, when you consider how long it took to build him up." With his understated Berlin humor, Mattick refers to Apel's misguided celebration of the party's leadership as a "trinity," and implies wryly that Brandt might make an excellent replacement for Kurt Waldheim as UN Secretary-General but not for Zeus.

"He surely had become a father figure. He enjoys adulation and is very happy with applause. Unfortunately, the monument he has permitted himself to become is deeply rooted in the problems of his youth. Politically, he has not quite learned that the dreams of a guy in his twenties could not, and probably should not, be maintained at forty."

Mattick attributes the disintegration of the party to Brandt's weak leadership. "As a party chairman you have to concern yourself with personnel policies, the placement and advancement of people. This became his downfall. If somebody organizes against the interest of the party, then something has to be done to stop it. Willy has an entirely wrong attitude toward party politics. It is patterned along the lines of the Swedish model where you can let things go. Our Jusos are only part of his problem."

Among other things, Mattick holds Brandt responsible for the party's left-leaning tendencies.

"Actually, many of our party resolutions were framed and forced on the membership by the left-wing Jusos. These resolutions made all the headlines and were attacked by the press as party doctrine. Once I tried to talk to Willy about the radical leftist drift of the Jusos. To my astonishment, he asked me: 'But what shall I do?' " Mattick breathes a deep sigh before he continues.

"The trouble started at our party convention in Nuremberg in March of 1968. It was there that the extraparliamentary opposition, as the left-wingers, mostly students, called themselves in those days, started to demonstrate against the war in Vietnam and the Grand Coalition [the coalition of the SPD and CDU/CSU, formed in 1966]. It ended with a violent fist fight in front of the convention hall, not just verbal attacks on Brandt, Wehner and other party leaders. The party gave the nod to the radical leftist camp. This was wrong, because it turned the workers off and away. The radicals stream into our party because they know they can exert a certain influence. We must try to get them out again. We need a purging process."

Mattick, who is not loved by the leftists, is not surprised that many of the young voters, repulsed by the irrationalism of the radic-libs fostered in the universities, decided in favor of the CDU/CSU.

The outspoken Berliner belongs to the few SPD politicians who openly express disappointment with the results of Ostpolitik.

"I, for one, had expected more. More normalization of the visiting routine. More visiting days instead of just one at a time. I never dreamt that the German Democratic Republic would double its entry toll—even temporarily. A regulated tension, the contractual order of German tension, more is not in it," he maintains sceptically. He regards the Bahr-Brandt slogan, "Change through rapprochement" which led to "fraternization" with the GDR, particularly ill-conceived.

"Quite to the contrary, this concept started all the irritation in the GDR. It is difficult to imagine why Willy supported this. A rapprochement that would cause a change in a Communist country—you might think about this, but you would never openly speak about it." The theory was that by way of rapprochement the democratic West would effect a change, a watering down of Communist doctrine in the East. Mattick does not believe that the interest-free credit the Federal Republic grants the GDR is as important to her as the West thinks.

"What is important to them is the constant hacking away at the Berlin condition. Honecker and his SED have the Berlin situation on their minds every day. Even though they enjoy full sovereignty it is hard for them to get around the fact that two-thirds of their capital, Berlin, is situated outside GDR territory. The recovery of West Berlin presents itself as a daily challenge to Honecker."

He is not certain whether the degree of confidence Brandt extended toward the GDR was warranted. "We will have to bridge the existing distrust with more treaties and political safeguards. On the other hand, I find the negativism of the opposition, which has gone astray in every way, as dangerous for the CDU/CSU as for the Federal Republic. What the CDU/CSU is doing in regard to Ostpolitik borders on sabotage. Their more enlightened leaders are too weak to take matters into their own hands."

The iconoclast from Berlin thinks nothing of the party's holy cow, its cherished "long-range program," a conceptual platform devised for the next decade.

"So many rapid changes take place in our society that it is foolhardy to set tomorrow's priorities, let alone those of 1985. Who would have dreamt a couple of years ago of an oil crisis or the mounting environmental problems facing us?"

Brandt's greatest service to the country?

"Well, he has brought the Federal Republic out of its navel-gazing

I position. Adenauer was a highly esteemed gentleman, internationally speaking. Brandt, however, has formulated policies that include other countries in their overall strategy. He has worked within the framework of other nations and created a position of trust for himself and Germany. He has enhanced the reputation of the Federal Republic among our neighbors like nobody else." His look as he speaks is one of surprise that anyone would ask a question for which there is so obvious an answer.

Brandt's Weaknesses Cannot Be Adjusted Without Ruining His Strength—

Egon Bahr

Wednesday, July 10, 1974, is a happy day for Egon Bahr. When the date for our meeting was set ten days earlier, during a break in the Bundestag debate over the Czechoslovakian treaty, nobody in Bonn had an inkling that he would receive me as Schmidt's newly appointed Minister for Economic Cooperation. Since Bahr belongs to Brandt's innermost circle, the surprise appointment was interpreted by insiders as a conciliatory gesture by cabinet-reshuffling Schmidt toward the Brandt camp and the SPD's liberal wing.

Bahr was born in 1922 in a little town in Thuringia (today part of the GDR), son of a school teacher. A journalist by trade, Brandt's press officer in Berlin and later chief architect and negotiator of his Ostpolitik in Bonn, he has often been described as the *éminence grise,* Brandt's Kissinger. Like America's "foreign minister," he has a Jewish grandmother. Not of pure Aryan descent, young Bahr became a hapless outcast in Nazi Germany. In contrast to the bouncy Kissinger, Bahr is a reserved and modest man. He is a man of ideas, of sharp intellect, whose reasoning powers—cutting straight to the core of the most complex conceptual arguments—are well matched by a quiet, persuasive eloquence. He is not averse to the controversial art of Kissinger-style secret diplomacy. His clandestine talks with Italian Communists in 1968, and his various still-undisclosed missions to Moscow and East Germany have made him a disputed figure and target of continuous attacks by the opposition press as "tricky Egon," political dilettante, or worse, "helper of Soviet Westpolitik."

Egon Bahr's triangular-shaped face, all forehead, lights up with a wide smile as I enter his spacious ministerial office. It had been just an hour ago that he had taken the oath of office as a member of the Schmidt cabinet and he was dressed for the occasion in a dark suit. That afternoon there had been a short but cordial ceremony with his ministry's upper echelon officials, who had few tears to shed over the abrupt departure of his unloved predecessor: pedantic, ideology-preaching Erhard Eppler.

In celebration of the event, the new minister nurses a whiskey and pours one for me as we conclude the preliminary small talk.

"Did you really cry during Brandt's official resignation speech?" I immediately regret the question. Thunderstruck, Bahr's gentle smile freezes into a hurt expression. His amazingly clear green eyes turn misty. For a moment, he seems off balance. But he recovers in a split second.

"Yes," he replies simply.

"Were your tears for the man or the cause?"

"I cannot remember that anymore," he says haltingly. "I guess I actually wanted to wipe out those last seventy-two hours before the resignation. I don't want to remember them ever, if I can help it." The genuineness of the emotion in the low voice of the man renowned as a cold, intellectual and Machiavellian strategist, warms up the whole, sterile, status-conscious room: cleaned-out bookcases, bare desk and blank white walls still bearing shadowy traces of the former inhabitant's pictures.

Memories of the tragic circumstances leading to the fall of his friend and boss seem to be so shattering and gruesome that Bahr refuses to bring them back by talking about the experience now.

He will talk about Ostpolitik. It should be mentioned that Bahr's new chancellor has not held back from introducing a note of skepticism on the subject. Only a few months before the signing of the Moscow Treaty, in August 1970, Schmidt emphatically warned of "exaggerated hopes" concerning Bahr's renunciation of force negotiations. As it turns out, the negotiator belongs among the few prominent Social Democrats in Bonn who admit to not being satisfied with his Ostpolitik.

Bahr's Points

"Firstly, it would be really bad, if one were satisfied. I certainly am not happy with the results of the Basic Treaty with the GDR." Bahr finds the treaties unsatisfactory "measured by the demands they make on themselves and the inherent claims that remain."

"Secondly, measured by the position and expectations at our point of departure, more has been accomplished than the skeptics thought," he swiftly modifies his own critique to the point of cancelling it.

"Thirdly, those people who believed that Ostpolitik would ring in a condition of harmony and frictionless bliss have been disappointed. Concerning the GDR, I have said at the conclusion of the Basic Treaty: Until now we had no relations—in the future we will have bad relations. We'll have to get through this phase. It takes a long time for a rusty mechanism to get going again—years! I have never cultivated any optimism." During an earlier talk with the German press corps in Washington, Bahr actually envisioned outright "trouble" instead of nonrelations with the GDR.

Because it was an isolated country, the Basic Treaty meant a "revolution" to the East Germans, he explained. The fact that suddenly this "locked up country" was to open its doors filled its leadership with apprehensions. The avalanche of visitors—several million West Germans visited the GDR in 1972—brought along a mass of "information, ideas and new interests to the population of the GDR that created an element of unrest." Discussions on all levels were stimulated and began to multiply. Many of the sheltered party functionaries could not cope with the sudden input of alien ideas. Unquestionably, Bahr had psyched out his conversation partners on the other side.

"But I am very optimistic about the Transit Agreement [for the first time since 1966 West Berliners were allowed to visit East Berlin] and the Traffic Treaty [for the first time West Germans were free to travel to the GDR at the invitation of friends rather than family only]. Hundreds of thousands have visited since the restrictions were lifted. The people have already become used to it. Tens of thousands have gone on day visits. Everybody takes telephoning for granted now. In April 1970 forty new telephone lines were installed between West and East Germany; they were a tremendous success. But, of course, people would rather speak of the things which have not been attained. The upcoming air traffic agreement is enormously complicated.

"Even more so is the cultural treaty, because here we get to the very kernel of the whole conflict: What is German culture? For example, it was possible to put together a commission with Poland to align the texts in our history books. It would be impossible to do the same with the GDR, because this is another topic which touches directly on the 'nation question,' that is, the consciousness of nationhood. Topics such as those simply have to be left off our agenda."

Bahr is equally willing to talk about the origins of Ostpolitik. He remembers that one of the initial inspirations came from Kennedy's *The Strategy of Peace.* Its powerfully stated thesis provided him with a fresh outlook on the complex problem of the German question.

"That a change in the relationship between East and West could best be effected by turning toward each other instead of turning one's back, impressed me as a reasonable premise," he asserted.

His own "policy of change through rapprochement" was proclaimed first in a speech at the Protestant Academy in Tutzing in 1963. It called for an end to the stale formulas for German reunification, and for normal relations by means of communication instead of confrontation with the neighbors in the East. Inadvertently it fanned hopes of toppling Walter Ulbricht by isolating his Communist regime. In recognition of the realities of the days, reunification was to be regarded as a slow "process of many steps and many stations." The acceptance of Bahr's heretofore unthinkable thought of "two Germanys" paved the way for the recognition of the GDR —if de facto or de jure depends on the interpreter. It did lead to membership in the United Nations, but not to reunification.

GDR Foreign Minister Winzer, at the opening of the UN session in September 1973, could not have been more blunt:

"The adverseness of the political and social orders leads to the necessary conclusion that a reunification of the German Democratic Republic and the Federal Republic of Germany will never be possible."

Impact of the Wall

"But the most important date in the annals of Ostpolitik is August 13, 1961: the building of the Berlin wall," Bahr continues. "In Berlin we became aware at that time that it is not enough to have a rightful claim. Suddenly, the trappings were gone and what we saw was an empty stage. From that time on, the activities of the West consisted of exhausting itself in protest notes. More than anything else this experience made us realize that entry permits to East Berlin were available only by cooperation with Moscow—this actually happened two years later. What we also learned then was that the permits would not be obtainable in Washington, but in East Berlin by way of stimulating German activities."

In a television interview in August 1970, Bahr described the dramatic lesson of the Berlin wall even more strikingly:

> The reality then [in August 1961] was that the Governing Mayor of Berlin had to wait for a relatively long time before Allied patrols came. It also took a long time before merely a protest was sent to Moscow. That was the reality. In Berlin it became clear, in the most brutal way, where the border lies between East and West, and that no one could reach beyond the wall. And the question was: if you cannot do away with the wall . . . then one must make an attempt despite the wall so that the people on the one side could visit again their relatives on the other side. In a nutshell, the attempt was to come to terms with the realities despite the realities.

Contrary to the accusations of his political opponents, Bahr maintains that he is not and has never been a proponent of any theories for convergence of the capitalistic and socialistic systems.

In a scathing article, "The Grand Design of Egon Bahr," Professor Walter Hahn of Philadelphia sums up Bahr's alleged viewpoint in *Orbis:* "Yet it [reunification] did not have to be discussed because Bahr's assumptions seemed clear. With Soviet [and American] power removed, a process of political convergence would undoubtedly grip the members of the collective security system. At the very least, the importance of borders among them would dwindle. The German 'nation' would thus become once again a fact, if not a formality."

"I have never believed in a convergence of the two systems," Bahr protested when I confronted him with Hahn's deductions.

"Professor Hahn surprised me a great deal," Bahr commented soberly. "He introduced himself as a man of the U.S. administration. I must confess, I did not mind the discussion of our game plan. He has never talked to me about making public use of it. Then—two or three years later—he informed the opposition about it. That was shortly before the vote of no confidence."

Bahr's inference about the timing is clear.

The game plan could easily be written off as professorial contrivance if it were not almost identical to a document labelled "Model C." Although the inception of Model C goes back to 1968, it became the subject of a bitter parliamentary debate led by CDU/CSU floor leader, Karl Carstens, in October 1973:

> The writer of the document [Egon Bahr] anticipates troop reductions in the near future. He offers several different models as basis for subsequent negotiations and decides finally on Model C . . . the dissolution of the alliances [NATO and Warsaw Pact], the withdrawal of Soviet and U.S. troops, the establishment of a collective security system in Europe with a membership of seven nations such as: the Federal Republic of Germany, the German Democratic Republic, the Netherlands, Luxembourg, Poland, and Czechoslovakia. According to the paper, Great Britain and France could join the security system but probably would not do so. All further considerations are based on that premise.

Professor Carstens was outraged that Bahr and Brandt, contrary to their repeated declarations, seemed to prefer the Soviet proposal for a collective European security system to the political unification of Western Europe and the Atlantic Alliance.

For Professor Hahn, on the other hand, the comparison of Bahr's "blueprint" with the "general scope" of the Rapacki and Gomulka plans for a "club of nonnuclear powers," formulated during the late 1950s, reveals a resemblance too close for comfort. Bluntly he asked if the Bahr-Brandt Ostpolitik, with its "alleged accomplishments that represent little more than West German concessions to the demands of the Soviet bloc," could have been prearranged with the Communists. In a more lofty but equally damaging vein he voiced yet another supposition: that Bahr, unlike Bismarck, has fallen prey to a "German propensity for overestimating their own ability to shape, manage and exploit their political environment on the Continent."

Professor Hahn apparently has no difficulty seeing Bahr and Brandt kowtow before the Soviets while seized with a typically German case of illusions of grandeur.

"I suppose the massive attacks and insinuations about Ostpolitik took their toll on Brandt's nerves and wore him down," I venture.

Bahr, a man not given to gesturing, flings out his right hand in surprise. "No," he replied quietly, "I never have had the impression that Brandt was tired of his job. Sure, he often complained about the bureaucracy, about the cumbersomeness of the administrative apparatus. But he certainly had not tired of his office. We even used to have an ongoing thing about the length of time of his government. We tried to figure out if he would be in for eight or for twelve years."

"Under those circumstances the Guillaume affair must have come as a terrific shock for Brandt?"

As soon as I mention the spy's name, Bahr's face takes on the same pained look I had detected earlier in our conversation.

"Well, let's say the man has lived up to Brandt's concept of complete treachery," Bahr counters with a wry little smile. "I simply cannot understand why he was kept around. Brandt should have said, 'No' when the security people wanted to send Guillaume along on his trip to Norway. Of course, he would carry the responsibility when things went wrong. This decency of his—you know, it is his great strength and his great weakness. And it's impossible to adjust his weakness without destroying his strength." Bahr falls silent as he slowly sets down his empty glass. His moral verdict is a reluctant one.

He does not seem to think much of the idea of a united Europe under the banner of the social democrats, socialists, or any other party.

"You cannot make European politics under the guise of party politics—whether socialistic or conservative—this is utter nonsense. A European union can only be shaped by people who feel and think European. Actually, it strikes me as anti-European to think of unification as a venture in party politics. The question is, however, are the socialists willing, if they could do something in Europe? But that is a different proposition."

Bahr has frequently stressed that European security cannot be attained without the backing of the Atlantic Alliance. In wanting to elevate the principle of renunciation of force to an all-European doctrine, he never has lost sight of his favorite dictum: Trust is good, control is better.

It is hard to imagine this extremely alert and *Realpolitik*-oriented man intellectually outwitted. With unexpected nimbleness, Mr. Bahr

—who is not an athletic type—jumps to his feet and sees me to the elevator. He makes light of my reference to his new title when I say, "*Auf Wiedersehen, Herr Minister.*"

"What kind of nonsense is this? My name is Bahr," he replies jovially. German officialdom, in essence, has not touched Egon Bahr.

5
The Ladies' Man

"Power is the ultimate aphrodisiac," Henry Kissinger used to philosophize in reference to his sudden success with the ladies after his arrival at the White House. Burly, homely Henry, of the owlish look, certainly was not the first powerful public figure to experience this age-old phenomenon.

The correlation between sex, power and politics has been the favorite topic of immortal Greek dramatists and ephemeral cocktail gossips. Strangely enough, it is still absolutely tabu in official and unofficial biographies of politicians and in political science classes. In their bulky volumes on Kennedy, neither Ted Sorensen nor Arthur Schlesinger found space for chapters on their subject's active sex life.

JFK's frolicking, lusty rompings in the White House of an afternoon, his many girl friends, and the merry, secret weekends in Palm Beach or in brother-in-law Peter Lawford's California abode, brightened by Marilyn Monroe and other lovelies of the silver screen, offend the sense of propriety of our most liberal and liberated historians and professors. They choose to perpetuate the illusion of their hero's moral fortitude and unassailability. Stories of a politician's sexual mores are quickly cast overboard as "salacious material" and relegated to cheap magazines.

In Willy Brandt's quasi-official biography by his devoted fan, Terence Prittie, only 4 of 464 pages deal with the women in his life; surely, an insult to the women—two shared his life as wives—as well as to the man. Or are we encountering just another instance of male chauvinism on the part of male authors wanting to enshrine their Willy Brandts, LBJs, JFKs, and FDRs, together with other successful collectors of the female vote, in the traditional, fragmented images of neutered, saintly leaders?

VOTE APPEAL—SEX APPEAL

How dare they distort historical records! After all, it is precisely this carefully erased sex appeal that translates so well into voter appeal in the realities of the political world. When young, handsome Willy Brandt was chosen over Erich Ollenhauer, the leader of the SPD, as chancellor candidate in 1961, it was because of Ollenhauer's poor marks in physical attractiveness or sex appeal. After careful analysis, the cruel verdict was that the ungainly, grey little functionary would never be able to capture the female vote. Pollsters and political scientists have known it all along: Politicians are professional seducers—and not just of women.

So obvious was the SPD's all-out effort in its pursuit of women voters in 1969 that the party changed its symbolic red color to a stylish orange. According to the SPD public relations chief, orange exudes a "certain degree of eroticism." Famed novelist Heinrich Böll took the time to compose his often cited "Open letter to a German Catholic woman," in the hope of swaying the ladies to cast their ballots for Willy.

Nobody was more fully aware of the vital role of women voters in his campaign than Brandt.

"There can be no doubt that new votes are to be gained also among women and senior citizens," he wrote in his diary on August 19, 1972. In his otherwise superterse "notes from August to November 1972," Brandt devotes a whole entry to recording a modicum of a female groundswell during the previous election campaign:

> Sunday, November 12th. Infratest-telephone poll (November 3rd to 6th) shows sympathy growth for SPD (five plus points with women). Essential change in the course of the campaign: the portion of those who count with an election victory for the coalition has grown further.

If in modern Germany or any other Western society, the female votes with specific feminine reasons in mind is yet another question.

It seems hardly fair to ask a stylish sex symbol to act the eunuch once he has won the elections. When Brandt's extramarital escapades accidentally surfaced during interrogations in connection with the East German spy affair, the German public was stunned but not really shocked. On the Bonn cocktail circuit the ominous list of Brandt's playmates aroused more interest than all of Egon Bahr's secret trips and talks. One publicity-minded lady of the press went so far as to suggest to a fellow journalist that he "expose" her name to instant fame. And an attractive society columnist—who supposedly held place number 17 on the intelligence agency's list—amused by the mistaken inclusion of her name, remarked: "Under such circumstances, one almost has to act as though it were true—for professional reasons."

As usual, the "revelations" promised in the inch-thick headlines were not forthcoming in the small print. Spy-knows-lovelife magazines blurted the names of two or three minor television personalities over their pages garnished with photographs of Willy hand in hand with a smug-looking blond. Others referred to flaming affairs with a platinum blond, cigar-smoking Swedish journalist; the sturdy, sometimes witty, reporter for a Rhineland paper; and one or two career-minded wives of government officials. The boulevard press was especially hard pressed for scurrilous sensations. Under the headline, "And There Was Also a Girl," it offered the warmed-over Susanne Sievers story of the 1950s in new dressing. The girl who had told all in her book of the same title, cramping Brandt's campaign style in 1961, had made a sudden comeback. Yet curiously enough, nobody so much as mentioned a writer who had put together a book of glamorized legends about her once adored Willy.

What seemed really to intrigue the public was Brandt's security officer's testimony concerning the tête-à-têtes in the chancellor's luxurious railroad car. Sex on wheels powerfully stimulated the readers' imaginations. This salon car was well known to every journalist who had ever travelled with Brandt on any of his many campaign trips. Brandt's distinct preference for campaign by train was known to the public, if not its reasons.

Willy's technique for enticing a lady to visit his private compartment followed a three-step game plan from which a graceful retreat was possible at any stage. When his roving eye spotted an attractive member of the press, a rather immediate process, he would manage to sit next to her in the dining car late in the evening. After a few drinks—while talking about the faltering Common Market or the possibilities of détente—there would be an accidental touching of hands. The next step, several drinks later, was entirely unexpected and far more imaginative. Without taking his eyes from the eager conversation partner across the table, his foot suddenly pressed hard against the sole of the lady's shoe. If there was no negative reaction, she was ready for step number three: holding hands under the table and a whispered invitation to a cognac away from the crowd.

Since all this silent wooing went on under the watchful eyes of his personal aide, Guillaume's task of fattening the dossier on Brandt for his puritanical Marxist bosses in the East was not an arduous one. It was *Bild* which raised the question as to whether the porno-loving Guillaume was able to mix his duty as a spy with that of a photo buff's simple pleasure.

The Don Juans of this world have always been more envied than despised. In Germany's permissive society no number of girls could have brought about the fall of Willy Brandt had his government been in better shape. To be sure, there were bigots with their raised eyebrows and taxpayers resentful of the socialist playboy. Then, of course, there were those who demanded moral rectitude in their political leaders. Most importantly, there were those believers in the wholeness of the personality, who comprehend moral weakness and self-indulgence not as a flaw that can be compartmentalized, but as a flower of evil that pervades the entire human psyche.

Mother remembers

The dictum that powerful men are sexy because they are powerful holds only partially true for Brandt. The truth is that tall, stately Willy, well-endowed with masculinity and dimpled charm, was a lady killer long before he came to power. Throughout his adventurous, recklessly lived life, there was always a girl, and another girl, and another. Since the age of puberty, women were a compulsion and a challenge to him. Restless, ambitious Brandt loved the chase, the conquest. At the same time, the man instinctively sought to compensate for the scarcity of warmth and love during his childhood and early youth. The introverted, socially insecure Brandt, born into this world as Herbert Ernst Karl Frahm, had never known life with a father. At best he remembers a somewhat remote relationship with his hardworking salesgirl mother, Martha Frahm. Living in the provincial town of Lübeck in 1913, the nineteen-year-old Martha probably felt the humiliation and the shame that straitlaced Christian society used to attach to the private predicament of which the presence of her robust son bore constant witness.

Long before he became Willy Brandt, the good-looking youngster learned fast that women were not competitors; they could be trusted and were helpful along the way. Brandt's mother, eventually married to a stonemason from Mecklenburg, Emil Kuhlmann, remembers well that her son, Herbert—she could not bring herself to call him Willy—had always been fond of girls. "As a three-year-old he had eyes only for the daughter of our butcher, a child of the same age. Herbert wanted to show his affection by biting her cheek one day," Mrs. Kuhlmann recalled in 1967, two years before her death. "The little one cried terribly and Herbert was cured of women for the time being."

Mama, a stout, housewifely woman, had a wide and open face that vaguely resembled the features of her famous son. With her grey hair neatly brushed back, she resembled many kindly German grandmothers. But there was a difference. She was proud of her working-class background. Her father joined the Social Democrats during Bismarck's time. She became a party member at the age of twenty. Her Herbert was a "loner," but he wanted to know much and he learned fast, she observed.

Mama vividly remembered another pretty girl, Gertrud Meier. Herbert met her at the romantic campfire outings of the Socialist Youth Union. In his memoirs *My Way to Berlin,* published in 1960, Brandt refers to her as the "girl for whom I felt a strong attachment." He could talk to her openly without fear of being betrayed. Gertrud was hopelessly in love with "wild" Herbert, a tremendously attractive male even at seventeen, with his unruly mane of blonde hair. He liked to walk around wearing a sailor's cap and acting the worldly he-man in those days. He had started to smoke a pipe and enjoyed the reputation of loving a beer, or something stronger, as well as the "favor of a pretty girl." He knew how to use his elbows and had become the unchallenged leader of the radical Marxist-oriented Socialist Workers' Youth of the SAP. A bit of a bully, he was known to carry his socialist political arguments against the Nazis from the smoke-filled beer halls into the dimly lit streets of Lübeck.

In the spring of 1933, Willy—who worked in a shipbroker's office as a clerk by day and produced resistance leaflets by night—decided that the time had come to leave Lübeck and Hitler's Germany behind. It did not take much persuasion for him to obtain Gertrud's promise to follow the nineteen-year-old into exile. Meanwhile, the leftist SAP had been outlawed by the Nazis and Herbert, who had attended a secret meeting of SAP functionaries in Dresden under the name of Willy Brandt, had accepted a party offer to establish a liaison office in Oslo "after the man first picked for the job had been arrested on the Island of Fehmarn while attempting to leave the country." Whatever the "local circumstances" that prompted his decision, he set out to conquer new frontiers in April. Faithful Gertrud, to whom he sent letters filled with resistance slogans, written in invisible ink, was summoned by the Nazis. Remembering a compromising letter in her pocketbook the courageous girl is said to have swallowed it on the spot to escape suspicion of involvement in clandestine political activities.

The Comrades Frahm

Gertrud's arrival in Oslo "created order in my somewhat unhinged bachelor's life," Brandt confessed. The two thoroughly modern Socialists from Lübeck set up housekeeping. In their political circles they pass as Mr. and Mrs. Frahm or, simply, the "comrades Frahm." Gertrud, an intelligent and even-tempered girl, helped him over the first difficult hurdles of adjustment. Willy had a severe run-in with the Norwegian Labor party (NAP) which had served him as a firm base in exile. He had ignored the NAP's moderate course—it had cut its ties to Moscow—and had associated himself with an extremist opposition group. It was up to Gertrud to smooth things over and encourage him to carry on. She also was wise enough to ignore his many flirtations, recognizing, intuitively perhaps, his consuming inner need to prove himself. This unquenchable craving, root of his driving ambition and receptiveness to sweeping visions as well as controversial compromises, never left him, even after he had reached the stars.

Mrs. Kuhlmann and Gertrud's mother went to visit the young couple in Copenhagen in 1935 after Brandt's grandfather committed suicide. But the two mothers' blessings had little effect on Willy's freewheeling lifestyle. As a party functionary, he was obliged to travel frequently to Paris to SAP headquarters, and to Prague where the Social Democrats in exile had set up shop. Sometimes his continuous missions to Holland, Barcelona, Berlin, Copenhagen and England, where he was sent to promote the popular or "unified" front, a joining of Socialist and Communist political forces, kept him abroad for weeks, even months, at a time. Gertrud, who had left her home and country for the man she loved, saw less and less of him. She could not, however, close her ears to rumors that everywhere virile Willy went he seemed to have lived up to his reputation.

"Paris in the summer of 1937, more beautiful, gayer than I have ever seen it before, bubbling with joie de vivre," Brandt rhapsodizes in his memoirs. His illegal journeys, made under cover names such as Willy Flamme, Willy Brandt, Karl Martin or Gunnar Gassland, were not all fun and games. The inherent element of acute danger and constant fear in these conspiratorial activities is described by Brandt in connection with his visit to Berlin during the 1936 Olympic games.

"Very soon I had become accustomed to the life of an 'illegal person'—I called myself Martin—this permanent pretense and deceit; the necessity never to show one's true feelings; the mistrust that makes one fear an informer in every person sitting next to one at the table and suspect a traitor in every comrade from former times; the organization of 'contacts' and secret meetings—one's head is full of figures and code words, and they persecute me in my sleep." No wonder the writer sought escape from the intense stress by relaxing with a bottle of whiskey or a pretty girl.

The relationship with Gertrud finally broke up, after much suffering on her part, but hardly for the reasons Brandt's friendly biographers indicate. It was not his "excessive workload" that prevented him from marrying his childhood sweetheart after all those years, but his excessive demands for freedom from all personal ties. Besides, he had met a Norwegian who seriously attracted his attention.

CARLOTA

Nine years his senior, Carlota Thorkildsen was the well-educated daughter of a prosperous engineer. She had studied sociology and languages in Paris and economics at Oslo's university. Like many other intellectuals the tiny dark-haired Carlota was involved with radical leftist groups, largely pacifists, who later became resistance fighters during the Nazi occupation. It was she who opened many a door to important political and intellectual groups that would otherwise have remained "off limits" to the young German immigrant.

Carlota introduced him to the comforts of a Norwegian middle-class home in her parents' apartment. For the first time in his life, Brandt not only "moved in 'bourgeois' circles," as he puts it, but lived in them, a fact that was instrumental in his amazingly swift integration into Norway's leading highbrow crowd. With his great linguistic talent, his Norwegian was soon fluent and he was able to write and lecture in that language. Carlota's contacts at the Institute for Comparative Cultural Research, where she was employed, provided new intellectual stimuli.

An engaging portrait of Brandt in those days, sketched by a young British socialist, is included in Terence Prittie's biography. Brandt appeared as a friendly, extraordinarily good-looking young man of "genuine shyness and undivertable decisiveness." Others were aware of his readiness to help, his talent for handling people, and his ability to make himself popular with the "right" ones.

The harmonious relationship, accentuated by idyllic vacations in a friend's snow-draped cottage in the mountains, was brought to a rapid end. On April 8, 1940, the Norwegian radio announced the approach of the German fleet. Carlota was pregnant when Hitler's troops, aided and abetted by Vidkun Quisling's *Nasjonal Samling,* invaded Norway. There was no time for marriage. Brandt, deprived of his German citizenship in 1938, was not yet in possession of a Norwegian passport. As a stateless person the SAP official was unprotected from the Nazi authorities.

Like thousands of other refugees, Brandt left Oslo. In a borrowed Norwegian soldier's uniform, he found himself promptly arrested by the German occupation troops and interned in a prisoner-of-war camp. Weeks later, when the gallant Norwegian resistance effort broke down and King Haakon had departed for exile in London, Brandt was dismissed and allowed to return to Oslo, his "hometown." Due to the accusations of his political enemies, he later found it necessary to establish in a Berlin court that he had not fought against his German countrymen with a gun but rather used the Norwegian uniform as a protective camouflage.

Back in Oslo in June, security once more was foremost in Brandt's mind. He found it necessary to go into hiding at a friend's summer house on one of the far-off islands in Oslo fjord, where Carlota visited him from time to time. The hermit's existence was not for the firebrand activist. Without taking the time and the risk involved in formalizing marriage to Carlota, he took off toward the end of July for an illegal border crossing to seek refuge in neutral Sweden.

After being routed through a refugee center, the stateless Frahm was finally granted asylum. Carlota, since October 30th the mother of a baby girl, was instrumental in introducing him into Stockholm's Norwegian community. Despite contacts with German socialist and refugee groups, Frahm lived in a "Norwegian milieu." During those months, his activities seemed to center around disseminating information for the resistance movement. Carrying a false passport, he surprisingly returned in December to Nazi-occupied Oslo from which he had barely escaped. While the expediting of his Norwegian papers probably counted as the most pressing reason for his daring return, he chose to emphasize unspecified "political considerations" in his memoirs, as well as "the wish to see his daughter, Ninja."

"Illegal border crossings were nothing new for me. I was no longer the amateur in conspiratorial work I had been at the beginning of the Nazi regime," he wrote in his memoirs, explaining away the risks. After his return to Stockholm, he ran into complications. He was arrested for suspicion of abusing Sweden's neutrality. As a SAP functionary, he stood accused of illegal intelligence activity in the service of a foreign power, according to Brandt's friends, the Norwegian government in exile; according to his foes, the Soviet Union. The intervention of Swedish Social Minister Gustav Möller cut short this unpleasant episode, which was glossed over by friendly biographers and takes on espionage thriller overtones in the writings of his opponents.

When Carlota and Ninja arrived on the Stockholm scene in the spring of 1941, Brandt had not quite found his footing in the Swedish capital. It was up to Carlota to create an atmosphere conducive to the exchange of ideas. Willy set the wedding date for June 30, 1941. Carlota, however, did not become Mrs. Brandt, but Mrs. Herbert Frahm, even though in the process of naturalization a legal change of name to Willy Brandt, the name he used as a SAP functionary and publicist since Lübeck, would have been a mere formality. They settled down in a new house among the pine trees of the suburb Hamarbyhöjden. And Brandt's only complaint was a "bad conscience from time to time" for leading a relatively "normal existence in such a normal country."

These years became an extremely busy and rewarding period for him. More than half a dozen books credited to Brandt were published before the end of the war in the Norwegian language, three of them about Norway and the war. Because most of Brandt's later books were coauthored (even his memoirs, *My Way to Berlin*, were written with Leo Lania, former editor of the Communist magazine *Kommunismus*), the question of the extent of Carlota's contribution has always been a matter of speculation, especially since she established herself as a respected literary agent in later years.

The conjugal bliss in the "modest but comfortable" home was of short duration. Burning with energies and ambition, Willy threw himself into new activities. He opened a Swedish-Norwegian Press Bureau that, according to an OSS report, doubled as an intelligence gathering agency. He became executive secretary of the "Small International," a socialist group committed to the fight against the Nazis and advocating far-reaching controls of the economy in postwar Germany. Its membership could not have held greater international promise. Projected into the future, it included chancellors, Nobel Prize winners, foreign ministers, and other to-be-distinguished leaders.

The secret reports of the American legation in Stockholm noted that Brandt "maintained close relations with the Norwegian Labor Party circles and with the Soviet legation." If some of his adversaries claim that Brandt was too friendly with the Soviets, the files of the U.S. State Department document an even closer contact with the German-born Norwegian journalist.

Brandt also kept in touch with the men of the resistance in Germany, the progressive men of the Kreisauer Circle, and the officers around Count Stauffenberg, who were deeply involved in the attempt to assassinate Hitler on July 20, 1944. Brandt believed that the July plot was launched prematurely. After negotiators failed to convince President Roosevelt and other world leaders that the German opposition deserved their support, it was only through action that the resistance leaders could prove their existence and their sincerity to the Allies. Rumors had it that Brandt, the devoted resistance fighter, also recruited paratroopers among the emigrants, a strictly illegal activity in neutral Sweden.

Enter Rut

Meanwhile, Willy had met a remarkably enchanting young woman. Sparkling, pretty Rut Hansen-Bergaust, described by him "as almost a girl," was his latest conquest. Actually 24, the tall, slender girl with an extraordinary zest for life came from Hamar, a small town in Norway. She was married to Ole Bergaust, a railwayman-turned-resistance fighter. Ole had found a job as a courier at the intelligence center attached to the Norwegian legation. What the willful chauffeur's daughter lacked in education, she made up in feminine charm and a refreshing naturalness.

Carlota, who also worked at the Norwegian legation, had met her sexy, long-legged young rival. By making a friend of the exuberant girl, sixteen years her junior, who liked to sing, dance, drink, and stay up all night, she hoped to save her marriage. Tenseness invaded the Frahm household as fun-loving Rut entered their lives. Bitter, irretrievable words were spoken. In the end, the couple suffocated in deadening silences. When the older woman realized that she had lost the battle, she quietly accepted the inevitable. By 1943, Carlota and her child Ninja had moved into the Norwegian legation. They remained there until their return to Norway in the summer of 1945.

Brandt's review of his behavior toward Carlota was couched in pensive, even melancholy, reveries. In his memoirs, he skirted the upsetting private events by artfully shifting into a more general gear: "The year 1944 was a turning point in my life. My marriage broke up. To a great degree the impact of external circumstances probably hastened our estrangement. Life in exile is a hard test for any human relationship. We were obliged to recognize that we had drifted apart. I reproached myself. Should I have married at all? Politics eats one up totally. Did I have the right to tie a woman to myself?"

In this official version of his life, designed for the voting public of 1961, Rut's appearance is postponed until a vague "toward the end of the war." He continues, candidly: "We felt a strong attraction for each other and stayed together." Understandably, he does not want to shock his prospective voters—whom he assumes to be old-fashioned enough to take offense—with the news that both of them were still married to other partners when they set up housekeeping.

Still more hypocritical and yet more honest in its revelation was the comment of Brandt's friendly biographer Prittie: "Failed marriages only concern the partners," he lectured his readers, "therefore a minimum needs to be said about this at this place."

After some rhetoric about war and separation, and the unusual circumstances, Prittie launched into a defensive attack. Advancing the astounding idea that Carlota might have been unhappy at the thought of Brandt's return to Germany after the war—in actuality Brandt had never been too specific about this—he goes on to worry about the effect of the difficult war years on a woman and her child. A man at least can bury himself in his work, he asserts, entirely overlooking the fact that Carlota was a working person also. After this preparation, he finally let the male chauvinist cat out of the bag. "Brandt was, as is well known, an extremely independent person and never ready to be put on too tight a leash. He greatly valued his independence. . . . Was Carlota, perhaps, not only intelligent, sensitive, and lively; was she, perhaps, also overly possessive?" In other words: the break-up of the marriage was not due to the errancy of the husband but to the possessiveness of the wife!

It can be safely assumed that Willy the activist felt much more comfortable with the bubbly Rut, who appreciated the simpler joys of life, than with the educated Carlota and her ever-questioning critical intellect. With only a grade school education, Rut proved to be a skillful manipulator. Somehow she had obtained an apartment in the exclusive suburb of *Hamarbyhöjden,* no small achievement considering her husband Ole's lowly position and the acute shortage of housing in refugee-packed Stockholm during these war years.

Encouraged by Willy, Rut gave up her job as housemaid and babysitter to study English and typewriting. By the spring of 1944, when her husband began to show symptoms of tuberculosis, she was already working in the photo archives of the Norwegian legation press office. Her job was to paste photos on press releases, but on occasion she seized the opportunity to make her own captions.

Rut and the Resistance

Rut, one of four daughters of a poverty-stricken chauffeur whose widow supported the children by working in a dairy, had always been an enterprising girl. In her toughness and keen sense for self-improvement and advancement, rough and tumble Willy had found his match. She left school at fourteen to earn money at a bakery as a maid and salesgirl. She became a housekeeper for her grade school teacher, and a seamstress in a tailor's shop. She was exposed to and eagerly soaked up Marxist doctrine. The "new" ideas of class differences, the injustice of a world with Haves and Have-Nots, struck a sympathetic chord in her. Had she been less pretty and popular with the boys, she might have become seriously interested in communism. But Rut, being Rut, attended the workers' youth meetings primarily for the dancing and the promise of meeting new boys. Politics became a synonym for dancing and companionship in Rut's vocabulary.

In the effort to obscure leftist leanings in her youth, much has been made in the German press of her past as a "resistance fighter," especially during Brandt's campaigns. Once more reality is less heroic, despite Rut's dreams about the Soviet "workers' paradise," and her hatred of the German Nazi occupiers and the "Quislings." A group of boys from the Labor Youth, declared illegal by the Quisling authorities after the German invasion, formed Hamar's resistance organization. Reluctantly, they allowed Rut, who managed to charm her way into the all-male group, to perform minor tasks in the distribution of illegal flyers urging the German soldiers to put down their weapons.

It was Ole Bergaust, her steady boyfriend at that time, who aroused the suspicion and attention of the Gestapo. While he and his coconspirators were forced to flee into neutral Sweden, Rut and her sister Tulla, whose journalist boyfriend belonged to the same group, were quizzed by the Gestapo on the boys' whereabouts. Rut and Tulla "escaped" to Sweden in 1942 to join their sweethearts and marry them.

———

Even before Rut had met and fallen in love with Willy Brandt, who "meant more than anything else" to her, she had heard about him. His outrageous private life was the talk of the small, inbred Norwegian community. As a political figure, his inscrutable professional activities, shrouded in the secrecy of sudden comings and goings, gave rise to differing assessment and intriguing gossip in this circle. Rut, like Willy, found it necessary to give an explanatory account of her background when the political limelights were focused on the two "Norwegian left-wingers" in Berlin.

Their self-serving "memoirs," produced in the late 1950s in preparation for the big jump from Berlin to national politics, were both "as told to" versions of their eventful lives written by professional journalists.

By the end of the war, Ole Bergaust was a very sick patient in a tuberculosis sanitarium in Sweden. Although the Norwegian community shrank from day to day, Rut had no desire to return home so long as Willy remained in Stockholm. Officially she stayed on so that Ole was not all alone. But when Ole was transferred to a sanitarium in Norway, she still was unable to give up Stockholm. "In Sweden I had met the man who would influence my whole life: Willy Brandt. Old bonds were torn, a new one was tied," she stated.

Assignment Nuremberg

Restless Willy, still the young man in a hurry to get places, shuttled back and forth to Oslo. Despite all his party contacts and connections, he seemed to be looking in vain for a rewarding political opening, possibly in Norwegian politics. Early in the fall of 1945, Rut and Willy finally departed for Oslo together. He managed to find Rut a job as secretary for the Norwegian Labor party. While his emigrant friends packed to return to Germany, Brandt could not decide what to do. "Once more he was very much alone," his friendly biographer Prittie commiserated. A strange comment, considering that Rut was by his side and Carlota and daughter Ninja lived across town. In lieu of a more enticing task, Brandt accepted an offer to become an observer-reporter for the party press at the long-lasting German war crimes trials in Nuremberg. The result was a book of harsh judgments published in Norway and Sweden only. *Criminals and Other*

Germans generated an undue amount of hostility in Brandt's early political career in postwar Germany.

The Nuremberg assignment gave Brandt a chance to visit his mother, not seen for a decade, his stepfather, and half-brother Günter. His mother provided us with a description of the dramatic reunion scene.

"I sat at this place and looked out of the window," she told a magazine reporter in 1967. "Suddenly a huge car stopped in front of our little house"—it was the official car of Bremen's mayor, Wilhelm Kaisen—"a gentleman in an elegant [Norwegian] uniform got out and rang the door bell. 'Who are you and whom do you want to see?' I asked. 'But mama, don't you know me anymore?' he replied. I did not recognize my Herbert," she confesses unabashedly. Looking back, she could ascertain that "he was the same—a thoughtful boy who had sent her flowers from exile" despite his hardships.

Willy Brandt also used his time in Germany to establish contact with leading Social Democrats in Frankfurt, Hamburg and Lübeck, where he made his first official political speech at a Social Democrat meeting in May 1946. While mercurial Rut emerged at the photo archives of the *Arbeiderbladet's* new magazine, *Aktuell,* where she sometimes tried her hand at reporting, Willy was still waiting for suitable job offers.

In spite of assurances by friendly biographers that Brandt was overwhelmed with job opportunities, a chance to become an editor at a German news agency did not materialize. Nor did he pursue the politically promising mayor's post in Lübeck. However, after his friend Halvard Lange emerged as Norway's foreign minister, a position as a press or cultural attaché in the Norwegian embassy in Paris became the subject of discussion. Eventually, an opening was found in the press office of Norway's newly established military mission in Berlin. "I did not hesitate long in giving my 'yes.' But only toward the end of the year were the formalities taken care of," Brandt comments happily.

During these tense summer months spent worrying and waiting, Rut had helped him "to forget the sorrows and the disagreeableness." Often, when his plans and dreams were stunted by seemingly insurmountable obstacles, tough, indomitable Rut provided courage and comfort.

"She has given me that [courage and comfort] even before the ten years I spent as governing mayor of Berlin—years in which I had a difficult time politically," he states in 1971, "for a rise in politics is hardly easy for anyone. For me, at any rate, it was not. One has to elbow one's way up and at times one stands all alone. There also will be bad backlashes. In this my wife has helped me very much. She did not gloss over the situation, she did not belittle it. But she made it clear that one must not take oneself too importantly and that there are things which are quite as significant as politics."

When Willy put on his smart Norwegian major's uniform in December 1946 to assume his position as information officer in charge of observing the East-West political developments, especially those of the Soviets and their zone, he received the title of press attaché, even though the actual press attaché and Brandt's chief in Berlin was Jens Schive.

Rut, a widow since Christmas when Ole succumbed at the sanitarium, was the third woman to follow Willy Brandt into unknown territory. Rut had more stamina and more charm and, perhaps, more patience than the others. She knew how to handle this headstrong self-made man—with a show of temper, if necessary. She understood his relentless drive, his work, his will to succeed. She knew "instinctively that he needed a certain *Spielraum* [leeway] of absolute independence," as Prittie put it.

Rut, also sporting a new uniform, joined Brandt as an employee at the press section of Berlin's Norwegian mission in the spring of 1947. Soon bombed-out Berlin became her oyster. In the city's landscape of ruins, where 60 percent of the houses were destroyed and the rubble was piled in veritable mountains, where the black market blossomed, hunger was rampant, and coal so scarce that the desperate Berliners used their furniture as well as the trees in their beloved city parks for firewood, Rut began her exciting, giddy life with Willy.

The foreign diplomats and Allied personnel who invaded Berlin led secluded, ghetto lives centered around the Allied clubs, swimming pools, an everlasting supply of alcohol, and an eternal round of parties. Outgoing Rut started to learn German and make friends among the cosmopolitan Berliners. Wherever she appeared, she radiated freshness and gaiety. If anybody could persuade the men to dance, it was Rut.

"What Brandt probably liked best about her was that she took direction without putting a claim on him. This corresponded to his inherent wish for independence and a life that exactly followed his wishes and plans," is Prittie's analysis of their seemingly lopsided relationship.

Rut's perseverance was indeed put to an endurance test. Brandt did not worry about a divorce from Carlota Frahm until 1948. When Rut finally became Mrs. Brandt, that totally political creature Willy had exchanged his Norwegian passport and position for German citizenship under the name of Brandt and a job with the Social Democrats.

"I want to try to help lead Germany back into Europe and, if possible, to become part of that third force that will be necessary to avert the greatest catastrophe of all times," Brandt explained his unexpected decision in a letter to Halvard Lange. It cannot be determined whether the repeated attacks of certain Scandinavian newspapers on Brandt's personal integrity had anything to do with his change of direction.

For Rut, the Norwegian patriot who saw to it that Norwegian was spoken in the home, the surprising change from pampered diplomatic status to a German housewife's lot might have been far more unsettling had her mind not been occupied with more vital things. Before her first son Peter was born in October 1948, the Brandts had moved into a small house provided by the party in the elegant *Halensee* district. In order to continue the worldly lifestyle to which the couple had so quickly become accustomed, the two children of the proletariat were looked after by a German maid and a chauffeur.

The honeymoon was over when Rut entered the delivery room in the company of the chauffeur instead of father Brandt during a dark night of the Berlin blockade. The precious electric current had been shut off and the hospital had to rely on its emergency lights. As a prelude to her husband's national campaign, Rut recalled these stark moments in her memoirs, which were published in 1960.

"I was taken into the delivery room. I was just lying there and staring into the dim glare of the emergency lamp. . . . If I had only known what kind of torture that is, I thought." At last Willy put in his appearance: "He was so excited that he almost squished the bouquet of flowers in his hands. . . . At the sight of his son his face became nonplussed. 'He is very tiny, isn't he?' he said. 'But he will grow.' With this statement he seemed to want to encourage himself."

Willy had quickly fallen into his old lifestyle of long evenings out, not all on the party's business. It is entirely to the credit of Rut's sociability and natural skills as a hostess that their house became a place where Social Democrats could meet with members of the Allied forces and old emigrant friends in the informal and agreeable surroundings Rut had created. No matter how stormy the marriage, how rough the fights, spirited Rut proved to be a formidable political asset for Brandt. And Rut—partial to expensive superchic designer dresses, limelight, vacations in grand hotels and luxurious guest homes, and just good fun—learned to stand her ground in the battle of wills. As time wore on, her charm turned into steel and the mischievous, carefree smile became an habitual mask of gaiety. The flight from loneliness turned the middle-aged mother of three sons —Peter was joined in 1951 by Lars and in 1961 by Matthias—into a devout pleasure seeker.

The tough little girl from Hamar compensated for the humiliating Waterloos she suffered from her husband's infidelities. Rut lived a life of her own. She assembled a small, tight circle around herself and, were it not for her glamorous, much publicized outings, she almost became a recluse. At the same time, Rut was always there when Willy needed her, fiercely loyal to him and not without vindictiveness toward the people who have harmed him and his career. One would be tempted to refer to their arrangement as an "open marriage" if Rut were not secretly still fighting for her man.

"My wife is my best friend," Brandt once said to an interviewer. It was the understatement of the year.

Brandt's SPD liaison position in Berlin came to an end in 1949 when Bonn was declared the Federal Republic's "provisional" capital. Although he had a chance to join Mayor Reuter's Berlin administration, Brandt preferred a change of scene. As one of eight parliamentary representatives from Berlin, he headed for Bonn. If he saw the Bundestag as a shortcut to political advancement, or if the prospect of getting closer to the Social Democrat's chairman, Dr. Kurt Schumacher, who from the beginning had openly shown profound reservations toward Brandt, was the motivating factor, remains to be analyzed in another context.

For Rut, Willy's absence during the week and many a weekend, meant loneliness and a new exercise in self-reliance.

SUSANNE

Bonn had not waited for Willy Brandt. And the tensions between him and Schumacher did not diminish at close range. Bonn is a conservative town where contacts are not easily made. Brandt, with his disorderly lifestyle and past, was regarded politically and socially as a quixotic outsider, a man tolerated but not quite accepted. Soon Willy was a well-known figure in Bonn's few provincial bars and it did not take long until a steady girlfriend shared his evenings and drinking bouts.

Ambitious Susanne Sievers was thirty and an attractive, bright brunette, on the make in more than one way in the hastily chosen capital. An editorial assistant in the Bonn office of a small Westphalian newspaper when Willy met her, the brainy woman was soon issuing her own newsletter, not immodestly named *Confidential Information from the Federal Chancellor's Office and the Ministries.*

Popular Susanne started her Bonn career as secretary to a special investigation committee of the Bundestag. Her connections in the tight little political circles of the capital were superb. The tall divorcée, whose two children lived with her parents, was as much a girl about town as Brandt was the unknown newcomer. She was the perfect guide into the secret ins and outs of Bundeshaus politics and cabals. Saucy Susanne, who became "more than only a passing fancy," as careless Willy emphasized in one of many handwritten love letters to her, knew everybody worth knowing. She befriended the most influential members of the press as well as the powerful Franz Josef Strauss. "She possessed a lot of charm—and she knew it," she commented about herself in her revealing book based on her famous affair with Brandt. The trenchant exposé that haunts Brandt to this day was written under the pen name, Claire Mortensen.

If pipe-smoking Willy knows women, sharp-eyed Susanne knows men. Her article about "politicians at 50" caused a small uproar in the sleepy town on the Rhine. ". . . they stand at the threshold where youth ends but age has not yet begun, where a father complex and the feelings of a Romeo complement each other so magnificently. But because they know how to swim about like merry little fish in the waters of everyday life and its gallant opportunities, they possess the sex appeal of maturity."

The attractive "new couple" soon was the talk of the town. Susanne wrote of Willy's "winning" behavior and a boyishness, tinged with timidity, that was irresistible to women. "Alcohol transports him into a conqueror's mood, blocking out complexes which he had to fight every now and then," she wrote. Because his dimpled face reminded her of a bear when he laughed, Susanne affectionately called him "bear." She was well aware, of course, that a dancing bear was an emblem in Berlin's coat of arms. When she discovered that Willy the Bear, who could outdrink any of the barflies, was an awkward dancer, she promised to rectify this shortcoming.

In order to still the gossips, more and more time was spent in Susanne's flat in Reuterstrasse. When parliament recessed in July of 1951 and the lovers said their sad *Auf Wiedersehen,* Susanne was convinced that she was the only woman who counted in her "bear's" life. Willy chose a book of tender love stories as a parting gift for Susanne. A splendid bouquet of flowers arrived on her birthday, followed by a letter written in his small but fluid hand, in which he expressed regret that the flowers could not convey his "hot birthday kiss." While he did not encourage an exchange of letters, he let Susanne know that "he thinks of her" and cannot get her out of his mind; that he hoped he was not forgotten before his return in September.

Susanne's summer was as difficult professionally as emotionally. She was accused of being a lobbyist by a major magazine and obliged to drop the catchy but perhaps misleading title of her successful newsletter in favor of a less intriguing *Bonn Information Letter.*

The cheerful note from her "bear," announcing the end of the summer's hibernation and arrival in Bonn, missed Susanne. She had decided to attend Leipzig's famed trade fair. A week later, the disappointed "bear," who had turned into a veritable pen pal, reported that Bonn without her was much more *triste* than he would have imagined. Waiting for her from 9 P.M. to 1 A.M. at Streng's wine restaurant, he had no choice but to "tank up" slowly but thoroughly.

There would be many letters from Willy to Susanne and the only remarkable thing about them was how unremarkable, how pedestrian they were as far as expression and style was concerned. From the embarrassingly platitudinous phrases, one could never conclude that the writer had a "literary" intellectual background. At best, one might suspect the undeveloped hand of a student or a semieducated clerk.

The reason for Susanne's trip to East Germany was not at all clear. It is hard to imagine that this knowledgeable woman was naive enough to try to sell her newsletter to East German customers. This trip, more than anything else, led to the rumor that she was an East German spy and her target was none other than Willy Brandt.

When Susanne's *Bonn Information Letter* made the bold announcement in the spring of 1952 that Willy Brandt was the prospective and most able successor to Ernst Reuter's job as Governing Mayor of Berlin, the news was based on wishful thinking.

Brandt had received no such encouragement from the Social Democrats' leadership. Dr. Schumacher's negative attitude toward him had not changed. Brandt's arch rival Franz Neumann—SPD chairman for Berlin and longtime confidant of Schumacher—whom the newcomer had unwisely tried to unseat, had been reelected with an overwhelming majority. Moreover, Brandt had not cut an impressive figure in Bonn's Bundestag.

End of an Interlude

Thoroughly depressed by the continuous attacks on him, Brandt became irritable and withdrawn. Susanne got to know his rapid changes of mood—his mental uptightness, the stereotype smile assumed when he thinks he is watched—as reliable symptoms of oncoming lows. "The hours they spent together often became a torture because they really consisted of just drinking." His breath always smelled of alcohol and cigarettes in those days, Susanne recalled. Still Susanne loved her virile "bear" even if he drank himself into a stupor. When his drinking problem became a political issue in his career he tried to combat it in a sanatorium in the Taunus. Meanwhile, Susanne—like Gertrud and Carlota and Rut and other women before and after her—shares Willy's problems and endeavors to give him the necessary self-confidence to weather his defeats and continue the battle.

Since Brandt did not bring Rut to Bonn during this period, Susanne even overcame her great jealousy. Brandt seemed to reason that the freedom he allowed his wife entitled him to keep her out of his territory, as it were. As had other women in Brandt's life, Susanne saw charm and tenderness suddenly crumble into insulting indifference. She suffered through his impulsive flirtations and was elated by assurances that he liked her "too much." According to her memoirs, he sorrowfully wished to be remembered fondly—even as an "inattentive and ungrateful boy."

When the relationship showed signs of strain in the spring of 1952, and Susanne became increasingly disenchanted with the bear's moodiness and jumpiness and his reluctance to dissolve his marital ties, he fanned the passions anew by asserting that though "reason speaks against hinting at my love, it is almost grotesque how often my thoughts turn to you."

Their long relationship came to an unexpected, horrifying end. For unspecified reasons Susanne drove to Berlin. According to her story, she lost her pocketbook with practically all her papers at the East German border checkpoint, Berlin-Babelsberg. She returned to notify the GDR border guard of the theft and got into a dispute. Following the advice of her business partner, she reported the theft and the insulting behavior of the guard to the people's police in East Berlin. Allegedly, they kept her interzone passport, the only document not stolen because it was in the car's glove compartment. Susanne was asked to return for it the next day. Mysteriously, her pocketbook, packed with papers for her next newsletter, was found by a truckdriver and returned to her West Berlin hotel. On June 25, 1952, after another telephone conference with her business associate in Bonn, she decided to retrieve her interzonal passport and apologize to the East German police. Before departing by metro to East Berlin, she tried to contact Willy Brandt, as she had done several times. Again, he could not be reached.

It was four years before Susanne again saw West Berlin. After being locked in a room at police headquarters, she was imprisoned in a villa and interrogated for days. Allegedly, the East German authorities' center of interest was Willy Brandt. It soon became clear to her that the interrogators knew of their intimate relationship and that she was being sounded out on the possibility of acting as intelligence agent for East Germany's State Security Agency in Bonn, "reporting" on Brandt and his American and Norwegian friends.

Susanne's tale is a strange one, worthy of those slightly out-of-joint thrillers that never completely unravel. In hopes that Willy would come to her rescue she managed to get a message to West Berlin. The SOS note, concealed in her powder compact, was flung out of her window and picked up by two young men. Miraculously, it reached its destination. But West Berlin's sensation-hungry papers got hold of the story. The news that Sievers was prisoner in a villa on Imkerweg in Berlin-Schmönckwitz was spread all over the front pages. Disclosure of her attempt to contact the West did not ease her situation. The evening that the sensational news stories appeared, Susanne was transferred to less comfortable prison quarters.

It was months before she was finally charged and sentenced as a spy for the Social Democrat's unofficial intelligence agency, the Ostbüro, and its "key spymaster" Willy Brandt. The director of the Ostbüro at that time was Stefan Thomas, but it was no secret that many SPD officials were actively involved in its operations. Since the SPD's Ostbüro records went up in flames one day, it is no longer possible to ascertain whether or not Sievers was on its payroll, as the GDR charges.

Frustrated in the abortive recruiting attempt, the state security officials covered up their mistake by another turn of the screw. At least that is the way Susanne Sievers explained the incredibly traumatic events. Hilde Benjamin, vice president of the supreme court of the GDR, knew no mercy. For spying for the "American agent, Willy Brandt, and the Ostbüro of the SPD" Susanne Sievers was sentenced to eight years in the penitentiary. She was released after four years. When she arrived in West Berlin on August 17, 1956, she had but one thought: she must see Willy Brandt! According to her account, the unfortunate woman, looking haggard and grey after her excrutiating ordeal, had to wait 24 long hours before Brandt granted her an audience.

If the years had been disastrous for Susanne, they had been good for Brandt. As so often happened in his life, Brandt dealt in good luck once more. With Schumacher's death in August 1952 and the death of his friend, Berlin Mayor Ernst Reuter, in 1953, Brandt's sagging career was given a considerable boost. Schumacher's death had undercut Franz Neumann's party support. Reuter's death, on the other hand, opened up an unforeseen avenue for Willy's ascent to President of Berlin's municipal parliament, a post up to then occupied by Dr. Otto Suhr, who had been slated as Reuter's successor. Although Brandt's candidacy for a seat in the SPD's presidium was defeated by the Social Democrats' congress in 1954 and 1956, he nevertheless broadened his support among the party comrades sufficiently to be elected vice chairman of Berlin's SPD. The combination of these two positions proved an ideal vantage point and platform for launching Brandt's meteoric rise into national and international politics.

In the anteroom of Willy's imposing new office in West Berlin's city hall, Susanne had plenty of time to study the elegantly paneled door—it remained closed for a long time. When she finally confronted him, seated behind an enormous desk, she agonized over his frosty reception. In the presence of his aide, Brandt supplied her with 100 West German marks, a free flight ticket to the West—all political prisoners from the GDR are eligible for this—and pressed for a speedy departure. Except for a reference indicating that he was instrumental in negotiating her release, there was no private conversation during their brief encounter, the physically and emotionally shattered Susanne recalled bitterly.

According to Sievers, there were letters from Willy and a few more secret meetings in Bonn but no help in collecting and putting together the pieces of her fractured life. She supposedly visited the Ostbüro to find out something about the organization that caused her such excessive grief; but there was no restitution for the loss of years of her life. She turned down a job as an informer among the right-wing organizations to which she would have access as an Eastern "refugee." Finally, when an offer to work for the Berlin representative's office in Bonn arrived, it was Willy who put obstacles in the way. He was afraid that such an arrangement might cause gossip. Susanne concluded that Brandt was not willing to compromise his political chances for the welfare of an old sweetheart.

Susanne tried her luck as a freelance journalist. Since she wrote about matters of defense, she came in contact with her old friend Franz Josef Strauss, now advanced on the political ladder to minister of defense. The warm welcome and the recommendation she received from Willy's august foe were not entirely happenstance or a mere beau geste. After all, Susanne was a precious source of information as far as Brandt's personality was concerned. And Susanne, a woman clearly hurt and scorned, no longer had reason to be protective of Willy. Before long, she held a position in the CDU/CSU dominated Federal Intelligence Service.

Susanne's Revelations

When Willy Brandt, Berlin's governing mayor since the death of Otto Suhr in 1957, made his first effort to capture the chancellor's office from Konrad Adenauer in 1961, Susanne had a chance to pay her debt to her benefactors. She wrote her memoirs. In ... *There Also Was a Girl,* she told what she knew of the private life and background of the candidate. Perhaps Susanne simply took her belated revenge. But it is also conceivable that the disappointed woman, who idolized Brandt at one time, felt an obligation as a citizen to reveal to the public those parts of the politician's "secret life" which she believed had a bearing on the assessment of his character and judgment. Since she portrayed herself quite honestly as a "woman scorned" in the book, the public was forewarned to regard her view as jaundiced.

The appearance of the small explosive volume caused a sensation during the campaign. Understandably, the SPD and Brandt were furious about the "indiscretions." Since Susanne's publisher shrewdly insisted on the inclusion of Brandt's letters in facsimile, his campaign managers were unable to write off the nuisance as pure fiction. Brandt decided to play rough. He took legal action for invasion of privacy and pressed for an injunction against distribution of the damaging book. For the trial in Munich the publisher had lined up forty witnesses to establish that his author told the truth in her sensational volume. The witnesses were never called to the stand. A compromise was reached. The court ordered the book withdrawn from the market because of the facsimile letter reproductions. Sentence was suspended. Instead of setting the record straight in reference to the events leading to Sievers' arrest, Brandt kept his silence. Counterallegations that Sievers was a spy for the GDR, detailed to Brandt, made the rounds and remained as unsubstantiated as the claims in the book. Hysterical party officials charged the opposition with a campaign of defamation, a "dirty tricks" campaign. The issues raised in the book were never aired or refuted.

Eventually, the storm blew over. Brandt had lost his premature bid for the highest office and Sievers was literally shipped off on a slow boat to China. Whether the firing of Susanne Sievers from her position as a BND agent in Hong Kong by Brandt's paladin Ehmke in 1969, after Brandt had moved into Bonn's Palais Schaumburg, was accidental or in repayment of past disfavors is anybody's guess.

The fact is, however, that Sievers haunted Brandt even after his fall. When the story of her substantial severance pay from the Federal Intelligence Service surfaced in the German press, the long forgotten affair was juicily spread before the public once more. But it was a different public in 1974, a public sooner amused by Willy's legendary derring-do than shocked.

Once more, excited accusations about a smear campaign were issued by overreacting SPD officials. Once more, Susanne Sievers promised to tell all in a new book, without pulling punches because of circumstances or the persons involved. The morally relaxed public, however, would just as soon turn to a hard-core porno show or a girlie magazine for entertainment.

Willy Brandt may not have written many love letters since that time. After a sampling of his ill-fated experiments in this oversensitive mode of communication that has always required the touch of a poet or of extreme youth, one concludes that neither would-be recipients nor his biographers will suffer from this privation.

6
The Rivals

"Schmidt the Lip"

"Yes," said Helmut Schmidt without blinking an eyelid when I asked him, on a hot summer day in 1966, if he would like to be chancellor. I had talked to the most prominent representatives of all the parties that summer for a series of profiles on German politicians. Most were potential candidates for the highest office, but none was as disarmingly candid as Helmut Schmidt. At that time he was the SPD's acting parliamentary floor leader and party whip, renowned for his stunning eloquence and managerial efficiency. Even the ebullient CSU chairman, Franz Josef Strauss, certainly no paragon of bashfulness, and itching to get a crack at the chancellorship, garnished his answer with the profuse verbiage of false modesty.

As the SPD's most quick-witted star debater, the economist from Hamburg had earned the sobriquet, "Schmidt the Lip." To the dismay of his colleagues, the pragmatic "will-do" politician often displayed his brand of disarming and at the same time infuriating honesty in the Bundestag. While Schmidt's friends never cease to admire this frankness, his enemies criticize it as blunt, arrogant, crude or even authoritarian. Wishy-washy statements are not Schmidt's style, not as party whip and not as chancellor. By daring to call a spade a spade, the clear-thinking technocrat, whose commitment to visionary or dogmatic party ideology is zero, has not endeared himself to all factions, especially the left-wing Jusos.

Unafraid to take on young, addle-brained theoreticians, Chancellor Schmidt challenges them to go into the factories and listen to the workers' actual worries instead of framing theoretical testimonies. Rather than thinking about the pressing problems of a worldwide economic crisis and unemployment "you philosophize about nationalization [of industries]" and the "crisis of your own minds," he chides. "You are about to preach the church empty." Such bluntness could never be expected from Brandt, a romantic radical left-wing functionary early in life, given to socialistic visions in his later years. That Schmidt on occasion is applauded by the opposition and labeled a "conservative" by his own party must be considered a handicap as well as a credit to his career.

Brandt had promised "New Frontiers" with his reform program. Chancellor Schmidt is more modest. His policy statement of May 17, 1974, promised nothing but pledged to deal with the most urgent needs.

"No government can work miracles, but it must do everything in its power to achieve what is possible," Schmidt said. "In this respect we are concentrating our energies on what is essential today."

The *New York Times* sees in Chancellor Schmidt an "all-round politician whose diligence—usually meaning an 18-hour day—determination and willingness to take expert advice, have enabled him to perform credibly in a wide variety of assignments." Although Schmidt clearly counts as one of the fathers and promoters of Ostpolitik, Moscow's *Pravda* is less exuberant in its praise. The official Soviet paper, which ascribes Brandt's fall to "machinations of reactionary forces," nevertheless feels obliged to point to Schmidt's "knowledge and experience."

"Pragmatic action is aimed at a goal, a purpose one sets for oneself that actually is accomplished with the means at one's disposal," Schmidt once said pointedly before he became Brandt's successor. The super-sober Schmidt is as impatient with pomposity as with inefficiency. As "expression of his independence as floor leader," he refused to address Kurt Kiesinger as "Mr. Chancellor." When Schmidt saw Brandt arriving at a party convention with an escort of several police cars and motorcycles and an entourage resembling a small army, he did not spare his sarcastic observations about such nonsense and promised as chancellor to do away with it. He did.

Parliamentarians and coworkers who cannot think or follow a

complex thought process as fast as the intelligent Schmidt often become the victims of his public tongue-lashings. When the "twerps," "ignoramuses" and "know-nothings" complain about his high-handed behavior, it is Herbert Wehner, the SPD's unchallenged boss, who has to play the mediator.

"You are supposed to say what our ministers are unable to express —but not against them," Wehner admonished him once. Wehner is just about the only party bigwig whom the irreverent Schmidt respects intellectually. Convinced of Brandt's emotional appeal but not of his intellectual capabilities, Schmidt recommended early in 1966 that the best solution to the party's problems would be to promote Foreign Minister Brandt to the decorative office of Federal President in the next elections. Brandt, who has never felt comfortable with intellectuals at any period of his life, never quite trusted the "bright young man" from Hamburg.

Since aggressive polemics and sharp reasoning are usually followed by prompt actions, Schmidt has been accused of talking and acting before taking time for contemplation. Whereas Brandt could sit through the most long-winded debates with a far-away, glazed look in his eyes, a posture often interpreted as tolerance, Schmidt begins to bluster out of sheer impatience in the face of rambling monologues. Günter Grass comments astutely that "for Schmidt, the intermission before Brandt starts to act is often too long."

Sommer comments

Theo Sommer, editor of the progressive *Zeit* and an avid Schmidt fan, has a different view of the new chancellor's decision-making practices. Sommer, briefly an assistant to Schmidt, then Secretary of Defense, was surprised how much time his boss took before reaching a decision:

"How many committees and people you occupied with this; how you took care that the prescribed procedures were followed—no shortcuts which would only cause confusion or disturbances; no quick shooting from the hip. Often enough, when I already had formed an opinion after a briefing, you still pressed further, dug deeper, weighing the pros and contras. Never have I seen you so grumpy as when someone tried to put you under time pressure on important decisions which did not seem quite ripe to you."

Sommer goes on to admire Schmidt's talent for organization, and for problem identification, the preciseness in his definition of necessities and possibilities. He lauds the discussion of the proposals in their different stages when the minister, sitting among his trusted advisers, acts as the recipient of feedback from below and above, and not as head of the house hierarchy. Sommer, one of Germany's top journalists, marvels at Schmidt's rare ability to formulate a decision in such a way that it is ready to go to the printer after hours of analytical discussions and at his supervision of its execution. Not everybody is as impressed with Schmidt's self-discipline as Sommer. Schmidt's "undisciplined attacks" on his rival Schiller, economics and finance minister, shocked the good professor into resignation and literally drove sensitive Chancellor Brandt out of the charged cabinet meetings.

Schmidt openly confesses that he is not altogether in agreement with his party, and the party not with him. While Brandt and his leftist circle advocate a democratic socialism, conservative Schmidt keeps talking of social democracy.

"In the first years after the war, the socialist component carried more weight in my political concept; today, the democratic one is more important," he admitted frankly in 1966. "The functioning of democracy and the functioning of the constitutional state is infinitely more important, in my mind, than some exaggerated notion of socialistic meticulousness."

He knows full well that this makes him even more suspect with the radical Jusos who distrust him as an "American slave" and a law-and-order man. Yet the protests are no less vociferous when Schmidt admonishes the U.S. government for its Vietnam war, "This war must be ended," or warns of the negative effect the replacement of the American draft with a volunteer army might have on European partners. It is up to Brandt to point out that Bonn has no intention of advising the Americans on the organization of their Armed Forces. As far as the Jusos are concerned, Schmidt can do nothing to please. When he argued, as finance and economics minister, that 5 percent price increases are better than 5 percent unemployment, his socialistic stance was shrugged off as sheer demagoguery.

As he demonstrated in the case of the moribund SPD tax reform bill, a complex three-inch-thick document that relaxed the tax burden slightly for lower- and middle-income groups, Chancellor Schmidt, in contrast to Brandt, is not averse to negotiating a compromise with the conservative opposition.

Each federal government, no matter whether social-liberal or Christian-democratic, has first to attend to the "classic functions of the state." Such functions are "the stabilization of its achievements." Schmidt means that the solution of the energy crisis and ensuing world economic problems have priority over "reforms" and "moral future hopes."

Since Schmidt made this concise statement, Brandt has dropped all references to classical state functions. Chancellor Schmidt's matter-of-fact approach has been appreciated by the confused voters. He is not out to conjure up new illusions but to build trust and confidence in his new government.

"We don't want to turn the whole world upside down. We also don't want to turn the whole society upside down in four years or overnight. We'd rather take one step after the other," he tells his audiences.

For the opposition, Schmidt becomes the most acceptable SPD politician. "A right leftist," Springer's *Welt* calls him; "The only vote-catching future hope of an SPD sliding downhill to the left," another paper chimes in. Schmidt is markedly different from Brandt, party officials and voters observe.

Dynamic Schmidt, only five years younger than Brandt, is indeed of a different generation and a different world. Like so many other German politicians of his vintage, he has no emotional or intellectual ties to the Social Democrats' past; not to Marx, not to Engels, not to Bebel, not to their class struggle or their desperate fights in the Weimar Republic. He comes from a white-collar family background. Yet even if his parents had not belonged to the bourgeoisie, the most important experience in his life still would be Hitler's war.

Handsome Helmut's background

Handsome Helmut Schmidt with his full head of hair and distinguished Anthony Eden looks was recruited to be groomed for the top job by Herbert Wehner after the SPD's chancellor candidate, Willy Brandt, suffered his second bitter defeat at the polls in 1965. Wehner, the party's ruthless, powerful vice-chairman and dedicated secret master as well as its ingenious strategist, had handpicked Brandt in 1960 for reasons of his own against considerable resistance within the party's top echelon. When Willy failed to catch on with the voters during his second round, Wehner decided the time had come to build up two other candidates as replacements. This time Wehner promoted two intellectuals with bourgeois backgrounds: Helmut Schmidt, Hamburg's charming, decisive and photogenic Secretary of the Interior; economics professor Karl Schiller, Berlin's Secretary of Economics, blessed with the same vote-getting qualities as his rival and one-time student Schmidt.

The bait used to lure both of these high-powered politicians and economic experts from their snug positions was nothing less than the highest office in the land. Wehner, who had sworn to lead the SPD out of its perpetual opposition into the limelight of the governing benches, was no longer willing to bet on one horse only. Besides, the hellbent-for-power manipulator probably reasoned that a little competition could only benefit the party.

Compared to Brandt's inscrutable past, Schmidt's life is an open book. He was born in Hamburg, in the largely "red" working-class district of Barmbek on December 23, 1918. Father is a teacher, uncle serves on Hamburg's school board. His younger brother teaches and so does his wife, Hannelore, his junior high school sweetheart whom he met as an eleven-year-old boy and married as a first lieutenant in the middle of the war. He was fourteen when Hitler came to power. At fifteen, the captain of a rowboat crew, he was automatically detailed to Hitler's navy youth. He advanced quickly, but as a student in the progressive, liberal arts oriented Lichtwark high school, he repeatedly got into disputes over the Nazi concept of "degenerated art" and was subsequently punished by being suspended from his functions in the Hitler Youth.

At an age when Brandt had mastered the first hard lessons of politics, Schmidt wanted to become an architect and city planner. He paints and draws well and plays the organ and piano, preferably Bach, Handel, Scarlatti and other baroque composers. He has reportedly selected Pachelbel's *Canon and Gigue* to be played at his funeral. As versatile in music as in politics, he plays Gershwin during a TV appearance and, when in the mood, improvises medleys of waltzes, folk or pop music, and spirituals.

He graduated at the top of his class, was drafted into the Reich

Labor Service and, half a year later, into Hitler's armed forces. When World War II began, Schmidt was twenty years old. On duty in an antiaircraft artillery battalion, he wrestled with an inner conflict spared the generations before and after him—the realization that ". . . to know, on the one hand, one must defend one's country, which we did and did willingly; and on the other hand to know each day and each week final defeat delayed in this way meant only a prolongation of a regime that was lastly and unequivocally to be condemned." Unlike the self-exiled Brandt, who never faced a day of field combat, Schmidt found himself in a tank division rolling toward Leningrad and Moscow, behind a desk in Göring's Air Force Ministry in Berlin, in the Battle of the Bulge on the western front at the end of the war, decorated with the Iron Cross second class, and a prisoner of the British.

When the war ended in 1945, he was twenty-six. Like many of his soldier comrades he had "no positive idea of democracy" or the "order of a constitutional state." His first concept of what a state ought to be evolved during "endless discussions" with other prisoners-of-war. There, "under the influence of older officers I became a Social Democrat," Schmidt writes. Looking back, he realizes that the moral principle upon which the "valuable experience of comradeship" was based served as a bridge to the Socialist's moral principle of solidarity. Unlike Brandt, it was not the class struggle that motivated Schmidt to become politicized and join the SPD.

"I have never pondered the thought that any other party was to be considered," he asserts. Rather, it was the traumatic impact of the war, the "senselessness" of it all, that drove him to study political science and economics and to choose political activism. Before long he was national chairman of the Marxist-oriented Socialist Students' League, the same SDS that became one of the prime movers during the violent student rebellions of the 1960s. As SDS chairman he supported the nationalization of basic industry and land reform of big estates. The Jusos' chief quarrel with Schmidt is that he deserted these early convictions.

The Schmidts' daughter, Susanne, was born in 1947. Two years later he handed in his thesis, "A comparison of Japanese and German Currency Reform," and graduated at the head of his class. His economics professor, Karl Schiller, an SPD member since 1946, secured a job for his top student in the economics department of

Hamburg's city and state administration, which he headed. Soon afterward, Schmidt took the big leap into politics.

As the SPD representative from Hamburg, he specialized in economic, transportation and military affairs in the Bundestag. The fact that Schmidt was not opposed to rearmament and was a captain in the reserves of the Federal Air Force does not sit well with today's anti-NATO Jusos. Nor did such action find approval of the SPD's leaders in 1958. "One cannot believe it possible. How can a Social Democrat put on a uniform?" Wehner fumed. Schmidt smartly countered that officers' clubs should be populated by Social Democrats like other organizations; he was voted out of the party's parliamentary executive committee. When the chance to head Hamburg's Department of Interior came his way in 1961, he felt relieved to get away from his frustrating, inactive existence on the opposition benches.

Crisis Management

As was the case with Brandt, Schmidt's career and reputation enjoyed a decisive upturn because of a crisis. Brandt's persuasive qualities came to the nation's attention during the Berlin uprisings against Soviet intervention in Hungary in 1956. Schmidt emerged as Hamburg's heroic flood fighter when single-handedly he commanded helicopters, police, Red Cross, army battalions and the Workers' Samaritan League in the dramatic rescue operations on the night of the catastrophe, February 16, 1962.

Three years later, Wehner brought Hamburg's popular "can do" idol back to Bonn. "If there is to be a fresh breeze, then not in Hamburg but here [in Bonn]," Wehner reasoned.

Schmidt really did not want to leave his hometown. He thought of the loss of his secretary's pension and the salary reduction he would have to take in Bonn. Actually, there was still another reason for his hesitancy in accepting Wehner's tempting offer. Schmidt sincerely questioned the wisdom of a politician who "in the long run—does not just live *for* politics but lives *of* politics." He wondered if, for a while at least, he should not consider a job outside politics, in industry. Wehner proved to have the stronger argument. He needed Schmidt's eloquence, his rationality, his activism and buoyant confidence, even his caustic wit, to beef up and glamorize the party's grey functionary image in the Bundestag. He persuaded his comrades to ante up the necessary marks so that Schmidt could afford to become the party's whip.

And elegant Schmidt, partial to neat British blazers, striped ties and an ever visible pipe, is no disappointment. With his quick mind and repartee he becomes an instant Bundestag celebrity as a man of unusual versatility. He often outstrips Brandt in the popularity polls. In 1965, long before the female readers of a boulevard paper vote handsome Helmut the German "Sexy-Mann, No. 1," England's *Sunday Express* comes to the conclusion that the name of the German chancellor of 1975 is Helmut Schmidt.

The open rivalry between Brandt and Schmidt actually starts with Schmidt's grand debut in Dortmund in 1965 before his return to Bonn. Wehner has put Schmidt next to Brandt as a speaker at the party's convention. Schmidt gives a performance with his critique of CDU/CSU weaknesses that is immediately downgraded by Brandt, who remarks, "The voters don't want an Olympics of griping." From that moment on Brandt knows, and the party knows, that Schmidt represents an alternative to Brandt.

Wehner's plan not only set Schmidt and Brandt on a collision course, but also programmed similar courses for Brandt and Schiller, and Schmidt with Schiller. Upcoming party leader Hans Apel and other party members agree that Brandt and Schmidt each possess all the qualities of a party leader: "physical stamina, passion, team spirit, and a great rhetorical talent."

Brandt, who is given to resignation after losing "the dirty election campaign waged against his person," is to play into luck again. Not long after he declared: "I shall serve my party best by giving up my candidacy for 1969," the political tide turned in favor of the SPD and Brandt. As the political wizard Wehner predicted, the loyal party delegates reelect as chairman the two-time chancellorship loser, Brandt, almost unanimously at their 1966 convention. During the regional elections, the Social Democrats swell into the biggest political party in the Federal Republic. A slight recession has undermined confidence in CDU/CSU Chancellor Ludwig Erhard as an economic miracle worker.

In the SPD presidium, Wehner raises the specter of a grand coalition with the floundering CDU/CSU. Brandt takes another view.

"Those who suspect us of trying to squeeze into a state of mere co-rulership just because our strength has grown are mistaken," he proclaims in September 1966. Long before Brandt grasps the enormous advantage of such a political marriage, Schmidt is strengthening Wehner's hand. When Erhard is ready to resign, the Social Democratic representatives huddle in a meeting that lasts until 4 A.M. Fifty-eight comrades have spoken when Schmidt steps up to the microphones. His pragmatic argument that the grand coalition presents the SPD with its first chance in 36 years "to free itself of the odium that it is unable to govern," and his strong opposition to a minicoalition with the unreliable Free Democrats as "arithmetical nonsense" are thoroughly convincing. The doubters are persuaded with a humanitarian appeal: Mass unemployment and a grave economic and national crisis are imminent if Erhard is not speedily relieved of his office.

Schmidt's brilliant maneuver, however, remains unrewarded; at least for the time being. The reluctant Brandt—"please believe that I settled for a temporary 'grand solution' only after a bitter struggle with myself . . . this is no great leap into governmental authority for we Social Democrats"—becomes the Grand Coalition's vice-chancellor and foreign minister on December 6, 1966. Professor Schiller takes over the Ministry of Economics and Wehner the Ministry of All-German Questions. Only the Ministry of Transportation is left for Schmidt. Rather than settle for the booby prize, the ambitious Schmidt decides to keep the relatively independent and highly visible party whip position. "Only one person can be parliamentary floor leader; a minister is one among twenty," he consoles himself.

Party whip

Like his CDU/CSU colleague Rainer Barzel, he makes a formidable party whip. "They will be sorry that they did not let us into the cabinet," the two floor leaders are supposed to have said. Schmidt eventually is voted into the party's presidium in March 1968. Once more his hopes are raised of becoming the party's No. 1. Schmidt makes no secret of what he thinks about the slow-moving coalition government. Kiesinger and Brandt are "miserable administrators," the cabinet ought to be reduced from twenty to twelve ministers, and the elevated government bench should be brought down physically to the same level as the parliamentarians' seats, he says. Unless he is nominated for the chancellor's office, he will think of taking a lucrative position in industry, he intimates to his friends after sharply criticizing Brandt's failure to draw a line between the party and the Marxist student left.

Brandt is furious. But mindful of his statesmanlike public image and the successful launching of his Ostpolitik, he keeps his cool. Privately, however, he needles Schmidt with a curiously patronizing letter on the rival's fiftieth birthday: "The patience of those pressing for activism is always put to a severe test in a democracy, a party and in a state." It would be a pity if "creative impatience" played itself out with age, he adds ominously.

No love is lost between the two politicians. "I asked him for his friendship and he refused," the bruised Schmidt complains, fifteen years after he had attempted to make a friend of Brandt. The elections of 1969, when differences between Chancellor Kiesinger and Foreign Minister Brandt turn into open hostility, bring a short-lived truce to the inner party power struggle. On the matter of another coalition, Brandt and Schmidt find themselves once more on different sides of the fence.

Brandt, who "is no longer in the mood" to serve another term as a "figurehead" foreign minister in a Kiesinger cabinet, negotiates with the Free Democrats. Schmidt prefers to keep an open mind. This time, Brandt is faster than anyone else. Before the CDU/CSU can get to the Free Democrats during election night, Brandt has made a deal with liberal Chairman Scheel. Once more, a defeat has been turned into a victory for Brandt. In that historic election, Kiesinger's CDU/CSU has actually polled 46.1 percent of the votes to the SPD's 42.7 percent. Still Willy Brandt becomes the first Social Democratic chancellor of postwar Germany.

Brandt decides to keep his dangerous rival under close control in his new cabinet. Instead of allowing Schmidt to continue as freewheeling party whip, he talks the reserve captain and military expert into becoming Minister of Defense. Schmidt does not keep a low profile as defense minister. Building an international image, he travels around the world, mostly to Washington, and makes headlines as a staunch supporter of NATO and the Atlantic Alliance. Schmidt's "Strategy of Balance"—his book bears that title—parallels Henry Kissinger's "Balance of Power" concept.

"The politics of relaxation of tension is nothing other than . . .

supplementation of the security politics of balance with other means," the defense minister paraphrases Clausewitz. As long as Schmidt is in the government there is no danger that the SPD-FDP coalition will be dominated by "unworldly peace apostles." The *Frankfurter Allgemeine Zeitung*'s praise was not music to all SPD ears.

In the fall of 1971, more people have a good opinion of Schmidt (67 percent) than they have of Brandt (60 percent) or Schiller (57 percent), who topped the list in 1969.

When the SPD minister of finance resigns in 1971, Schmidt's foes hold his refusal to trim the ever climbing defense budget (an 11 percent increase for 1972) responsible for the lack of funds for reforms and stabilization of the federal budget. Schmidt in turn blames Economics Minister Schiller, and his antidirigistic free market policy toward the onrush of devalued U.S. dollars, for the inflationary trend. Brandt, who has steadfastly resisted a merger of finance and economics in his cabinet, is now almost forced to combine the two ministries into one powerful superdepartment with Schiller in charge, to offset Schmidt's clout.

If the part Schmidt unwittingly plays in strengthening Schiller's power base does not literally make him sick, as some of his critics claim when Schmidt suffers a serious case of thyroid disfunction, it can hardly be a cause for joy either; especially since rumor has it that Brandt is trying to rid himself of his uncomfortable defense minister. Brandt actually is only contemplating the replacement of his sick rival, who "seems worn out" and unable to perform strenuous tasks "for an indefinite period." When a pale and puffy Schmidt at last returns to his desk, he shows distinct signs of irritability. In some circles, the resignation of the minister of science, due to a substantially slashed budget, is once more placed at the doorstep of the strong defense minister, who presides over the fourth costliest military budget in the world.

Feud with Schiller

The grand clash between Schmidt and Schiller, in the spring of 1972, over the long-due tax reform bill shakes Brandt's government to its fragile foundations. After Schmidt undiplomatically reminds his former economics professor to submit to party discipline, Schiller leaves the room without saying a word. The newspapers report an irreconcilable split in the party leadership. To make matters worse, Schmidt calls the Schiller ministry a crazy house and the willful economics professor super-crazy.

Brandt has governed with a slim majority of six seats in parliament. This majority crumbles to nothing when some of the more conservative representatives of the social-liberal coalition go over to the opposition, mainly in protest against Brandt's Ostpolitik. Aware of the coalition's inner and outer weaknesses, the opposition stages its big coup on April 27, 1972. But the vote of no confidence that is supposed to topple Brandt and his government falls short by two votes. CDU/CSU floor leader Rainer Barzel fails to become the new chancellor, yet he manages to defeat Brandt's enormously increased budget with a 247 to 247 vote in parliament the following day. The coalition's grounded ship can only be set afloat by new elections. The stalemate does not prevent a second, even more widely publicized, clash between Schmidt and Schiller. Schmidt accuses Schiller of being responsible for the financial crisis. He reluctantly goes along with Schiller's proposal to stabilize rising prices by trimming the controversial budget by 2.5 billions, except for the 800 million marks reduction in his defense budget which, in addition to Star Fighters, Phantoms and helicopters, at one time included 1 million marks worth of hairnets for long-haired soldiers. Since Schiller's professorial arrogance and his appointment of his brother-in-law to a high government position are causing renewed friction in the SPD leadership, Brandt comes to Schmidt's aid. "We have to keep in mind that the expenditures for the defense of the country are not reduced further than is recommended by the defense minister himself," Brandt counsels. Schmidt's friend, Georg Leber, minister for transport, warns that "security policy must not be made dependent on market policy."

When Schiller's suggestion for combating the dollar crisis by floating the mark is also turned down that summer by the cabinet in favor of Schmidt's and Federal Reserve Bank president Klasen's short-term dollar-blocking recommendation, he is so outraged that he resigns in a huff.

Brandt realizes that the timing of the departure of this highly esteemed and independent expert, who had given much intellectual luster and stature to his cabinet, could not be more unfortunate so shortly before the crucial elections. The Schiller crisis, preceded by the resignations of two other cabinet officers, is interpreted by the press as evidence of Brandt's weakness and inability to govern.

Only Schmidt, Schiller's unchallenged successor to the vital cabinet job, does not believe Schiller's exit will damage the party's chances in the election.

"Schiller voters, who are they? They are no longer in existence," he maintains. The outcome of the elections proves him to be right.

For Brandt, Schiller's political suicide is "a victory of vanity over intelligence." Confronted with the choice between two prima donna ministers vying for an opportunity to ease their way into Palais Schaumburg, Brandt has eliminated the less popular one.

Schmidt, the talented all-round man, becomes the most powerful politician of the coalition government. Possibly, Chancellor Brandt —who thinks of the unloved Schmidt as "inevitable"—just plays for time. He knows that time is Schmidt's worst enemy. "He is actually, if I don't make it this time, too old," Brandt had commented spitefully in 1969. "Does he hope to circumvent Schmidt by pushing young Horst Ehmke up the political ladder?" insiders ask each other.

Meanwhile, the papers speculate that Schmidt cannot lose in the November 1972 elections no matter how they turn out. If Brandt's coalition wins, Schmidt is bound to be more than a mere successor to Schiller; if it is defeated, "Brandt is hardly the man who would take over the continuous leadership of the opposition in the Bundestag. Herbert Wehner ponders the thought of writing his memoirs. Then Helmut Schmidt would be the opposition leader and possibly chancellor candidate four years later," *Spiegel* magazine prognosticates. It is not the only periodical that dwells at length on the rivalry between the two SPD leaders. The prestigious *Zeit* already addresses Schmidt as "co-chancellor." Whereupon the pro-Brandt *Frankfurter Rundschau* comments that a junior chancellor is not yet provided for in the constitution. Brandt remarks dryly that Schmidt's switch from defense to finance has saved the government and the taxpayers some 2 billion marks. As finance minister, Schmidt advocates precisely what Schiller had suggested: a budget cut of 2.5 billion marks!

Even Schmidt's antagonists express approval of the less professorial, more active, zippy Schmidt style. "What actually matters to me is to set things into motion and to move that which one moves better than the predecessor or the successor, or the next man,"

Schmidt once defined his brand of active pragmatism. Schmidt knows he has to win friends—especially among the leftist Jusos and ministers—and influence people if he is to attain his immediate goal: finance and economics merged into a single department of the treasury.

Challenging Brandt

Both Schmidt and Brandt find it difficult to conceal their animosity in public. When Schmidt is asked in a TV interview about the chancellor's weak leadership, he adroitly shoots back that nobody would expect him to comment on this if this were the case. He then proceeds to characterize Brandt as an "extremely comradely" man whose sense of comradeship and friendship toward this or that member of the cabinet has landed "all of us in the present situation." Brandt, on the other hand, likes to tell his audiences what the party does not need: "coldblooded managerial behavior and intellectualism without heart."

After the SPD's clear-cut election victory, Schmidt presents Brandt with a seventeen-page letter in which the conditions of his takeover of the "department of the treasury," up to then unknown in German government, are spelled out. Besides his demand that he be put in charge of tax, budget, customs, credit, monetary, currency and economic policy making, he advises Brandt to get rid of yes-saying courtiers, such as the chancellor's chief of staff, Horst Ehmke. If these conditions are not met, he would rather withdraw to his former position as floor leader in the Bundestag Schmidt coolly announces.

Brandt, notably strengthened by the highest voter mandate in the SPD history (46 percent), cannot suppress his irritation. A simple "no" would lead to the third resignation of a finance and economics minister and, possibly, revolt by some of Schmidt's numerous backers within the party's old guard. Unwilling to face the risk, Brandt has to try another tack. He asks Herbert Wehner if he would vacate his present position as party whip for Schmidt in exchange for the more prestigious but decorative office of parliamentary president. The crusty Wehner declines. He has no intention of sacrificing the efficient Schmidt on the altar of Brandt's ego.

Having lost this round, Brandt declares the ambitious Schmidt "first man of the SPD in the cabinet of Willy Brandt." At the same time, he and his palace guard figure out how to curtail Schmidt's powers; they introduce strong-willed politicians into the cabinet. Ehmke is supposed to head the important Ministry of the Interior, and the FDP's tough Genscher is to share Schmidt's Finance and Economics Ministry. As expected, Brandt is aided by FDP chairman Walter Scheel in denouncing a "department of the treasury" as "unjustifiable." He is joined by critics of the former "super-minister" Schiller.

Meanwhile, Schmidt's forces are not idle. Genscher is persuaded to forego Finance in favor of Interior. Rival Ehmke is downgraded to Minister of Research, Technology, and Post and Communication. Schmidt is not Minister of the Treasury but of a finance ministry with extended jurisdiction, out of which only a small hunk is carved for the new FDP economics minister, Friderichs.

Brandt in effect has lost his second round, also. Schmidt is first man in the cabinet; all other ministers are more or less dependent on his largess in the execution of their programs and reforms. The failure of his plans enrages Brandt. He talks of the "sabotaging" of his cabinet reform and of divided loyalties within the party. Indignantly, he makes it clear that he has no desire to occupy the office of federal president in 1974 or to retire from active politics in 1976.

During the course of the year, the eloquent Schmidt—not as convinced as Brandt that the "unrest of the youth, especially the Jusos, is productive"—becomes Brandt's severest critic and official challenger. As SPD fortunes decline during the regional elections, Schmidt accuses Brandt of "neglecting the citizens' need for economic and social security" and fostering the Jusos' anticapitalistic politics.

Brandt is disenchanted with Schmidt's professional performance. The chancellor maintains that Schmidt neglected to develop a policy for improving market conditions. Rather, Schmidt concentrated on budgetary policies and international monetary problems, with which he improved his image at international conferences. When Brandt's devoted ally Klaus von Dohnanyi, Minister for Education, comes forth with the suggestion that a "co-chancellor" would substantially lighten the chancellor's burden, Brandt is convinced that Schmidt is behind this move to undermine his power.

Leadership Credentials

For all his ambition and his belief in his own ability to do a better job than Brandt was doing as chancellor, Schmidt does not want to make history as being responsible for scuttling the chancellor when the Guillaume affair assumes the dimensions of a Watergate. He does not advise Brandt to resign. On the contrary, he urges him to keep the party's chairmanship. Privately, he says that under Brandt's leadership the party has become a mess.

Ironically, Brandt is forced to nominate his old rival for the chancellorship. The decisive Schmidt is perhaps the most qualified chancellor-aspirant the Federal Republic has ever had. Everything in his long career seems to have prepared him for the difficult job. Besides being a political expert, he can look back on his experience as traffic and military expert for the party in parliament, Secretary of the Interior in Hamburg, floor leader in the Bundestag during the Grand Coalition, minister of defense, and minister of finance and economics. No politician can have a wider understanding of government and a wider professional range. Schmidt is at home in the whole sphere of politics. "Except for agriculture, I don't feel incompetent anywhere," he admits without coyness. One of his friends remarks: "This is the first federal chancellor of whom one can say that he was trained for the job."

Schmidt is astute enough to admit that things are not going to be easy. "We have reached a low that nobody would have thought possible since 1957," he complains after Brandt's fall. His recipe for recovery sounds more like a stern command to the dejected comrades: "Out there everybody has to make it clear, if you please, what we have achieved and not just lament about multinational corporations and capitalism."

His friends praise Schmidt for telling it "like it is." Even leftist critics like Representative Dietrich Sperling plant themselves solidly behind Schmidt with their appeal to party solidarity. *Spiegel* finds it "impossible not to be fascinated by Helmut Schmidt."

Only Theo Sommer seems to sense that the Brandt-Schmidt rivalry is anything but dead. He identifies a series of built-in friction points that could trigger an explosion any time. "There is the party chairman, Willy Brandt. I cannot imagine that the twin top arrangement—here Chancellor Schmidt, there Chairman Brandt—can come to a good end. Even in normal times one cannot expect that. It is wholly impossible when the chairman above all wants to work off resentments and enmeshes himself in legends about his fall. His public statements about his own 'potency' are unappetizing; the reference to the 'decent Germany' is hardly in keeping with the delicacy of the situation."

Sommer's comments do not stand alone. As soon as Schmidt is installed in the Palais Schaumburg, the betting on the duration of Brandt's party chairmanship is brisk. Mention of the subject brings on Brandt's unrestrained ire. "Schmidt told me to be party chairman," he says with a sarcastic grin. Brandt, for his part, is not ready to give up his last vestige of power without a fight to the finish.

Karl Schiller: Superstar

"Brandt's fall began with my exit from his cabinet," Karl Schiller, well-heeled head of the multinational investment firm Economic Development of Equatorial South Africa (EDESA)—"but only free African nations"—soberly insists. "He should not have tolerated my departure." Brandt's former minister of finance and economics is in a contemplative mood. Our conversation in his unostentatious office overlooking Bonn's picturesque market square easily weaves back and forth from present stagflation, which the all-round economic Wunderkind would combat with a policy mix, to his spectacular past as one of Brandt's most dangerous rivals. As the celebrated fighter of the Grand Coalition's inherited recession, he became the acknowledged vote-getter and secret winner in 1969. The SPD's additional six seats in the Bundestag enabled the party to form the first Social Democratic coalition government in 39 years.

The small, slender professor, veteran of three marriages, was Germany's youngest university president at age 44. Often mistaken for a student in his teaching days, Schiller has hardly lost his politically marketable youthful attractiveness at 63.

The end of the SPD's Callas

"Brandt should have done something about my resignation. Our factual disagreement over the stabilization of prices and medium-term finance policy could have been ironed out. As a matter of fact, my recommendations were just about carried out to the letter by my successor." The professor's amused half-smile that used to drive students and antagonists to distraction returns as he shrugs his shoulders in a gesture of futility. Everybody who had dealt with Brandt in those days was aware of his inclination to put off troublesome decisions as long as the course of least resistance was still open.

Schiller had not anticipated Brandt's fall.

"I was quite surprised. Brandt's advisers are to blame for letting him stumble into this whole ghastly affair. He had the wrong advisers—and in the wrong places." During our conversation, it becomes obvious that Schiller bears no ill will toward the fallen Brandt. When he learns of my talk with the exchancellor only a day or two earlier, he inquires about his health and general outlook with sincere compassion. He seems on the verge of giving me a conciliatory message to his former boss and rival but suddenly has second thoughts.

"We had many a discussion during our association that began in Berlin after the wall was built. I still have a warm feeling for Brandt. It is amazing how fast a politician is forgotten in this country. It happens faster and faster." Schiller's voice holds a distinct element of surprise. The SPD's former superstar still seems stunned by the speed with which he has been turned into a political nonperson, a forgotten has-been.

The party has done its utmost to eradicate the professor's name from its records and his impact from the public mind. Schiller's dramatic resignation from Brandt's cabinet and even more sensational renunciation of his party membership shortly before the elections had caused a major embarrassment for the Social Democrats in 1972.

"It is the duty of the government to look beyond the rim of the election dish and tell the population in time what has to be accomplished and what is required." Schiller is harsh in his criticism of Brandt's unwillingness to tackle medium-term budget planning, correlative to job security and savings, before the elections. Inexplicably, the professor's explosive five-page letter of resignation as minister of finance and economics finds its way into the public domain. His refusal to support a policy "which on the outside gives the impression the government lives by the motto: After us, the deluge," is quoted in every newspaper.

The party has neither forgotten nor forgiven the damaging charges and indiscretions of its most prominent renegade.

In retrospect, the clash between robust Brandt and cerebral Schiller appears to have been inevitable. Except for a burning ambition and a mutual admiration for John F. Kennedy—also shared by arch rival Schmidt—the two politicians have little enough in common. Brandt is deeply impressed by JFK's "conscious control" of himself by "disciplining his thoughts and his will to act, but never impulsively"; Schiller admires the "fast forward-driving spirit as a source of power, ideas and inspiration"; what matters to pragmatic Schmidt is that Kennedy gave "the courage to have ideals" back to youth.

To the aid of Berlin

After the Berlin wall went up in 1961, Governing Mayor Brandt hired the economics professor away from Hamburg to preserve and build up Berlin's cut-off economy, otherwise destined to dry up and die on the vine. "The economic and cultural extension" of isolated Berlin was Schiller's "peaceful answer to the East's challenge" of the wall. Schiller was probably the first politician of postwar Germany who fully understood and successfully instrumented the interrelationship between politics, economics and the media as a powerful tool for action! Even in Berlin the willful professor threatened to resign when unimaginative comrades rebelled against his innovative Berlin aid program, a mixture of family and building loans, investment credits, and tax reductions to attract industry and workers into the divided city. When he learned that his comrades referred to him as the "SPD's Callas," mostly because of his highhanded methods, he responded wryly: "I would just as soon be Onassis! He is a shipping tycoon and a man and not a prima donna!"

The first cloud on the Brandt-Schiller relationship probably appeared when Schiller's humble attic apartment on Olivaer Platz replaced Brandt's stodgy mayor's villa as the "in" place for intellectuals, writers, artists and academicians, among them Günter Grass and young leftist publisher Klaus Wagenbach. The rivalry became deeper and more pronounced in December 1966. At that time, the Free Democrats let it be known that they were ready for a coalition with the Social Democrats, provided their brilliant economics expert would be the chancellor-designate. The FDP of those days was not partial to supporting a professional party functionary like Willy Brandt.

By 1969, the personal relationship had deteriorated into formal, strictly utilitarian teamwork for a common good and purpose. During that election campaign, the self-assured Schiller could not suppress the remark that "Brandt overdoes his statesmanlike role a bit." Doubts of Schiller's future position lurk in the mind of the interviewer for the well-informed *Spiegel.* "Will the SPD hold on to Karl Schiller as minister of economics no matter with whom it forms a coalition?" *Spiegel* wants to know from Brandt. In responding, the party chairman's endorsement of the professor could hardly be more detached and noncommittal from a personal point of view.

"That is for sure, on the basis of what Schiller has accomplished. We will not sacrifice him to the CDU/CSU. Our people are selected by us. Besides, we will not deceive the voters. One cannot let a man like Schiller just take a walk."

CDU Chancellor Kiesinger, who had presented his friend Schiller with a four-leaf clover—"May it bring us luck"—a few years earlier, had concentrated his election rhetoric on the SPD's undisputed star. Schiller's advocacy of the revaluation of the mark, after Kiesinger had publicly rejected these proposals, ripened into a tenacious feud. Charging that Kiesinger had actually caused the new wave of inflation by impeding Schiller's revaluation formula, the professor became the chancellor's foremost and deadliest adversary. To Herbert Wehner, the once sought-after coalition partner Kiesinger was now simply "a dilettante" who prevented the "right decision out of political vanity."

It must have hurt more than Schiller's pride to hear Brandt flippantly downgrade his substantial achievements on behalf of the party a few years later with his angry comment: ". . . as if prices always went down under Schiller and now go up because Schiller no longer is minister." Perhaps even more wounding were Brandt's gruff personal attacks on the man to whom he had entrusted the nation's economic and financial affairs. The minister's resignation was not referred to as a political decision but as Schiller's "psychological" problem.

In his diary notes of August 21, 1972, Brandt attempts an account of his side of the story:

"The expected letter from Schiller that ends his membership on the party's executive committee came today. Yesterday afternoon he came to the Venusberg [Brandt's official residence] for a three-hour-long calm, but certainly not friendlike, talk. I will not throw stones at a longtime coworker. Yesterday I sought clarification as to whether he will and can stay in our party." Brandt asks himself if the conflict could have been avoided. He insists—contrary to Schiller's point of view—that the disputed factual difference did not play a principal role in their parting. Brandt notes that the break was caused by those "peculiarities of this talented man" which had set the whole cabinet against him and undermined the party representatives' confidence in him. The public reproach of his indecisiveness and subsequent prolongation of the smoldering Schiller affair is dismissed by Brandt with the argument that a wait-and-see attitude was necessary, since the matter had to be handled in the "most undramatic" manner possible.

After a perusal of the papers of that year, filled with sensational headlines about the disunity of the party's leadership, it is difficult to imagine more awkward and unprofessional management of the bad news. In all its intended and unintended distortions by the press, the Schiller exit blossomed into a spectacle of all against all in the functionaries' relentless haggling for power.

Worst of all, the quarrel took on ideological overtones. Prompted by the floating of the British pound, Schiller wanted to float the mark, preferably in unison with the French franc and other European currencies, in an effort to stop the inflationary onslaught of weak U.S. dollars and to stabilize the European market economy. Helmut Schmidt and Federal Reserve Bank President Klasen, on the other hand, persuaded the cabinet to vote for the control of foreign capital flow. Schiller regarded the cabinet's unanimous vote against his proposal as a conspiracy. Schmidt had finally outmaneuvered him. And Brandt sat silent as a sphinx. Schiller's position had become untenable.

Economic Principles

The heated controversy highlighted the juxtaposition of the Social Democrats' official "social market economy" and Schiller's ingenious blend of imperative liberalism and Keynesian economics vis-a-vis an inchoate and unofficial tendency toward a more controlled socialistic system espoused by the party's left wing.

The age-old conflict which had cracked the party's solidarity during the SPD's stormy tax convention the year before (1971) was laid open once more. Schiller's iron principles of a social market policy, ascribing to stability and growth the function of main guarantors of social justice, did not incite enthusiasm amidst proposals for workers' "collective investments," participation in profit sharing, or "equal partnership for work and capital." The Jusos, who wanted to "test the carrying capacity of the economy," voted resolutions calling for drastic hikes of high income and corporate taxes.

When it dawned on Schiller that "they" really wanted a "different republic," he tried to reason with the young anticapitalists. "Comrades, let's not lose your marbles!" But his jovial approach found little resonance among the Jusos, who suspected in Schiller a displaced CDU conservative and a bourgeois mentality that "lived past and beyond the consciousness of the party."

Since the SPD ascent to power, based largely on Schiller's antirecession and antiinflation feats and his appealing personal image reflected time and again in the popularity polls, Brandt and Wehner lent their support with noticeable reluctance. The "undercooled intellectual," not in the habit of playing buddy-buddy games or drinking with the comrades till the early morning hours, stood alone. Brandt kept his distance from the formidable "shadow chancellor" and maintained an impenetrable silence. Schiller's friends spoke of a glass wall between the two politicians.

In the end, Schiller commanded two ministries with 50,000 employees. Yet, his "combatants," as he liked to call them, were no help in the final showdown.

"The crux is whether free market policy and competition actually still form the dominant principle of organization for the economic and finance policy, as the government's policy statement of October 28, 1969, promised. This is the central question, and it remains unanswered by the federal government," Schiller writes Brandt in his much publicized letter of resignation from his party membership of twenty-six years.

Two years pass before the professor receives an answer. It is an ambiguous one. In *Beyond the Day,* Brandt qualifies his "yes" to a social market economy by a number of negative definitions. It must not be: a camouflage for "antisocial actions"; its "social obligation" must be more than a dolled-up theory of "Weltanschauung"; it must not be understood as a "new edition of laissez faire," where the state plays no more than a nightwatchman's part; "renunciation of planned action does not stand for freedom and liberalism in our time but lack of responsibility"; renunciation of planning does not necessarily mean free play of the acting forces "but chaos." In conclusion, Brandt finds himself in agreement with his often cited, anonymous "political friends" that market economy has to be "more than a capitalism with limited liability" and a cover for the "inviolability of privileges."

Without making a single negative reference to Helmut Schmidt during our conversation, Schiller conveys an attitude that suggests a rather dubious opinion of his former student and friend. Still, remembering Schmidt as one of his most vocal sparring partners in a discussion group known as "Schiller's Kindergarten" in Hamburg in the 1950s, Schiller admits: "Schmidt is the right man for this hour. He is energetic. He knows how to use his elbows." Schiller has profound doubts about Schmidt's tolerance for Brandt as party chairman.

Not surprisingly, Schmidt's famous statement about the preference of a "5 percent price increase to a 5 percent unemployment rate" as the lesser evil, is mercilessly torn to shreds by Schiller as a "phony alternative," a demagogic minimizing of the "actual inflationary development" that hampers the task of stabilization. Schiller remains adamant: "A consistent policy of stability cannot be replaced by anything." He admits "a policy of stability hurts at first."

Unlike Brandt or Schmidt, the economics professor has never had to fight or jockey for position. From the moment he graduated summa cum laude from Heidelberg University in 1935 he was, so to speak, condemned to succeed. Consequently, he finds it difficult to understand the barbarous infighting for a place at the party's top.

"I don't know what the decisive event was that gave rise to Schmidt's negative attitude towards me. I really cannot assess it and actually don't want to do so," Schiller declared after his resignation.

It seems never to have occurred to the SPD's erudite superstar that his independent thinking and open show of intellectual prowess were despised as arrogance, ego-tripping and opinionatedness by the run-of-the-mill functionary. This alienated comrades and turned the consentient tide against him. Long before it became apparent to the others, Herbert Wehner was well aware that unmanageable Schiller, who had "joined the party more or less by accident after the war when a friend of student days invited him to become a member," would never be a proper *apparatchik* and submit to party discipline. Although Schiller had nailed down the economic tenets for the SPD's reform platform at Godesberg in 1959 by replacing Marxist-style planned economy with "social market economy plus global steering" that converted what was then a narrowly based workers' party to a modern people's party, he had remained an outsider. The comrades accepted his catchy slogan, "Competition as far as possible, planning as far as necessary," but the party did not give him a seat on its presidium until Brandt prevailed on them to do so in 1966.

Jockeying for Promotion

If Brandt had mixed feelings about the extension of the presidium from a membership of nine to ten to accommodate the professor, he had no qualms about turning down his rival's second request. As a reward for his outstanding performance and contribution to the SPD election victory in 1969, Schiller coveted a promotion to the nonexistent post of second vice-chancellor, next to Scheel, or the creation of a third party vice-chairmanship, next to Schmidt and Wehner. Brandt did not have to defend his decision. The comrades, who rarely glimpsed the professor during the grinding routine of in-house work sessions, had always resented his demand for special treatment. "He lacks the smell of the stable," one of the functionaries, unconvinced of the economist's socialistic commitment, unhappily observed. Others remembered, with varying degrees of discomfort, the "brown spot" in his past. Until the elections of 1969, it was one of the best-kept party secrets that Schiller had joined the SA, Hitler's brown shirts, in 1933. The most penetrating criticism came from the progressives, who were convinced that the "friend of industry and big business" was sacrificing their treasured reforms for the sake of his bourgeois "stability."

Recognizing Brandt's inability to lead the party to victory by himself after the crushing defeats of 1961 and 1965, Herbert Wehner devised and built up a dazzling supportive team to carry him along in 1969. The problem of how to remove incipient prima donnas from the stage was to be resolved later. Wehner did not relish the Brandt-Schmidt versus Schiller row so shortly before the premature 1972 elections, brought about by Barzel's vote of no confidence maneuver, which failed to oust Brandt but stalemated his fragile coalition government. Yet Wehner dealt with the disagreeable situation head on. Media-conscious Schiller would exit neither fast nor silently (like Finance Minister Alex Möller before him). The most effective defense was to sidetrack the damaging economic controversy fanned by Schiller with a broadside personal attack.

Charging that Schiller's reason for resignation is a "myth," a smoke screen for obscuring the truth, Wehner launches his counteroffensive. Schiller is forced to admit that he asked Brandt, indeed in vain, for a guaranteed seat in parliament and in the cabinet at the 1972 elections. Naively, he wonders publicly how far "Wehner wants to push things."

Schiller's precipitous move was allegedly in response to Wehner's devilishly divisive remark: "Schiller has already led one campaign against his federal chancellor." With this reference to the professor's successful campaign against Kiesinger, resolute Wehner meant to alarm the lackadaisical Brandt. Panic-stricken that the professor who resigned in piecemeal fashion, first his cabinet post in July and then his party offices in August, will renounce his party membership in September with the usual flurry of publicity, the party, in anticipation of the next blow, does its utmost to disqualify him as a querulous malcontent, treacherous egomaniac and potential turncoat.

Wehner boldly bases his case on the unwelcome fact that both of Schiller's confidential resignation letters—brimful of recriminations on government tardiness in adopting antiinflationary measures and Brandt's weak leadership—surface in the opposition press. Brandt is furious. He maintains that Schiller's letter rests securely in his briefcase and insinuates an "indiscretion" on the professor's part. Schiller in turn professes surprise and innocence. Suspicion that his brainy, aggressive third wife, Etta, civil servant careerist and doctor of law, had something to do with the scandalous publication is laid to rest by his assurance: "She does not know where I keep my copy." Self-assured Etta, who liked to talk of her substantial part in her husband's hiring policies, had ventured that her Karl would be better appreciated in the CDU/CSU.

Since the name Guillaume was not a household word in the summer of 1972, and the country was not yet preoccupied with spy stories, the guessing game about the letter went on unresolved.

"Was it possibly Schiller himself who wanted to make the document of self-defense available to a larger circle of readers?" the respected *Stuttgarter Zeitung* speculated idly. "But the letter could have just as well been leaked by the anti-Schiller circle," it mused, to show how difficult it was to work with a man who accuses the government of an "after me, the deluge" attitude.

After the signal "to get Schiller" was out, Wehner in public could benignly praise the professor as a "brilliant Socialist" whose expertise would be most useful to the party in the future. Party chairman Brandt's commendation of Schiller's splendid services, however, is tempered by a biting story about especially intelligent army recruits who believe all others are marching out of step except themselves. Novelist Günter Grass is "a little ashamed of Karl Schiller." He feels that Schiller has misused Brandt's tolerance, till Brandt agreed to his resignation. Grass thinks it "inexcusable" that his former election campaign comrade found his way to talking with opposition leader Rainer Barzel. Only Horst Ehmke, Chancellor Brandt's ambitious chief of staff, gives away the show by beaming, according to *Quick* magazine, ". . . we will never get rid of him [Schiller] so cheaply again."

Schiller and the CDU

Schiller plays right into Wehner's hands. Twice he meets with Barzel and each time the papers are bursting with rumors of treachery. Headlines blare: Schiller has joined the CDU! Schiller makes a deal with the CDU! Schiller wants to found his own party! Schiller intends to campaign against the SPD! Is Schiller kicked out of his own party? Schiller is offered a ministry in Barzel's cabinet! Schiller is not offered a position in Barzel's cabinet.

The CSU boss, Franz Josef Strauss, takes full advantage of the rare political windfall. "Let Herr Schiller remain what he is, a Social Democrat. Facing the radicalization of his previous party he can defend and represent this point of view only in the CDU/CSU," he gloats.

As hostilities intensify, Schiller charges that the SPD is not "capable of governing." His resolute wife does little to polish her husband's rapidly tarnishing image. After all, it was her brother-in-law for whom her husband had provided the lucrative government job, the press argues, that cost the German taxpayers an estimated million marks in instant pension pay. In its cover story, "Cherchez la femme," *Spiegel* blames Etta, the "blond Rasputin," for Schiller's self-destructive wanderings between the parties. Etta, known to boast of her friendship with Mrs. Connally (wife of Nixon's controversial Secretary of the Treasury) as being worth cash to the Federal Republic, unexpectedly becomes the target of the media. *Spiegel* discloses how she had berated CDU's Barzel as a "triumph of mediocrity" and Schmidt as "sick" and ripe for a mental institution. Do the Schillers think of editing the story of the Connally party switch for German consumption? the tabloids ask.

The *International Herald-Tribune* summed up the SPD's precarious situation: "If Mr. Schiller should cross the floor, it would tip the balance of the parties in parliament in favor of the opposition and possibly upset the prospects of new elections this year, informed sources said."

Soon SPD headquarters is bombarded with telegrams from outraged members demanding that the party put an end to Schiller's damaging behavior.

Schiller heatedly assures reporters that he is not a turncoat like the FDP chairman Erich Mende. "Has everyone gone crazy?" he asks in desperation. But few people believe him when he sets out with the CDU's faded *Wirtschaftswunder* Chancellor Erhard at his side to campaign, as a lonely and not altogether believable independent, for the "recovery of economic stability."

To this day it is not clear if Schiller ever sought a cabinet post with the CDU or if that party ever considered the able professor for any position. Reportedly he was offered, but turned down, the minor traffic and science ministry. It is hard to imagine that Strauss, who also considers himself an expert in the field of economics and finance, would have supported more than a come-on lure. After the fact, the CDU/CSU consensus seems to be that Schiller's resignation in itself represented the maximum benefit for the Christian Democrats.

When Schiller's last hope of reconciliation with the party collapsed after his three-hour visit with Brandt, he apparently no longer harbored any illusions of a future in politics. He rejected the offer for a SPD candidacy for parliament in the state of Nordrhein-Westphalia because that would not be "convincing." "Can't you imagine," he said to reporters, trying to end all further speculation, "that, for example, Schiller just wants to make some money?"

Denial follows denial.

After the elections are won by the SPD-FDP coalition, *Stern* magazine steadfastly reports a Schiller-Barzel deal: Schiller was to be CDU/CSU chairman of a "stability council."

Schiller has given me his word that he never joined the Christian Democrats. I have known Schiller since his days as a Berlin senator, as a candid person and—after checking with the CDU, as he himself suggested—I have no reason to doubt his version. Yet to this day the SPD papers refer to the ex-superminister as a "member of the CDU."

Rumors die hard. So do memories of past political glory. Schiller, with offices in Zurich, Swaziland, Bonn and elsewhere, was one of the first politicians to send the fallen Brandt a heartfelt note of encouragement. He had not forgotten the pain. And Brandt, perhaps drawing parallels between the methods used by the manipulators in his superminister's and his own fall, publicly appreciated the "very decent letter."

"It is terribly hard for people who once have been in power to find their way in another situation," Schiller's secretary confides. "Most of them never quite get over it."

7
Uncle Herbert Pulls the Strings

In the Bundestag they share the same bench. But somehow, exchancellor Willy Brandt and the Social Democrat's most powerful parliamentary floor leader, Herbert Wehner, manage not to sit side by side. They sit back to back. They do not speak to each other. They never so much as glance at each other. When the session breaks up, stonyfaced Brandt heads straight for the aisle at his right, while Wehner, his broad forehead lowered like a charging bull, exits to the left.

Long before his actual fall, Brandt had sworn to keep an "iron silence" vis-à-vis Wehner. Since the chief strategist's outraged attack on Brandt's cavalier attitude toward the East and Berlin treaties, the two top SPD leaders have been on nonspeaking terms. To ensure that his devastating comments about the "laxity" of Brandt's leadership would not be lost on the public, the wily Wehner used his first official visit to Moscow, with an all-party parliamentary delegation, as a platform.

"What the government needs is a head," the SPD's strong-arm politician, who had determinedly helped Brandt into power, lamented between secretive visits with highly placed Soviet officials. Moscow is not unknown territory for the former Communist functionary Wehner. Together with top Communist leaders like Yugoslavia's Tito, Italy's Togliatti, and East Germany's Ulbricht and Pieck, the refugee from Nazi Germany and trusted member of the Comintern spent several years (1939–41) in Stalin's capital.

Power has made Brandt and his team "haughty," almost "Adenauer-like" but without the "capability," Wehner tells a *Spiegel* journalist in Kiev. The detection of a standoffish, dilatory note in the extension of cheap credits to Poland and the Soviet Union, as well as limited active support for cooperative industrial ventures, distress him. He is afraid that the Germans overestimate themselves, as they have done often before.

"We are neither de Gaulle nor his successor," he soberly observes. His worries that the coalition partners, the Free Democrats, are slowing down the momentum of the SPD Ostpolitik with incessant demands for more elastic interpretations of the treaties are intensified on Russian soil. He feels that the attempt to make "old Ostpolitik with new treaties" is not sufficiently checked by a peace chancellor with his head in the clouds, grown slack and self-satisfied from too many ovations and honors.

Bonn's position toward the touchy question of West Berlin's integration into the Federal Republic is "overdrawn," Wehner charges.

"I share the opinion of those who believe one should do something to strengthen Berlin. But the Four Power Agreement happens to be the legal foundation. If some people try to undermine and damage this agreement, I will have nothing to do with it. I will represent this point of view even if I am stoned to death for it. The Federal Chancellor knows my position."

The disagreement over government policy concerns full consular representation of West Berlin by the Federal Republic. While the agreement permits persons to be represented by Bonn, the representation of firms, agencies or institutions remains unspecified. Brandt and his foreign minister Scheel take the position that it was the intention of the negotiators to include "persons in the judicial sense" as well.

Once the bombshell is exploded, Wehner tries to soften its impact. Deploring the general tendency to try to "cash in" in advance for Berlin in international regulations, Wehner advises: If one is not satisfied with the negotiated (Berlin) treaty—which as far as he is concerned was the best deal possible under the circumstances—grievances should not be addressed only to the Soviet Union but to all four of the victorious powers.

The rude reprimand from the fearless parliamentary floor leader takes Brandt by surprise while on a visit to the White House and the

United Nations. Expressing "irritation" at Wehner's "incredible" behavior, the chancellor unexpectedly departs for Bonn after his maiden speech for the newly admitted Federal Republic to the UN in 1973. The American visit is cut short by at least 36 hours.

Back on the Rhine he lets it be known what he really thinks of his treacherous comrade, an associate since their Paris underground days in 1936. There, the two of them—Communist Wehner and radical Socialist Brandt—had endeavored to stitch together a German popular front, the integration of Communist, Socialist and Social Democrat groups into one antifascist and anticapitalist front. Intimating that the "guy" must be "mad," that he probably has succumbed to the "romantic notions of his youth" and should be eliminated from office, Brandt goes so far as to allude to Wehner's Communist past, a tactic usually reserved for conservatives of the ilk of Franz Josef Strauss.

The opposition, never quite trustful of the crafty Wehner, is delighted. Remembering Adenauer's warning that "Wehner is a dangerous person and much more than a Communist," the opposition press wonders if the old exfunctionary, ousted from the Communist party after his sensational arrest and imprisonment as a Soviet agent in neutral Stockholm in 1942, had perhaps reverted to the Communist line during his latest exposure to Soviet air. They had, of course, conveniently forgotten Adenauer's later and considerably more mellow assessment. As early as 1960, Adenauer's trusted friend and CDU/CSU parliamentary floor leader Heinrich Krone comes to the sober conclusion: "Wehner has the power in his party. He would govern if Brandt should become chancellor."

If the heated Wehner-Brandt controversy stirred up old fears of a possible revival of the SPD's abandoned course of political neutrality, it also confirmed the public's suspicion that all was not well in the Palais Schaumburg. Wehner, not loved by many but respected for his selfless devotion to the party that had borne his imprint since his election to the vice-chairmanship in 1958, once more had to play the "bloodhound," as he put it. The independent vice-chairman had not acquired his reputation for ruthlessness without some justification. This was the man who had dared to force SPD chairman Erich Ollenhauer to relinquish his traditional claim to the party's candidacy for the chancellorship in 1961 in favor of Brandt, had also dared to demolish Henry Kissinger's half-baked Atlantic Charter scheme advanced in 1973, with a single word, "monstrosity." When his mounting disappointment in the performance—or rather, lack of performance—of Willy Brandt had forced him to conclude that the chancellor was a liability to his party, Wehner did not hesitate to chip away at the pedestal of the "gentleman" with the taste for "high living."

Once Wehner had broken the tabu on open criticism of the party's idol, even his conciliatory remarks about the difficult "historic period of regeneration" the party has to undergo in the 1970s under the stewardship of Chairman Brandt do not silence the voices of discontent. All of a sudden, it is not only the cynical Wehner who suspects that Günter Grass's pertinent observation about Germany's silent majority "agreeing to help itself by helping Brandt" might well have worked the other way around. Long before the comrades see the waste of precious time and power in the initiation of "precise, practical and accountable programs," Wehner had pointed an accusing finger at the tasks undone. What the politically sensitive bloodhound had sniffed out soon became evident to all: Their emperor wore almost no clothes.

Brandt had invited open critique: "We do not seek admirers; we need people who critically share with us the thinking, the decisions and the responsibility." However, he was not ready for the demolition crew.

When the friction between Brandt and Wehner turned into an open feud, analysis of the ambiguous love-hate relationship between the two leading Social Democrats centered around the dictum that they did not fit together but that they complemented and needed each other.

Wehner's record

Herbert Wehner's singular career was at least as unorthodox and astounding as Willy Brandt's. There was only one major difference. Because of his "Commie" past, Wehner could never aspire to the highest office in democratic postwar Germany. Therefore, Brandt and Wehner were never rated as rivals—they could only become enemies. In contrast to Brandt, who never outgrew a certain awe and uneasiness in the face of power—often confusing or transfiguring it with a missionary zeal or a sense of history—Wehner's thorough

Communist indoctrination exquisitely prepared him for the uses and manipulation of power.

If the irascible vice-chairman had learned anything in particular in his long, zigzagging career, it was the power game. More than any other politician, the SPD's foremost troublemaker and troubleshooter managed to forge the party's upward spiralling trend with a rare skill and foresight. Actually, Wehner had battled for twenty-three eventful years to bring the party out of the ideological doldrums. If dubious methods were required on the road to victory, he would use them without compunction. No matter what detours he was forced to take, the goal remained steady. It was finally realized in the election of 1972, when the SPD became the strongest parliamentary party in German history.

"Democracy and socialism first had to be sacrified in order to push through democracy and socialism; an operation, it is understood, of deadly uncertainty." *Spiegel* publisher and editor Rudolf Augstein's cutting commentary appears under the heading: "Wanted: A Strategist."

To Konrad Adenauer, the SPD's most intriguing, most controversial and most enigmatic personality became the "party's demon." To the comrades, the ex-Communist with the questionable past became the guiding light, the inspired mastermind with the Machiavellian touch. To the general public, he became the chief strategist and tactician who coaxed and coerced, shaped and pummeled the Marxist-directed, class-warfare conscious workers' party into a middle-of-the-road people's party until it had earned its mandate to govern.

Speaking about "Uncle Herbert," as he is called with affection and awe by the party functionaries, superlatives inevitably seem to crowd into the descriptive vocabulary. One senses something excessive in the stern vice-chairman's psychological makeup. A total lack of flamboyancy suggests a fanatical trait. His abstinence betrays an affinity for the absolute. His craggy face reflects a tortured life. He has been likened to a volcano which erupts from time to time, especially in Bundestag debates when he showers his adversaries with insults and obscenities meriting a call for an exorcist. Friends who pretend to know him swear that the choleric outbursts of this iron-willed man are as calculated as his somber silences.

With his "proletarian grin," as the conservative *Welt* once described the curious lift he gives one corner of his mouth, and his shrieking voice, sirenlike in decibels, Wehner has become the party's provocative negative symbol. Likened to Adenauer and Ulbricht in political craftsmanship, he becomes the dark foil for Brandt's shining Siegfried.

A BOOST FOR BRANDT

It is perhaps to his credit that Wehner never pretended to be impressed by Willy Brandt, the party's lightweight "beau," the sonny boy, who in his opinion had little else in his head than "horses, women, and champagne." This harsh appraisal of the obliging Brandt personality, however, did not prevent his giving full backing to the party's chancellor candidate for 1961. Whatever Berlin's smiling mayor was, or was not, he certainly looked like the only SPD functionary with enough voter appeal to put the party on the map.

Unlike other Social Democrats, Wehner did not take comfort in the glory of representing a moral but impotent political party. He seemed more than ready to compromise party morality for power. When lesser functionaries followed his pragmatic examples in the 1970s he was horrified. "They believe they could make politics without morals," he scolded. Still there was one principal lesson the battered old functionary would never forget: social justice and social change could not be achieved by a party habitually condemned to find its place in the opposition.

"Our problem is how do we arrive at socialism by means of democracy. The decisive democratic means is the SPD's victory at the election," he said in 1959 after streamlining and adjusting the party in the bourgeois image of the Christian Democrats. If it was necessary for the party to abandon its Soviet-oriented policy of neutrality to gain power, it would do so. It would embrace Westpolitik . . . the NATO concept, the Atlantic Alliance, the European Economic Community, the church, emergency laws, even private property. It would endorse rearmament, even though Wehner had publicly declared that the "SPD will abolish the draft when it comes to power. This resolution is irrevocable." When the SPD came to power, no such thing was done.

Did the means justify the end—to govern? It looked this way to the general public.

Wehner remains flexible. Any claim that the solution of a problem can be attained *only* this way or *only* that way is regarded by him as a typically German tendency. The "art of superior statesmanship" can best be realized by allowing "different possibilities to compete." Wehner endorses the possibility of experimentation "in the best sense," in order to find out, perhaps in the span of a few years, what works best.

His part in framing the reforms of the Godesberg Program in 1959—with more than a dozen collaborators—consisted mainly of freeing the party from its role as executor of its inherited economic and historic constraints and rules. Marx, Engels, Bebel, Lassalle and Bernstein, the revered party godfathers, had to make room for a modern political pluralistic community of common will and values, brought together for the realization of certain political goals.

Without the Godesberg reforms, the grand coalition with the CDU/CSU (1966) would have been impossible. Yet a grand coalition is very much on Wehner's mind. After stating that a common ground with the "mendacious people at the top of the CDU" does not exist for the SPD, barely a year elapses before he solemnly reminds the Bundestag of the "mutual obligation of the Social and Christian Democrats." Brandt seconds Wehner's hidden coalition proposal in 1961: "In spite of all animosities, we start with the basic truth that we are one family."

The incident of the Berlin wall sharply boosts the idea of forming an all-party government. Adenauer is not interested. Nor is Brandt, who would rather work with the FDP. Only steps three and four are missing from Wehner's four-step strategy to bring the SPD to power via a grand coalition with the CDU, followed by a minicoalition with the FDP, and prove to the voters its ability to govern. Provided there was such a plan, the next step would have been a majority SPD government and subsequent development of a democratic socialism patterned after the Swedish model.

Willy Brandt belongs among those politicians who doubt that Wehner is more than an ingenious tactician. As Peter Koch reports in a series of articles on Wehner in *Stern* magazine, Brandt revealed his disbelief in his vice-chairman's fabled long-range strategy by answering the question, "Where does Wehner stand?" with a telling gesture. After putting his finger in his mouth, he held it—sailor fashion—in the air. This little demonstration signified, of course, that

Wehner shifts and adjusts his position according to the winds of current consensus.

Does Wehner in effect subscribe to Machiavelli's counsel and observation that the politician who adapts his policy to the times prospers? Was Brandt, a phenomenally bad judge of character and men, mistaken? Or was he riled to such extent by the vice-chairman's extraordinary reputation that he gave in to the self-serving need to diminish it?

THE REAL LEADER

Vice-chairman Wehner's decisive contribution to the party was duly acknowledged by the opposition and its press. In its official campaign brochure, the CSU recognizes the shrewd functionary as the "real" leader of the Social Democrats who runs the state and Brandt's government from the back benches with the "cunningness and unscrupulousness of the experienced party functionary."

Wehner had not changed his opinion of Brandt when he offered to help him and build him up. "Firstly, you can always count on me when the object is to make a real reform party out of this party and to develop it as such. Secondly, you can also always count on me when the object is to oppose those who believe it to be enough to put on some 'rouge'," he wrote Brandt before the 1961 campaign. This was a promise as well as a warning. He kept that promise until he became convinced that his trust had been misplaced.

He knew from the very beginning that Brandt was wanting in decisiveness. On the other hand, he was certain that only Willy would be able to sell the party's program. As it turned out, the independent Schiller was as successful in illuminating and winning the voters for the party's various concepts, and the eloquent Schmidt was never far behind. By 1966, Wehner had built a brilliant team around Brandt, a team designed to outshine the CDU/CSU coalition partners. If Kiesinger wanted to win the elections of 1969 he would not just have to fight Brandt, but Schiller and Schmidt as well. In concert with these two strong politicians, practically anybody could run the government.

Paradoxically, Wehner had preferred Brandt as head of government precisely because of his "weaknesses." Politicians with an inclination to be dazzled by their own role in history tend to become aloof to current needs and too busy to concern themselves with party trivia. At the same time, they are likely to respond to guidance and prove less troublesome in showdowns and in the enforcement of party loyalty and discipline than strong functionaries, especially if their dossiers are slightly scandalous. Besides, the self-confident ex-mayor of Berlin, who had boasted that his "calling card was not the worst" one could hand out in the world, was by far the best-known Social Democrat around.

When it came to people, Uncle Herbert was a cynic.

When it came to Willy Brandt, he was resigned to accepting him as he was. As a birthday greeting, Wehner wrote Brandt years ago that he had given up "wishing him what he wished from him." Wehner remembers Brandt to have "gulped that up," especially since the note also assured him of Wehner's continued support.

Brandt is not necessarily intrigued by Wehner's celebrated tactical qualities either. "Does he have manners!" Brandt once gasped in despair over his party whip's persuasive methods. "Whenever he talks with our partners of the CDU, he first refers to all other Social Democrats as assholes!"

Like Brandt, Wehner has become a legend in his lifetime. Like Brandt, Wehner does as little as possible to destroy myths and rumors concerning a past that for the most part still lies shrouded in secrecy. To this day, both of them have shied away from revealing their revolutionary political background to the public. In his official biography in the Bundestag directory, Wehner forgets to mention his membership and meteoric rise in the Communist party. Not only was he a Communist representative in the Saxony state parliament at the age of 25, he also became the personal aide of Germany's *Kommunistische Partei Deutschlands* (KPD) leader Ernst Thälmann, as well as editor of *The Party Worker,* in 1931. Aware that it is hardly possible to go "unpunished" in German politics as a former Communist, he also skips over his anarchosyndicalist period.

Neither does he think it necessary to burden his fellowman with any reference to his work for and attachment to anarchist leader Erich Mühsam, one of the initiators of the short-lived Communist Bavarian *Räterepublik* (Council's Republic) in 1919, then Wehner's spiritual mentor. As early as 1926, young radical Wehner had advocated the "destruction of the state." He encouraged the workers to take over the factories, weapons in hand, to put an end to their "unfreedom," and "to gather all forces for a battle against the republic and the state, against Parliament and all other institutions that are instruments of power in the hands of the capitalists."

Wehner, born in Dresden in 1906, comes from a solid working-class background, like Brandt. His father is a shoemaker. Not being blessed with the luck of Willy Brandt, Wehner does not have the benefit of a higher education. He left school at 15, enrolled in an administrative course, and held assorted jobs as a farmhand, at a motor factory, and in an advertising office. He was fired from the Zeiss-Ikon works because of his alleged "Communist agitation" among the workers in 1927. After that, Wehner made a living as a Communist functionary. He had joined the SPD's Socialist Worker's Youth in 1923 but switched to the Communist party in 1927. As a labor union member, the hard-working young man also worked as editor of Communist union papers.

From Moscow to Stockholm

As soon as Hitler came to power and the KPD became illegal, Wehner went underground. Together with other activist KPD functionaries, he helped to organize, under Moscow's direct control, a vast Communist network of communication, intelligence gathering and sabotage in Western Europe. It was designed as resistance to Nazi Germany and for the eventual establishment of Communist-dominated governments. On instructions from Moscow-based Comintern headquarters, he attempted to promote a "popular front" or "Red front" in the Saarland that opted for the continuance of separation from Germany in 1935. Since 90.5 percent of the population voted for reunification with the Third Reich, Wehner's impact appears to have been negligible.

Wehner met with better luck in Paris, where he assembled Communist volunteers for participation in the Spanish war. It is not certain if he was acquainted with the fact that Moscow used the Spanish battlefield, among other things, for the liquidation of undesirable comrades. During a popular front conference, he briefly met Brandt, then a functionary of the Marxist revolutionary Socialist Workers' Party, whom he saw "on the horizon," an encounter that is not remembered by Brandt.

Shuttling back and forth between Communist espionage centers in

Paris, Berne, Zurich, Amsterdam, Brussels, Lisbon and other places, he frequently changed quarters and names, like James Bond. He travelled with forged passports, code books, and the constant fear of being discovered by Hitler's Gestapo. After a short taste of Stalin's infamous Ljublanka prison, Wehner's road led straight to the top of the Communist hierarchy. As a trusted member of the elitist Comintern and personal aide to its almighty chief, Georg Dimitrov, he received a thorough indoctrination in the advancement of the Communist world revolution, political espionage, psychological warfare, and total subjugation to party discipline.

Not surprisingly, the exemplary professional revolutionary, who is said to have displayed no tolerance for deviation from the Soviet-ordained party line, survived all the purges that shook up Moscow's emigrée elite from time to time. Wehner's unwavering loyalty did not go unrewarded. He was asked to lecture at the international Lenin school where high echelon party functionaries received their training and was granted another rare favor: publication of articles in *Pravda.*

Wehner hated to leave Moscow, where in 1941 the world's top Communist leaders were gathered. He had been ordered to take over the Comintern center in Stockholm to uncover suspected intelligence leaks and to serve as editor of the Communist German language weekly, *Welt.*

The circumstances of his arrest for political espionage on behalf of the Soviet Union in February 1942 have puzzled many an expert. How this experienced functionary could be trapped by the Swedish political police in the apartment of a Communist woman whose husband, one of his agents, had just been arrested, remains a mystery. Since a professional like Wehner would have known that the place was under police observation, substance is given to the charge that he deliberately provoked his own arrest, perhaps because of his next assignment. He had been directed to organize resistance cadres in Berlin, a deadly mission. Just the illegal crossing of the heavily guarded German border was considered a great risk.

During his trial in Stockholm, Wehner made a second grotesque mistake, actually a tragic one and not in keeping with his superior talents. In his testimony he revealed the names of a number of his agents and collaborators, not knowing—so he claims to this day—of the existing cooperation between Hitler's Gestapo and the Swedish political police. The consequences were devastating: a wave of arrests by the Gestapo; among the prisoners were Swedish sailors who had helped German antifascists. Wehner was sentenced to one year in the penitentiary.

Contradictory statements also tend to obscure his "break with communism." Wehner swears that his political conversion took place in penitentiary cell 314. But some of his former comrades are equally sure of his attempts to rehabilitate himself in Moscow after his release. This fact is certain: Wehner's brilliant political career came to an unforeseen end in the summer of 1942 when he was excommunicated by his party because of "non-execution of party resolutions, proven denunciation, and of conduct negligent and damaging to the party."

When Wehner came knocking at the door of the German Social Democrats in 1946, he was no more welcomed by Chairman Kurt Schumacher, who had spent most of the Hitler years in concentration camps, than was Willy Brandt. Both, in a sense, remained prisoners of pasts they anxiously tried to conceal from their comrades and the public. Wehner's younger brother Rudi had waited for him to come home—their father died early and their mother and only sister were killed in the historic, brutal bombing raid on Dresden—but Germany's Social Democrats were waiting neither for Wehner nor Brandt.

Nobody quite trusted men who had been accused alternately of being agents of the Soviet KGB, America's OSS, or the British Secret Service; men who had only marginally shared the German fate, the fear of Hitler's concentration camps, the war years, the suffering from hunger and cold, and the intellectual deprivation. What made matters worse was the disturbing fact that most of the more serious allegations and innuendos originated in the circles of the regular returned emigrants and refugees. Wehner, as well as Brandt, was vilified and humiliated with every derogatory word in the German language.

They were outsiders in their own party. The comrades kept a safe distance because they felt there was always the chance that some grisly unearthed fact would make them liabilities. Only after the stern anticommunist Schumacher died were Wehner and Brandt given room to breathe. Their ascent began in 1958. Hard-working Wehner was elected the SPD's vice-chairman, and Brandt, Berlin's newly elected mayor, was finally voted into the party's presidium.

Strangely enough, the kinship of these two unusual men was strengthened by their isolation, although their isolation was not broken down by their kinship. "Brandt does not know even today what it means to have once been a Communist," Wehner complained in reference to Brandt's lack of empathy. Even after his installation as the SPD's respected "éminence grise," Wehner's self-pity was undiminished. "I am not a man who attracts moths like light," he grudgingly admits. He is famous for rudely dressing down people in public yet he is ultrasensitive to slights and hurts where his own person is concerned. When he found his customary chair next to Brandt occupied by Scheel during one of the weekly coalition luncheons at the Palais Schaumburg, he immediately felt rejected. "They are not going to hurt me," he said, bitterly hurt.

The idea that Brandt, whom he helped along the way to power and glory with his winning brainchild, the Grand Coalition, suddenly wishes to build distance between them does not fit into Wehner's indelibly ingrained concept of loyalty. It is not the first and certainly not the last time that Wehner has felt let down by comrade Willy. Since both men carry with them the fundamental insecurities and anxieties accumulated in their youth, compounded by excessive feelings of inadequacy and pronounced complexes of persecution in early manhood, there is little chance for a rebuilding of bridges once they are broken.

Brandt's constant fear of psychological exposure, of appearing undignified or wanting, resulted in an exaggerated sense of dignity that enhanced his isolation. With his mania for offensive language and public self-accusation, Wehner, on the other hand, had learned to exploit his temper in order to hide his mimosa-like sensitivity. Under that grouchy, consciously cultivated proletarian exterior, however, close observers have found an ardent lover of baroque music who has mastered several instruments, including the guitar and mouth organ; a collector of rare books; a friend and admirer of intellectuals like Georg Lukacs, stage director Piscator, novelist Theodor Plivier and lesser writers, as well as painters of the caliber of Otto Dix; a devoted husband nursing his ailing second wife, widow of a Communist murdered by the Nazis; a workhorse starting each day at 5 A.M., who writes his own speeches and articles; a passionate politician for whom the party is everything; and a compassionate superior who takes time to visit and comfort dying functionaries, big shots and others. He sat at the bed of Brandt's dying speechwriter and friend Leo Bauer, another ex-Communist turned Social Democrat, who kept asking why Willy was not coming.

As Brandt made use of his international experience and connections in his political career, so too does Wehner know how to benefit from his controversial sojourn in Moscow. Years before he is appointed committee chairman and Minister of all-German affairs, Wehner is known as the SPD's foremost Kremlinologist. Arguing that Adenauer's Westpolitik—reconciliation with France and Bonn's integration into NATO and the Atlantic Alliance—is blocking the hoped-for reunification of divided Germany, he becomes the chief proponent of a course into neutrality that proves to be forerunner of the Brandt-Bahr Ostpolitik.

"A reunification will come only under the aspect of democratic socialism, or it will not come at all," Wehner maintained in the early 1950s at the height of the cold war.

Did the dedicated Socialist, who loathes the United States as a fortress of "sinister forces" of capitalism, dream of reunification by means of the establishment of a popular front? Did he indeed believe that a merger of the two Germanys could be worked out between the SPD and the SED with his old Communist comrades Ulbricht, Pieck or Honecker who ruled over Germany's eastern half? Rejecting the CDU/CSU's "power politics without a trace of power," Wehner challenges Adenauer's western integration policy as a betrayal of reunification for a mere "twelve divisions." For a while, Wehner beats the drums for Molotov's plan for a "provisional government," half Bonn, half East Berlin, "if it exclusively pursued the preparation of elections for a constitutional and legislative national assembly" in 1954.

The Germany plan

In all of Wehner's reunification schemes, from the "small solution" to the four-step plan of 1958 and the "Germany" or "Wehner plan" of 1959, elements of previous Soviet proposals can be recognized. Controlled disarmament, thinning out of troops, the creation of a demilitarized zone encompassing both parts of Germany, Poland, Czechoslovakia and Hungary, the withdrawal of NATO and Warsaw Pact troops, and eventual abandonment of the military alliances for a European security system, as well as the establishment of all-German institutions for a political and economic rapprochement of the two half states, are tirelessly promoted by Wehner.

Aside from its principal objection to German neutralization with its implicit recognition of East Germany and the eastern borders, the CDU/CSU is aghast at the idea that sixty million West Germans and seventeen million East Germans were to be represented by an equal number of delegates. For the opposition, the "Wehner plan," linked as it was in their eyes to the intention to push "socialism through the back door," once more demonstrated the "national unreliability" of the SPD.

One year later, the ill-fated plan is buried by Wehner himself. "This Germany plan . . . is a proposal that belongs to the past," he announced to an applauding Bundestag in June 1960. The SPD's new foreign policy pointed westward, parallel with the modifications of Godesberg. Even before the building of the Berlin wall, the CDU/CSU's Westpolitik is in; Soviet-oriented politics are out, at least for the time being. Willy Brandt's 1961 campaign is built on Wehner's "adjustment" strategy. Instead of the "against each other" the "with each other" is stressed. Marxist class-warfare slogans are replaced by assurances of security, stability, order and prosperity. As the "without me" becomes the "me too" party, offering a minimum of alternatives, the idea for a grand coalition is carefully planted and prepared psychologically. By 1965, the average citizen can hardly distinguish the two parties. When Wehner's dream was finally realized in 1966, the Jusos angrily voiced their protests against the party's "adjustment" to militarism, lack of democratization, and assorted CDU goals and values by supporting the left-wing students' "extra-parliamentary opposition."

It is typical of Wehner, who warned against a "primitive crusade-like anticommunism" after the Hungarian uprisings in 1956 and in connection with the issue of the treatment of Soviet Jews following Solzhenitsyn's hero's welcome in the West in 1973, that on occasion he also liked to point to the "danger of a negative front toward the democratic forces in the West, in which America plays a prominent part."

Playing it both ways becomes Wehner's trademark. Although recognition of the GDR never rated as a consequential issue for the politician who advocated the establishment of diplomatic relations with Poland and other East bloc nations in the middle of East-West tensions in the fifties, he suddenly began to sound like a cold warrior after the "adjustment."

"A peace order with a fixed division of Germany carries the seed of discord and, at worst, war," he predicted in 1963, and a few years later: "Recognition [of the GDR] would be the final seal on the division of Germany." Acting outraged at de Gaulle's recognition of the Oder-Neisse line as Germany's eastern border, he scolds the CDU/CSU government for "pussyfooting" in the matter that "coldly touches my heart." German people want to join German people and will indeed do so, he promises at a time when the idea of reunification has been shelved by the party for its new Ostpolitik: coexistence of two German states within the existing boundaries.

Like the GDR's Honecker, Wehner initially rejected the Bahr-Brandt theory of "change through rapprochement," even though it suited his belief in the convergence of Socialist, Communist, and capitalist forces.

Father of Ostpolitik?

With the aid of Brandt's cold war rhetoric, CDU suspicions of the SPD's clandestine meetings with Italian Communists were quickly allayed. To the shouts of "betrayal," the conservatives learned much later of the top-secret meetings scheduled by Wehner, Brandt and Bahr between the SPD and SED functionaries, with Italian Communists serving as go-betweens in preparation of the East treaties in the event that Brandt became chancellor in 1969.

By 1955 the Swiss *Die Tat* recognizes in Wehner the political figure who "more than any other single politician determines the Social Democratic party's foreign policy." In 1973, the *Deutsche Zeitung* arrives at the same conclusion. It is "Wehner who will be discovered one day as the real father of Ostpolitik," it soberly observes. The detection of an uncanny resemblance between the results and the direction of Brandt's Ostpolitik and Wehner's old neutralist plan for reunification, led its editor to suspect that SPD foreign policy is still being molded in the image of the original guidelines.

While Wehner and Brandt don't openly clash over the use of funds in the all-German ministry headed by Wehner from 1966 to 1969, friction reportedly existed. Wehner's urgent sense of socialist commitment is repeatedly offended by Brandt's nonchalant attitude. "I have tried to find out, in conversations with him, if he actually is a Socialist," Wehner tells Peter Koch. "We now have set in motion some things in foreign policy, but domestic policy is pressing. Where is the concept, how, what opinion exists about health care reform or profit sharing? Are you by chance a secret Socialist?" the testy Wehner asked his silent chancellor, according to Koch.

By the time Brandt became party chairman, following the death of Erich Ollenhauer in 1964, the powerful vice-chairman Uncle Herbert was in full command of the party apparatus. With Ollenhauer's influence waning since Brandt's nomination for chancellor candidate in 1961, the leadership vacuum at Bonn headquarters was quickly filled by Wehner. His reorganization was total. Reducing the unwieldy thirty-three-man presidium by a third, Uncle Herbert also saw to it that its members were selected by the executive committee rather than being elected by the convention of delegates. Of the six departments he created, the four most important were kept under his own control and jurisdiction. Profiles of prominent functionaries from the 20 districts and 8,000 precincts were carefully assembled in secret dossiers. All officials had to answer a series of questions which ranged from supplying the names of relatives in the GDR to their personal financial status.

When the press got wind of Wehner's undemocratic way of running Europe's largest party (with approximately 1 million dues-paying members in 1974) all hell broke loose. Wehner did not appreciate the comparison of his methods with those "he had learned as a Communist cadre chief." Suspecting leaks in his own organization, he demanded a full investigation. Willy Brandt promised his help in uncovering the informants and calling them to account. However, aside from a vote of confidence for Wehner from the party faithfuls and his denial of having implemented a "dictatorial instrument of power" for himself, nothing happened. Once more Wehner felt let down by his protégé.

What the press did not learn at that time was Wehner's intimate relationship with Günther Nollau, president of the Federal Bureau for the Protection of the Constitution. The official explanation of the close cooperation between the party and the security agency was the detection of possible Communist agents and informers within the party's ranks, persons such as the SPD parliamentary representative Alfred Frenzel.

The vice-chairman had carefully cultivated the connection with Nollau, who was born in Leipzig, East Germany, escaped to West Germany in 1950, and whom he met about 1960. At least, Nollau proudly confided: "I have good reason to assume that I possess the confidence of Wehner." What Nollau knew about the party politicians would also be known to Wehner. It was no secret that the top functionary dropped subtle hints as to the general direction the agency should take toward certain anticommunist groups and individuals in times of détente. The prevention of a collision with the policy of diminishing East-West tension often hinged on an updated definition of the term "subversive" activity.

WIENAND-STEINER AFFAIR

Wehner's derogatory remark about Brandt's past, "Whenever there was dirt, he was a journalist," was fairly bold considering the fact that Wehner's name was linked with one of the most unsavory party scandals. True, it was Brandt's chief of staff, Ehmke, who was suspected of supplying the 50,000 marks from the chancellor's slush fund as a bribe for CDU representative Steiner. Julius Steiner, known for his intense dislike of CDU chairman Barzel, admittedly voted for Brandt in the Bundestag's vote of no confidence, initiated by Barzel. Only 247 votes were counted for Barzel's resolution on April 27, 1972, two less than the number required to topple Brandt's government, which had come under severe attack during the debates of the East treaties. Whether Brandt's government was indeed saved by a bribe could not be ascertained by the Bundestag's investigative committee. Bonn's Steiner affair did not become its Watergate.

Steiner, a self-confessed double agent, did not deny the mysterious deposit of 50,000 marks in currency in his Bonn bank. According to his unsubstantiated testimony, it was placed there by Wienand. The "friend of Ostpolitik," as the CDU politician called himself, had an exaggerated notion of his role as a spy. Some three weeks after his secret talk with the SPD's efficient parliamentary executive secretary, Karl Wienand, and one week before the constructive vote of no confidence, Steiner was approached by a GDR agent who, to his surprise, knew about Steiner's pro-Ostpolitik position. On counsel of West German security experts he strung him along, Steiner said. When he lost his seat in the Bundestag in the November 1972 elections the GDR agent supposedly offered Steiner a job as an informant on CDU party affairs in exchange for continued payment of his representative's salary.

Bonn's insiders have little doubt that the GDR's Ministry of State Security was tipped off by the trusty Guillaume about Wienand's friendly conversations with Steiner.

Karl Wienand, the SPD's efficient all-round manager, Wehner protégé and unofficial deputy, changed his testimony during the hearings. After assurances that he was hardly acquainted with Steiner, he allowed—under pressure from several witnesses—to frequent contacts and clandestine meetings, but denied talk of "buying members of parliament." Because of "security risks," Ehmke was unable to testify how the 50,000 marks he had withdrawn two days before the fateful April 27 had been appropriated. On the witness stand, Wehner took the offensive as usual by simply dismissing the whole affair as a sinister plot against the SPD engineered by CSU boss Strauss.

Suspicions lingered. If the esteemed Wienand, war veteran and amputee, was lying, was Wehner implicated also? The German press, not equipped with the long-range tenacity or the means to ferret out facts in the manner of a Woodward and Bernstein, and lacking a determined newspaper publisher like Katharine Graham of the *Washington Post* to patiently back them, only kept talking of a coverup. However, if anything was clear in this murky affair, it was that Wienand, the unofficial liaison between Chancellor Brandt and the party's commander, Wehner, would not act without orders from his superiors.

Wienand had been involved in shady deals before. Wehner had thrown his full support behind his man when he was accused of illegal lobbying for Paninter, a private airline, in 1971. "I tie my fate to that of Wienand," Wehner bravely announced. When the full confession of Paninter chief Trommer made headlines in the summer of 1974, the party had little choice but to send Wienand, allegedly guilty of false testimony and tax evasion, on "sick leave."

The all-knowing *Spiegel* speculated that Wienand's fall would put an end to Wehner's career as well. But by pointing to the fact that Wienand was promoted to his present position by Helmut Schmidt, when he held Wehner's position as party whip, the astute politician gave a different signal. For emphasis, he had only to hint that early retirement would afford him ample time to write his memoirs. Wehner let it be known that he did not share Ollenhauer's reluctance to hurt feelings and reputations. Statements of this nature, placed in the press with precision timing, were guaranteed to send chills down the spines of half of Bonn.

Wehner had no intention of resigning. For "personal reasons," he withdrew from the office of party vice-chairman shortly after Brandt's memorable victory of 1972. Plagued by severe diabetes, the 68-year-old Wehner certainly had reason enough for curtailing his activities.

It should be noted that Wehner departed in a blazing triumph. He was reelected to the party's executive committee with 419 votes, 15 more than Willy Brandt. His urgent warnings to refrain from navel-gazing and absorption in intraparty debates, were as much addressed to the Jusos as to Brandt. Thanks to the SPD-FDP majority vote, he pointed out, the passing of laws was now actually feasible if the lost momentum could be regained.

Everybody knew, Wehner being Wehner—especially after his attack on Brandt from Moscow—that the unexpected step was taken primarily for tactical considerations. The wily Wehner needed a free hand. The mortal blow against the chancellor could not come from his vice-chairman, according to those who understand Wehner's stern code of party discipline. To keep the party in power he would compromise on Helmut Schmidt as successor to a "purged" but not demolished Brandt, although Schmidt was loved neither by Wehner nor the Jusos.

Seeing Wehner and Schmidt huddling in long conversations, whispering together at official functions like two conspirators, made Brandt and his courtiers extremely jumpy. Such open displays of a united front were doubtlessly an integral part of the functionary's psychological warfare.

In view of Wehner's changing positions, it has been said—especially by the opposition—that the Communist renegade cannot be trusted and his allegiance has not changed. To the extent that Wehner has not forgotten the lessons of his Communist teachers, this may be true. He has always been ready for compromises, adjustments, zigzags and the other detours necessary for attaining his ultimate goal: the seizure of power.

That a man with the characteristics and the background of Herbert Wehner, who could hardly have made it to first base in American politics, rose to the very top shows that contemporary Germany is not short on civic tolerance and faith in a democratic system. At the same time, the authoritarian Wehner figure casts a dark shadow over the political emancipation of the German burgher who still seems to harbor a propensity for the adventurer-politician with a potential for myth and legend and deliverance.

Recognizing those lingering needs, the aging Brandt—converted from smiling Willy into a benevolent father-statesman figure—set out to fill them.

8

The Legendary Adventures of Herbert Frahm

From the tempestuous Lübeck years to exile in Norway

"Those who have a sense of history will not take lightly the fact that a man of my origins and conviction has become German Foreign Minister," Willy Brandt stated on December 1, 1966. Nobody who knows anything about Brandt's background will quarrel with that contention. After two rejections at the polls as candidate for chancellor, he finally had acquired a firm grasp on the famous "mantle of history."

In fact, not much was known of his origin or of the origins of the convictions of Willy Brandt at that time, and little still is known. Since the SPD's charming party chairman, or its driving force Herbert Wehner, had decided at some point in his career that the adventure-filled Brandt story was unorthodox campaign material, likely to turn off the narrow-minded, average, bourgeois voters, editions suitable for public consumption were released from time to time. Served up in dribbled bits and pieces with deletions here and proper emphasis there, Herbert Frahm's coyly shrouded odyssey as a leftist party functionary blossomed into a veritable hero's tale.

Occasional discrepancies can be found in the various accounts of events that led to Herbert Frahm's transformation into Willy Brandt, his sudden exit from Nazi Germany, and his clandestine activities between 1933 and 1945 in the service of the radical Marxist Socialists. His change of position from cold war politics in the early

1960s to one of prodigally placating the Soviet bloc in the course of his Ostpolitik also became hotly debated sources of unending rumors. They stimulated the curiosity of the public and the press and kept Brandt's name in the headlines. Denials, charges of defamation by a ruthless opposition, threats of lawsuits and court orders footnoted Brandt's political rise. As many of the lingering questions were clarified, the contours of the central figure were further blurred. In the end, it was difficult to distinguish truth from fiction, false allegations from false rebuttals.

The public fracas underlined one fact: Brandt was no ordinary man and as many such men, lived an extraordinary life. He was either a great rascal or worse, or the innocent victim of one of the most malicious smear campaigns postwar Germany had seen. Thus an intriguing myth was born, highly welcomed and skilfully exploited by Brandt and his team. It provided the politician with an almost impenetrable shield.

On the surface, at least, Brandt seemed perfectly comfortable with his turbulent past. "If I had to start over again I would approach things from the same attitude and philosophy," he once declared. At his Nobel Prize press conference in Oslo, he reiterated his self-revealing belief, "My fundamental convictions have not changed."

If he meant to stand by those words, however, it remains entirely unclear why the controversial questions were dodged. If he felt he had nothing to hide, then his reluctance to make accessible to the public his whole fascinating life story, including the sealed records, makes no sense.

As a politician, he has repeatedly asked for honesty and openness. A clean breast from the start would have crowded out of the picture those ambiguities and ugly speculations that kept undermining trust in his political and private forthrightness. Curiously, he did not heed his own advice that even "small lies in daily life can destroy the confidence of the people in politics, especially if a nation like ours has carried—not long ago—the big lie of a dictatorship like a disease and almost died of it."

THE MYTH STARTS AT BIRTH

The public's right to know certainly has not been met by Brandt's memoirs, *My Way to Berlin,* ghosted by Lazar Herman under the nom de plume Leo Lania and published in 1960. Had the coauthors omitted less and revealed more, they might conceivably have freed Brandt of a past that was to become burdensome, instead of keeping him its prisoner, and, incidentally, might have produced a more interesting book.

There is no disputing that Willy Brandt, a Sagittarius, entered the world as Herbert Ernst Karl Frahm on December 18, 1913. The mother of the strapping—to judge by existing photos—baby boy was the attractive nineteen-year-old Martha Frahm, daughter of a farm-hand, who worked as a salesgirl at a Lübeck co-op store.

The father is unknown, apparently even to his son. "I don't know my father. I never felt the desire to know him. In fact, I never asked what I might have inherited from him," we learn from Brandt-Lania. Later in the book, Brandt tries to amend this statement. "The name would indicate Hamburg or the Scandinavian north," he remembers. More than ten years later he tells the Italian newspaperwoman, Oriana Fallaci, that he did not suffer from not knowing his father's identity. "Besides, it is not quite correct that I did not know who my father was. I have told nobody up to now but I knew it. I knew his name. However, I always refused to meet with him. After the war he was still alive, but even then I had no interest in a meeting."

Regrettably, it has to be reported at this point that in his early career, Brandt was mercilessly assailed by certain Christian bigots—and there seemed to be a good many of them in Germany in the 1950s—because of his illegitimate birth. For a while, these perfidious attacks, held to be libelous by the authorities, unexpectedly bottled up all further inquiries into Brandt's political background as well. On the assumption that certain charges and harsh criticisms were based on the circumstances of the politician's birth, the press and outraged citizens hurried to the defense of the man who had started out in life under so grave a social handicap.

It did not take long for the SPD leadership to take the cue. The conversion of Brandt's personal misfortune into a political advantage was quickly accomplished. Whenever old Konrad Adenauer struck out against his younger, virility exuding opponent by referring to him as "Herr Brandt alias Frahm," the backlash against the holier-than-thou Catholic could be heard throughout the media.

Adenauer, of course, was eager to acquaint Commie-hating German burghers with Brandt's controversial political activities in exile, his cooperation with the Communists, and his acquisition of Norwegian citizenship. Adenauer was still part of that stout-hearted patriotic generation quite unable to imagine that the Germans would ever accept as their chancellor a man who, technically at least, had become an alien.

The twilight zone that settled on Brandt like a gift from a mischievous fairy the moment he caught his first breath, evolved from controversy and doubt. Shuttling back and forth in time, the connective psychological momentum weaves its own myths.

Since the SPD proposal in 1970 to make Chancellor Brandt an honorary citizen of Lübeck, his official place of birth, still another part of the politician's beginnings became clouded. Brandt, who should know best, of course, asserts that he has always carried with him "a piece of Lübeck" wherever fate led him since he left the town in 1933. "Here I was born and raised, here I have experienced important orientations for my life," he says. The polite applause during the solemn ceremony that made him an honorary citizen of his hometown after two years of heated controversy with the Christian Democrats could not entirely erase the persisting doubts in some minds.

Whether Lübeck's Christian Democrats tried to block the bestowal of this honor on Brandt for political reasons, or whether they actually possessed evidence that Brandt was born in Schönberg village in the state of Mecklenburg remains unresolved. Long ago, the SPD-dominated city fathers of Lübeck decided to keep the Frahm file, meanwhile lost without a trace, off limits to press and public. Neither the opposing CDU nor friendly journalists trying to determine the precise hour of Brandt's birth in order to forecast a horoscope in the 1969 elections were able to get any information from the office of vital statistics. The speculation doubtless grew out of the fact that his grandfather, Ludwig Frahm, came from an unnamed village in Mecklenburg. When one considers the prudery of pre-World War I Germany, it is not inconceivable, on the other hand, that young Martha preferred to finish her confinement out of sight of gossipy neighbors in Lübeck.

Only the *Lübecker Nachrichten* blithely assured its readers that Brandt's birth was properly registered and that the files contain no secrets. If this was actually the case, then the withholding of the information, an issue only because of the puzzling fact that it had been withheld, seems utterly capricious and ill-advised.

"Of the boy Herbert Frahm, of his first fourteen years, I have only very vague recollections. An opaque veil hangs over these years, grey like the fog over the harbor of Lübeck. . . . Figures and faces are like shadows—they rise to the surface and disappear again, like flotsam on the waves of the northern sea," Lania, Brandt's alter ego, informed his readers.

Certainly no one has ever questioned Brandt's assertion that his childhood was "not an easy" one. His mother, who had to earn a living by standing behind a counter from 8 A.M. to 7 P.M., recalls a heartbreaking scene of the day she tried to enter three-year old Herbert in a kindergarten.

"But that was not easy. He cried violently when I wanted to leave. He clutched onto me. I did not bring myself to leave him there. But my father was in the [military] service [the year is 1916—the middle of World War I] and I could not leave the boy alone at home. Then, thank God, I found a woman who took care of him by day. The boy trusted her."

Martha Frahm, married to Emil Kuhlmann in 1927, confesses that she did not even have time to knit a pair of mittens for her son. During the war clothing was hard to come by. "Herbert's shoes were worn through. He had to walk in wooden shoes from the tram station to the house of the woman—at age three! But it did not hurt him," Martha Kuhlmann consoles herself. Often the child was left alone for hours. According to Brandt-Lania, the boy had practically no playmates.

Papa's tales

All this changed when Herbert's grandfather returned from the war. Little Herbert had found a father. "Papa," a committed Socialist and avid follower of August Bebel's teachings, had joined the Social Democrats in Bismarck's time. His grandson proudly recalls that Papa boasted of being the first "red" in his village in Mecklenburg.

Widowed Papa was a truck driver at Lübeck's Dräger Works. Humiliating experiences with the landed gentry had made a class-conscious militant out of him. For grandfather, "Socialism was more than a political program; it was rather a kind of religion," Lania comments. Grandfather's father had been subject to corporal punishment on the estate of a Mecklenburg aristocrat.

Seething with fury, Papa tells young Herbert of his former employer's control of voting by the distribution of brandy and other unsubtle methods. On election day, the farmhands had to line up in the living room of the overseer's house. They had to pass in front of their boss, who took down their names as they cast their ballots into a soup tureen, one on top of the other. Grandfather was so exercized by this infringement of the workers' civil rights that he overturned the tureen, as if by accident, to enforce the secrecy of the election.

Sitting on grandfather's knee, Herbert listened to fascinating tales quite different from those of the brothers Grimm. They were not peopled with beautiful princesses and Cinderellas waiting for irresistible Prince Charmings, but with striking workers who disarm the police and form a militia, dignified proletarians who refuse to accept charity from the "rich enemy," exploited classes refusing to be bribed by the exploiters, and revolutionary heroes like Karl Marx, August Bebel and Ferdinand Lassalle who promised a glorious future for the working class. Because all men would be brothers one day, all injustices in this world would be eliminated; even the need for money would disappear since everybody would receive as much as they needed.

Grandfather apparently was an excellent raconteur. As they sat in the kitchen of the "modest worker's flat" that was home, little Herbert could not hear enough of Papa's Socialist paradise. Instead of Mother Goose songs or church hymns, they happily hummed the revolutionary song of the workers, the *Marseillaise.*

Brandt did not exaggerate when he commented that he was "so to speak, born into socialism." Later in life he gives equal credit to his mother for his early Socialist indoctrination. "If I were asked today how I became a Socialist, I would answer: through my mother. She was pretty young then, and women were not even allowed to participate in political meetings, but my mother was an active trade unionist. At age eighteen she already belonged to the trade union's youth. . . . This way I was not just born into the Socialist movement and into trade unionism—but I grew up with them. With very firm roots. You understand, the credit is not mine but hers," Brandt explained to Fallaci in 1973.

From the children's group of the working men's sports club and the Social Democratic *Kinderfreunde,* Herbert Frahm advanced to the Workers' Mandolin Club and the Red Falcons. Before long he became the leader of its Karl Marx group. At the age of fifteen he became chairman of the Socialist Workers' Youth Union. The desperately lonely boy, always an avid reader, had slowly learned to fend for himself and to seek companionship in organized group activities. The intimate family of three proved, unfortunately for Herbert, of short duration. It abruptly ended when Papa married again. Herbert apparently stayed with him but never developed a liking for his new wife.

"Mother visited them once or twice a week. She tried to spoil the boy within the limits of her modest means," we know from Brandt-Lania. The memoirs offer no explanation of why the boy did not move back to his mother after her marriage to the "tall, sturdy, and warm hearted" bricklayer whom Herbert called uncle. The answer his mother provides years later, after her son had become Germany's foreign minister, is as unexpected as it is simple: "His [her father's] heart would have been broken if I had taken the boy!"

BORN INTO SOCIALISM

Herbert seems to have come to the conclusion at an early age that the misfortune of the individual and all personal problems springing from it are somehow rooted in the existing social order. In his article, "We and our parents' home," published in Lübeck's Social Democrat paper, *Volksbote,* the sixteen-year-old boy vented his accumulated resentment against the so-called bourgeoisie. From Marx and his Communist Manifesto he deduced that the concept of a family, based as it is on capital and private income, can only exist for the bourgeoisie. Since the proletariat lacks the economic underpinnings necessary for founding a family, the designation "proletarian family" has to be regarded as a contradiction in terms. In Marx, Herbert had found at long last a "scientific" answer to the question of why he had been deprived of a real family: because he was poor and belonged to the proletariat.

The youth's unquestioning acceptance of so sweeping a thesis illustrated more drastically than anything else, how alone, how isolated a life he must have led. Otherwise, the fact that even poor working-class boys can enjoy the physical togetherness and comforting benefits of spiritual support a family unit has to offer could not have totally escaped him.

In his article, the introverted boy performs an extraordinary psychological striptease:

> The youth from the all-proletarian home seeks attachment. The easy explanation is that in his parent's house he most likely is not going to find it. Why is it that young people from our groups lead entirely different lives than those of their buddies of the same street and of equal age? The reason is that the youth organization provides the comrades with a backing, a support that the buddies do not find in the streets. The youths of the all-proletarian household will therefore easily fit themselves into the commune. This is important for the movement, even if we have to recognize that these comrades will not be able to accustom themselves easily to order and discipline. However, that too can be explained, because of the general conditions of the proletarian class the feeling for these prerequisites of the commune has no chance of being established. . . .

Brandt's political position, with its focus on a basically anticapitalistic revolutionary socialism as answer to the *condition humaine,* will be amended from time to time as the years pass by. Still, its accent on socialism rather than democracy is never substantially changed.

In observing the youth's political posture, it does not come as a surprise that he felt like an outsider at the *Realgymnasium* among his new classmates, with few exceptions the sons of middle-class families. His good grades had brought him a scholarship at Lübeck's prestigious high school, the Johanneum, where for the first time he encountered a world that was "if not hostile, nevertheless a strange one."

The comradeship in the Socialist youth movement, with its song fests, hikes and camping trips to the North Sea and the Rhine, compensated for the largely self-imposed isolation at the *Realgymnasium.* Herbert, by no means a docile boy, defiantly sought to make an impression on his middle-class environment, often by provocation. To the dismay of his teachers he showed up at school from time to time in the blue shirt and red tie of the Socialist Workers' Youth. The teacher's warnings "to keep her son out of politics" were, needless to say, ignored by mother and son.

His favorite subjects were German and history. The biography makes quite a point of his top marks in religion. Although he could not stand "organized religion" and loathed "piousness," he began to take a keen interest in the history of religion. Looking back, he remembers the appeal of "Christian ethos" as well as the realization that a true Socialist is also a "better Christian." Brandt's opponents as a rule interpret these passages as an effort to gloss over his antireligious tendencies for fear they could offend the broad mass of German voters. Mindful of the new conciliatory attitude toward the church taken by the SPD at the Godesberg party convention, they dismiss such recollections as pure window dressing.

Herbert did not grow up in a religious household. At Easter, in 1928, the "Red Pioneer" received the atheist's *Jugendweihe,* the youth consecration practiced by radical Socialists and Communists, rather than be confirmed in the Christian faith. His sudden interest in the philosophy of religion, however, need not be the obliging author's afterthought. Quite the contrary, it could be argued to be genuine precisely because the boy was brought up as an atheist and was guided by sheer curiosity into his studies of the sources of Christian ethics.

Youthful activist

Natural aggressiveness paid off for Herbert in the youth movement. Together with his gift for organization, he developed a considerable facility in public discussions and speaking. He spoke for the group whenever a spokesman was needed. It was "Herbert who was selected by his comrades to give a report about camp life among the Red Pioneers in a radio program," one of his friends recalled. That was in the summer of 1930. It was Brandt's first radio speech. Those who still remember the handsome youngster with the magnificent head of blond hair are agreed: He had distinct leadership qualities.

Although the lanky youth had managed to write occasional reports about local party events for the *Volksbote* since he was fourteen and had even earned a prize for his writing, a leather-bound copy of J. F. Cooper's *Leather Stocking Tales,* he was by nature an activist. He loved to swim and to travel. In Denmark on a student exchange program, he had a chance to travel elsewhere in Scandinavia and had taken a liking to Norway, whose people impressed him with their natural dignity and "unforced friendliness."

He was equally at home in face-to-face confrontations with the Nazis. In the Reichstag, Hitler's men were able to increase their number of representatives from 12 to 107 in 1930. By that time, Frahm was "strongly committed" to the fight against them. The tumultuous encounters at the meetings were often carried out into the narrow streets of Lübeck.

But the bloody fistfights did not save the Weimar Republic. The shocking Nazi victory of the September elections, swollen to landslide proportions by mobilization of the youth and nonpolitical sections, referred to as the "bitterness vote," had already turned the political tide.

"We met with the Hitler Youth, debated with them, and sometimes fought it out. In the night hours, many a street became a fighting arena," Brandt reports. Charged with assault in 1930—he was barely seventeen—he had to stand trial in Lübeck's municipal court. He was released because of lack of evidence. That time, he testified, he was not even at the scene of the fight.

"I was a wild-eyed youth," Brandt said of himself, reflecting on that phase of his life.

Under the steadying influence of Dr. Julius Leber, editor-in-chief of the *Volksbote* and prominent Social Democrat who represented Lübeck in the Reichstag, young Frahm abandoned the idea of joining the navy in favor of being a "newspaper writer." Reportedly, he preferred the German word *Zeitungsschreiber* to the foreign term journalist. Leber, a political moderate who fervently fought against all forms of radicalism as well as bloodless idealism, was a true champion of the little people. "The workers regarded him as one of their own. . . . Here was a man who never compromised, not a fanatic, but a real fighter," the biography notes.

Leber, who sponsored Frahm's membership in the SPD, is often assigned the role of "spiritual father," especially since Brandt in retrospect, in the early 1960s, encouraged such interpretations. Young Frahm's association with the respected Leber, one of the genuine heroes of the German resistance forces against the Third Reich, was readily enlarged by friendly biographers for good reasons. Throughout the Hitler years, the committed Social Democrat was in and out of prisons and concentration camps. He was actively involved in the plot to assassinate Hitler on July 20, 1944. Julius Leber was sentenced to death by the Nazi "People's Court" in January 1945.

Leber was highly critical of the inadequacies and half-measures of the Weimar Republic. Nevertheless, he endorsed its parliamentary institutions even after the dissension-torn Social Democratic coalition government of Chancellor Hermann Müller fell apart over a disagreement about the distribution of unemployment insurance costs for the three million army of jobless in September 1930—a figure that doubled within two years. The inherent danger in a situation where the Nazis ranked as the second strongest party after the Social Democrats was obvious to Leber, who thought it prudent to tolerate the government formed by Chancellor Heinrich Brüning of the Catholic Center party. Its severe austerity policies, decreed by emergency power, failed to solve the insurmountable problems of a worldwide depression; they could neither stay the corrosion of the republic nor renew confidence in the democratic process.

No doubt, Leber had taken an interest in the enterprising fatherless boy who, in turn, admired his intellect and great compassion. Whether a "sort of" father-son relationship really developed between the intellectual and the teenage fireband, as friendly biographers claim and Brandt occasionally intimated, is open to question.

"His was a decisive influence on my life," Bolesch and Leicht quote Brandt. However, young Frahm does not seem to be the least influenced by Leber's desperate efforts to strengthen the SPD in its fight for survival between the totalitarian fronts to the Communist left and the Nazi right.

By broadening the party's base, which at that time was limited by the parochial concept of class struggle, Leber hoped to open it up to the middle.

"He wanted the Social Democratic party to be 'a home for the youth of the middle class who had lost its way in the battle and was searching for a new fatherland'," Brandt-Lania explain. They also report that he was called a "Rightist" by the Socialist Youth, whose members were "naturally Leftists."

In joining a May Day demonstration in 1931, Herbert Frahm chose a different course. "The Republic does not mean much—our goal is socialism" read the big banner the young man was proudly carrying through the streets of Lübeck. According to official biographers Bolesch and Leicht: "He was hoping for the revolutionary breakthrough of the working class." His disenchantment with the Weimar Republic and the SPD angered his grandfather. "How can you be so ungrateful!" he scolded his rebellious grandson. Many years have passed by when Brandt confesses: "I only realized much later what he meant."

Enter Socialist Workers Party

Even less pleased with Frahm's shift toward the radical left was the man who supposedly had made such a tremendous impact on him. Leber tried in vain to dissuade the young hothead from joining the radical leftist splinter group founded in October 1931.

The Socialist Workers' party originated from a long standing dispute between the right- and left-wing members of the SPD that culminated in a sharp controversy over Brüning's budget proposal, containing funds for a new battleship. When the left-wingers refused to go along with the SPD majority, the lines were finally drawn. In the party's program, the destruction of capitalism and the seizure of power by the socialists, either by way of democracy or proletarian dictatorship, are named as goals.

The SAP pledged to support the Soviet Union against aggression by capitalistic nations and to uphold the "best traditions of the prewar social democracy." Its leader, Max Seydewitz, a high official in East Germany's political hierarchy and Minister President of Saxonia after World War II, became one of the key figures of the Comintern's popular front strategy. Aside from discontented leftist SPD members, the SAP also attracted Communist deviationists of "Trotzkyist" persuasion. Among them was Jacob Walcher, one of Brandt's closest friends in exile. When Seydewitz switched over to the Communists in 1933, Walcher assumed leadership in the SAP.

As is so often the case, Brandt's memoirs barely illuminate the reasons for his significant political decision. He merely allows that the "gap between us young ones and the leadership of our party" was widened by the "continued radicalization of the left, promoted by the provocations of the Nazis and the sharpening of the economic crisis." He thought Leber's arguments to dissuade him "unjust." In an allusion to hunchbacked Seydewitz, Leber called the party an association of cripples. What was a normal young man who appreciated a good book, a good bottle of wine, and a pretty girl doing among those sectarians, those impotents, who escape into radicalism because they are aware of their physical and intellectual incapacities, the agitated Leber wanted to know? It was a rare occasion when he lost his cool. "We separated in bitterness," Brandt-Lania report without a show of regret.

The role of Leber in Brandt's life has been marked by ambiguity.

Asked about it after the "fall" in the summer of 1974, the exchancellor bristles with irritation at the suggestion that Leber was one of his mentors.

The parallel between young radical Brandt and today's leftist Jusos has been pointed out. By keeping a polite distance from the conservative image of his fatherly counsellor, Leber, Brandt seems to indicate that the differences between him and the young radicals of today, as well as yesterday, are slight indeed.

The friendly biographers are at a loss. Bolesch and Leicht think it was not "only political inexperience" that made the impatient, radical youngsters overshoot their target, but their "Socialist idealism." Hans Dollinger, author of *Willy! Willy!,* on the other hand, clearly blames Leber for "having gone too far."

In a television interview in 1964 with Günter Gaus who, ten years later, becomes the Federal Republic's first diplomatic representative to East Germany, Brandt explains his controversial party switch this way:

"It was Bebel's social democracy which was alive in the young leftist socialists. It was that which my grandfather had actually told me, had communicated to us. And it was the dissatisfaction with the state of Weimar, we believed then—and this was the real error—that too little socialism was the problem; but the reason was too little militant democracy."

By leaving the Social Democratic party for the SAP, Brandt also put an end to his journalistic ambitions. He could no longer work for the *Volksbote.*

"This was not the only material disadvantage of my joining the new party. I had planned to go to the university; Leber had offered to help finance my studies. That was now out of the question," Brandt-Lania assert.

The SAP leaders must have been delighted to have the dedicated activist in their ranks. In spite of Frahm's youth he was made a political instructor. "As an organizer and speaker I was on the go day and night." Before long, as chairman of Lübeck's SAP he also headed its national youth organization. In order to earn a living he had to take a job as a clerk in the shipbroker's office of F. H. Bertling. The monthly salary was 30 marks. It was his first regular "civilian" job and just about his last. The remainder of his life was spent—with few noteworthy exceptions—as a party functionary.

The takeover by the Nazis on January 30, 1933, was accompanied by spectacular torch parades, chanting, singing, rousing march music and an instant wave of persecution of the new regime's opponents. Hitler's brown shirts arrested the most prominent in their homes. They came for their victims at dawn, loaded them on trucks and delivered them to prisons and concentration camps for "protective custody."

On the night of January 31, Julius Leber, on his way home from a meeting, was brutally beaten by Hitler's storm troopers. "The comrades of the 'Reichsbanner' who accompanied him as his bodyguard, offered fierce resistance. Leber was severely injured; he was carried off with a cut nasal bone. One of the assailants remained dead on the spot. Although he and his friends had acted in self-defense, and in spite of his immunity as a member of the Reichstag, Leber was imprisoned," Brandt-Lania report.

The citizens of Lübeck, above all the workers belonging to the SPD and SAP, were outraged. To force Leber's release, a general strike was demanded. As chairman of Lübeck's SAP, Herbert Frahm was a member of the delegation that took the proposal to the trade union leaders. These functionaries, however, refused to go against the new authorities who had declared strikes illegal.

After a two-week delay, a compromise was worked out. A one hour "protest strike" for Leber was carried out. Brandt-Lania provide this description: "Lübeck saw one of the most powerful demonstrations in the history of the city. Fifteen thousand people gathered on the Burgfeld. The threats of the new rulers could not frighten them. . . ." Leber's wife Annedore successfully effected a short-term release for her husband from the prison hospital. When he appeared at the rally, his head swathed in bandages, he shouted only a single word: "Freedom!"

It was the last time Brandt saw Leber.

Frahm's shipping clerk job was a dull one. But he enjoyed the "close contact" with sailors, fishermen, longshoremen and the firm's various Scandinavian clients. With his fine ear for languages, he picked up basic Norwegian on the docks. He also took the opportunity for improving his English and the other languages he had studied at high school.

Hazy Contours

Since the memoirs, apparently for the purpose of easing strain on the reader's patience, avoid overdetailed accounts of hard facts, such as specific designations of time, dates and places, the contours of some events often remain hazy. For that reason, even this part of the Brandt story has become the subject of speculation by the opposition. Young Frahm's defection from the SPD and his confrontation with Leber took place at the end of October 1931. Both friendly biographers Bolesch and Leicht, as well as Hans Dollinger, report how the gymnasium graduate looked for and found a job at the shipbroker's firm. However, in 1931, the political unfriendlies point out, Frahm could not have finished his high school finals. Were the writers mistaken? Or was it just sloppiness on their part that they failed to place due emphasis on the passage of time between the October event and Frahm's new job?

Other sources have since tried to clarify the confusing time sequence. According to them, Brandt became the proud possessor of the important diploma—still the main key for entrance into a German university today—on February 12, 1932, and assumed his new job sometime in May. A tempest in a teapot? Certainly. But until Brandt insists that the *Realgymnasium* open its records to the public—the school's administration has refused to give out information on student Frahm—the rumor that the young politico may have been a high-school dropout will hardly be put to rest.

From prison, Leber undauntedly wrote his friends: "For a good and just cause the risk of one's life is a fair price to pay."

The drama of the Reichstag fire of February 28, 1933, played right into Hitler's hands. To crush a "bloody uprising and civil war," Hitler promised no mercy. "Whoever gets in our way will be cut down. The German people will not put up with leniency." He vowed to shoot the responsible Communist functionaries. He would "not spare" the Social Democrats nor the members of the Reichbanner. Communist newspapers were banned, as were all publications and posters by the Social Democrats.

The *Gleichschaltung,* the forcible coordination of the political will of the people, states, political parties and labor unions with the will of the Nazi government, completed the "national rising"—a euphemism for the total takeover of power. With the passing of the Law for the Removal of the Distress of People and Reich, the so-called Enabling Act—opposed only by the Social Democrats—the function of the Reichstag legally ceased.

"The parliamentary system has capitulated to the new Germany," Hitler's *Völkischer Beobachter* jubilated. The authority of the Führer was established. Incredibly, dictatorship had entered the republic's front door, brazenly and unhindered. "The rapid, unopposed extinction of all political forces from Left to Right remains the most striking feature of the Nazi take-over. If anything could have demonstrated the sapped vitality of the Weimar Republic, it was the ease with which the institutions that had sustained it, let themselves be overwhelmed," Joachim C. Fest comments in his book, *Hitler.* By July, the liquidation and voluntary dissolution of political parties, groups and associations, in addition to the destruction of the unions, were accomplished facts.

"To be defeated in open battle is tragic—to capitulate without a fight turns tragedy into a farce. It robs the defeated of the last and most precious possession: self-esteem," Willy Brandt wisely observed later.

When Lübeck's SAP chairman attended the party's secret national convention that March, shifted at the last minute from Berlin to Dresden for reasons of security, the small party had already been declared illegal. It had only polled 0.2 percent of the vote in July 1932 and counted at best 15,000 members. In Dresden it was resolved that the party should continue its work underground.

In his book *In Exile,* published in 1971, Brandt explains the SAP's goal of a proletarian "unified front" in these benign terms: "I too was convinced at the time that Social Democrats, Communists, and groups between were in the last analysis members of one and the same socialist movement and that if the whole movement erected a unified barricade against Nazism it could not help but succeed in blocking its progress."

Actually, the tenor of his letters, written as head of the SAP's Socialistic Youth Organization of Germany from Oslo in 1935 and 1936, registered a marked difference. "The aim of our battle is the fall of Fascism and the destruction of the capitalistic system by way of the proletarian revolution. As students of Marx and Lenin we know of the need of a determined revolutionary party for the victorious battle of the working class." Clearly, the proletarian unified front was aimed as much at the destruction of the opposing bourgeoisie as of Nazism. In this correspondence, in which the word "democracy" is hard to find, Brandt also reminds the Communist Youth Association that we have the "task of bringing about the separation of young catholic workers from their priests. . . ."

Frahm into Brandt

The plan for underground operations provided for headquarters in Berlin, supported by branches to be established in Paris by Jacob Walcher, in Prague by Joseph Lang, and in Oslo by Paul Frölich. Rather than risk discovery by Nazi mail inspectors, all contacts and communication with Berlin would be by courier. Since some of the SAP comrades had already been arrested, methods of escaping persecution by going underground were discussed at some length. Familiarization with the techniques of conspiracy became a means for survival.

Herbert Frahm took the precaution of travelling in disguise. "My less than subtle costume was a brightly colored cap," he remembers in his memoirs. In the translation by Hank Keller, however, the disguise becomes a colored "student's cap." More important was the adoption of a different name as a cover for his identity, referred to in later interviews as a "nom de guerre."

"After discussing the matter with my closest friends, I called myself Willy Brandt" (Brandt-Lania).

Appropriately, it was "Willy Brandt" who stopped off on his way to Dresden to get his first "fleeting glimpse of the great city of Berlin."

Contrary to the contention by Bolesch and Leicht that from this moment on "Herbert Ernst Karl Frahm was a thing of the past," the name was not discarded for a long time. The SAP official was known in Oslo as Comrade Frahm. When he married Carlota Thorkildsen in June 1941 in Stockholm, Carlota definitely became Mrs. Frahm. While Brandt served as a party cover and pseudonym for the journalist, it was not legally taken before the reinstatement of Brandt's German citizenship in 1948; the official document bears both names. Dollinger's assertion that the name Frahm belonged to the past when he left Lübeck "and young Willy Brandt lived on in his stead," must also be dismissed as another instance of confusing literary license.

Nobody seems to know if Brandt first pondered the idea of leaving Germany immediately after the installation of the Third Reich. Even the actual date of his secret illegal departure for Denmark is still a mystery. The many versions of his "real" motives are legendary. Controversies over the terminology in connection with his exit from the German scene—should it be described as flight, escape, self-chosen exile, emigration or a journey into adventure—have dominated many a newspaper column and untold heated discussions.

The combined recollections of Brandt-Lania are as vague as they are wanting in congruity. They neither confirm nor destroy the impression generally fostered and accepted by the public and the media that Willy Brandt was a political refugee.

After his return to Lübeck from Dresden, young Frahm apparently continued his daredevil political activities. For the most part they centered on the clandestine production and dissemination of flyers and handbills with inflammatory appeals to the workers' solidarity, urging resistance to Nazi barbarism. According to SAP comrade Heinrich Wigger, Frahm typed the stencil for the May 1 appeal on his office typewriter. He had kept his job at Bertling's and could easily be found there by the authorities.

Undoubtedly, the activist SAP chairman was known to the Nazi secret police, the Gestapo. The fact that he was not on the initial list of the arrested SAP leaders may have had to do with his youth. Taking a long look back in 1972, Lübeck attorney Emil Peters, a friend and political think-alike of Frahm's in those days, tells newspaperman Bernd Brügge: "One day an associate, a defense attorney, said to me, 'Some of your people have been arrested and interrogated.' I went at once to the official who had drawn up the depositions. He knew, without asking, what was on my mind. He left the room, leaving the depositions on the table. I quickly glanced through them and saw with relief that my name did not appear, nor that of Herbert Frahm. But suspicion seemed to point in his direction, to him as the author of the handbills."

Peters also claims to remember—39 years later—a conversation in which Brandt alluded to his intention of going to Scandinavia for the SAP. It was young Frahm who was in charge of organizing the illegal departure of SAP leader Paul Frölich, who had been assigned to take over the Oslo branch and establish close contact with the Norwegian Labor party. But Frölich, a well known ex-Communist, met with bad luck. He was recognized and arrested on the island of Fehmarn before he could start his mission.

The reader can only surmise that Brandt was chosen by SAP headquarters as a replacement for Frölich. Brandt-Lania supply no factual clues.

"I had been warned of my imminent arrest and had to expect the worst because of local occurrences. It would be difficult for me to hide in another German town, for I had no profession which could serve as a cover and hardly a way to earn a living in Germany. As much as the big adventure lured me, saying goodby to Lübeck was not easy for me. . . ."

THE VOYAGE

Through a political confidant, a driver at the Dräger Works, contact was made with a fisherman in Travemünde, who also looked after Dr. Dräger's private yacht. Arrangements were made with his stepson, the fisherman Paul Stooss, to take Brandt across the Baltic Sea to Rödbyhavn, a little Danish town on the nearby island of Lolland.

During the night of March 31, 1933 (Bolesch-Leicht) . . . in April (Brandt, 1972) . . . the night of April 1 (Terence Prittie) . . . it was the middle of April (Bernd Brügge and SAP comrade Heinrich Bruhn) . . . in the night of April 3 to 4 (fisherman Paul Stooss in *Stern* magazine) . . . the boat, a small cutter equipped with motor and sails, set out for Denmark. Hidden in a corner behind barrels, boxes and crates was a nineteen-year-old man in a dashing trench coat: Willy Brandt.

Before boarding ship, Stooss and his passenger walked over to a pub for a leisurely glass of beer. While some sources indicate that Willy even danced a round on that occasion, the official version insists on an air of sobriety. In the smoke-filled sailor's hangout, Brandt encounters a situation fraught with danger—a former SAP comrade who had "deserted to the new masters." Since avoiding the man in the pub was out of the question, he greeted him very "warmly" and they exchanged some inconsequential remarks. Suspecting that the excomrade had guessed his intentions, Brandt spent some "long and anxious minutes" at the bar.

"When I left, I didn't know whether he would follow me, call the police, betray me."

They shipped out at dawn. Luckily, the customs inspector had not discovered the stowaway. It was a stormy morning and the voyage took five hours, almost double the normal sailing time. "It was the worst trip of my life. The weather was awful, the seasickness was almost unbearable. When we landed I could hardly stand on my feet. Several cups of strong coffee, to which my friend had added a large dose of Aquavit, brought me back to life. Thus Willy Brandt journeyed into freedom, with a few shirts and the first volume of Karl Marx's *Capital* in his briefcase and one hundred marks in his wallet."

It is interesting to note that the Nobel Peace Prize winner of 1971 is no longer burdened with *Das Kapital* in his briefcase in the American edition of *Willy Brandt, Portrait and Self-Portrait,* which was issued by Nash Publications in Los Angeles in 1971. "Thus I landed in the free world with a briefcase and one hundred marks," we read in that carefully edited version of the memoirs. Karl Marx, along with other pertinent clues to Brandt's radical leftist past, was found objectionable and dutifully eliminated by professional Brandt image-polisher and sometime speechwriter Klaus Harpprecht. As in many another instance, the practice of omission becomes important for the sole reason that it is of importance to Brandt and his crew. Instead of accepting his past for what it is and presenting it forthrightly to the American public, they engage rather—perhaps from compulsive habit—in political laundering on behalf of their hero even after he had made his spectacular home run.

The original description of the voyage by Brandt-Lania is not without poetic flourish.

The Stooss story

How it rated in accuracy became a matter of debate. Mr. Stooss, for one, remembered the dramatic escape differently. A couple of years after the publication of the memoirs he gave his story to the press. Compared with the Brandt-Lania colorful account, it was dull. There was no mention of a rough sea or secret hiding places, let alone the presence of a snooping customs officer or other spine-chilling danger signals. Even the unusual length of the voyage found its rational if undramatic explanation. Stooss had intermittently trimmed the sails so that the trawler would ride more evenly and the boy could catch some sleep. In the morning around seven o'clock, the cabin door swung open and out came the young man to jump happily onto Danish soil. Stooss took his charge, whose name he did not know at that time, to the railroad station. They sat comfortably in the station restaurant, drank coffee spiked with Aquavit and waited for the train that took the young man in the trench coat to Copenhagen.

Mr. Stooss, who allegedly left the Social Democratic party, claims to remember nothing of a visit from Willy Brandt after his return to Lübeck in 1947 to thank him for his valuable help and great kindness —as the memoirs indicate. Stooss saw Willy Brandt in 1947 as a speaker at a meeting, but denies that he ever shook his hand or was visited by him.

If Brandt left Lübeck to assume the task "of establishing one of the bases for our work abroad in Oslo," as he writes in 1966, then of course his "escape" becomes a matter of voluntary exile. On the other hand, he darkly hints of unspecified problems in the context of unspecified "local occurrences" which "might well have had dire local consequences."

Just as he tries to talk his girl friend Gertrud Meier into coming with him to Oslo, he hopes the evening before his historic voyage to persuade his friend and comrade Heinrich Bruhn to accompany him. It has been argued that a man fearing "imminent arrest" would hardly think of doubling the risk by teaming up with a friend equally suspicious to the Gestapo.

This rather casual behavior seems to be in line with Brandt's later observation that he was not certain whether his flight from Lübeck was "absolutely necessary." In the absence of hard facts, it is also quite conceivable that it was the powerful lure of the great adventure, the desire to flee from the gnawing memories of his "not so easy childhood" and the narrow confines of Lübeck with its limited outlets for his talents that prompted an escape meant to shed at least part of his youthful burden.

To ask, as has been done, what might have happened to Willy Brandt had he remained in his hometown amounts to idle speculation as long as the mysterious "local occurrences" are not clarified. Comrade Bruhn, who stayed behind, was soon arrested and released. Some of Brandt's political friends think it most likely that the nineteen-year-old SAP leader would have been treated in the same manner, because of his extreme youth.

The confusion about the diverging aspects—whether deliberately generated by Brandt and his inner circle or not—derives to a large extent from the discrepant autobiographical data in his writings, as well as material in the official Bundestag and Berlin House of Representatives directories. Unending speculation has been fostered by the opposition over the varying entries, such as "flight to Scandinavia" and "emigration to Norway," that lend a certain note of excitement and grandeur to early biographical versions. In later editions that touch of drama was unceremoniously dropped for innocuous statements like "historical studies in Oslo. 1933/47, journalistic and political activities in Scandinavia." But the intriguing inconsistencies, betraying either an untimely sloppiness or a timely opportunism, are not totally abandoned. In some editions of the directory he also becomes a student of philosophy, while in others, for variety's sake, one presumes, no mention at all is made of his "political" activities in Norway and Sweden.

The problem with loose biographical bookkeeping is that it leaves wide gaps that allow the ugliest of rumors to float in and out of the myriad crevasses.

Incident in Lübeck

One of the most vicious, underhanded of blows was dealt Brandt in the spring of 1972. At that time, a retired criminal investigator of the Gestapo from Hamburg by the name of August Naujock addressed a letter to Chancellor Brandt and the CDU/CSU executive committee of the Bundestag charging that the German chancellor had not escaped from Lübeck in April 1933 because of Nazi persecution but because of suspicion of second degree murder.

Naujock claimed to have knowledge of the incriminating contents of a police file he came across while on duty with the German security police in Esbjerg, Denmark, in 1944. He supposedly remembered that the name Herbert Frahm appeared in a file marked "Suspicion of Murder" as a suspect in the brutal killing of Willi Meinen, knifed to death in Lübeck's Hundestrasse on "January 31, 1933." In an attempt to substantiate his charges, Naujock's letter made reference to Frahm's activist political engagement.

"The fact should be noteworthy," he wrote the Federal chancellor, "that you were known in your Lübeck years [1930–1933] as the outright roughneck of your SAP group and therefore had to stand trial in the courts of Lübeck." Although Dollinger tends to confirm this accusation by reporting Frahm's acquittal because of lack of evidence and Bolesch-Leicht admit to "embittered street and beer-hall fights with the SA," Hitler's brown shirts, the former Gestapo investigator certainly did not have his facts straight. Actually, Meinen was stabbed to death on July 31, 1932, by several assailants, two of whom were eventually convicted and sentenced to death.

On the January 1933 night he mentioned, however, a Nazi named Rudolf Brügmann suffered fatal knife wounds in a street fight that involved an attack on Dr. Julius Leber. The description of the incident cited earlier in Brandt-Lania contains the key sentence, "One of the assailants remained dead on the spot." However, in a statement given under oath, the SPD witness Willi Rath, a retired official of the criminal police in Lübeck, reportedly maintained that the Herr Bundeskanzler Brandt was neither present during the "altercation nor had he initiated it nor did he know of it."

In a second letter, to all the members of the Bundestag, Naujock tries to rectify the peculiar mixup of dates and names and to restore his credibility by giving specifics of the Meinen slaying and the apprehension of the two suspects who allegedly named Frahm as instigator and accomplice. "Frahm was informed of the arrest of Fick and Kähding and drew the conclusions leading to flight," he writes.

To be sure, none of these charges would be proven. Brandt appeared to be satisfied with characterizing his accuser as a demented, perhaps senile person who had been in and out of mental institutions and was therefore not legally responsible for his words and actions. Naujock maintained that he was committed to a psychiatric clinic a few years earlier under very strange circumstances.

When asked about the "Incident in Lübeck" by a Herr Wilfried Lange from Eckhausen during a *Bild* telephone interview shortly before the November 1972 elections, Brandt answered:

> You now refer to this letter by a former Gestapo man who in addition comes under statute 51 [persons pronounced legally insane]. He has disseminated a handbill in hundreds of thousands of copies which meanwhile has been subject to confiscation by a decision of a Hamburg court. This means whosoever spreads this makes himself punishable under the law. The writer has once accused me of working

> with death rays. But back to the case: These accusations are without substance! The federal burghers need not believe that they vote for somebody who has a murder on his conscience.

As far as his foes are concerned, Frahm's fear of "imminent arrest" and his expectance of "the worst" because of undefined mysterious "local occurrences"—mentioned in the memoirs—tell their own tale.

Since the distressing Naujock episode erupted during the unexpected 1972 election campaign, it was easy to dismiss it as one more desperate effort to defame the leader, haunted by his nebulous past throughout his career, with one of the dirtiest of smear campaigns. Judging from the outcome of the election, the outrageousness of the unsubstantiated charges probably won Brandt some support.

One can easily sympathize with Brandt. But one would have occasion to admire his respect for democratic procedure far more had he seen fit to release the records in question to the public, especially after the charge was made by the opposition that all pertinent court and police files have mysteriously disappeared from Lübeck.

Why Brandt and his party shied away from public disclosure when he had everything to gain by it is not readily understood by those who believe, unequivocally, in the public's right to know. Was the aloofness that grew along with his steadily rising sense of power and invulnerability like an unseemly twin also blurring the contours of his often praised credo in an open democracy?

9

The Revolutionary Years in Exile

If the first nineteen years of Willy Brandt's life are difficult to trace and pin down, possibly because of an accommodating slippage of memory and the anxious efforts of his biographers to obscure unflattering personal and political details from the German public, the next twelve years spent in exile in Norway and half a dozen European countries as a top SAP functionary are very nearly impossible to delineate. While maintaining that Brandt came to "Norway on a political mission," Bolesch and Leicht solve the dilemma by devoting scarcely three pages to that period which Dollinger describes as the political maturing process of the leftist Socialist Herbert Frahm into the "European Democrat, Willy Brandt."

As usual, Dollinger bases his comments and observations chiefly on Brandt's recollections in *My Road to Berlin,* published in 1960, and Günther Struve's severely edited, admittedly "small but representative selection of Brandt's voluminous writings over the period 1933–47," published under the title, *Draussen*. In an introductory note to the English version, *In Exile,* mature Brandt tries to soften his radical left-wing posture of a "genuine Communist" by allowing that he had strayed "not a little into political dilettantism," a surprising remark for a professional party functionary "born into socialism."

Surely, it is a glaringly inappropriate term for the political activist whose whole thinking was geared to a life in party politics from his early teens. One might be tempted to call Brandt a number of things after reading his polemic Socialist writings of that period, but one would never dream of accusing that devoted pro of dilettantism!

In the same paragraph, Brandt makes an attempt to assure his basically anticommunist German readers of predétente days that "in the Norwegian language my political style shook off the [radical left wing] dross much more quickly than in my German correspondence with my friends at home. . . ." An unfortunate phenomenon indeed, especially since the reader has to take the author-politician's word for it so long as his original Norwegian writings are not made available to the public. Members of the opposition who have rummaged through the dusty bookshelves of Sweden's and Norway's antiquarians have returned empty-handed. The explanation was that all the Brandt books and brochures had been mysteriously bought up a long time ago.

Brandt's statement raises yet another question. If he had shaken off the radical left-wing dross of his "early years in Norway," as he remembers decades later, then it is incomprehensible why he did not quit his functionary's position with the SAP. After all, the SAP had not changed its anticapitalistic, antiparliamentarian revolutionary "genuine Communist" position. Like the Communists, it had no intention of fighting the Nazis for a restoration of democracy. Its goal—to fight for a proletarian revolution against the capitalistic world, to attain a socialism under the protective shield of the Soviet Union—had not changed. Yet the thought of making a clean break with the deplored "political dilettantism" into which he had "strayed" in his "early twenties," did not seem to have crossed his mind at this time.

Another intriguing question is, of course, how repudiation of his early political posture in 1966 can be reconciled with his prideful assertion of 1972, "I stand by the impulses of my youth."

Brandt's countless trips as a courier and organizer for the SAP with the mission of establishing a so-called popular or unity front out of a collective of leftist revolutionary groups were equally underplayed in later times. For the most part, they were coyly disguised as the by-products of various journalistic assignments. To this day, the average German believes what the official biographies state: Willy Brandt spent his time as a regular working journalist while in exile. His important political activities during those years were either not mentioned at all or passed over as spare-time occupations in the service of anti-Nazi humanitarian organizations.

The Refugee Federation and the Norwegian Labor party's (NAP) program for sending money and material to Finland, the Norwegian People's Aid, administered by Brandt, surely fitted the description. So did the Spanish Aid, even though the question has been raised whether it intermittently functioned as a "front" for SAP cadres. The "International Bureau of the Revolutionary Youth Organizations," on the other hand, a composite of predominantly Communist and radical Socialist youth groups, founded in February 1934 and cosponsored by Brandt, would scarcely rate a humanitarian label by any stretch of the imagination.

The accent on journalism proved to be an extraordinary asset to the budding political candidate. Notwithstanding the fact that eventually he forthrightly wrote about the "political task" he had taken on in Norway *(In Exile),* there was hardly a journalist in Berlin or elsewhere who did not approach Brandt with all the goodwill of a "colleague." Not only did the magic word journalism amply cover all the SAP functionary's occasional conspiratorial missions, it also generated an immediate, unsolicited climate of sincere sympathy among members of the press. The eternal bystanders at historic events were quite willing to give one of their own a boost on the way up. The reflection of the power and the glory swelled their own sense as instrumental power builders and enhanced their professional pride.

The "Scandinavian newspapers," to which the memoirs and biographies continuously refer as playing a part in the hectic life and travels of newspaperman Brandt, remain unidentified as a rule. At close inspection they turn out to be trade union papers like the Norwegian Labor party's *Arbeiderbladet,* or party organs like the *Marxistische Tribüne,* published in Paris, *Det 20de århundre,* Oslo, the SAP magazine, *Neue Front,* Paris, and the publications of the Socialist Youth League (SJV) *Sozialistische Jugend,* and *Kampfbereit (Ready to fight),* published on Brandt's initiative as representative of the SJV. In Barcelona, he also worked for the German language weekly, *The Spanish Revolution,* issued by the United Marxist Labor party *(POUM, Partido Obrero Unificado Marxista).* A number of his Socialist consciousness-raising and psychological anti-Nazi warfare contributions in pamphlet form were published by the Norwegian Labor party or the Socialist press.

SAP FUNCTIONARY IN OSLO

It is difficult to understand today why Brandt and company were so determined to avoid a clear reportage of his solid Socialist past, especially after his public recantation had drawn attention to it. What did they think was so objectionable about a young SAP functionary propagating his ideas about a new Socialist order in word and deed? Did they judge the German voters not "mature" enough to assess the experimental steps of a radicalized youth? Or had the evolving politician, raised in the constricted atmosphere of a stuffy Socialist-Communist world of conspiracy, who self-admittedly had come late to value the merits of the rough but free breezes of a democracy, not quite come to appreciate its all-round openness as the quintessence of the democratic system?

It would have been, for example, interesting to know whether the three brochures about Nazi occupation of Norway, *Norge Under Hakkorset, Norge Kjemper,* 1940, and *Norsk Front,* 1941, for the most part credited to Brandt and published in Stockholm by his Swedish poet friend, Ture Nerman, were indeed financed by the British Secret Service. Nerman, an ex-Communist allegedly changed over to the capitalistic Western front, is supposed to have been in the employ of the British.

Let us surmise, for the moment, that the charge was true. One wonders what about its revelation could have been so disgraceful or damaging for the Democratic Socialist twenty or twenty-five years after the fact?

Again, the confusion may be an outgrowth of the frenzied competition of too many overzealous image builders and their desperate rush to meet deadlines. What other explanation could there be for the strange discrepancies in the dates of the Nazi-enforced expatriation listed by Brandt and his official biographers? In a television interview with Günter Gaus in September 1964, Brandt gives 1936 as the year of his deprivation of German citizenship. Bolesch-Leicht, whose book was distributed free of charge by the Federal Press and Information Office, as well as Dollinger, maintain that Brandt's "German citizenship had been abrogated as early as 1938." Prittie concurs with Brandt's answer to Gaus. However, in a footnote, "Brandt was deprived of German citizenship on 3 September 1938," in his book *In Exile,* the editor contradicts Brandt's earlier statement.

In this maze of confusion and inaccuracies, it is impossible to determine from the writings of Brandt and friends how long a time the trench-coated youth who jumped off the cutter at Rödbyhavn had spent in the company of the socialist poet Oscar Hansen in Copenhagen. It must be explained at this point that Copenhagen had become an important base for the British Secret Intelligence Service after 1933. Its vast agents' network was directed from there with the full consent of the Danish Intelligence Service. It goes without saying that the legendary Nazi spymaster, Admiral Wilhelm Canaris, also operated a respectable intelligence setup in the Danish capital that was visited by Vidkun Quisling from time to time. Under the direction of the German Communist Ernst Wollweber, who was to become chief of the GDR's State Security Service, the Soviets supported an elaborate spy and sabotage center with jurisdiction over Norway and Holland, as part of the Comintern's famed international espionage network, *Die rote Kapelle* (The Red Orchestra). Leftist emigrants coming from Germany, among them a number of SAP and labor union functionaries, often made their first contacts with other emigrant groups through Wollweber.

Brandt apparently wrote and published his first anti-Nazi brochure in Copenhagen. From his own writings, we learn of frequent trips to Copenhagen for unspecified political rendezvous. Was it possible that young Frahm actually received the SAP directive to take over the party's Oslo operation after his arrival in Copenhagen? Had he already known or been assured in Lübeck that it would be forthcoming? Or was it issued to the surprise visitor? Was the footloose refugee accommodated only after his sudden arrival?

An answer to this question would most likely satisfy more than the reader's idle curiosity, inasmuch as it might provide a clue to the financial resources of the SAP. Brandt, unfortunately, never concerns himself with the financial affairs of the small splinter party that supported headquarters in Paris and offices in a number of places. Cut off, as it was, from its home base in Germany, it nevertheless kept dozens of functionaries travelling all over Europe. Moreover, it was able to publish a relatively lavish number of regular and special publications that must have cost an enormous amount of foreign money. Where did the money come from? Who were the generous donors? Instead of clearing up those matters, the memoirs have a tendency to fuel unnecessary speculation.

Mot Dag

There is no speculation about Brandt's contact in Oslo. Finn Moe, foreign editor of the NAP's *Arbeiderbladet* and Norway's representative in the United Nations after the war, was able to secure a small monthly allowance from the Norwegian trade union fund and a position in its secretariat for the German. In his eagerness to adjust to the new environment and get acclimated, Brandt confesses to a mistake by "rather overhastily" joining forces with the extremist left-wing youth group *Mot Dag* (Toward the Day), that acted at cross purposes to the Norwegian Labor party's Youth League.

The NAP as well as the SAP were Marxist-based parties. What they had in common was that both of them were in keen ideological and doctrinal competition with the Communists. The NAP had severed its connection with Moscow and the Comintern in 1923. By 1928, it had become Norway's majority party and was promptly asked by King Haakon VII to form a government. With the classic remark, "Gentlemen, I am also King of the Communists," Haakon resolutely overrode the objections of the Conservative opposition to entrust the Communist-inspired radicals with power. Their reign was of short duration. When the party made its comeback with its election slogan, "Jobs for all the people," during the economic crisis of 1935, its transition from a total commitment to Marxism to a broader democratic concept was well under way.

Instead of invoking the dogma of class struggle, it appealed to the common interests of "the working people." Such a shift of ideological emphasis was regarded as a move to the right in the radicalists' quarters with whom Brandt, undiplomatically, had allied himself, much to the disappointment of his benefactors in the NAP. The newcomer had committed a severe blunder which alienated him from the leadership of the party with whom he was to establish close contact on behalf of the SAP, at least on a temporary basis.

In retrospect, Brandt recognizes a distinct parallel between the new course of the NAP and the SPD's reform program of Godesberg in 1959. Moreover, the NAP's evolution from a left-wing Socialist party with a class platform to a Democratic Socialist party with a radical democratic platform, struck a responsive chord in him regarding his own political development. In admitting to swimming against the political current in his first years in Norway, Brandt succinctly sums up the whole experience in *In Exile,* ". . . but the path of the Norwegian Labor party . . . was, if I may say so, parallel to my own."

When, and under which prevailing circumstances, Brandt's cognition was converted into practical conclusions is difficult to ascertain. We know that he did not officially relinquish his SAP membership until its quasi-merger with the SPD in Stockholm in 1944. Brandt remains equally uncommunicative about his final break with the radical *Mot Dag* youth group. One can only presume that it did take place, since he repeatedly mentions his active collaboration with the NAP's Youth Federation.

Pure guesswork also obtains in evaluating the intensity and impact of Brandt's association with this influential leftist intellectual group. Faced with a lack of pertinent information, one tends to surmise that the encounter with the leading highbrow discussion group was not a satisfactory experience. Brandt dismissed his contacts with the academic theorists as "instructive, if problematical." However, he credits the *Mot Dagists* with encouraging his studies at the University of Oslo. He enrolled in courses in modern history, although he found it difficult to reconcile his political "obligations" with his classroom attendance. Whether he also studied philosophy, as Bolesch and Leicht and some of the directories of the Bundestag claim, is open to question. Brandt merely mentions good grades in the "qualifying arts examination in 1934," and the fact that he never submitted to any "final examinations."

Brandt's studies at Oslo University became the subject of a minor scandal in the mid-1960s. The CSU's propaganda brochure, *Rotbuch,* issued in Munich during the election campaign in 1972 and reissued in 1973, tried to make an unsavory affair of the 10,000 marks in restitution money the Governing Mayor of Berlin collected from the government because his flight from Germany had prevented him from getting a college education. As a refugee or exile, Brandt qualified for restitution of damages suffered from deprivation of a higher education.

Brandt had his own reasons for making use of the government's special educational fund. "In 1957 a lot of accusations were leveled at me," Brandt told me. "Actually, I made that official application in order to establish that I did not leave the country as a criminal. It was one way of letting everybody know that I had no record. I also saw to it that the 10,000 marks I received were put at the disposal of Berlin's students."

One of the chief benefits of Brandt's meeting the representatives of academe was the resulting acquaintanceships with leading left-wing personalities. Among them were Trygve Bratelli, known to today's readers as Prime Minister of Norway, 1971–72, and again since 1973, and chairman of the Norwegian Labor party since 1965; Halvard Lange, a future foreign minister; and Einar Gerhardsen, who was to be prime minister for many years after the war.

The energetic SAP functionary also made friends with writers outside his left-wing crowd. "I moved in 'bourgeois' circles as well," the author of *In Exile* concedes with a touch of obvious pleasure at his own openmindedness.

Willy's Norwegianization

Brandt's rapid, seemingly effortless adjustment and his ability to blend into the Norwegian scene elicited expressions of profound astonishment and admiration from everyone around him. After a few months, the young German had such a good command of the Norwegian language that he was able to address a public meeting in Norwegian. Friends still marvel at how quickly the language became familiar to him. He soon spoke it as though it were his mother tongue.

Early on, young Brandt had decided against the life of a political refugee. As chairman of the Refugee Federation, he had commiserated with the "sorrows and troubles" of hundreds of homeless fellow countrymen. He had watched their "spiritual and political isolation" with concern. He refused to share their lot as outsiders in the host community. "I realized the necessity of growing roots again," he wrote. "I could not and would not look only back into the past."

Instead, he plunged into the "political life of Norway as quickly as possible." Later on, he reflected upon that course of action which had opened a new existential option for him. Norway had become "more than an asylum for me. It became my second home." His ability to perform sudden, intuitively timed, almost instinctive shifts of adjustment, a talent probably developed and sharpened in early boyhood when the outsider was forced to look out for himself, without the substantial sacrifice of principal parts of position, was often considered by those thought to know him well—and they were few—as the secret of his successful rise in the political world. His friends would praise the prevalence of such inclinations as tactical strength. In the jaundiced eyes of his foes it smacked of nothing less than political opportunism.

The "Norwegianization" of Herbert Frahm in dress, mannerism, speech, thinking and girls, facilitated by an affinity for the people, the attractiveness of Oslo, and his love of the "beauty of the Norwegian landscape," held obvious advantages. Not only did it improve the SAP functionary's working conditions with a steadily increasing number of important contacts in the capital's political circles who would not necessarily have opened their doors to a transient refugee foreigner, it also afforded a perfect camouflage during his many illegal travels in Europe. Lastly, it held the promise and the key to a truly new life, a new identity, a different kind of existence in a country where the past counted for nothing and even the memory of the past was easily cordoned off by the simple demands for attention to austere everyday tasks.

Brandt seems to have been constantly on the go, smuggling "illegal" information, letters and pamphlets (sometimes printed on Bible paper), across the borders into Germany. The dissemination of anti-Nazi publications, involving cover addresses, invisible ink, coded messages, suitcases with false bottoms and hollow bookbindings, was risky business. Attendance at the various Socialist-Communist resistance group meetings was often just as dangerous, as Brandt soon was to find out.

It was in February of 1934, after a meeting of the International Bureau of Revolutionary Youth Organizations in Laaren, a small town in the Netherlands, that Brandt narrowly escaped being apprehended by the Gestapo. Laaren's authorities disapproved of the illegally held "communist" conference. Four German participants were arrested, taken to the German border, and handed over to the Gestapo. Others were unceremoniously dumped at the Belgian border, while some were taken to a police prison in Amsterdam, interrogated and then deported to Belgium. Brandt, the Scandinavian, travelling under the name of Willy Flamme and equipped with first-rate papers to prove it, belonged to that lucky group. After the Laaren meeting had blown up in their faces, a repeat performance supposedly to be held in Lille, but in fact in Brussels, was hastily scheduled. Again nothing came of the attempt to found of a "new Communist Youth International."

Although Brandt only touches on the Brussels fiasco, one senses a thorough frustration in the activist youth with the endless haggling over theories and methods, and the dogmatic differences among the various factions. The conferences did not "yield any results," Brandt resignedly came to conclude. Whether his disappointment led him to consider collaboration with the Social Democratic Youth league, led by London-based Erich Ollenhauer, or whether that decision was prompted by his disillusioning experiences in his work with Communists and Trotskyists during and after the Spanish Civil War, and finally realized in the wake of Stalin's revolting alliance with the Fascist enemy when he signed the Pact of Steel with Hitler on May 22, 1939, cannot be determined from his sketchy dateless outlines of these events.

In Exile notes that Brandt's SJV "gained the status of an allied organization to the Socialist Youth Internationale" in the summer of 1939, after he had severed connections with the Communist-dominated "International Bureau of Revolutionary Youth Organizations."

Pressuring the Nazis

Brandt was more fortunate with another mission. In Berlin, the leaders of the Socialist Workers' party, among them his friends Max Koehler and Stephan Szende—underground after Hitler's advent—had been brought to trial for "subversive activities." In an effort to avert possible death sentences, heavy protest campaigns were started abroad. Under the leadership of the German emigrant groups, the Nazi courts as well as the press were flooded with long petitions from protestors throughout Europe, bearing the full weight of the pressure of international opinion.

In Norway, Brandt had a part in the mobilization of judges and lawyers, among them Oslo's future mayor. The petition was read "in the courtroom during the trial," Brandt reports. "And the German judges mistook it for an official intervention of the Norwegian lawyers' association. The Attorney General fumed against 'these gentlemen who call themselves lawyers,' but it proved effective." The defendants were lucky enough to draw "relatively light sentences."

Brandt realized, however, that the success was achieved, partially at least, because of the timing. The year was 1934. Unlike the military, who obligingly proffered their unconditional loyalty to Hitler on the day President Paul von Hindenburg died (August 2, 1934), some of the judges had not yet knuckled under to the Führer's kind of conquistadorial order and its self-serving fascist law. Hitler's stranglehold on the judiciary was just beginning to tighten.

The massive group action in the case of Carl von Ossietzky was another instance of political pressure instigated by refugees abroad trying to help Germans persecuted inside the Third Reich. Ossietzky, the pacifist editor of the radical leftist weekly *Weltbühne,* had already served a six-month prison sentence in 1932. Because of his public stand against secret rearmament, he had been indicted on charges of "treason and betrayal of military secrets." As soon as the Nazis seized power, he was arrested once more on the night of the Reichstag fire in February 1933.

Ossietzky, taken into "protective custody" as a "criminal traitor," disappeared in Hitler's concentration camps. Appeals and protests from colleagues throughout Europe, including official inquiries by English politicians, tended to irritate the Nazis and intensify the situation. It became clear to Ossietzky's friends that a more subtle approach had to be found.

The first attempt to call the world's attention to the imprisoned pacifist by proposing him for the Nobel Peace Prize originated with a colleague who had emigrated to Strasbourg. The nominations for 1934 were already closed. By 1935, the press and information campaign for the fairly unknown antimilitarist journalist had gained momentum. Among the international notables backing the political victim's nomination for 1935 were prominent Nobel Peace Prize recipients, American Jane Addams (1931), and German historian Ludwig Quidde (1927), a daring foe of sword-rattling German nationalism and militarism of the Wilhelmian pre-World War I era and chairman of the German Peace Society until 1929.

In Norway, it was primarily up to SAP functionary Willy Brandt to keep the campaign moving. His urgent advice was that the pressure for the courageous publicist be continued with "full force," even though he was not overly optimistic about the outcome of the effort in the bleak November days of 1935.

Nobel Prize Campaign

Brandt's correspondence gives the reader fascinating insights into the mechanics of the illustrious Nobel Prize committee, the psychological areas of sensitivity of its members, and the surprisingly significant role of outside pressure in the decision-making process.

Brandt knew that of the Nobel Prize committee of five appointed by the *Storting* (Norwegian Parliament), Dr. Christian Lange would be the most sympathetic to the cause. Since he was also the most accessible—Brandt was acquainted with Lange's son—the SAP functionary decided to single him out as the foremost target of his persuasive powers. With a lengthy article on Ossietzky for the NAP's *Arbeiderbladet,* reprinted in most of the provincial party papers across the country, Brandt launched an impressive press campaign in the summer of 1935. In the fall, however, its impact had leveled off.

To his friends in Paris who initially had asked for his support on the decisive Norwegian front, Brandt complains of a lack of progress. Not enough important people have come to his aid, he laments. Ossietzky is only known because of his imprisonment by the Nazis and not for his journalistic achievements, which should form the basis for qualifying him for the Nobel Prize.

"Even among pacifists he was hardly known," Brandt writes disconcertedly about the difficulties of securing proper backing. Still, he asked his journalist friend, Hilde Walter, in Paris to keep forwarding information on the condition of Ossietzky, a frail man who had been in poor health most of his life. In the hope of convincing the "gentlemen who are close to the Nobel Prize committee" to take action, Brandt intends to go on writing and placing articles in the Norwegian as well as the Danish and Swedish party press.

The strongest contender for the prize in 1935 was Thomas Masaryk, first president and liberator of Czechoslovakia and one of the most tenacious opponents of German and Austrian encroachment.

Brandt wondered if Masaryk could possibly be persuaded to share the prize with the unsung journalist who bravely suffered the terrible consequences of his convictions. In the end, no Nobel Peace Prize was awarded that year.

"We are all fully aware that the situation is very grave for O. Just now, however, an unexpected occurrence has come to our aid: Knut Hamsun has penned a shabby attack against Ossietzky in Oslo's newspapers *Aftenposten* and *Tidens Tegn. . . .*" Brandt sensed correctly that the tide could be turned if swift, concerted action were initiated. The Nobel Prize winning novelist's public insinuations—Ossietzky's choice of staying on in Nazi Germany was an act of provocation designed to provide fuel for continuous agitation from enemies abroad—evoked such a strong wave of indignation in the vocal intellectual community and in the press that its effects became totally counterproductive. Unwittingly, Hamsun's ill-considered remarks had prepared precisely the favorable climate needed for a renewed airing of the "Ossietzky Case."

Brandt went to work at once. The time seemed to be opportune for a direct approach of the Norwegian Labor party's sixty-nine parliamentary representatives. If they could be persuaded to nominate Ossietzky instead of the former mayor of Stockholm, Carl Lindhagen, the NAP's favorite nominee over the past several years, then the battle could be won. Brandt's letter of January 21, 1936, reflected great optimism.

By now, he knew the ropes. The tactical ins and outs of the meticulously circumscribed nomination process were no longer a mystery to him. The whole strategy boils down to an orchestration of apposite international contacts. And Brandt had those contacts; they constituted part of his job.

Mrs. Lunden, who had written a piece on Ossietzky for the *Dagbladet,* was to take care of convincing the liberals of the merits of Ossietzky's case. Brandt would see to it that the NAP representatives in the *Storting* would speak out as one voice. In Sweden, the petitioning for Prince Carl had to be torpedoed by the Social Democrats. The central committee of the NAP also dispatched a resolution. In his letter of January 24, Brandt was able to assert that his optimism had been warranted.

"It was partially due to my hard work that sixty-nine members of the Norwegian *Storting* and fifty-nine deputies of the Swedish *Riks-*

dag signed a formal petition," Brandt remembers proudly in *My Road to Berlin.*

One hundred and twenty-four Swiss parliamentarians, and three hundred European and American legislators helped to guarantee the Nobel Peace Prize for Ossietzky. Together with the letters of nomination from more than thirty professors eligible to place such nominations and the petitions from International Peace Offices, an avalanche of mail from around the world descended on the august committee. Its decision of November 23, 1936, presented the Nazis with a major political and moral defeat.

Ossietzky, a physical wreck at the time, once more had occasion to show his immense courage. He defied Field Marshal Göring by insisting on acceptance of the prize. Knowing that the eyes of the world were watching them, the Nazis relented. Ossietzky was transferred to a small hospital of his choice, where he died in May 1938. The day after the prize money—the equivalent of 100,000 Reichsmarks in hard-to-come by foreign currency—reached the Reichsbank, Hitler decreed that from then on no German citizen would be allowed to accept the Nobel Prize.

When the news broke of the announcement of the hard-earned prize for Ossietzky, Brandt was in the midst of a quite different mission in Berlin. The SAP's Paris headquarters had sent him there in the summer of 1936 to take charge of "Organization Metro." The designation "Metro" meant Berlin. He travelled into the Nazi lion's den in the guise of a Norwegian student who loved German culture. His expertly forged passport was made out in the name of Gunnar Gaasland. His memoirs tell us that he entered the sleeping car that took him from Paris to Berlin "not free of fear." We also learn that his kindly landlady's name is Frau Hamel; that by accident he runs into a Nazi ideology admiring "Norwegian countryman" who might become suspicious of his accent and give him away; and that the Berlin of the grand Olympic games, festooned with thousands of swastikas and humming with the marching rhythms of parading brown shirts "mirrored the megalomania of the dictator."

Berlin Mission

No doubt, operation "Metro" was young Brandt's first major conspiratorial mission. From the detailed discussions of the assignment with his comrades in Paris, he knew that the underground work with Berlin's resistance groups was a dangerous task. Brandt makes no effort to hide the "sobering effect" the "continuous quarreling and wrangling" among the comrades had on him. He succinctly sums up his disillusionment over the lack of solidarity with an offhand remark about a "rather unpleasant refugee atmosphere."

Presumably, Brandt's important work, for which he was willing to "risk his life," consisted of the organization of cadre cells and connecting channels of information between the underground and the outside world. Unfortunately, the reader only has short glimpses of secret contacts in department stores, memorized passwords, codes and cover names—he called himself Martin—perpetual disguise, fear of informers, sleepless nights and long mornings spent at the "university library" partly as a coverup and partly in the pursuit of a thorough knowledge of Nazi indoctrination material. From Hitler's *Mein Kampf* to Alfred Rosenberg's pernicious ideological doctrines on race theory and his intellectual galimatias on the evils of Communism and Jewry echoed in his voluminous *Mythos des 20. Jahrhunderts,* young Brandt tried to digest everything pertaining to Nazi ideology, organization and politics.

The sole note of amusement in this sober, strangely noncommittal chapter from *My Road to Berlin* is provided by the later-published *In Exile,* in which the author insists on having "profited greatly from mornings spent in the Prussian State Library." One wonders what happened to the good old university library in the intervening years.

What troubled and upset Brandt more than anything else was the problem of keeping alive the flagging spirit of resistance. The economic boom and the grandiose mass spectacle with its breathtaking light shows designed by the ingenious Albert Speer, choral singings, mass rallies and mass oaths, mass hysteria and mass euphoria, worthy of any Cecil B. De Mille production, slowly dimmed the voices of dissent and discontent.

The Western powers had benignly looked on as Hitler proceeded to assert his will by the flagrant abrogation of one international agreement after the other. The majority of the conservative segment of the population gave up opposition to the upstart dictator when they realized that support from the free world was not forthcoming. Brandt still finds "cadres of trustworthy comrades in the big factories," but he wondered how "certain quasi-legal kinds of opposition groups could be developed" under these unfavorable conditions. He recommends sports clubs for the young Socialist unbelievers in the "providence" that presented Hitler to the Germans, and attention to the material needs of the workers already suffering from indigestion of "isms" and political theories, and more efficient dissemination of information.

What kind of specific demands were made on the twenty-two-year-old SAP functionary, and what the actual results of his mission in Berlin were, have kept his biographers—as well as his opponents—guessing. Only Brandt knows if a simple courier's routine trip was dramatized into an important-sounding mission for the sake of adding a note of excitement to his memoirs or if the innocuous accounts of inconsequential happenings were meant to cover up an intelligence operation of a nature and proportion no longer classifiable as mere "political activity."

Some commentators have argued among themselves whether Brandt's Berlin excursion could not be construed as sufficient evidence against the claim that he was persecuted by the Nazis—or by the criminal police for that matter—and facing arrest before escaping from Lübeck. In these circles, it is believed that his SAP comrades would hardly have run the double risk to their man and their organization by dispatching to Germany somebody who was already on the Nazi political wanted list and therefore twice as likely to become subject to detection by efficient surveillance teams.

Brandt must have done well on his mission to the big city that was to assume vital importance as a stepping stone into the world of international politics at a later stage in his career. Toward "the end" of the year, he receives orders to travel to Brünn via Prague to participate in a conference that Otto Bauer, chairman of the Austrian Social Democrats, had set up in cooperation with the Sudeten Germans living in Czechoslovakia.

For reasons of security, the gathering was called the "Kattowitz Congress" although it actually was held in Mährisch-Ostrau. Brandt excels in his customary vagueness when it comes to a listing of the participating parties. Fortunately, he is less reticent about the issues discussed by the "representatives from home and in exile." Foremost among them was the formation of a German "popular front."

POPULAR FRONT DRIVE

The collaboration between Communists, Socialists and left-wing bourgeois Social Democratic forces was decreed by the Seventh World Congress of the Communist International in Moscow in 1935. The establishment of antifascist popular fronts and the promotion of proletarian unity fronts by the indigenous Communist parties of Western Europe and the sudden deemphasis of the inherent revolutionary aspects in capitalist nations constituted a radical departure from revolutionist-oriented Communist policy.

It was based on the assumption that the previously detested bourgeois Social Democrats, who had obstinately failed to accept the Marxian doctrine of class warfare and thereby blocked the way to Communist victory, were subject to changing positions in a number of capitalistic countries. The tactical shift of the Comintern was the topic of much debate. And many a Social Democrat, unwilling to go along with the Communists' proposal because of a refusal to take orders from Moscow, was accused by the Communists of opposing the prime objective: the "party or the state of the proletariat."

United Front tactics had already been adopted by the Comintern's Third Congress in 1921. In principle, it was a strategic device to gain access to the proletarian masses by cooperating with non-Communist groups and organizations in collecting these left-oriented forces into one Communist-directed movement or Unity Party.

The Popular Front advances by the French Communists were eagerly taken up by Léon Blum, chairman of the French Socialist party, who succeeded in forming a Popular Front government in June 1936 with the help of the radical Socialists as third coalition partner. Shortly before, in the general Spanish elections of February 1936, a Popular Front government under Don Manuel Azaña was swept into power. Out of 470 seats the left-wingers, composed of the Republican left, the Republican Union, Socialists, Syndicalists, Anarchists, Marxists and Communists, had captured 260 seats, 166 more than in the 1933 elections.

Understandably, German left wingers in exile, all of them impassioned opponents of the Third Reich, were especially interested in gathering their scattered forces into one single potent Popular Front. One of the chief proponents and initiators of the Committee for the

Establishment of a German Popular Front was Herbert Wehner, leading German Communist in exile in Paris and trusted member of the Comintern. Together with Willi Münzenberg—who had the brilliant idea of bolstering their effort by the recruitment of luminous personalities among exiled artists and intellectuals—he prepared the first meeting scheduled for February 2, 1936, at the Hotel Lutetia in Paris. Some of the names of the 118 participants were straight out of Germany's literary *Who's Who.* Novelists Heinrich Mann, brother of Thomas Mann, Lion Feuchtwanger, Ludwig Marcuse, Emil Ludwig, dramatist Ernst Toller, as well as Klaus Mann, Thomas's son, had gone to mingle with prominent journalists and leftist political leaders.

Although the executive council of the Social Democrats in exile consistently refused to make common cause with the Moscow-directed Communists, the party was well represented at the historic meeting. The result was a flaming appeal to the German people, but not much else. The demands for "peace, freedom and bread" and the destruction of the "brown tyranny" with its racial persecution and brutal power and war politics exhausted themselves on paper. The "new Germany" would eliminate the enemies of the people. It promised to nationalize the war industry and the big banks. It would know how to prevent the attempts at sabotage by big capital with the sharpest of measures. It advocated disowning the "Junkers" and their kind as saboteurs of the people's food and freedom. Aside from the great spirited disputes, little substantive progress was made toward a common guide to action.

The desperate appeal bears the signatures of Willy Brandt and Jacob Walcher, among others, for the SAP; of Herbert Wehner, Walter Ulbricht and Wilhelm Pieck from the ranks of the Communists, alongside the names of approximately twenty Social Democrats and thirty writers and other "civilians."

Interestingly, Brandt insists that he was still in Berlin and not present at the meeting. Therefore he could not have signed the paper together with Ulbricht, even though Wehner remembers having seen Brandt "at the horizon." Apparently, Brandt's friends made use of his name "which they were entitled to do according to the terms of the time." Brandt admits he "would have signed the paper myself if it had been placed before me."

MACABRE EVENT

Among the Popular Front congresses he attended in those days was one held at the Hotel Lutetia in Paris during the fall of 1938. It was chaired by the celebrated novelist Heinrich Mann who, Brandt writes in his memoirs, served as a figurehead of the enterprise. With great distress, the sharp-eyed young SAP functionary saw "how the Communist wire-pullers of the congress abused the political naiveté of the novelist for their own aims." Since Mann also came from Lübeck, Brandt seized the occasion for an exchange of ideas about the prospects for the future with the prestigious representative from his hometown. Mann gloomily summed up the hopelessness of curbing the rising tide of Nazi barbarism in one sentence: "We may never see our Lübeck again."

In retrospect, the Lutetia meeting described by Brandt as a "macabre event since it lacked inner veracity as well as clarity and strength," bears an uncanny resemblance to the descriptions of the founders' congress, also headlined by Heinrich Mann, in 1936. The obvious difficulty in distinguishing one popular front congress from another reveals the frustration of the movement; the same people talking on the same topics year after year.

Brandt comments that his "own group affirmed its support for a unified front of Social Democrats and Communists and took the view that a 'revolutionary but independent' unity party could develop at a later stage." These lines were written by the author of *In Exile* in 1966. The SAP functionary's ambiguous position vis-à-vis a unity party was the cause of considerable misunderstanding in postwar Germany, especially among those who regarded the differences of political nuances between democratic parliamentarian socialism of Western provenience and the socialism of the people's democracies godfathered in Moscow as manifestations of an interreligious war within the Communist "church," a controversy among members of the same family.

In 1936, in the *Marxistische Tribüne,* Brandt advocated a "genuine communism" and proletarian party of the masses. In order to achieve this objective, the SAP was to combine its efforts to fight for proletarian unity and for revolutionary reforms. The revival of the "discussions on the unification of German Socialist and Communist youth organizations" that had been "pushed out of the public mind" by the war in Spain was still praised by him in 1937 in the *Socialist Youth* of November-December. The single most sobering effect is reflected in his bitter condemnation of the Comintern and its "corrupt functionaries who blindly danced to Moscow's tune" after the Stalin-Hitler pact.

While Brandt decries the "dependency" the Comintern had created in relation to the Socialist movement in 1939, the disillusionment over the failure to work together constructively was just as keenly felt on the Communist side. The readers of the French Communist newspaper *L'Humanité* probably felt equally embittered about the conclusion that Stalin was correct when he said capitalism could only be defeated if the Social Democrats were eradicated from the working-class movement. The writer was none other than the Comintern's Georgi Dimitrov.

Looking back in 1966, Brandt expressed the thought that he "regarded the Communist party as part of the German Socialist movement, and as an important part at that." His experiences had caused him to "modify" his opinions. Without referring to the personal attacks launched on him by the Swedish and Norwegian Communists during the war, he admits having gained a better understanding of the "nature of their party machine." Although he later was to challenge the Communists' contention that only they put forward a viable concept, Brandt "still did not drop the idea of a unified socialist movement" at that time.

EMIGRANT GOSSIP

In his book *Forbrytere og andre tyskere (Criminals and Other Germans),* published in Stockholm in 1946, he justifies this decision by pointing to the attitudinal change of the Communists who "in contrast to former times are assuming a positive posture toward democracy and parliamentarianism." This positive assessment does not prevent him from strongly denouncing the "compulsory amalgamation of the Social Democrats with the Communists in the Russian zone."

Since he became the target of what he calls "emigrants' gossip" and "absurd suspicions" that undermined his credibility among Social Democrats upon his return to Berlin after the war, Brandt found it necessary to clarify and define his previous and present position concerning the controversial popular front issue. In a letter to the SPD's ardent anti-United Front chairman, Kurt Schumacher, in December 1947, Brandt wrote ". . . in my time I have been a supporter of a unified Socialist party, which should be independent and rest on a democratic foundation."

Brandt's Social Democratic affidavit satisfied the distrustful Schumacher. It should have laid to rest existing doubts and suspicions once and for all. Somehow it did not. Brandt's affinity for the Socialist camp became a major national issue when his closest associate, Egon Bahr, proclaimed a new approach to Eastern politics in 1963 by "change through rapprochement." Brandt's insistence on "democratization" and a collective security system as an instrument for securing peace, a pet idea since the 1940s, also espoused by the Soviets, his nonchalant treatment of Germany's borders in the East, combined with his thesis of a "social balance of power" and vague visions of a united Socialist Europe at the end of the road, instilled an intangible uneasiness concerning the "renegade" politician in Western-oriented Democrats of the middle-of-the-road bourgeoisie.

Indubitably, the book of memoirs, *By Order of the Party,* by top SED functionary Karl Mewis, published in East Berlin in 1971, was bound to renew the "emigrants' gossip," casting doubt on Brandt's heralded "modified" Socialist commitment in certain quarters. Mewis, intimate of Herbert Wehner and other Communist notables in Berlin since the 1930s, member of the International Brigade in Spain, where he met Brandt, and arrested in Stockholm in connection with the Wehner espionage affair in 1942, had quite a different impression of Brandt's political credo. Evidently, the two men had been in contact in Stockholm during their years in exile. Mewis recounted:

> Although Brandt was executing an official task for the Norwegian government, he regarded himself as a German anti-Fascist in the negotiations with us. We felt a justified distrust that was further strengthened by the close relations Willy Brandt maintained with the U.S. embassy. But in the fight against Hitler, we had worked together with inscrutable Germans before and we knew how to safeguard ourselves. The cooperation, however, soon fizzled out. I only saw Willy Brandt again in 1946.
>
> At that time the state headquarters of the SED in East Berlin was

> already located in Behrenstrasse. I worked there as a secretary for agitation and propaganda. Some weeks after the unification [of the Communists and Social Democrats into the SED] a Norwegian officer, who greeted me happily, appeared in my office. It was Willy Brandt. He spoke with enthusiasm about the SED and declared that he looked upon working for the unification [of the political parties] in West Berlin as his main task.

Declaration contradicts declaration. Given the ambiguous attitude of East German SED functionaries toward West German Democratic Socialists, Mewis's "total recall" may well be marred by imperfections. As a case in point, his assumption that Brandt worked in an official or quasi-official capacity for the Norwegian government-in-exile while in Stockholm has been widely debated. Attesting only to a "working relationship" with Brandt, Jens Schive, press attaché at the Norwegian Legation during that period, has emphatically denied official collaboration on a government level. However, secret U.S. State Department records, declassified in 1974, shed a different light on the situation. In confidential dispatch No. 3142, dated April 17, 1944, Herschel V. Johnson of the political section of the American Legation in Stockholm explains the true function of Brandt's Swedish-Norwegian Bureau. "This Bureau is ostensibly an independent Swedish one, but is actually completely controlled by the Norwegian Legation."

From the ideological warfare thicket of the multitudinous disputes about popular and unified fronts, an issue that severely handicapped Brandt's soaring ambitions in Berlin's anti-Communist climate after the war—we must return to the turmoil and chaos, the unprecedented terror, destruction and lawlessness that was visited upon the Spanish people by the Civil War. It began in July 1936 when insurgents under the leadership of General Francisco Franco launched their carefully prepared surprise attack on the republic's impotent, faction-ridden Popular Front government.

Knowing something about Brandt's efficacious political commitment and his extraordinary predilection for being wherever the action is, it is not surprising to find him on the way to Barcelona in the midst of the crossfire of the Spanish republic's inordinately painful struggle for survival.

The Spanish chapter

When the twenty-three-year-old, starry-eyed activist appeared on the Spanish scene in February 1937, together with hundreds of young idealists, adventurers and agents from all over Europe, as well as publicists of the stature of Ernest Hemingway and Sefton Delmer, the putsch of the generals had already lost the dimensions of a civil war. The internal conflict soon assumed the aspects of an ideological sparring contest between the forces of fascism and communism on an international scale.

After the Popular Front government had turned to France and the Soviet Union for support, Franco's contact man, Canaris, encountered little resistance in convincing Hitler and Göring to come to the aid of the "nationalists" with planes, tanks, matériel, advisers and the Condor Legion, ready for a test in battle. The christening of the new weaponry climaxed in one of the most shameless firsts in history when German bomber planes descended on defenseless Guernica on April 26, 1937. In two hours the tiny old Basque town was wiped out, and with it 1,654 civilian lives—whose martyrdom is immortalized in Picasso's shattering canvas of mass death, *Guernica.*

Despite official concurrence with the British Five Power pact proposal of nonintervention, also advised by the French, the Germans followed Mussolini's footsteps into Spanish territory by according recognition to Franco's regime. The Soviets favored the Republicans. Their operational basis was established in Barcelona. Here the International Brigades, collected for the most part by Communist organizations in Paris, were organized and dispatched. Here the Communist-oriented organizations set up their headquarters. Among them was the SAP's Spanish counterpart, POUM, a smallish radical group with Trotskyist characteristics. Brandt had met POUM's president in Paris the previous year.

Brandt had ostensibly travelled to Barcelona as a correspondent for unnamed "Scandinavian papers." Primarily, however, he was on another SAP mission for Jacob Walcher, his friend and mentor, who had taken charge of SAP operations in Paris. Brandt has been extremely reluctant to specify the purpose of his journey "as trusted delegate of my political friends in exile" with the "task of keeping up political contacts in Barcelona for my SAP friends, which was a quarrelsome and thankless enough chore." Such artful vagueries, not surprisingly, invited the wildest of speculation about the five-month Spanish interlude.

During Brandt's race for mayor in Berlin in 1957 the charge was made, among others, that he had been a Communist, fighting with the "Red Brigades." It was easy enough for the SPD candidate to establish the falseness of such off the mark accusations in court. But when respected papers like *Die Zeit* eagerly jumped to the conclusion that Brandt—since he was not a Red Front Fighter—participated in the Spanish war solely as a newspaperman, they were equally off the mark.

In Exile provides the first veiled clue to the direction of the author's real efforts: "To bring together all the youth leagues under one heading." What this means is clear. He was sent out to promote the Popular Front and to persuade the resisting POUM to fall in line. Brandt's success must have been negligible. He writes of "friction with every single group" and his active role in the endless verbal fights carried out by him in the halting Spanish acquired as a fourth foreign language at Lübeck's *Johanneum.*

The Socialist and Communist youth leagues were no boy scout troops. Like the young Falangists, they were organizing on paramilitary lines. It is possible that the rumors about Brandt's combat service stemmed from his intensive work with these groups.

The wayward POUM was dubbed a "Fascist agency" by the Communists because of its refusal to submit to Moscow's orders. Interestingly, some SAP members had come to share this view, thereby causing a split from the Walcher circle that the small splinter party could ill afford.

Contrary to the Communist comrades, POUM was hell-bent on the social revolution. The directions of the Comintern, on the other hand, gave precedence to extension of Communist influence over the police, the Republican army, and the war effort as a whole.

Whatever the modest initial inroads Brandt mentions were, they were completely wiped out when POUM staged a house revolt and went into open attack. The rebellion was brutally squashed by the forces pledged to the Comintern. Brandt describes the bloody week in May that raged in Barcelona aptly "as a civil war within a civil war." As with all infights between believers, the punishment of the heretics was merciless.

POUM's leaders, together with the antihierarchical anarchists and syndicalists, "were persecuted and dragged before the courts, or even murdered by the Communists," Brandt reports. He "regarded it his duty to intervene" on their behalf. Brandt describes how he forced his way into the office of the German representative of the Comintern in an effort to pressure him into releasing young Mark Rein, who had been kidnapped, imprisoned, tortured by the Communists and was eventually liquidated. It was this bold intervention, Brandt reasons, that resulted in the Communist wrath and their denouncement of him as a "Franco agent."

This is all the more remarkable inasmuch as the author accuses POUM of "sectarian conduct." He is convinced that its leaders had "taken a false position on virtually every practical issue." On the other hand, he claims to have disagreed "even more violently" with the Communists' exploitation of the "discipline which the military situation demanded by establishing a system of one-party rule." Asked by *Spiegel* in 1961 if he still feels a commitment to Popular Front politics, he answers with a qualified "yes—the one of that time."

The young SAP functionary-about-Barcelona admittedly found these thoroughly confusing events, from which he "learned a great deal," hard to explain. From his own and his comrades' accounts, one gathers that he had recklessly plunged into the murderous situation, thereby incurring, quite innocently, the wrath of both factions. To extricate himself from the snake pit of collective vengeance he nimbly retreated, perhaps guided by an instinctive sense for self-preservation acquired in his youthful bouts in Lübeck, into a neutralist position by showering criticisms at both sides.

To be sure, the Communists are less than pleased with his conclusion that they "acted exclusively as auxiliaries of Moscow" with Stalin "no doubt, interested in defeating Franco" but not willing to allow the Spanish people "to decide for themselves about their own future." But the "bourgeois" democratic side had no cause to rejoice either. In a speech, *One Year of War and Revolution in Spain,* given before the SAP in Paris after his return from Barcelona, preserved in the Archives of Amsterdam and the CSU's *Rotbuch,* Brandt shows no signs of budding sympathies for traditional bourgeois institutions:

> The tasks of the civil revolution were solved for the most part during the first attack. A purging storm has cleansed churches and

> monasteries. The power of the church as a socioeconomic factor has been broken. The nobility, the big estate owners, have disappeared, likewise, a great part of the corrupt reactionary crooks of the bureaucracy. With them departed almost all big business people and banklords. Wherever they did not hurry we helped them along. With the attack of the civil forces the first steps of the social revolution were taken.

Brandt's inclination to consider both sides, his conscious preference for the "not only . . . but also" instead of a clean-cut "either . . . or" becomes even more pronounced in later years. It is undoubtedly the basis for his growing reputation as a mediator and a practitioner of noteworthy tolerance and moderation thought to be rooted in the exhilarating experience of Scandinavian democracy. At the same time his amazing political flexibility was also labeled opportunism or waffling by his opponents.

In his television interview in 1964, Günter Gaus comes straight to the point but, losing courage, blunts it by self-consciously referring to his question as "maliciousness": "Occasionally one has, if one reads that book of yours [*My Road to Berlin*], if one listens to your speeches—however, not just during your speeches, but certainly not limited to your party—the feeling that one trait predominates, I mean, the urge to say something to everybody. Don't you fear, Mr. Mayor, that this way the airing of political adversary conflicts is thwarted in favor of the most effective permanent publicity appeal possible?"

Mayor Brandt allows "there is something to it," before he assumes a defensive posture that fails to address the issue of muddying the political waters with skilled political double-talk. He cites an enormously clever man in a foreign land as having said: "Today one can only be a good realist if one believes in miracles." As Brandt argues confidently that this, too, represents a "not only . . . but also" position, the stunned listeners have time to decide that Gaus won his point.

The eventful Spanish chapter closed on a tragic note. In the supercharged emotional cauldron where tempers rose quickly and accusations were hurled at random, the relentlessly persecuted POUM and SAP leaders began to question each other as to why Willy Brandt, of all people, had been spared from Communist brutality. It did not occur to them, apparently, that the tough Communist fighters were hesitant to lay hands on a twenty-three-year-old, thoroughly vexed young man.

What had whipped up an atmosphere of hysteria, where friend turned against friend, was the abduction and unsolved murder by unidentified Communists of Kurt Landau, former secretary to Trotsky and one of the chief anti-Stalin ideologists. Landau had investigated the causes of the May revolt and had documented his findings that they grew out of brazen provocations by the Communists. Allegedly, five copies of the compromising paper were sent out to POUM and SAP leaders. It is said that Landau's friends immediately suspected a connection between his subsequent murder and this document. In an effort to establish a lead, the five copies were recalled. The copy sent to Brandt was supposedly missing.

Contrary to rumors circulated among German emigré groups, Landau's widow, Katja, had nothing to do with the charges hurled at young Brandt during an airing of the mysterious case before the party leadership in London. Brandt told me that he has in his possession a letter from Mrs. Landau, written years later as testimony to prove this point in a court action for libel initiated by candidate Brandt.

However, there is little doubt that Brandt met with undisguised hostility because of the "Spanish affair" at the international Socialist conference held in Letchworth in August 1936, where the Independent Labor Party summer school convened. Brandt complains bitterly of the "malicious distortions" about his behavior in Barcelona.

"There were cavilers who sought to stir up trouble because of my attitude in Barcelona, but after I had expressed my views in detail, the conference chairman, the M.P. Campbell Stephen, declared the matter closed." His SAP comrades Walcher and Frölich had vouched for him. When an Italian "sectarian" tried to bring the matter up once more in a session the following day, there was a "painful scene," Brandt reports without going into the substance of the allegations. The robust young man obviously lost his cool and called his accuser a "mad dog," an outburst he excuses as a lack "in parliamentary experience."

"Katja Landau was not even in London," Brandt explained to me during a meeting in March 1975. "But Jeanne Maurin, the wife of POUM's imprisoned leader was there urging and insisting that the whole thing must be stopped," he remembers. "As far as POUM's political position was concerned, I was as much for it as I was against it. I certainly sympathized with them."

Brandt intimates that he was the victim of a chain of tragic coincidences. It perhaps would have been wiser had he cleared the air by forcing the whole disagreeable story out into the open, instead of allowing rumors and suspicions to settle on it like so much mold in a jelly jar.

Who would cast the first stone at an ambitious twenty-three-year-old hothead, even if he had blundered into a serious mess? Why did Brandt put so little faith in the generousness and understanding of human failings by his fellow man?

Ultimately, the profundity of his distrust becomes the existential trauma that blurs the outline of his personality.

10

Apprenticeship in Socialism —Scandinavian Style

The precarious Spanish adventure apparently had a sobering effect on the feisty functionary. If there had been lingering shreds of romanticism about The Revolution, they were most likely knocked out of the young man after the London flap. In spite of the disheartening experience in Spain, neither Brandt nor the SAP had given up on the Popular Front policy. Variations on the theme—one of them the founding of a "Socialist concentration"—proposed and discussed at meetings in Paris and other places, slowly played themselves out.

Europe's leaders stood paralyzed, watching Hitler's incredibly fast political footwork in changing the continent's power relationships, from the Berlin-Rome-Tokyo axis to the annexation of Austria in March 1938, and his relentless assaults on the Jews. The placating of the Western powers with the Munich agreement in September that enabled him to "bring home" into the Reich 3.5 million Sudeten Germans was a performance that in turn smoothed the way for the invasion of Czechoslovakia in March 1939. The persistent barrage included the forced cession of the Memel region from Lithuania the same month, the signing of the assistance and nonaggression pacts with Stalin in May and August, sealing the fate of Poland with time bought by the Kremlin.

The lightning actions mesmerized the German masses into a state of contrite apathy. The momentous credulousness and disarray of

Hitler's European adversaries, their torpid fascination with his asseverations of a peaceful quest for new living space or *Lebensraum,* was directly reflected in the dictator's impudence and breathtaking momentum.

As Hitler's world expanded, Brandt's grew smaller. He had become more active "on the educational side" of the Norwegian Labor party, its Youth League, and functioned as full-time secretary of the Norwegian People's Aid, the *Norsk Folkehjelp,* that was supported by the trade union. Every morning he worked in the small office he had set up, preparing lectures and articles, and maintaining international contacts through a massive flow of correspondence.

No doubt, the intellectual climate of the pacifist circles in which Carlota was at home stimulated his work on *War Aims of the Great Powers and the New Europe,* a study of the problems "which would confront Europe after the downfall of the dictators." If living with liberal Carlota and her family was Brandt's first intimate experience with the comforts of life enjoyed by the upper middle-class bourgeoisie, it had no sedentary effect on him. Being taken into the family fold without legal ties did not inspire complacency. Nor did Hitler's instant victory in Poland afford peace of mind.

"The nerves are tense, you are in a strange state of agitation, the restlessness is like a poison in your blood," Brandt wrote shortly after the outbreak of war. It was a war he had sensed for a long time. If Hitler maintained "the horoscope of the times does not point to peace but to war," Brandt accurately concluded in 1933 that the "victory of fascism in Germany" was bound to bring a "marked increase in the danger of war, even if the Fascist leaders themselves are afraid of war."

Now that his prophecy had come true, he felt as "paralyzed, helpless in the grip of a dull fatalism" as the people taken by surprise. He busied himself with a monograph, *A Short Study of Latvia under the Soviet Occupation,* basically a report of the terror regime inflicted on the population by the KGB, and research for a *History of the Youth International.*

In a commentary on the Soviet-German alliance, Brandt criticized the German Communists for not intervening on behalf of their leader, Ernst Thälmann, who had been imprisoned by the Nazis in Berlin and left to die in the concentration camp at Buchenwald. Brandt held out little hope for the preservation of Norway's neutrality. Still, the Nazi invasion of Denmark and Norway, a "precaution" against English aggression from along the Northern front following the attack on France, the notorious west offensive with its blatant abuses of the neutrality of Luxembourg, Holland and Belgium came as a shock to Brandt.

Five years later he was to witness the verdict of the Nuremberg war trial court as a correspondent for Norway's *Arbeiderbladet.* The judges ruled that neither the safeguarding of bases for the German navy or air force in the battle with England, nor anticipation of allied occupation of Norway, nor the disruption of the shipments of Swedish iron ore and nickel qualified as "defensive measures." In the judgment of Nuremberg, the invasion of Norway and Denmark therefore constituted acts of aggression in defiance of international law.

The judicial intricacies of international warfare were of small concern to Brandt on April 9, 1940, when German battleships were spotted in Oslo Fjord and German troops began to invade Norway at seven strategic points along the coast. As members of the *Storting* assembled in Hamar and decided to retreat further to Elverum, Brandt joined the stream of refugees on their way north. They ended up in Lillehammer, where his colleagues from the People's Aid had escaped. A civilian without valid papers, and the functionary of an antifascist party, who had undoubtedly attracted the attention of the Gestapo during his many missions abroad, Brandt was in a precarious position.

The application for naturalization in Norway, after his forcible expatriation, was still being processed. Since escape on skis over the mountains into neutral Sweden promised "no chance of success," Brandt and his friends came up with an idea for his rescue that would enrich any espionage thriller.

In a Borrowed Uniform

It mattered little that the Norwegian soldier's uniform of his friend, Paul René Gauguin, grandson of the famed artist and himself a painter, hung much too short and far too wide on Brandt's lanky frame. "As one of thousands of Norwegian soldiers I could hope to be treated as a prisoner of war, and probably I would soon be released. As a civilian, on the other hand, I had to expect the worst, once my true identity was established," Brandt commented.

The plan worked to perfection. There was only one surprise element in it for Gauguin, who appeared in a Copenhagen court in 1963 to tell the whole story once more. This time it was in defense of chancellor candidate Brandt, who was accused by German and praised by Scandinavian newspapers of having fought, weapon in hand, against his own countrymen.

The blitzkrieg against France, an updated Schlieffen Plan—basically an offensive built on the idea of bypassing the heavy fortifications along the German-French border—began on May 10, 1940. It ended on June 14 when Hitler's troops marched into Paris through the Porte Maillot and the tricolor that topped the Eiffel Tower was lowered to halfmast.

Defenseless Norway had not seen a war in 125 years. It was invaded on April 9 and bravely resisted almost two months, until it surrendered to the brutal thrust of German forces on June 7. In his many writings on the exemplary Norwegian fight for freedom, Brandt deals with the different aspects of the invasion, the occupation, and the role of Major Quisling, the Norwegian Nazi chief who played "a decisive part in the preparations leading up to Hitler's occupation."

Brandt was twenty-six years old and not sure if his life had been a failure. In the seven years he spent in Norway, his asylum had become his second homeland. Now the life he had built for himself in Oslo was shattered by the Nazi takeover. "Hitler took away my country for the second time," Brandt says with understandable bitterness. Unless he stayed in hiding, there was no guarantee of safety or freedom.

Once more, the young man was obliged to pull up stakes. Assuring pregnant Carlota of a wedding in Sweden, he caught a train to Björkelangen, located within five miles of the Swedish border. Guided by a reserve officer, a farmer familiar with the schedules and routes of the German border patrol, he marches through hilly pastures and open woodland at dusk in search of the meandering man-made abstraction stretching unmarked and undistinguishable between grey rocks and yellow buttercups . . . that was his Rubicon.

When Brandt started out to rebuild his network of connections and contacts at home and abroad in glittering Stockholm, filled to the brim with refugees, resistance fighters and agents of every imaginable nationality and persuasion, he could not know that the interim existence would last five long years. Thanks to his talent for adjustment, the process of acclimatization was a brief one. Although he soon acquired a good command of Swedish, he kept in close touch with his exiled friends from the Norwegian Labor party—who had established a second center in Stockholm as a counterpart to their London bureau—and became part of the tight little colony around the Norwegian Legation.

Since the neutral Swedes were anxious to avoid any provocation of the Germans, his political activities were sharply curtailed and had to be executed with the utmost discretion. By necessity, they therefore often became covert affairs. With the commission for a series of articles about the Norwegian campaign, the skeleton for his later books, and plans to open a Swedish-Norwegian Press Bureau, primarily for collecting and passing on information about Nazi-occupied territory, and processing top-secret intelligence for the resistance movement, Brandt could not complain of lack of work.

The combat lines of the informational front, manned by publicists whose efforts for the most part were as generously financed by the British as by the Soviets, comprised an equally important component of Stockholm's hectic climate during the war as the espionage agents' trade, with its acts of sabotage against war operations and war matériel transports, its provocations, its transmitters, and all-round intelligence work.

"Through Swedish correspondents, business men, representatives of the Church, also occasionally through government officials," Brandt kept informed about Germany and the resistance. His friend August Enderle, liaison man for the International Federation of Transport Workers, "tried not without success to organize a system of underground communication with German sailors." To help their persecuted comrades they smuggled forged papers and ration cards into Germany.

The American connection

It was well known in Stockholm's American Legation that Brandt "maintains close relations" with Soviet diplomats. Perhaps it is because of this fact that the Americans tried to encourage his information-sharing visits. After one such session, on August 31, 1943, Herschel V. Johnson cabled back to Washington as top secret the resulting conclusions: "Brandt mentioned man called Furubottom was still most active communist leader in Norway but he did not know this man was identical with Gubben."

Gubben was the cover for Norway's Communist leader and head of the party's five-man central executive committee in charge of underground resistance work against German occupation forces. According to U.S. Dispatch 2663, Gubben worked through *Arbeidernes Inlandsbyraa,* ostensibly a nonpolitical home front made up mainly of labor unionists. Johnson's informant described its activities as sabotage, particularly in factories, the organization of guerilla units, and the military training of about 30,000 men in Norway. In Sweden, Gubben's representative kept in secret touch with the Norwegian and the Soviet legations, from whom orders reportedly were received regularly. Gubben was at odds with the Norwegian government in exile in London over the issue of guerilla warfare.

While one informant denied knowledge of any campaign to enlist Norwegian recruits in Sweden for guerilla activity—a highly punishable crime in neutral Sweden—another source implicated the *Utlandsbyraa* under the direction of Martin Tranmael, Norwegian labor leader in exile in Stockholm and Brandt's protector. While Gubben's men maintain covert contacts with the Soviets, Tranmael met openly with his old friend Soviet Ambassador Madame Kollontay. Although Tranmael's supporters, among them Brandt, frequently lectured in refugee camps, Johnson doubts that they had anything to do with the recruitment of guerillas.

Apparently, the American OSS (predecessor of CIA), reporting "that Brandt is one of the ablest in the entire lot [of refugees] and is the one most likely to play some role after the war, in spite of his Norwegian nationality . . ." (Document No. 3399) was even better informed than the young activist. Nevertheless, his opinions and observations were highly valued. "Brandt gave impression Norwegian communists and Labor Party while cooperating in nonpolitical underground activity are at the same time engaged in real political struggle to gain control of masses," Johnson cabled. For him, this piece of "inside" intelligence seems to have come as a major revelation.

According to Dispatch 4027, Washington learned from Brandt—after the attempt to assassinate Hitler failed on July 20, 1944—that it was the executed Count York von Wartenburg who served as liaison between the military group and the civilian opposition movement. Brandt also revealed that one of the leaders of the resistance movement, the executed Adam von Trott zu Solz, an official in Hitler's Foreign Office and friend of Julius Leber, had come to Stockholm in June to establish contact with the British legation but that the contact with the Soviets could not be made before his departure. From Brandt's memoirs we know that it was Julius Leber who sent Trott his way.

Since antimilitarist Brandt had always held a low opinion of officers in general and a "mere" officers' revolt against Hitler in particular, he found himself in complete agreement with Adam von Trott about the organization of the resistance on the "widest basis possible." This knowledge of the existence of an alliance of leaders from political, economic, military and religious groups from "the Right to the Left," as well as representatives of the labor movement, was duly passed on to information-hungry Washington.

As the German troops marched on the French capital, most of the SAP members fled to the United States or to London. Paul Frölich and Jacob Walcher, who had chosen exile in America, soon parted company when ex-Communist Walcher reverted to the old Communist line.

In London, the SAP's strengthened contacts with the SPD found expression in the mutual work toward a "Union of German Socialist Organizations." In Sweden, the SAP was headed by ex-Communist August Enderle, who was to play a significant part in the rebuilding of the German Federation of trade unions. The small party kept in close touch with the "Club of Austrian Socialists," led by Bruno Kreisky, and became associated with the so-called "Small International," an "International Group of democratic Socialists." When the Socialist Workers' party merged with the SPD in October 1944, a proposal to christen the joint venture the Socialistic Unity party came under serious consideration.

Double Emigrant

It would seem that the double emigrant, "a German who had fled to Norway and a Norwegian who had escaped to Sweden," had to come to Stockholm to discover the extent of the Norwegianization of Willy Brandt. His affinity for the natural, totally unaffected reserve of the Norwegians grew in proportion to his ever diminishing appreciation of the suave formality, the cool politeness of the Swedes.

For a while, after Carlota and the baby had joined him in the spring of 1941 and terminated his precious bachelorhood, it looked as though restless Willy would settle down to enjoy the blessings of family life. "For the first time I could devote myself to my family," Brandt-Lania paint a cozy picture in the memoirs. In his letters to his friend Herbert George, he writes like any proud father about the great joy little Ninja brings into their life. Ninja, "a little more than two years old already talks a lot, mainly in Swedish," Brandt was not above bragging a trifle.

With members of the Norwegian resistance mostly from the Socialist movement, and members of the intelligentsia visiting often, the couple's social life is an active one. Brandt widens and enhances the circle with "interesting personalities," college teachers, journalists and writers he meets during his lectures on international affairs. Driven by the gnawing ambition to prove his worth and make a name for himself, he becomes more and more absorbed by the many projects in which he involves himself.

Brandt's ability to work hard and long seems to have been as capacious as his knack for arousing controversy. His critical study of the changing concept of guerilla warfare in reference to the iron laws of the Hague Rules of War on Land, dating back to 1874 and ratified in 1907, shocked the military as well as conservatives and liberals because of its implications. The author of *Guerillakriget,* published in 1942, correctly observed that "contemporary warfare has decisively swept aside the distinction between combatant and civilian" and therefore concluded that the "old provisions of international law no longer offer a viable basis for judging present-day guerilla warfare."

Arguments such as, "Something is amiss with a nation which takes the view that it cannot conduct a war of liberation because its regular army has been wiped out," or the question, if the bombing of defenseless individuals is not just as inhuman as "men willing to sacrifice themselves setting out, often under skillful leadership, to attack enemy troops?" were interpreted in later years as a brief for international recognition of irregular warfare and sanction of guerilla warfare against the German occupiers of Norway in particular.

"Rules against irregular wars as the Nazis fought them were worthless. The Nazis didn't care about the Hague rules; therefore it was legitimate to fight against them with any means available," Brandt told me in the spring of 1975.

Paradoxically, some of the Norwegian Communists attacked Brandt as a German for "renouncing" a guerilla war in Norway. Among Brandt's opponents in Germany, however, the fact that guerilla warfare is advocated solely by the Soviet Union was enough to fan old suspicions.

If *Guerillakriget* irked the conservatives with its inferred challenge to the validity of the Hague Convention, his next book *Norges Tredje Krigsår (Norway's Third Year of War),* which appeared one year later, angered the Communists. Although the story of Norway's suffering under Nazi occupation was widely praised by the Swedish press, the author's account of the metamorphosis of Norway's Communists from eager Quisling collaborators to intransigent resistance fighters against all forms of fascism elicited furious attacks from the illegal Communist newspapers *Ny Dag* and *Friheten.*

Brandt's reproach that Norwegian Communists did not act like Norwegians before Moscow joined the war was taken as an impudent defamation of Norwegian freedom fighters who died as heroes on the battlefield while the author, protected by an opportune Norwegian passport, sought safety in neutral Sweden. With his "denouncement of Norwegian patriots" the writer stood accused of trying to split up the Norwegian freedom front. Furthermore, by his betrayal of the International Bureau of the Norwegian Working Class as a cover for the Political Bureau of the Communist party he had supposedly "delivered the best sons of Norway to the Gestapo and the occupation authorities." Lastly, his association with POUM was dredged up once more as proof that he belonged to "the most embittered enemies of the Soviets within the ranks of the labor movement."

Mr. Herschel Johnson of the American Legation, who is keeping an official eye on Brandt, reports the incident to Washington. Dispatch No. 2253 contains the charges and their refutations. Johnson is satisfied that the true function of the International Bureau of the Norwegian Working Class was indeed "well known in labor circles." As concerns the last charge, Johnson paraphrases a passage from Brandt's own defense, published in *Trots Allt* in August 1943: "Brandt emphasizes his interest in the Soviet Union and its great achievements, and draws attention to the stress laid in his book on the necessity to collaborate with that great country."

POSTWAR POLICIES

More than anything else, Brandt's longstanding love-hate relationship with communism and the Soviet Union seems to be at the bottom of his evolutionary development toward the interim step between social democracy and communism. The resulting theory of democratic socialism as a permanent political force that endeavors to change society by means of "democratization"—whatever that means—is not an easily defined hybrid. Its interpretation stimulated the liveliest of disputes among the framers of the SPD's "long range" program in 1975. For the time being it is, perhaps, best delineated as an opposite to "authoritarian socialism."

Inspired by the discussions about a viable policy for postwar Europe and Germany and the intellectual input by the distinguished members of the Socialists' international study group, Brandt issues a number of memoranda, sometimes in collaboration with Irmgard Enderle, pamphlets, and a book entitled *Efter Segern (After Victory)* on that subject. Each uses identical language, often repeating whole sentences, paragraphs and lengthy passages.

In view of the powerful figures of the future who formed the braintrust of this international study workshop—Nobel Prize winner Gunnar Myrdal, professor of economics and longtime head of the European Economic Commission of the UN in Geneva; his wife, Alva Myrdal, who was to become Swedish ambassador to India; Bruno Kreisky, the present Austrian Chancellor; Torsten Nilsson, later Swedish foreign minister; Martin Tranmael, affectionately called the "grand old man" of the Norwegian Socialist movement by Brandt; and German Reichstag deputy and leader of the Woodworkers' Union, Fritz Tarnow—Brandt's reflections deserve to be appreciated as mirror and synthesis of its collective consensus.

In all these writings the exiled Brandt exposed his scant understanding of the extent of the suffering of the German people during the terrors of Hitler's war by making the monumental error of predicting a revolution. Apparently, neither he nor the other members of the study group were able to imagine the utter demoralization of the German masses, after years of apocalyptic total war and the gradual destruction of civil liberties, cities, morale and family life. The population was much too dispirited, much too weak from hunger, cold, and the constant fear of death from bombings to contemplate, much less stage, a revolution.

Brandt, sitting cozily in Sweden, takes a bloody revolution in tortured Germany for granted. To him it becomes the purge "which unfortunately was not fulfilled in 1918–19" after World War I. "A revolution like this is bound to have social consequences," he stated in the treatise *Future Developments in Germany and Possible Sources of Future German Leadership as Viewed by a German-Norwegian Journalist* that is promptly forwarded to the U.S. Legation.

"If one shrinks back from these consequences, one endangers democratic improvements. One of the first demands will be to confiscate the estates of the 'Junkers.' These will either be divided or transferred to the Labor Unions."

One can readily picture the surprise on the face of the State Department official at Brandt's extraordinary concept of "democratic" improvements, as he reads on.

"Heavy industry and finance are also responsible for the war. The indispensable purge will leave many factories ownerless. If one wants to break the influence of German pro-war monopoly capital, one has to put the cartels and financial institutions in official hands. A guaranteed democratic control of industry also gives one of the most essential foundations for a real demilitarization of Germany."

In his memorandum *Forces of the German Revolution,* it becomes quite clear that the connotation Brandt attaches to the term democracy is derived strictly from socialistic criteria. In this piece, he suggests that the estates be "administered collectively." Since heavy industry and high finance are partially responsible for nazism, their power has to be broken by the collectivization of "cartels, et cetera." In Nazi-owned factories, the workers will take over the management.

A position in favor of the transfer of the raw materials industry, public utilities, coal and chemicals to public ownership—either national or municipal—runs as a leitmotiv through Brandt's theorizations, although the socialization of all industry is not a point of discussion. On the other hand, democratization from below is to be achieved by the establishment of work councils, while the National Parliament is supposed to have the final decision in all broad economic-political questions. Cooperative control of industry will be the natural consequence of a serious anti-Nazi movement and an essential condition for disarmament and the reconstruction of Europe.

While approving of unilateral German disarmament in principle, the author nevertheless is doubtful whether such unilateral steps present a solution in the long run. The idea of industrial dismantling is repeatedly rejected on pragmatic grounds. In an appeal to the self-interest of the victorious nations, he argues that the dismantling of heavy industry, chemical and electrical plants would lead to an economic ruin in Germany that would benefit nobody.

All "executives, judges and police [of the Nazi era] will be banished, imprisoned or killed." Brandt's tolerance at age thirty-one is certainly not that of the future peace chancellor. "Nazi criminals must be ruthlessly exterminated and all public institutions purged, SS-men, Gestapo et cetera, interned and put to hard labor."

Together with "radical social reforms" he demands a "new order" created by "naturally reliable men." Such leaders can only be found in the laboring classes, which have never cooperated with the Nazis. In the factories, these leaders "could form the basis for democratic trade unions." They would replace Hitler's "Work Front." Some of the new democratic leadership, however, could be recruited from intellectuals and working-class youth who have grown up under the influence of their working-class parents.

Brandt is certain that the rebuilding of a new German democracy will not be achieved by the conservatives or the bourgeois parties who collaborated with Hitler. In order to disqualify the bourgeois elements from participating in a future democratic society, Brandt levels the absurd charge that some of them "advocate a restoration of a monarchy." One wonders how the author obtained such inaccurate intelligence. Had his knowledge of the German scene not been secondhand, preposterous historical distortions of this kind would be hard to forgive.

Presumably, a dearth of intelligent and informed labor leaders is to be expected. Therefore, the returning emigrants will play a large part in the labor movement, Brandt suggests in *Forces of the German Revolution.*

Historians will be delighted by the comments of Mr. Johnson in Dispatch No. 3142, dated April 11, 1944. "It must be remembered that this judgment is expressed by an emigrant, but one who is not expecting to return to Germany, so far as the Legation knows," Mr. Johnson observed. Happy to have found such an unbiased source of counseling, he passes on Brandt's advice that the American government should look into the matter of establishing "close and friendly relations with emigrant German labor leaders."

From Mr. Johnson's continuous comments about Brandt and his ideas, one can readily detect a fairly good rapport between the American officials and the German-Norwegian. It is without doubt this secret and, up to the release of the State Department's top secret records to the public in 1974, carefully hidden relationship that nurtured later, never subsiding rumors about Brandt's American connection. One could hear it in the 1950s and one can hear it now in Germany: Brandt was brought to Berlin by the Americans, was installed as the city's mayor by grace of the CIA, and was propelled into the chancellor's chair compliments of Washington.

It was not until Watergate changed the public's attitude toward secret operations conducted at home, in Allende's Chile and elsewhere around the world in the name of national security, that the opprobrious atmosphere surrounding the touch-me-not intelligence agency was lanced by an overdue airing. In the course of the ensuing investigations before and after Richard Nixon's fall, the *New Republic,* the *Wall Street Journal,* and other highly respected publications have boldly printed what Victor Marchetti, former executive assistant to the deputy director of the publicity-shy CIA, was forced by court order to delete from his controversial book, *The CIA and the Cult of Intelligence,* the statement that Willy Brandt belonged to the collection of European politicians who in the parlance of the international espionage trade are referred to as agents of influence.

In his column of May 5, 1974 Jack Anderson managed to fill in some of the blanks "with the help of our own CIA sources." The Victor Marchetti-John Marks manuscript, he wrote, "also contains some big names, among them that of West Germany's Chancellor Willy Brandt. Like many other world leaders, he received money from the CIA when he was an aspiring young politician. At a White House state dinner for Brandt in 1971, the high and mighty were puzzled about one nondescript guest whom no one recognized. The manuscript originally identified the mystery man as Brandt's old CIA contact, whom the chancellor had asked the White House to invite for sentimental reasons. The CIA got this reference censored out of the book, ostensibly to spare Brandt's sensibilities."

Marchetti, who had been assigned to West Germany during the fifties, had gleaned this piece of "news," which was not exactly news, from his contacts as well as from the records the CIA accumulates. Until Marchetti quit the CIA, the superthick dossiers on Willy

Brandt and his nemesis Günter Guillaume were fully accessible to him.

During the broadcast "The Fifth Estate," aired by the Canadian Broadcasting Company in 1974, former National Security Agency intelligence officer Winslow Peck stressed the fact that the CIA preferred funding non-communist leftist parties and politicians in Europe and everywhere else to fight the Communists because "they were thought to have a broader appeal to mankind." Naming Henri Spaak and Henri Frenay, the Belgian and French socialist leaders as recipients of CIA support, Peck also pointed to leaders of the CDU. Marchetti, a panel member of the program, concurred: "They [the CIA] did this for many politicians in West Germany at the time — Social Democrats, Christian Democrats. They did this for similar politicians in Italy and France. This was the cold war and they were trying to support reasonable candidates who could cope with the then strong drift towards communism in these areas. Willy Brandt to my knowledge never made a profit in a direct sense out of this sort of an activity. . . . Well, ultimately he has risen to a very high position and the CIA's connection with him, I guess, as a clandestine thing, ceases to exist. He now has overt connections with the United States government . . ."

As expected, CIA officials kept mum. "Marchetti has a bad memory," one of them ventured to say. But before I had a chance to remind him that the CIA's memory was less than perfect, he retracted that statement as if by habit. "It is not for us to confirm or deny. In our business a confirmation can be a denial and a denial can amount to a confirmation." If the pipe-smoking agent from Langley, Virginia, meant to sound like the oracle of Delphi, he had certainly succeeded.

"Just one clue, for what it's worth," he offered as I turned to make my exit. "If a person once worked for or with the CIA, then it is most likely that he still does. The CIA is not in the habit of letting its collaborators out of sight."

Democratic revolution

In the illuminating pamphlet, *Concerning the Post-War Policies of the German Socialists,* a collaboration with Irmgard Enderle, the sole function ascribed to the generals and the Wehrmacht is the signing of the armistice conditions and the acknowledgement of their defeat. The authors reiterate that from the truly middle-class groups no replenishment of "dependable and consistent leadership of a democratic movement" can be expected. Middle-class youth has to be thoroughly reeducated.

Even though the opposition of the church reflects firstly the discontent among country people and the middle class, "its important part in the revolution" is assumed by the authors. A differentiation in the churchly strata is necessary in view of the great number of Catholic priests who actively cooperated with the Nazis. Also, mindful of the Bishops' Conference in Fulda in the summer of 1940, when the faction that supported Nazi war policy was victorious, the authors display considerable skepticism about the full support of the Protestant church.

In the chapter entitled "The Course for the Democratic Revolution," the two Socialists reveal themselves as skilled practitioners of *Realpolitik.* In their opinion, the new government cannot be formed "on the basis of a purely socialistic program." To be accepted by the moderate elements in Germany it will have to embrace a "wider and less radical set of aims." The post-Hitler regime will have to fulfill four points to smooth the way for the new order.

Firstly, it must "root out the Nazi criminals," lock, stock and barrel. Secondly, an immediate restoration of all basic democratic rights has to be implemented. Freedom of thought, religion, organization and of the press and the "worth of the individual" must be reestablished as the basis of a new democracy.

Thirdly, the pressing social and economic needs and problems have to be addressed. Bread, work and shelter for the population are more important in that context than ideological arguments concerning the question of "complete socialization or free initiative" and competition. In *Forces of the German Revolution,* however, Brandt clearly envisions a planned economy from the very beginning. He thinks it essential that its "administration is in the hands of reliable people" and satisfactory democratic controls are established. In his view, the "cooperative production and distribution agencies must play an important part."

Lastly, one of the main tasks will be the democratization of public administration and the legal and educational systems on every level, along with the restoration of local self-government. Cultural and administrative decentralization "must be coordinated with increased centralization in the economic sphere."

In all these overlapping writings, Brandt rejects the idea of a government based entirely on labor unions or a free and united trade union movement. Instead, a political coalition with the staunchly anti-Nazi Social Democrats, who "have not let themselves be cajoled or forced into collaboration with Hitler," seems to be preferred. Not surprisingly, Brandt's old dream of a unity party is as alive and well as ever. Provided the German Communists are willing to abandon their concept of class warfare and the "dictatorship of the proletariat" dictum, the unification of all progressive elements, Socialists, Democrats, Communists, and other leftist groups into one single "United Socialist Party," based on a democratic socialist platform, is advocated as feasible and an assured way to overthrow the last vestiges of fascism. Brandt clearly recognizes that the creation of free parties and free organizations will have to take precedence over parliamentary elections.

Interestingly, Brandt and Enderle hold "the narrow-minded policies of capitalistic self-interest" as responsible for the war as Hitler and his supporters. "We know that the war might have been avoided through the use of the principle of collective security and that the circles then ruling in England and France not only sacrificed Abyssinia, Spain, Austria, Czechoslovakia and, in part, China, and condemned the League of Nations to impotence, but also that they would not have been averse to a German expansion against the Soviet Union." For this reason, the authors are convinced that the success of Germany's development along democratic lines depends to a great extent on the attitude of foreign countries toward the German revolution and its foreign policy.

Commenting on Brandt and Enderle's chapter, "Considerations of Foreign Policy," Johnson finds in their exposition as much of an "attitude of repentence and admission of guilt and humble desire to make a new beginning" as could be expected from human beings, "particularly from Germans!" Only some points of the general outline for "radical" removal of the foundations for German imperialism, the rebuilding of Europe as a contribution to make good on Nazi crimes, and recreation of a new confidence in the peaceful character of the new government by working with the Allies "for a peaceful reconstruction of Europe" are specified in his dispatch.

The thesis that the new Germany cannot survive in a vacuum and therefore must collaborate with the rest of Europe in order to reshape its foreign relations is sometimes prophetic and other times pathetically hypothetical. While Brandt emphasizes that the time has come to minimize the importance of national boundaries in favor of international interdependence and "collective security," he is unable to foresee a conflict of interest resulting in a rift or a cold war period between the Soviet Union and the Western Allies after the war. In the interest of world peace and security, he recommends an uninterrupted continuation of the present working coalition among Great Britain, the Soviet Union and the United States. It is up to the new Germany to fit her foreign policy into this framework.

In view of Brandt's Ostpolitik, it must be recorded that his conversation with an American diplomat in September 1944 on the question of Germany's Eastern boundaries was prefaced by a singular statement about his lack of nationalistic feeling and sentimental attachment to any particular boundary. Did Brandt already envision a United Socialist Europe, neatly tied together by the collective security system the Soviet Union, he and Herbert Wehner had advocated all along? To be sure, in a united Europe of whatever stripe or color, considerations of boundaries would definitely not rate as prime questions.

Drawing the borders

In his report to Washington, Johnson merely stresses Brandt's fear of possible negative effects caused by an imposition of ethnically, economically and historically unacceptable borders between Poland and Germany. Continuing grievances, he believes, would play into the hands of "nationalist agitators." Brandt's overall policy for postwar foreign affairs impresses today's reader—conditioned to a partitioned Germany and the harsh lessons of Soviet *Realpolitik* learned in 1953 (the uprising of East German workers crushed with the use of Soviet tanks), 1956 (crushing the uprising of the Hungarians by the same means), 1961 (erection of the Berlin wall), and 1968 (crushing the uprising in Czechoslovakia following the thaw of the Prague Spring)—with its unabashed optimism.

Brandt sets forth the following goals: disarmament and the surrender of war criminals must be accepted; expedition of the repatriation of foreign workers and prisoners; participation in the rebuilding of Europe; the enactment of a peace policy that permits the creation of conditions under which Germany can be readmitted into the community of free nations. Given this foundation, "the other Germans" will have a chance to build the European Federation and to harness the spirit of nationalism and militarism so deeply ingrained in "German feeling."

All annexations of territory made by the Nazis must be renounced. This includes Alsace-Lorraine. Austria will become an independent country by decree of the three great powers but also because Nazi excesses have alienated even the Austrian Socialists from their former pan-German ideals.

Czechoslovakia must be restored to its pre-Munich borders. Wholesale transfer of the Sudeten Germans is not recommended by Brandt and Enderle because the supply of Nazis in Germany is more than adequate. The conversion of Germany into a democracy will not be easier if the country becomes a collecting place for Nazis and Quislings, the authors argue.

In the East, a continuous border is contemplated. The Corridor would presumably go to Germany along with Danzig and a small part of East Prussia. The eastern part of East Prussia, including Königsberg, would go to Poland. Danzig would be available to Poland as a seaport. The complete exchange of the population that is recommended in certain areas seems a reasonable suggestion in the U.S. Legation's opinion—especially since it comes from a German.

The writers are definitely not supporting the cession of Silesia or Pomerania to Poland. They advise against giving the whole of East Prussia, Danzig, and the Corridor to Poland because of the fear that such drastic measures would be unacceptable to most of the Germans and thus become the basis for future problems. In this connection, Brandt asserts that East Prussia does not constitute an economic necessity for Germany since its value as a granary was entirely dependent on high protective tariffs before the war.

The Socialist writers theorize blithely that Poland's future will not depend on military or border considerations but on its close cooperation with the Soviet Union and a democratic Germany. Such abstract expressions of Socialist idealism make one wonder if the international study group that met regularly in the remoteness of the building of the Swedish trade unions—far, far away from the reality of the passions, the fears, and the dying—was not just an incestuous intellectual exercise, a form of collective shadow boxing were it not for the echoes in Chancellor Brandt's reform and foreign politics.

Last, but indeed not least, it must be mentioned that Brandt and Enderle took a strong position against Vansittartism. Lord Robert Vansittart held that all Germans are basically Nazis and therefore irredeemable. Germany's power had to be utterly broken. Vansittart wanted a Germany of full warehouses and empty arsenals, a Germany occupied for seventy-five years and partitioned into smaller states.

Although Vansittartism may be directed against a militaristic and nationalistic Germany, the two Socialists charge it also aims to "prevent a Socialist German Republic." In another flight of Socialist fancy, the authors allege that the reactionary circles in the Rhineland and in Bavaria would be the most likely groups to foster separatist thinking in hope of curtailing the rise of socialism. They are honest enough to state that their intense disapproval of Vansittart's theories center mainly around the political measures prescribed to beat the working population into submission while sparing reactionaries and big capital. As far as splitting the country is concerned, they see in such action a great disservice to the economic reconstruction of Europe. At the same time, they fear any partition would serve to stimulate the quest for national unity and exacerbate not-so-latent nationalistic tendencies.

It would be an inexcusable omission to allow to go unrecorded the subtle mellowing in Brandt's thinking and vocabulary that occurred within the next decade and is generally looked upon as the maturing process of the firebrand activist into a responsive and responsible politician.

Some fifteen years later, when Lania restyles Brandt's recollections under the impact of the prevailing political climate in Adenauer's Federal Republic, the contemptible procapitalistic qualities of Vansittartism are all but forgotten. "We oppose it because it is, if consistently executed, nothing but Nazi race policy in reverse," Brandt-Lania remember in *My Road to Berlin* in 1960. At that particular transitional period, even the word socialism has a tendency to slip into oblivion. Like an old soldier, it fades away with the meritoriousness of anticapitalism and socialization.

When dealing with scandal-prone Willy Brandt, the assumption that the shadows of shocking events would eventually be cleared away by time's passing proves to be sheer folly. Stockholm's little Norwegian colony, tightly knitted in togetherness, had barely recovered from Brandt's brazen affair with the couple's pretty, flirtatious, sometime babysitter Rut Bergaust, when rumors of a different kind began to enliven the cocktail conversations once more.

New suspicions

A book exposing some of the ultrasensitive details of the background of the assassination plot against Hitler, *Misslyckad Revolt (The Plot That Failed),* had appeared on the market in 1944. Published anonymously in the form of "Ten letters from Berlin," it was feared to have inadvertently provided information about clandestine resistance activities to the Gestapo. The original letters were supposedly written by a prominent member of the resistance who had fled to Stockholm.

As a political writer, and one in touch with the German resistance moreover, Brandt was immediately suspected of being the editor. Brandt issued a vehement denial of the charges. According to Brandt's admirer Struve, the material was based on writings from several individuals, among them Fritz Tarnow and Willy Brandt, "who was involved in the writing of a few sections only." Not so friendly sources wanted to know of Brandt's visit with the participant of the July 20 plot, in a Stockholm hospital, where the refugee handed him the papers for safekeeping.

The vexing story was to haunt Brandt even after his return to Berlin. In a thoroughly underhanded attack, the East German Communist paper, *Neues Deutschland,* added a footnote of its own on February 5, 1950, with a brand new twist. Charging that the publication of the book was motivated by "sheer love of sensation and greed," the paper reports that the editor's identity was discovered by a Social Democratic functionary who came to Stockholm direct from Germany. In this version, the procedures against Brandt within the SPD, initiated by the functionary, were brought to a halt when Brandt objected to them on technical grounds: As a Norwegian citizen he could not be a member of the German Social Democrats.

So much for the stories, myths, defamations, accusations, the intriguing air of mystery—combined, all somehow contributed to building and enhancing the captivating Brandt mystique. Ironically, the scorn of the Communists and conservatives—often finding themselves in the same camp where the Brandt personality was concerned—transformed itself into one of the most prized of political assets: Brandt became the underdog.

The day Hitler committed suicide, May 1, 1945, Brandt was addressing the International Workers' Council and various groups of refugees at a mass meeting in Stockholm. He had been handed a note with the news before stepping up to the lectern. "When I announced it to the audience, a deep silence was the answer; no applause, no joyful shouts. It was as though the people could simply not believe that the end had actually come.

"And at the same time a question stood almost physically in the room: Hitler's dreadful challenge to all mankind—had it really ended this way?" The Brandt-Lania entry in *My Road to Berlin* may not impress the reader as immortal literature, but when seen from an historical vantage point, its grave impact is undeniable.

Despite the rapidly changed and changing political scene, Brandt's road to Berlin appears to be an excruciatingly slow and cumbersome one. Delayed by fateful circumstances, self-doubts, and intricate detours along uncertain, rocky paths rather than roads covered with the proverbial roses, he does not manage to reach the destination that became his destiny until a year and a half later—Christmas, 1946!

At thirty-three, Willy Brandt was not only a man with a past but one with a future. Seasoned in the art of survival and politicking by twelve years in exile, crammed with the widest range of experiences that would take a lifetime to acquire under normal existential circumstances, he was equipped for the fight to the top like nobody else.

The tough kid from Lübeck—double emigrant, Nazi fighter, revolutionary, provocateur, writer, womanizer, functionary, charmer, politician, tactician, opportunist and visionary—had prevailed against the world's vilest attacks in the end. There were times when Brandt, with seeming justification, felt invulnerable.

11

From Berlin to Bonn— The Bumpy Road to Success or: The Luck of Willy Brandt

With the *Götterdämmerung* of the Nazi "Thousand Year Reich," when Hitler chose "death to escape the disgrace of removal or surrender," an epoch had clearly come to an end—not only for destroyed Germany but also for raped and humbled Europe. It was now up to another generation to deal with what Hitler termed the "soulless" assaults of American capitalism and "inhuman" Russian bolshevism.

For Willy Brandt, the time of political apprenticeship was over. "The impulses of my radical youth had not been shaken. But much had grown on to them," he reflected decades later in *In Exile.* As his Norwegian friends returned to their homes from Stockholm, he was faced with the uneasy question of his own progress in life. Since there was no particular position waiting for him in Oslo, he restlessly shuttled back and forth to Stockholm all summer long. Rut was patiently waiting there. Besides, helping hands were always needed at the Swedish Red Cross, which had a part in the release of deported Danes and Norwegians from German concentration camps as well as the organization of a drive to provide CARE for starving Germans and vacations for the undernourished children of Berlin.

Just as Hitler was dead sure that Germany would survive "even me," Brandt had no doubt that it "will live on." In a letter to Ernst Winkler from Stockholm on August 23, 1945, he astutely assessed the German situation: "Apart from the senseless far-reaching frontier changes, the Potsdam agreement represents from a political view, an advance from the previous state of affairs."

In the same letter, his personal problem was briefly illuminated. Although he knew "I shall always feel bound to Norway by the closest ties," he had "never given up Germany." In another context he relates how his Norwegian passport was "more than just a useful travel document." He repeatedly comes to the conclusion that it would be easier to "remain in Norway." But he cannot "make up his mind to do this."

One can appreciate the conflict between loyalty to his mother country and loyalty to the country which gave him shelter and new impulses on politics and life and became his second homeland in the formative years between youth and manhood. These conflicting loyalties certainly played a role in shaping his cosmopolitan European outlook. "Someday a Europe in which Europeans can live together in harmony will surely become a reality," he emphasized. Seen in this personal frame of reference, Brandt's hopeful prognostication strikes one as more substantive than the usual phony politician's United Europe rhetoric.

If Brandt had learned anything in his extravagantly uneven existence, it was to roll with the punches. When no place opened up in politics or in Norway's newly formed coalition government of all parties, he accepted an editor's job with the *Arbeiderbladet.* This position enabled him and Rut to return to Oslo in September on a seemingly permanent basis. A job for Rut as secretary at the NAP and later on as clerk in the photo archive of its magazine, *Aktuell,* was quickly promoted. In October, Brandt was off on an assignment to Nuremberg to cover the war trials.

As usual, the energetic man made the best of a not altogether promising situation. In the process of accumulating the background material for his articles, he began preparations for a new book. *Criminals and Other Germans,* published in Stockholm in 1946, gave him a chance to distinguish between the theory of collective guilt of the Nazis and collective responsibility of the Germans and anti-Nazis. The thesis that all Germans must assume responsibility for Nazism because they "cannot escape the consequences of Nazi war and murder politics" did not make him popular in postwar Germany.

Postwar Germany must neither align herself with the Soviet Union nor with the Western powers, was Brandt's contention. In order to avoid tipping the balance of power in favor of one party, a friendly cooperation with "both east and west" is mandatory. The premise and essence of his future Ostpolitik was clearly foreshadowed in the following passage: "The Nazis sought to Germanize Europe after their fashion. Now the task is to Europeanize Germany. This cannot be done by partition or by playing one group of Germans off against another. The problem of Germany and Europe can be resolved only by a rapprochement between east and west—and the territories in between."

But Brandt did not spend all his time behind a typewriter. He travelled to Lübeck to see his mother. He visited with August and Irmgard Enderle in Bremen, and other emigrant friends. He stood aghast at the sight of the "surrealistic vision of the destroyed cities," and the psychological effects of "brown gangsterism" on the population. Reports of what happened in the concentration camps and occupied countries made his "flesh creep." He objected to the Soviets sitting in judgment at the international tribunal "pretending to represent the perfect constitutional state." He became aware that such "hypocrisy was grist for the mill of the cynics" who coldly remarked that the Nazi leaders "had not been executed because they started a criminal war but because they lost it."

Brandt, who showed up in Germany in a dashing Norwegian uniform, spent much of his time digging up old political contacts. After he returned from a short Christmas vacation spent in Copenhagen with Rut, he had his first meeting with Dr. Kurt Schumacher, head of the reestablished Social Democratic party, in January 1946 *(In Exile)* or in February *(My Road to Berlin).* Schumacher, who was occupied with the reorganization of the shattered party, had emerged from Hitler's concentration camps as the single most dynamic force in the reconstruction of the new democratic and socialistic Germany.

Seeking out Schumacher

Long before the mayor of Cologne with the name of Dr. Konrad Adenauer became a national figure, the crippled Schumacher was the acknowledged representative of the new national conscience. The politician, who had lost his right arm in World War I and his left leg later on, was dying alive. Those who knew him attested to the fact that his very existence was an act of sheer willpower and self-control.

To Brandt, the outsider, he may have symbolized the "suffering and sorely afflicted Germany," but to those who remained behind, Schumacher's case was an inspiring example of mind over matter.

Little is known of their first encounter in Frankfurt, except that Schumacher, bloodied survivor of twelve years of concentration camps, showed little interest in the young man who had taken the road to Norway and chosen to return in the role of a foreign observer instead of a participant in the work of reconstructing democracy. Brandt, in turn, was not overly appreciative of Schumacher's sterling qualities. He found him a "rather difficult person." His self-effacing asceticism impressed the robust and lusty Brandt, with his outspoken fondness for the ways of the world, as "fanatical," even "authoritarian."

It is obvious that Brandt had never met a man as uncompromising and independent as Schumacher in his life among the refugee politicians. In spite of the personality clash, he had to respect the man who dared to reject any compromise with the Communists. By thwarting the Communists' "united front" strategy, Schumacher had "barred their way to the West of Germany, and laid the foundation for their defeat in Berlin." Brandt leaves no one guessing about Schumacher's lack of popularity among the Allies. To the Russians, he was Enemy Number 1, for the Americans he was "too socialistic," and for the French, "too German." Schumacher's resolute refusal to be influenced by or to defer to the wishes of Washington, London or Paris in building his free Social Democratic party in a free democratic Germany was understood by Brandt as a shortcoming attributable to a dearth of foreign experience.

Brandt and Schumacher saw each other again in May 1946 during the SPD's first convention in Hanover. Attending the meeting as a reporter for the Norwegian Labor party press and as a guest delegate for German Social Democrats in Sweden and Norway, Brandt noted with some displeasure that the whole conference was dominated by Schumacher's personality.

At the historic gathering, the delegates from Berlin were the heroes of the day. Only the three Western zones were represented.

The delegates from the Soviet zone were missing because its SPD had been swallowed by the Communist party. Otto Grotewohl, SPD leader in the Soviet-occupied zone, opted for the unification of the two parties for fear that otherwise it would be forbidden by the Soviet authorities.

Schumacher was frantic. Using a British military plane, he flew to Berlin to avert the "united front" that Walter Ulbricht, German boss of the Soviet zone and Wilhelm Pieck, Unity Party leader and later President of the German Democratic Republic, promulgated on directives from Moscow. Together with a small group of Berlin's Social Democrats around Franz Neumann, a countermove was hurriedly initiated. The controversial merger would be decided by a plebiscite.

Ulbricht and Pieck were not eager for the popularity test. The plebiscite was cancelled shortly before elections in the Soviet sector. When the ballots were counted in a West Berlin occupied by the Western powers, it turned out that 82 percent of the party's membership had voted against SED, the Socialist Unity party.

When even the persuasive Schumacher did not succeed in convincing Grotewohl to rescind his consent to form the united front, the opposing group broke with him and constituted a new Social Democratic party in Berlin, still undivided at that time, under the stewardship of the crusty Franz Neumann, who had fought like a lion for the party's independence and a clear line of separation from the Communists. Like Schumacher, he felt that the idea of socialism had been perverted into a dehumanized and dedemocratized "formulistic state religion" by the Communists.

Brandt, who was of the opinion that German socialism should fight against capitalism and totalitarianism without engaging in a campaign against the Soviet Union or any form of "aggressive antibolshevism," never shared Schumacher's uncompromising position, which bordered on outright hatred toward Stalinist communism. Schumacher was well aware of that. From the gossipy emigré circles he and his party's leadership knew that Brandt had previously supported the idea of a unified Socialist party. He had read Brandt's critical comment on his own position: "But flexibility is perhaps not his [Schumacher's] forte. His orientation in foreign affairs seems to be rather one-sided. His attitude in regard to the unity question appeared negative."

Besides, Brandt's visits with his former SAP mentor Jacob

Walcher, a strong proponent of the Unity Party who had cast his lot with East Berlin and the Communists, seemed to confirm suspicions that he was still secretly espousing the same ideas.

In fact, Brandt had to wait well over a year before Schumacher could overcome his profound aversion to the young man with so inconsistent a past. Actually, Schumacher was never able completely to dismiss his apprehensions in Brandt's case. Brandt's idea of working with the Communists and winning them over appealed as little to Schumacher as Brandt's inclination to close an eye when it came to an examination of the developments inside Stalinist Russia.

The resolute Schumacher was much too upright and firm where moral standards were concerned to appreciate tactical considerations such as this: "Also in judging the development in countries within the Russian sphere of influence I should be inclined to give central importance to the historical and social background of present events. . . ." Brandt's statement in a letter to Schumacher must have sounded like the worst of political doubletalk to this paragon of straightforwardness and decency, who proclaimed precisely the contrary at the party's first convention: "There is no primacy for tactics. One cannot change society with small maneuvers and cleverness."

Schumacher had won the first and perhaps most decisive battle for the future of Berlin.

In a later analysis, Brandt was to conclude that the unification with the "Social Democrats would have made it much easier to incorporate the city into the Soviet zone, and most probably the 'Anschluss' would have been an immediate consequence." Even if the Western powers were not cognizant of the implications of this fight, as Brandt intimates, the Social Democrats had held the bastion called West Berlin that was to become the embattled symbol of freedom and democracy.

Brandt was anxious to go there, where the action was. So while reluctant Schumacher kept his reserve, Brandt did not remain idle. He saw Erich Ollenhauer, back from exile in London to assume the SPD's vice-chairmanship; he visited with Annedore Leber, widow of the executed Julius Leber; he met Herbert Wehner in the office of the Social Democrat paper *Hamburger Echo.* He talked to Fritz Heine, in charge of the party's press relations, who advised him to seek a position with one of the news agencies in the American or British zone because, in the party's view, "this would be a useful field of work" for him. Reportedly, after a speech in Lübeck, Brandt turned down an encouraging offer from Schleswig-Holstein's prime minister to become mayor of his hometown, because he found it "too restricting."

A Norwegian diplomat

Berlin faded clear out of reach during that summer with Rut in "the most beautiful spots in Norway." It was still out of sight in the autumn, spent crisscrossing the dilapidated German countryside with mounting concern over his career as the Nuremberg Tribunal closed its files and its doors, and the arguments about its moral significance died down. Whatever mental agonies Brandt suffered during this most painful waiting period, luck was just around the corner. It swept away an onset of depression, a psychological condition that was to plague him all his life and become the root of what was commonly known as his drinking problem.

Halvard Lange, Norway's foreign minister and Brandt's friend from the days of the resistance, had come up with a tailor-made job: a one year term as a diplomat with a special assignment at the newly established military mission in Berlin. As *In Exile* reports, somebody was needed "to keep an eye on the way the east-west problem was developing there." By January 1947, Brandt was installed as temporary press attaché with the rank of major and the task of reporting on "political matters." It was a delicate assignment and a perfect vantage point for evaluating and coming to grips with the political situation and its possibilities. As one of the Allies, he moved unencumbered between the missions of the Western powers and the Communists in East Berlin. Jacob Walcher, for one, was not beyond luring Brandt to follow his path with promises of "high offices" in the SED, the Socialist Unity Party of East Germany.

Before the year was over, Brandt's decision was made. His lobbying exercises with various leaders of the SPD had resulted in softening Schumacher's attitude. In Berlin, the well-trusted Kurt Mattick, influential member of the city's SPD executive committee, put in a good word for him, even though Berlin's party chairman, Franz Neumann, a simple man with all the attributes of a diamond in the rough, instinctively rejected the aggressive, dandified intruder in Norwegian uniform. It is hard to imagine that the courageous party leader, celebrated as the "storm bell of freedom" among Social Democrats and Berliners, actually sensed a deadly political rival in the unknown Brandt at that time. It seems more likely that the older Neumann, proud of his working-class background as a mechanic like his friend Kurt Mattick, and behaving, speaking, thinking and living like the workers he represented, resented this newcomer because of his cosmopolitan airs.

Brandt's willingness to give up a cushy diplomatic career for the uncertainties of politics and the personal risks connected with a position in demolished Berlin, barely held together by the thin legalistic thread in the hands of the four powers, had not failed to impress Mattick and a number of other functionaries. After he and Rut, by now a widow and through the good offices of press attaché Jens Schive employed at the Norwegian mission as well, had attended the second postwar party convention in Berlin, the majority of the key functionaries decided that the energetic young Brandt was precisely what the party needed: an infusion of new blood.

It was not until autumn that the SPD leadership came around with an offer. Contrary to friendly biographers' legends, Brandt was sent to Berlin not as the SPD's or Schumacher's "special representative," but as office manager for Berlin's SPD executive board. Among the duties of this assignment was liaison between Berlin's SPD headquarters and the Allies stationed in Berlin. The cultivation of contacts with the Allies was a task that did not differ substantially from his previous activities executed under the Norwegian banner.

The position, vacated by Erich Brost who eventually went to the Ruhr to start the successful *Westdeutsche Allgemeine Zeitung,* Germany's biggest newspaper today with 700,000 subscribers, was difficult to fill for another reason. As tensions with the Communist regime in the Soviet-occupied zone mounted, the assignment took on a precarious activist aspect that had to be handled with the utmost delicacy because of its close collaboration with the SPD's so-called *Ostbüro.*

This "East Office," then headed by Stefan Thomas, was the party's intelligence gathering bureau. While its confidence men collected information in the Soviet zone—later on, throughout Eastern Europe—they also smuggled illegal material from the West into the zone where it was distributed among the remaining Social Democrats. The Communists regarded this whole operation as an outrageous attempt of political provocation if not sabotage; they trapped and imprisoned the participants as regular agents. When Willy Brandt, with his experience in covert activities, was chosen for the party's liaison work in Berlin, he soon rated as the favorite target of their most venomous attacks.

The charge that the *Ostbüro* was generously supported by the CIA and that the American agency benefitted from its intelligence work did not necessarily originate in the East. The controversial "office," later on disclaimed by its own party in a legal sense, folded its tent shortly after a fire broke out in the wing of the SPD's Bonn headquarters, destroying most of the records that were stored. Alert observers noticed that the timing, 1966, coincided with the dawn of the détente and Brandt's rise to foreign minister.

Once more a German

Just as Brandt sat down in November 1946 to explain his decision to join the Norwegian military mission to his German friends, who might find it "odd that I am going to Berlin as one of the Allies," he faced a similar task in February 1948. This time he meant to justify his new switch to his Norwegian friends, among them Foreign Minister Lange, who were assured that "it was not easy for me to make up my mind." As he had soothed the feelings of his German friends before: "my personal attitude toward the German Socialist movement is the same," he placated his Norwegian benefactor: "No artificial lines of demarcation can prevent me from feeling that I am part of Norway."

In his letter of resignation he confirmed the rumor that all was not as well as it should have been. Brandt assured Lange that on his part "there is no hint of bitterness." Brandt's diplomatic appointment had been the subject of savage attacks in the Norwegian press. That an ex-German was sent to Berlin to inform the Norwegian press and the Norwegian foreign ministry about German affairs offended a number of citizens who wanted to know if the position had been publicly posted and why Brandt was selected over Norwegian-born candidates.

When the newspaper of the Farmers' Party, *Nationen,* learned that this was the same leftist Brandt who had written unkind comments about Norway's conservative farm population in one of his books, the appointment became a volatile political issue. Notwithstanding Jens Schive's gallant defense of his "temporary" colleague's great services to the Norwegian nation, insiders maintain Brandt's resignation came just in time to spare the foreign ministry further embarrassment.

No matter what so-called informed sources said, Brandt's decision in favor of Germany and German politics was as much a conscious one as one out of conscience. Had he wanted to remain in the diplomatic circuit, he only needed to have accepted Professor Myrdal's offer of an opportunity to go to Geneva as "public relations man" for the United Nations Economic commission. Work for the UN had been on Brandt's mind from time to time.

Basically Brandt was an activist. The job at the SPD's Berlin headquarters afforded him that unique, long awaited opportunity. "After many years of preparation and commentary from the sidelines, I long for active involvement," he wrote to Schumacher in December 1947. "It would be all the easier for me to take over responsible work for the party, as I am aware of your programmatic demand for a rejuvenated German Social Democratic party. Tradition means a great deal. But respect for what has been handed down should never go so far that the errors and mistakes of the past are not admitted. How else can the party grow from within?" Brandt had firmly expressed his credo. Further up on the rungs of the political ladder he called it "living democracy."

In preparation for the new job—he was convinced he entered a "decisive phase in his life"—he was busily putting his own house in order. In January 1948 he asked Carlota for a divorce. On the advice of Schumacher, he regains his German citizenship in Schleswig-Holstein and makes application for an official change of name from Frahm to Brandt, which is granted by Berlin's chief of police. In due course, he marries vivacious Rut and looks forward to becoming a father for the second time.

Known as a bohemian in his political circles, he is determined to eradicate that image by ardently embracing a bourgeois lifestyle. To rid himself of the ambiguities of a disorderly past, he covets respectability and all the existential trimmings that enhance his mental picture of a rising politician and solid German citizen. He had firmly resolved that from now on his life would be an open book—if possible.

Brandt was thirty-four years old when he started his new life among the compatible Berliners. In experience he was twice that age.

When he unequivocally declared that he would stand by the principle of democratic socialism and his party's policies, he put envious exile gossips on notice that he was ready to fight back—and fight hard. "I am no longer in the mood to take it calmly when one spits in my face," he wrote Schumacher in answer to the partly open, partly hidden "insinuations" that he was "not quite trustworthy."

The couple had scarcely settled down, Brandt had barely become acquainted with the duties of his new job, when the Communists, backed by the Soviets, struck out in Czechoslovakia. As Czech Foreign Minister Jan Masaryk jumped to his death from his apartment window, Communist party leader Klement Gottwald hoisted the Red flag on Wenceslaus Square. The test of strength between the concepts of Eastern and Western democracy had clearly been decided by February 1948 in favor of Premier Gottwald. After securing control of the coalition government, Gottwald forced a Communist takeover that was accompanied by one of the most ruthless purges in modern history.

The Communist coup in neighboring Czechoslovakia deeply shocked German leftists and liberals, including Brandt. In one of his first speeches at a SPD functionaries' meeting that March, Brandt draws rousing cheers with his tough stand against the encroachment of communism: "The result of Prague separates totalitarian communism from democratic socialism. For the Communists all those who will not capitulate unconditionally are regarded as enemies." It is Brandt's first official cold warrior speech and a prelude to what is commonly depicted by political observers as a "shift to the right."

Whatever might have remained of his secretly harbored illusions about a Popular Front was certainly shattered by the putsch in Prague. "Whoever joins the Communist United Front will perish of it," he warns, advocating national solidarity to prevent a second Prague and collaboration with the "other" Democrats. As a consequence, he prescribes for Berlin a coalition with Adenauer's conservative Christian Democrats as more than a "tactical" move.

For Brandt the internationalist, the events in Prague signaled an all-out alarm. Had the average Berliner not been so busy—with clearing away the mountains of rubble, finding shelter in the city where 60 percent of the houses were destroyed, growing potatoes and vegetables in ridiculous garden plots, trading his last earthly possessions for a pound of flour, coffee, butter or a can of Spam on the black market, where the currency was cartons of cigarets, preferably American; looking for lost relatives and jobs in a town where half the able-bodied population was still unemployed; optimistically hoping for a change and cracking their wry sophisticated jokes—there probably would have been a mass exit to the West, a development, by the way, that would have been heartily welcomed and encouraged by the Soviets. On the other hand, knowing something of the stamina and the indomitable spirit of the Berliners and their love for their city from having lived among them, it is more than conceivable that they would just as soon have stayed on for the hell of it, and to show the world that Berliners will not be pushed around.

BERLIN BLOCKADE

As it was, however, the Berliners were far too preoccupied with staying alive to notice that the cold war had begun, and that Berlin —the most eastern outpost of the West—had become a frontier town. They should have known that the Western counteroffensive against Soviet advances in Europe was born when the "Truman Doctrine" to save Greece was proclaimed in March 1947, or when General Marshall proposed economic aid to Europe in his Harvard address that summer. But at that time, American strategy and tactics designed to halt sovietization as the balance of power was forcefully tilted were still in the process of taking shape and therefore recognizable only to the pros. From a Communist point of view, psychologically drained, strategically indefensible and politically vulnerable Berlin, ruled by an extremely malfunctioning Four Power occupation administration, must have looked like an easy conquest. Judging by the disputes in the *Kommandantura,* the Control Council, the Western powers were a pushover for the Soviets.

It was Ernst Reuter, rightfully elected mayor of Berlin in June 1947 but blocked by a Soviet veto because of his "anti-Soviet attitude," more likely, however, because of his defection from communism earlier in life, who anticipated and prepared the worn-out Berliners and easygoing Allies for the Communist onslaught on their city, a state of siege that made history as the Berlin blockade.

The Social Democrats had decided on a show of solidarity against the Communist Unity party when they staged a mass rally in front of the old burnt-out Reichstag building. Some 80,000 Berliners had assembled that cold, damp day of March 18 to stand up and be counted. "It was Prague's turn, Finland next, whose turn is it now?" Reuter questioned. "It will not be Berlin's turn. The Communist flood will break on our iron will. Then the nations of the world will know that they must not leave us in the lurch, and they certainly will not leave us in the lurch." The strong applause was more than an expression of acclamation. It was the spark that "kindled the will of resistance still glowing under the cold ashes of fright." Brandt's language became inspired by the moving event.

Neither the skeptical Reuter nor General Clay, the originator of the Berlin airlift, would have guessed that the tough endurance test was to last 322 days. When the blockade was finally lifted by the Soviets on May 12, 1949, more than two million tons of food, raw material, machinery, and even coal had been flown into the beleaguered city. At the peak of the operation, a plane landed every 63 seconds at its airports. The unloading crews managed to take off ten tons of freight within five to six minutes. In the battle for the freedom of Berlin, thirty-nine Englishmen, thirty-one Americans and nine Germans lost their lives.

The squeeze had started with the massive defeat of the Communists at the first postwar elections in October 1946. The Soviet Union, expecting to influence the political developments in Berlin under any given circumstances, resorted to exerting heavy pressure in its attempts to bend to its will every law, every decree or directive passed by the Municipal Assembly. It did not discourage Communist members of the council from hassling their non-Communist colleagues. In the Soviet sector, provocative acts, often resulting in illegal arrests and kidnappings, became frequent occurrences. Arbitrary road controls and delays were enacted from time to time to test the reaction of the Allies.

The already tense situation came to a boiling point when the three Western powers, the Americans, the English and the French, decided to unite their zones and institute the long overdue currency reform necessary to halt inflation and revitalize the German economy. The Soviets opposed both moves on the ground that they would revive German militarism and fascism. Their representative walked out of the meeting of the Control Council and declared the

Four Power administration of Berlin ended. Marshal Sokolovski decreed a currency reform for the Soviet zone and all Berlin. The whole city was supposed to be put under Soviet "protection."

The Western powers hurriedly invalidated this decree for their sectors. It was up to Ernst Reuter to convince the Allies that circulation of the Eastmark in Berlin amounts to an incorporation of the city into the Soviet orbit. When all railway traffic, highways and autobahns leading to the island that is West Berlin from West Germany and the Soviet zone are suddenly blocked on June 24, 1948, it happens under the pretext that some of the roads are impassable and a bridge near Magdeburg is under repair.

When the horrifying nightmare, that kept the whole world holding its breath as it saw itself suspended between war and peace, is over, Berlin is a divided city with two different currencies, two differing municipal assemblies, two mayors, two universities and a totally disrupted communications network. Its obvious heroes were the brave participants in the legendary airlift and the inventive General Lucius D. Clay. Yet even more important were the unsung heroes: the indestructible Berliners who, in total isolation, had suffered without complaint the hardships of a life without sufficient food, heat, electricity or jobs in exchange for political and personal freedom.

In the admirable qualities displayed by the steadfast Berliners during the blockade, Brandt discovered the very attributes he had come to praise in the Norwegians:

> It was, however, not the astonishing 'normality' of those months that impressed me most. It was the simple manner in which the Berliners demonstrated their allegiance to common basic values; their knowledge that they stood for each other and could rely on each other; the determination they manifested in the defense of justice and freedom of speech and press; their acceptance of individual responsibility. All that reminded me of the admirable resistance the Norwegians had offered nine years before to all attempts to break their will and their spirit. As I felt then that Norway had never been greater than in the time of its hardest distress—just so I experienced now the real greatness of Berlin.

REUTER'S MAN

The single most potent force among the powers of the resistance was the man with the black beret, Ernst Reuter. He had been acting mayor of Berlin from 1947 until his death in 1953—part of the time, when the Soviets rejected him, in the role of assistant to the officiating mayor, Louise Schroeder. The former SPD Reichstag representative and Mayor of Magdeburg had returned from exile in Turkey to the city he had served long ago as Counsellor for Transport Workers.

A professor of political science in Ankara during the Hitler years, he had specialized in municipal administration. He chose Berlin as the town to come home to because of his profound admiration of its people whom he found "remarkably thrilling, more open-minded than anywhere in Germany." He was elected city councillor and put in charge of the departments of transport and utilities. His energy in dealing with the tremendous workload, his patience in untangling bureaucratic thickets, his persuasive powers and his big-heartedness have become part of the legendary components echoed in the special vibrancy that is Berlin.

Brandt had met this extraordinary man at Annedore Leber's house and immediately sensed a kindred spirit in the fellow emigrant who looked "beyond the frontiers of his own country." Like Brandt, the popular Reuter, twenty-four years his senior, regarded the tasks of reconstruction as an intermediate step toward the ultimate objective of German social democracy: a United Europe. Reuter had been in the leftist camp before he changed into a fervent anti-Stalinist. Brandt, no doubt, felt an immediate affinity for the man who had given a brief performance as general secretary of the German Communist party in 1920–21. Not only did he see in him a comrade who would understand his own radical past but the "prototype of a humanist" whose goal was the abolition of conditions that "infringe upon human right and dignity." His aim was to create better living conditions for all. Most importantly, he was not striving for the well-cared-for robot but for the "free man, conscious of his dignity and his rights."

One of the facts that cannot be overlooked in the relationship between Brandt and Reuter is their position as outsiders in the cliquish functionaries' circles of their own party. Brandt, who was tolerated rather than welcomed by Franz Neumann in Berlin and Dr. Schumacher in Hanover, was accepted by the imposing Ernst Reuter. By building a case of the great contrasts between the Schumacher and Reuter personalities, Brandt identifies himself with the latter as the "comrade of the seekers and strugglers". They came from "completely different social environments, but we did not only have the same aim, we travelled the same road, for we had the same stars by which we steered our course."

Brandt's critics see it differently, of course. They are agreed that he hitched his off-the-track wagon to the star that was Reuter when he became Reuter's "young man." There was much to learn from this independent spirit, whose frankness and determination had played a decisive part in General Clay's recommendation to support the offer of resistance that safeguarded Berlin's survival.

Ten years later, at the "airlift thanks" memorial for the victims of the airlift, Berlin's mayor Willy Brandt raises an intriguing question in the presence of General Clay, Lord Atlee, and French Foreign Minister Robert Schuman. Was it really wise not to have seized the advantage after the suspension of the blockade? Should not the advanced position of the Soviets have been pushed back, thereby solving the German problem, instead of allowing them to consolidate their holdings in Central Europe? The unforgotten Ernst Reuter, "soul of the resistance," had asked these very questions.

A strong proponent of a political offensive, Reuter thought nothing of people who made their peace with the Hitlers of the world. It was certainly no coincidence most of the Berliners believed, that the signing of the NATO pact in April 1949, twelve Western nations manifesting the will to defend themselves, was instrumental in putting an end to the blockade.

After the Federal Republic of Germany was born in the West, holding its first national elections, and the German Democratic Republic was proclaimed in the East, Brandt's liaison work in West Berlin began to look like a dead-end road. No matter how sharply Reuter attacked the decision to make Bonn the federal capital, the Allies moved on to the Rhine. "If I were chancellor, I'd go to Berlin and set up the Federal government there," Reuter criticized Konrad Adenauer's preoccupation with his Western concept. "The Russians won't go to war over that," Reuter insisted and Brandt could not agree with him more. Both suspected that Rhineland-born Adenauer was not sufficiently interested in the restoration of Germany's unity or in forcing the incorporation of West Berlin into the Federal Republic as its twelfth state. By virtue of the Four Power Agreement on Berlin, West Berlin eventually acquired additional stability in the course of détente with guarantees for preservation and development of its ties to the Federal Republic which represents it abroad.

Although Brandt found himself mostly in agreement with Reuter's ideas, which fundamentally corresponded with those of Schumacher, his relationships with the party's chief and his faithful comrade in arms, Franz Neumann, were as remote as ever. Brandt began to feel trapped in Berlin and overshadowed by the party's two independent figures. While Schumacher and Reuter saw eye to eye on the necessity for abandoning the party's traditional concept of class warfare for conditional approval of national defense in place of "unrealistic pacifism," and a new Germany as a part of Europe, participating in European cooperation with the goal of an economic union instead of an isolated or nationalist nation-state, they had their differences.

In his determination to equip Germany's new constitution, the Basic Law, with as many Social Democratic safeguards as possible to prevent another breakdown similar to that of the Weimar Republic with its catastrophic consequences, Schumacher did not worry about delaying the formation of the new German Republic. In Reuter's opinion, on the other hand, the rebirth of the nation had priority over constitutional matters, because cutoff Berlin was in danger of being lost without the backing of a West German government.

Divergent assessments existed in regard to the Berlin situation. Whereas Reuter insisted on close legal and political ties between the SPD-dominated city and Adenauer's conservative government in Bonn, Schumacher and Neumann were inclined to favor an independent Berlin that was not bound to abide by the laws enacted in Bonn against the will and the votes of the Social Democrats.

There were people around Schumacher who thought Reuter much too independent. He would travel to London or to Paris on invitation of French Foreign Minister Robert Schuman, and even to the United States, without officially consulting party headquarters or informing it of the results. Schumacher might not always have relished the idea of his "prefect of Berlin," recommended by him to Berlin's SPD for the mayor's job, engaging in making his brand of foreign policy.

Admitting to occasional differences of opinion, Annemarie Renger, president of the Bundestag and long-time personal assistant to Schumacher, nevertheless insists that there was no ill feeling between these two remarkable men. "It is time to finally set an end to another legend, which is cultivated to the detriment of the party and its history, namely, the alleged rivalry between Kurt Schumacher and Ernst Reuter," she asserted in *Vorwärts* in September, 1973.

Watching the bitter physical and mental frustrations suffered by the immobile, crippled party leader, Neumann, a giant of a man of great physical strength, sentenced for high treason by the Nazis and, like Schumacher, experienced in the ordeal of imprisonment, made an unfailing display of loyalty his foremost task. Needless to say, his well-intentioned intercessions only sharpened the situation. Loyal Neumann, who was lacking in diplomatic finesse, quite undeservedly came to be known as Schumacher's watchdog.

As time went on, Brandt's relationship to Schumacher and Neumann worsened, even though he had done a commendable job in his lobbying efforts with the Allies. "My relations with Schumacher were not as good as before. He had the impression that I, instead of representing the Executive, had become 'Reuter's man.' Plotters and schemers, to be found in every party organization, tried to create distrust between us."

My Road to Berlin was replete with paranoid outbursts of this kind. Wherever Brandt was, he imagined rivals busily plotting against him by ferreting out his past. In his defensive effort to trace the components of his life for public inspection in his memoirs, he inadvertently created new rumors by holding back and hoping to get by with deliberately selected parts of the story. Being a very private and perhaps even a very moralistic burgher underneath all the bravado and elbow-bending ambition, he became his own worst critic and judge. Because he could not quite come to terms with himself, he deduced that others could not do so either. What he forgot, obviously, was that others, seeing him as a human being and not superman, were ready to take into account any reasonable quantums of human frailty.

Brandt underestimated Schumacher's generosity. He was offered a safe district in Schleswig-Holstein in the next elections. It certainly was not Schumacher's fault that he was unaware of Brandt's burning ambition. Always mistrustful, Brandt believed Schumacher intended to sentence him to oblivion by relegating him to the provinces. The offer was turned down by Brandt expressly for the reason that he wanted to stay on in Berlin. A plausible enough explanation, except for the fact that he also turned down Reuter's offer of a position as head of the transport department in Berlin's municipal administration. Community work had no appeal for Brandt, even under Reuter's inspired guidance.

Once more the "plotters and schemers" had it all figured out when Brandt packed his suitcases and departed for Bonn's Bundestag as one of the eight representatives of Berlin's Assembly. For them, Brandt's decision indicated an extraordinarily clever move: Using famed and troubled Berlin as a base and issue, the politician meant to build up his own reputation in the national limelight of Bonn.

Whatever the gossips assumed, Brandt knew that his position in parliament could only be secured by a positive role in Berlin's local party politics. If he could not win Neumann's goodwill, he would have to oppose him. Shuttling back and forth from Berlin to Bonn offered the tremendous advantage of direct contacts with Kurt Schumacher and the party's most prominent national leaders. Neumann's mediating services, or disservices, would be circumvented.

At the same time, Brandt would be able to cultivate the grass roots voters and functionaries at the home base precincts of Berlin. Before long, he managed to be elected chairman of the party local in Wilmersdorf and to secure the editorship of the SPD paper, *Berliner Sozialdemokrat,* later known as *Berliner Stadtblatt,* which regularly carried his editorials until it folded in 1952.

Extended democracy

Very much on the sidelines in Berlin, Brandt tries to widen his narrow base by constantly looking for other outlets to expound his ideas on the principles of democratic socialism. The newly established CIA-funded magazine, *Der Monat,* is one of them. In the February 1949 issue, editor Melvin J. Lasky presents among the contributions of the distinguished Lionel Trilling, Arthur M. Schlesinger, Jr., George Orwell, Christopher Rand, Ernst Tillich, and historian Golo Mann a fascinating article by unknown Willy Brandt on "extended democracy," which anticipates, in many respects, the whole complex theorems of the party's reforms, adopted ten years later as the *Godesberg Program.*

Here we find Brandt's whole seductively enlightened socialist smorgasbord from workers' codetermination to the refutation of the traditional concept of a collectivist planned economy as a guarantee for the victory of liberal-democratic elements on the political level. The thoughtful author stresses that the rejection of the outmoded primitive model of totally planned economy, as practiced in the Soviet Union or the People's Democracies, does not signify concessions to capitalism—where in its pure form does it still exist?—but a new approach to a regulated free market economy.

Brandt points to the fact that even the conservatives accept certain economic guidelines and controls. In order to avert the imminent danger of bureaucratization, socialization of industry is preferred to nationalization. Coal, iron, steel, chemical plants and big banks are slated to be stripped of private ownership and its power to influence the destiny of the nation or, in this age of interdependence, possibly nations. They will become public property, either in the hands of the federal government, the states, communities, public corporations, social unions or co-ops. In the new order of democratic socialism, freedom must not be suffocated by bureaucratic or totalitarian planning schemes of any kind. Furthermore, the promised humanization of society must not turn into slavery in the service of the state.

Brandt closes his argument with a flourish that is as grand as it is pertinent today. "In our time, socialistic democracy constitutes the only viable alternative against totalitarian communism, which must not only be fought but overcome. Yet one can only overcome it if one makes it superfluous, and that means the elimination of the soil in which social insecurity and economic injustice prosper."

His harsh critique of traditional Marxist-Leninist socialism had two not entirely unforeseen side effects: as the Communist East German press used every invective against him as a traitor to the socialist cause—from capitalistic slave to infidel who had never represented the interests of the working class—his stock went up dramatically in the capitalist West German press, which celebrated him as a devoted Social Democrat of bourgeois dimensions. Both were mistaken. Brandt always had been and would be a socialist, one who understands socialism not as a finished system but a process that seeks to define itself according to the conditions of the times, taking into account social changes as well as scientific knowledge.

It cannot be stressed often enough that the wrath of the Communist East German press became priceless political capital for Brandt in the cold war days of West Berlin and even later on, because it furnished him with the kind of unsolicited, controversial publicity no public relations firm could invent or buy.

In May 1949, he had a chance to test his "constructive reformism" before the comrades during the Berlin party convention. Reuter, to whom the ideas sounded not unfamiliar, was visibly impressed. Brandt's voice sounded hoarse and rough. He talked slowly and calmly, like someone who is very sure of himself and therefore could afford to be deliberate in groping his way to the listeners' minds.

By 1950, Brandt is established as a member of Berlin's SPD executive committee. In the *Stadtblatt,* he takes issue with certain proposals voiced within the SPD for a neutralized Germany. Such a Germany would be welcome prey for Communist exploitation, Brandt editorializes angrily. As Berlin's representative in Bonn's Bundestag, he makes headlines in 1951 by taking Reuter's lead in rejecting the suggestion that Berlin be transformed into a UN enclave. Like Reuter, Brandt wants to establish strong links between the Federal Republic and West Berlin but not a neutrality resembling the principality of Monaco.

Heady with the success derived from securing federal economic assistance for impoverished Berlin, Brandt plunges recklessly into a premature campaign against Franz Neumann for Berlin's party chairmanship in 1952. Despite Neumann's resoundingly defeated effort to block a municipal coalition government supported by Reuter, "Reuter's man" did not stand a chance. Neumann's argument that the SPD must "keep its pure socialist profile" and was better off on the opposition benches than being caught up in compromises with the conservatives did not convince the party leadership but proved effective at the polls. The plainspoken, plainly dressed champion of the proletariat, who had Schumacher's full backing, won the election handsomely with 196 votes to the 93 garnered by his dashing opponent in the expensive tailor-made suit.

Brandt is crushed.

"The obstacles I had to overcome in the Berlin party organization were not small. They were indeed bigger than I had expected," he complains in his memoirs.

His hour had not yet come.

ON THE SIDELINES IN BONN

After the blockade, Berlin was no longer interesting to the world. Instead of becoming the capital of the new Germany, as Brandt had anticipated when he chose to settle in that city, Berlin was reduced to taking a backseat to Bonn. If Brandt had hoped to dazzle the Bundestag with his knowledge and insights into international affairs and sage advice on the conduct of foreign policy, he soon found out that he lacked an appropriate platform.

Just as in Berlin, Brandt found himself once again stuck on the sidelines in the "temporary" capital on the Rhine. The physical proximity to Schumacher had not helped their relationship. The party chairman's doors were no more open to him here than they had been before in Hanover. He quickly learned that the only chance of finding any kind of an audience was when the freedom of Berlin was at stake. As Brandt's friends and foes were to discover with varying degrees of surprise, "Reuter's young man" was not the kind of politician who was easily discouraged by adverse circumstances. As the obstacles piled up, his tenacity automatically grew.

Though his colleagues in the Bundestag paid little attention to the lonely figure, Willy's boyish grin was a warmly welcomed sight in Bonn's few bars. More restless and moody than ever because of increasing frustrations, Willy could not bear to spend his evenings in his rented room in the Hausdorffstrasse. Alone or in the company of various attractive females, he dived into Bonn's underdeveloped night life by making his bar hopping rounds. Had Willy been less ambitious, his chances of ending up as a playboy might have been excellent. As it was, he licked his wounds, cursed his fate in a hoarse, hardly audible voice, nervously lighted one cigaret with another, glared at his dishevelled reflection in the dimly lit bar mirrors with reddened eyes, and sought solace in Susanne Sievers' arms.

Luckily, he managed to spring back with renewed energy from these bouts of mental and physical paralysis, rooted in melancholy and its alcoholic remedies.

From the difficulties Reuter had encountered within his own party organization, uncompromisingly loyal to Neumann, Brandt knew his whole political future rested on a broad base of support among the SPD membership and functionaries in Berlin. Reuter hated party work and paid dearly for his negligence in terms of endless time- and energy-consuming confrontations with Neumann's loyalists. Brandt would not repeat that mistake.

Patiently, he embarked on a systematic program of visits to regular precinct and district meetings. He spared no effort in getting acquainted with the comrades through discussions, workshops, or chats over glasses of beer in local pubs. Stressing the strategic advantages of his own "reform" program in comparison with Neumann's dogmatic views, he smoothly edged up on his less vocal rival, whose stronghold on the party was considerably weakened after Dr. Kurt Schumacher's death in August 1952. When Brandt made his second move to unseat Chairman Neumann in the spring of 1954, he was defeated by only two votes and subsequently assumed the office of vice-chairman of the Berlin organization.

His substantial gains in Berlin were not yet reflected on the national political scene. Although he became a member of the executive committee of the SPD parliamentary group in 1953, he was defeated in his bid for a seat on the party's executive committee in 1954, when Neumann received 270 votes to Brandt's 155, and again in 1956.

Once more Brandt displayed tenacity and perseverance—his favorite words—in pursuing his goal. Where many another politician would have thrown in the towel, Brandt stubbornly went on. His clenched fists and his stereotype smile would betray only to insiders his immense anguish and inner turmoil which easily reached boiling point. His self-control was put to a severe test before he succeeded at long last in 1958, well after his election as Governing Mayor of Berlin.

Schumacher's death did not magically open the doors to the party's hierarchy for Brandt, but it did help remove those stubbornly maintained barriers that would have made his rise in the party leadership next to impossible. Schumacher's devastating criticism of Brandt, charging that he was neither heroic enough nor consistent enough a Social Democrat to be admitted to the party's leadership, lost some of its bite after his death. It was never quite forgotten, even after Brandt had undergone a period of adjustment.

When the Soviets tried to intervene in the establishment of a European Defense Community in 1952 with a seductive offer of talks about German reunification on the basis of armed neutrality, Brandt voiced regret that the offer was turned down by Adenauer's government without an attempt "to put the Russian sincerity to a test." It was the first, and in fact the last, time the Soviet Union had consented to discuss Bonn's precondition of free All-German elections without substantial preconditions of its own.

In his memoirs, Brandt suspected that there "was reason enough" for the Western powers to reject anything that might disturb their own plans. In the same context, he cited John Foster Dulles as being in full agreement with the Soviets as far as Germany's inclusion in alliances was concerned. "He, therefore, thought it quite possible that in the end the Russians might accept the military control of Germany in the framework of NATO," Brandt reported. Could Foster Dulles, the eminent pastmaster of "brinkmanship" really have been so naive? Or had Brandt misunderstood?

Looking back, Brandt came to the conclusion that any progress the SPD might have made by taking independent steps in the full depth exploration of the possibilities of reunification at the opportune moment following Stalin's death in March 1953 would have been wiped out automatically by the East German workers' historic uprising on June 17. In their fear of a collapse of the whole Eastern bloc now bereft of its supreme commander Stalin, the builder of Socialist society, the East German Communist leaders increased their vigilance against the enemy within and without. With the stepped-up pace of Bolshevization and purges of "deviationists," the number of refugees rose drastically. In 1951, some 165,000 East Germans sought refuge in the West. That was before the East German regime tried to stay the tide by the creation of the 35-foot-wide obstruction along the border, the heavily guarded "forbidden zone" or "death zone."

In spite of the fact that the border guards were issued shooting orders, the mass exit was in full swing in the spring of 1953. Fifty thousand East Germans fled in March alone! When the grumblings of the discontented population and the threats of the workers finally could no longer be ignored, some of the more repressive measures were eased by the proclamation on June 9 of the "New Course" by orders of the Soviet Ambassador Extraordinary and Plenipotentiary, Vladimir Semyonov.

Not lifted, however, was the most unpopular decree: the 10 percent rise in work norms ordered on May 14 which substantially reduced the workers' living standard.

The New Course backfired. Instead of being grateful for the

concessions, the incensed population regarded them as a sign of weakness. The open protest started on June 16 with a demonstration by the construction workers of Berlin, who had been extremely critical of the SED's antistrike trade union policy. Chairman Ulbricht hoped to be able to localize the disturbance within that union, but he hoped in vain. The next day, isolated strikes and general unrest among the workers escalated into a mass revolt of such dimensions that it could only be squelched by Soviet tanks.

The news of the Berlin riots spread like lightning. Riots, demonstrations and strikes broke out simultaneously in 272 towns throughout the country. Even the party's red-faced officials admitted that more than 300,000 workers participated in the grand-scale rebellion. It was a conservative estimate.

Brandt's observations on the twofold character of the rebellion as a "yearning for national freedom" and "social liberation" are not notable because of their profundity. Rather, they serve to illuminate his ever hardening anti-Communist posture during the 1950s and early 1960s. "The workers—and they were in the vanguard and the body of the insurgents—rebelled against a system that had disguised slavery under the shabby cloak of an abused, so-called 'socialism'." Brandt argued correctly that the "unmasking of communism as the enemy of the weak, of the helpless, of the workers, whose advocate and guardian it always had claimed to be, had consequences which no countermeasures of the Kremlin could undo." As the examples of the Hungarian uprising in 1956 and the "Prague spring" of 1968 demonstrated, Brandt was too optimistic insofar as the influence of the riots on the "political development" in the countries under Soviet rule was concerned.

Curiously, he shrinks from applying the term "unsuccessful" to the uprising, despite its meager results: slightly reduced work norms; facilitated travel between East and West Germany, eventually revoked by an "inhuman passport law."

The event stimulates Brandt to a Bundestag address focussing on the "fight for unity." He insists that the struggle for German reunification in freedom must take precedence over all plans in foreign affairs because the eighteen million people in the Soviet zone cannot "wait till doomsday" for Western action. He severely criticizes the democracies for not seizing the "opportunity of June 17 to put political pressures on the Soviet Union."

The charge that the revolutionaries had understood the attitude of the Western powers and Adenauer's "policy of strength" as a promise for military assistance was heard again during the Hungarian rebellion. Brandt feels bitterly disappointed that the Allies had not made use of their chance for "serious negotiations" with the Soviets during the crisis following Stalin's death. Instead of strengthening the position of the West and lightening "the burden of the suppressed people in the East of Germany," they "seemed primarily determined to prove that they were in no way responsible for the East German rebellion," he records in his memoirs. Why the author fails to refer with a single syllable to the repetition of the Soviet offer for a discussion of the German question of reunification, tendered August 15, 1953, two months after the workers' revolt, is highly puzzling.

Like the note of March 10, 1952, this "one provided for the calling of a peace conference, the formation of a provisional all-German government, the holding of free elections, and some relief of financial and economic obligations connected with war damage," Heinz Lippmann informs the readers of his biography of Erich Honecker, leader of East Germany's Communist party.

The announcement that hit East Berlin's party hierarchy "like a bombshell" is not recorded in the official outline of "the development of the Relations between the Federal Republic of Germany and the German Democratic Republic" either. A startling phenomenon, considering Lippmann's description of the panic the all-German election scare created among Ulbricht and his comrades. The Communist leadership felt abandoned, even betrayed by the Soviet Union and contemplated a fight to the finish in the event that West Germany should accept the Soviet proposal "and, if it comes to the worst, die like heroes."

"They'd be complete fools not to accept that kind of offer at this time," Lippmann quotes the East German head of the division of all-German affairs, Erich Glückauf. "They know what we're up against now, since June 17. If they don't jump at the opportunity, they're really beyond hope." The East German officials clearly counted on and hoped for Adenauer's refusal of the offer. The question remains however: Why did Brandt and his party neglect to make an issue of this offer? Why did they keep silent?

The passivity of the Western Allies irks activist Brandt as much as Adenauer's overwhelming victory in the following elections, in Brandt's opinion, entirely a result of the "economic miracle." For the

Socialist, the *Wirtschaftswunder,* achieved by "means of high prices and low wages," was an expression of the population's "materialistic egoism." Although the amassing of huge fortunes had admittedly created a climate of general prosperity that benefitted the workers as well, the "income and wealth are especially unjustly distributed" in the Federal Republic, Brandt wrote.

REUTER'S DEATH

The year 1953 afforded Brandt the chance to make his first major public speech in Berlin on October 1, at a rally whose intense emotional impact gripped the whole country. Ernst Reuter, Berlin's beloved defender and hero of the blockade, had died at the age of sixty-four. The city mourned its mayor by lighting the sad dark night with burning candles in its windows. No one gave a signal.

In the same way that the American people experienced a personal sense of grief when President Kennedy was shot, so the Berliners felt they had suffered a personal loss in Reuter's death. The mayor had asked the Berliners to put candles in the windows the previous Christmas as a greeting to the unforgotten prisoners far away. Now the population responded spontaneously with the same gesture in memory of his bravery and warmth. "Those innumerable, flickering little flames behind the window-panes looked like innumerable glittering tears," Brandt remembered. "The Berliner wept wherever he received the news—at the radio, on the street corners reading the special editions. . . . A whole city was mourning for its dead leader."

Brandt praised in Reuter what he possessed himself: the rare art of expressing complex issues in a simple way without simplification. "Your words were simple, penetrating, human. . . . What would have become of Berlin without your undaunted will and without the faith that moves mountains. . . ." Brandt had been chosen as main speaker because Reuter's widow could not face party chairman Neumann, who had contributed to her husband's heavy burden, as a graveside speaker. Later on, however, when Brandt had loaned his name to a biography of Ernst Reuter in collaboration with journalist Richard Löwenthal and was hailed in public as Reuter's intellectual and political heir, Hanna Reuter, forever protective of her husband's memory, let it be known what she thought of the "opportunistic" admirer.

According to Mrs. Reuter, her husband had been deeply disappointed in the young politician. Apparently he was less disturbed by Brandt as an intellectual lightweight than by his immoderate ambition and restlessness. It was for similar reasons that his widow came to resent Brandt as a hanger-on, who chose to ride to fame on the coattails of her revered husband. Hanna Reuter, who died in 1974, lived to see Brandt's fall. Unrelenting in her judgment of character, she sadly confided to a longtime friend that she was not the least surprised by the chancellor's unseemly exit from the Palais Schaumburg.

As Schumacher's death weakened Neumann's position, Reuter's opened unforeseen avenues to the top for Brandt. After an interim CDU-FDP coalition government under Dr. Walther Schreiber, the Social Democrats gained an absolute majority in Berlin's election in 1954. Dr. Otto Suhr, president of Berlin's House of Representatives, became the governing mayor and Willy Brandt succeeded him by a vote of 36 to 25 within the SPD delegation. At forty-one, the politician had reached his first plateau.

The presidency was an honorary position. What it lacked in monetary compensation was made up in freedom and prestige. Brandt continued his parliamentary work in the Bundestag but his new position gave him the official stature he needed to establish a platform which would sufficiently impress the party's hierarchy. In order to strengthen his reputation as an expert in international affairs, he traveled abroad as much as he could. Together with Fritz Erler, Carlo Schmid, and Günther Klein, he was one of the first German politicians to visit the U.S.A. on a State Department "leader grant." He traveled to Belgrade, Stockholm, and Oslo to exchange ideas on European integration and problems related to a European Market Community. In contrast to most of the comrades from the SPD, Brandt was not against rearmament.

Even before the Western European Defense Community—advocated by the Christian Democrats and opposed by the Social Democrats in favor of an all-European collective security system—foundered because of French opposition, Brandt's advice is to "examine more carefully the possibilities of an association with the member states of the North Atlantic Treaty Organization." In the same interview with the *Neue Rhein-Zeitung* (July 17, 1954) Brandt makes it amply clear that a one-sided military engagement constitutes no solution for a reunified Germany. An all-German government must be given the option of considering a collective East-West security system accepted by Washington and Moscow as a guarantee for peace and the defense of its freedom. One year later, West Germany became a full-fledged member of NATO and the West European Union against the wishes of the SPD.

Berlin's new hero

Brandt's breakthrough into big time politics did not rest on a conceptual basis. Not surprisingly, it was the activist—used to leading Lübeck's SAP youth in its street fights against Nazi youth gangs and equipped, even then, with an uncanny know-how in handling angry crowds—who emerged with all the glory of a charismatic leader in an unexpected crisis growing out of a mass protest over the Soviet's brutal suppression of the Hungarian revolt.

"At the beginning of November 1956 I was pushed into the foreground in a manner quite different from what I would have liked. It was the reaction to an event which had occurred far from Berlin—the Hungarian revolt." Like many a true activist, Brandt was inclined to overestimate the role of the politician as thinker and philosopher. His craving to be recognized as an intellectual by intellectuals was one of the most Germanic traits and psychological hangups in the otherwise cosmopolitan makeup of the man from Lübeck.

In Willy Brandt, Berlin was to find its new shining hero. Reuter's man had become his own man during the mass demonstration of one hundred thousand agitated Berliners who had assembled in front of West Berlin's Schöneberg city hall on the evening of November 5. The tense crowd, remembering the East German workers' revolt, was not in a mood for listening to traditional speeches about Western solidarity and appeals for restraint in the face of the current outrageous intervention of the Soviet army in the internal affairs of other countries. They shouted down CDU chairman, Ernst Lemmer, and angrily interrupted Franz Neumann's well-meant speech with hissing and chanting for action. They wanted to march on the Brandenburg Gate at the border of the Soviet zone. They wanted to storm the Soviet embassy. "Out with the Russians," they demanded, not thinking of the grave consequences of such action.

Willy Brandt was not among the scheduled speakers at the rally.

He impulsively stepped up to the microphones in a desperate attempt to avert a bloody confrontation with the heavily armed East German border guards, backed by Soviet tanks hovering in the side streets of East Berlin. ". . . at first, I could hardly make myself heard by the crowd," Brandt related in his memoirs. "To prevent a wild march on the East sector, I asked the crowd to march with me to the Steinplatz and stage a demonstration in front of the Memorial for the Victims of Stalinism."

Brandt somehow accomplished the seemingly impossible. His call for unharmful action provided an outlet for the pent-up anger of the infuriated masses. Hermann Schreiber from the *Spiegel* was on the spot:

> Willy Brandt spoke anyway; off the cuff and exactly in the tone of voice that was sympathetic to the outrage of the impotent protestors and at the same time convincing them that it was best to go home. Those who did not go home then were chased by Willy Brandt from a police riot car. Armed only with a loudspeaker he herded the rebellious demonstrators away from the Brandenburg Gate and the rifles of the [East German] people's police into the direction of the Memorial. . . . There at last he brought the marchers to a standstill with new off-the-cuff remarks and the National Anthem. . . .

"In political situations, it is useful to remember that my German countrymen are fond of singing," Brandt remarked wryly. Modestly claiming "luck more than anything else" to be responsible for his successful operation, because "the actions of a huge mass of people are directed by its own laws," he nevertheless was well aware of the fact that the "evening certainly helped Rut and me to win the hearts of the Berliners." Sturdy Rut Brandt was at her husband's side during his dramatic initiation test.

The Berlin press was ecstatic. Brandt's presence of mind had saved Berlin, perhaps the world, from a catastrophe. If the Soviet troops had been attacked it could have meant war. Berlin's crisis had become Brandt's finest hour.

Brandt had been lucky once more. Luck, of course, had nothing to do with his masterful performance during the fateful crisis that enabled him to show his mettle. Under the pressure of mobilization, his dormant talents as a resolute swayer of masses had triumphantly revealed themselves. The compelling combination of homespun evangelist and cool Madison Avenue slickster fascinated the irreverent Berliners. It was the beginning of a long, rewarding and bittersweet love affair. The Berliners took smiling Willy to their big hearts, and Willy fell in love with the adoring Berliners. In the end, they got bored with each other. Meanwhile, the Social Democrats had been presented with a new political star.

It is always enlightening to check out the reactions of the functionaries in the Eastern orbit. How did a high official of the Socialist Unity party in East Germany, like Erich Honecker, explain the Hungarian revolt? According to Lippmann, he was quick to protest the "alleged attempts by the Western press 'to transform the counterrevolutionaries into heroes through the sensational slanting of the news reports'." Visibly on the defensive, Honecker cut the revolutionaries down to size in the context of the ongoing class struggle: "What those gentlemen really want is to restore the old relationship of exploitation." Admonishing the Hungarian Communists for making serious political and economic mistakes, he advises his own party to beef up its "vigilance against the reactionary forces of imperialism."

When we keep in mind this attitude, and the remarks made by Professor Dr. Fritz Baade, SPD member of the Bundestag, Brandt's action assumes a second, much more intriguing and important dimension. Professor Baade asserted that he felt in no way called upon "to liberate the Communist countries. . . . We especially refuse to participate in the policy of the rollback of communism in the countries dominated, as was advocated for a while by the U.S. State Department. This is not just my personal opinion, but it is shared by every influential Social Democratic politician. . . ." Professor Baade demands an end to the differentiations between the people in the East bloc and their governments.

Notwithstanding the glaring controversies and heated disputes with East Germany's orthodox standard bearers from Walter Ulbricht to today's leaders, Brandt and Wehner had built their hopeful concepts of German reunification primarily on the overriding affinities between the West's genuine socialism and its aberrant counterpart in the East. A reunification will come under the "aspect of democratic socialism or it will not come at all," Wehner boldly prognosticated in 1958. The dream of combining and unifying the two Germanys into one Socialist state within the general framework of a European Socialist federation is still cherished by the Jusos (Young Socialists in the SPD) today.

IN THE MAYOR'S SEAT

No matter how vigorously Franz Neumann counteracted Berlin's Willy vogue, everybody in the city knew Willy would be the next mayor. Before another year passed by, Berlin's new young governing mayor, no other than the popular forty-three-year-old Brandt, basked in the hot television lights.

Luck was becoming a constant companion. Reuter's successor, Dr. Otto Suhr, had died in August 1957. Louise Schroeder, who had occupied the mayor's office before Reuter's time, and would have been considered by the party, died two months before Suhr. Franz Neumann, a basic candidate for the prestigious job, had not sufficiently recovered from his fiasco during that November rally to dare throw his own hat into the ring. Berlin's press had decided to back the "worldly outsider." It was an image with which the proverbial elegant and cosmopolitan citizenry of the isolated city-state could easily identify.

The influential *Spiegel* disapproved of Neumann's "proletarian gimmick," on which his political career was built, forgetting and withholding the fact that his proletarian ways had nothing to do with calculating mannerisms. Neumann was a genuine proletarian and acted like one. On the other hand, *Spiegel* spared no effort to introduce Brandt as a sophisticated intellectual, at home in Norway's high society, and married to the widow of a "prominent Norwegian journalist." If *Spiegel's* research was lopsided, other papers were content to endorse the youthful anti-Nazi as the rightful heir to Reuter's august chair. The prestigious *Die Zeit* praised Brandt as a representative of the SPD "right reform wing," akin to Reuter's "nonconformistic attitude vis-a-vis the official course of the party." His skillful handling of the explosive situation, likely to reoccur in the excitable climate of Berlin, made him a natural contender for Berlin's mayoralty.

Above all, the paper agreed with Brandt's ingenious détente policy. "He belongs to those unorthodox politicians who stand for a maximum of professional and technical contacts (with neighbors in the East) in order to facilitate life on both sides." Charming Rut Brandt made headlines on her own as a "prominent Norwegian newspaperwoman," a fashion plate, or as an unhousewifely free spirit. The glamorous Brandts were the toast of the town.

Fighting the sails of the windmills of public consensus, Neumann became a tragic quixotic figure. In his luckless search for a candidate able to beat his hated rival, Neumann found that he was no match for the clever Brandt—who had seen to it that all the potential candidates, from Carlo Schmid to Herbert Wehner and Fritz Erler, were pledged to his support. As a last resort, Neumann presented Willi Kressmann, a local functionary with no particular assets, as a candidate. Brandt's followers immediately took the offensive by threatening party chairman Neumann with a vote of no confidence because of procedural irregularities. Neumann gave up grudgingly, and Brandt was elected in October 1957 with 86 of 118 votes to the office of governing mayor by Berlin's House of Representatives.

"With his strong hands Willy Brandt has now at the current climax of his blitz-career seized all levers of power within his reach," *Spiegel* commented. As luck would have it, it was the city-state's turn to furnish the president of the German Bundesrat, the Bundestag's upper house, that year. This meant that Brandt would receive additional public exposure as the deputy to the President of the Federal Republic during the next term.

It was an ideal situation for the rapidly rising politician. Berlin had to be rebuilt. The objective was to enlist active support, financial aid and psychological empathy for the reconstruction of the divided city, whose fate was inextricably tied to Brandt's. It was a systematic public relations job on the grandest possible scale. And Brandt, personable and eager to succeed, was equal to the difficult task.

Before he embarked on his ambitious rehabilitation program for Berlin, Brandt insisted on Neumann's removal as party chairman. He would not stand for any backbiting within the ranks of his own party. As the elections for Berlin's SPD chairmanship drew near in January 1958, Brandt had been in office less than three months. Taking full advantage of his position, he decided to beat Neumann with a spectacular political first: an official visit with the Soviet city commander of East Berlin, General Chamov. *Spiegel* reported extensively on the coup. Brandt had "argued and negotiated hard" about easement of traffic and visitors' permits while enjoying the Soviet general's vodka and champagne from the Crimea. The text of the official communique, stating that "questions of mutual interest had been discussed," appeared next to the photos of Willy crossing the border in his official limousine.

The Berliners, with their fine sense for theatrical flair and an independent, more mobile foreign politics than was generated in Bonn, loved Brandt's show of sheer bravado, even if it could not be sustained by visible results. Neumann's intimations that the excursion amounted to nothing more than a bit of social drinking was summarily dismissed by Brandt's icy remark: "I don't need to get into a discussion whether one vodka more or less was poured in Karlshorst."

The vote of 163 to 124 in favor of Brandt was the end of Neumann's political career.

After two futile attempts, Berlin's new political star was finally voted into the party's executive committee that year, which is well remembered by Berliners and West Germans alike for another reason.

Nikita Khrushchev had made a speech in Moscow that spelled new troubles for West Berlin. The gregarious Soviet leader supported the demands of East Germany's SED for a revision of the Potsdam agreement in order to create a "normal situation in the capital of the German Democratic Republic." In plain language, the demand meant a Soviet ultimatum to convert Berlin into a "free city" within six months. Brandt was handed his first full-blown Berlin crisis. The note of November 27, 1958, to the three Western powers included Khrushchev's threat of a special arrangement between the Soviet Union and the GDR to obstruct all military transports to West Berlin if the matter was not settled within the specified period.

Khrushchev's challenge gave Brandt a highly welcomed chance to establish himself not only as a tough fighter and expert on East-West affairs but as a statesman of great moderation with a novel approach to the German problem.

"There is no isolated solution to the Berlin question. If a contribution to the relaxation of tension and the reunification of Germany is supposed to be achieved, as the Soviet note states among other things, then the issue here and now is not the Berlin question but the overcoming of the division of Germany. We must negotiate about that and not about the change of the status quo of Berlin. . . ."

Once more Brandt had found the appropriate nuances and the right words to ward off the outbreak of panic among the jittery Berliners. The Social Democrats' overwhelming victory—52.6 percent of the votes to the SED's 1.9 percent—in the city's December elections was as much a vote of confidence for him as it demonstrated convincingly to the Soviets that the Berliners' allegiance to the West was unshaken and the time for a showdown was anything but opportune.

Berlin's ambassador

Soon the whole world knew about the plight of West Berlin—frontier town, show window of the West, bastion of freedom, island of democracy, bridge between East and West, or whatever the florid synonyms were for that singular cityscape concocted by limited military minds and unknowledgeable or revengeful Western politicians. The dynamic mayor and his attractive wife set out to conquer the world for West Berlin. While CDU Deputy Mayor Franz Amrehn minded the municipal shop, Brandt went on whirlwind tours around the globe luring dollars, visitors, industry and foundation grants to Berlin. His spreading of goodwill and sympathy for the Berliners and enlisting understanding of the German situation was by no means confined to New York, Ottawa, Paris, Bombay, Tokyo, London, New Delhi or Rangoon. It also meant meetings such as that in Westphalia with the Association of German Industrialists, whose membership is made up of the most influential tycoons and business men of the Rhineland, the Ruhr and elsewhere.

The results were more than satisfactory. The tide of the flight of capital from Berlin was stemmed, new orders poured into the city. The Communist threats failed to crush the incipient boom. Berlin's economic development progressed in spite of its state of perpetual crisis. The skill Brandt lacked as an administrator was made up by his superb salesmanship as the city's most vocal and persuasive spokesman and ambassador. By the time he left the mayor's office, West Berlin had emerged from mountains of rubble—estimated at 3 billion cubic feet—as the largest industrial city of prosperous West Germany, due in part to his having obtained substantial subsidies from the Federal Republic and the European Recovery Program (ERP).

What was good for Berlin was even better for Willy Brandt.

"Brandt was astute in his approach to things and did everything humanly and politically possible for Berlin." Eleanor Lansing Dulles, author of numerous books on U.S. foreign policy and long-time State Department expert on German affairs, still a consultant in 1975, is as knowledgeable about Berlin and Brandt as anyone can be. She remembers him as a kind, perhaps not tough enough politician, and a moody and restless man.

"Our objective was to hold Berlin. We knew how important Berlin was for the West." Ms. Dulles is convinced that Kennedy never understood Berlin politics, even after his celebrated visit there. Her professional involvement with Berlin, including two or three visits annually to the city on varying missions, spans the years between 1952 and 1959. "We helped Reuter and Suhr, and we helped Brandt," she explained.

Dulles knew Brandt as a bourgeois politician with moderate views. "I guess, today I would put myself to the right of his politics," she reflected in a talk with me in February 1975. When it came to conversations about politics or philosophy she admittedly preferred the intellectually stimulating conversations with Paul Hertz, genial holdover from a previous administration, to exchanges with Brandt.

The American diplomat, sister of Secretary of State John Foster Dulles and CIA director, Allen Dulles, was one of the few outsiders who intuitively sensed Brandt's enormous ambition.

"Brandt had his eye on Bonn ever since he got to Berlin. He was bored with Berlin," she observed. Well aware of his lack of talent in assembling good people around him, her attention nevertheless focused on him as the only younger promising politician in sight with a confirmed anti-Nazi background. Actually, long before Brandt began looking toward Bonn, the far ranging eye of the U.S. State Department and its OSS connection had been on him. Starting with Herschel Johnson's many dispatches and his report that one of the OSS representatives, "widely acquainted with German refugee circles in Sweden," found Brandt "one of the ablest of the entire lot," omnipotent State was to carefully scrutinize and often abet Brandt's progress as long as its interests were served.

Brandt's phenomenal international breakthrough during his first official visit to the United States as Berlin's mayor, which in turn enhanced his political standing at home beyond all imaginable hopes, was initially engineered by Eleanor Dulles. There was no reason for embarrassment for having launched this American debut. The attractive couple—Rut was invited along—made excellent impressions everywhere. Only the White House balked at receiving the Mayor of Berlin. But reluctant Ike had not reckoned with Eleanor's art of persuasion. In the end, President Eisenhower granted Brandt fifteen minutes for the exchange of greetings for the sake of Berlin. Those fifteen minutes with Ike made Brandt's political stock soar straight to the stars.

It may be trite to observe that nothing succeeds like success. Still its snowball effect cannot be denied. The knowledge that their Willy Brandt had impressed the Americans left a profound impression on the Germans with their secret love for all things foreign. The German language is the only tongue that has a word for the longing to be in faraway places: it is *Fernweh.* After his return to Bonn, the ambitious blockbuster of heretofore uncertain standing suddenly looked more like a chancellor candidate than any other politician, except Adenauer.

"I already knew in 1957 that Brandt would be chancellor," Dulles volunteered. When one considers the seasoned diplomat's position and connections, this is a statement of mind-blowing import.

If female intuition is ruled out, it could only be construed that Washington was keeping Brandt in the wings, grooming him and coddling him for the day that octogenarian Adenauer's chair in the Palais Schaumburg would stand vacant.

One wonders if anybody in Washington had predicted that the restless, newly reassured Brandt would hold his first press conference as the SPD's chancellor candidate against Adenauer in Bad Godesberg in October 1960.

Understandably, Dulles hesitated to deliver pronouncements. However, during our talk she seemed unable to hide her disappointment in politicians who rise to the very top but "do not grow."

12

Detours to Victory

Willy Brandt's lucky stars had a disconcerting periodicity of dimming. As if to test his newly acquired political self-assertion and the endurance of his personal stamina, Brandt's way to the levers of power in Bonn was paved with formidable obstacles. The humiliation of two defeats at the election polls would have crushed the spirit and ego of a lesser politician.

Amazingly, Brandt reeled back from the many political and personal knockdown rounds with the awe-inspiring elasticity of a champion prize fighter; a little punchdrunk, perhaps, but with the same stubborn determination to regain his equilibrium for the next cruel round that the poor boy from Whittier, California, used to display. The single-minded obsessive will to win that was Nixon's, despite renouncing publicly all ambitions, was a quality shared by Brandt who had struck the same pose on several occasions. In Nixon's case the fixation with the hard-won triumph over the enemy manifested itself in the imperial presidency.

Brandt's affliction after victory was of a different kind. Always unsure of being taken seriously by the "establishment," like Nixon, he overplayed the dignified statesman and finally, awed by his own dignity, froze into a national monument. The poor boy from Lübeck and the boy from Whittier were each obsessed with making history. They did. And for long stretches of the détente and the spectacular opening up toward the East in order to achieve that mystical balance of power between West and East—before the rules of the game were changed by the preponderance of economic realities—they occupied their rightful places in the world: center stage.

Adversaries have ascribed a "messianic complex" to the democratic socialist who wanted and still wants to change society and make a mark in the world. They tend to recognize a totalitarian trait in his moral claim of being the possessor of political and social truth without alternative.

Actually, Brandt, the eternal mediator, consensus seeker and compromiser, known to shy away from the harsh "either or" propositions in favor of dramatist August Strindberg's recommended "as well as" solutions, probably never looked at it this way. Filled with an unquenchable need to prove to himself that he could "cut the mustard," so to speak, in order to live with himself, he charged blithely ahead, hoping not too many portions of his fundamental principles would have to be sacrificed during the necessary detours.

Ultrasensitive, insecure, tractable Brandt, easily hurt, often offended and overreacting to imagined and real slights alike with prolonged indulgences in hostile silences and retreats from the cruel world, nevertheless was equipped with nerves of steel and the hide of an elephant in crucial situations. He is one of the most complex, brooding, puzzling, exasperatingly introverted characters since Hamlet. That the public man is even more private and less knowable than the famous Dane may be tentatively explained by the fact that Brandt suffered from a perennial poor-boy complex.

The year 1961, a crisis year because of the erection of the Berlin Wall by the East German regime, should have been a good year for Willy Brandt. The horoscope for Berlin and its mobile governing mayor, who was campaigning against incumbent Konrad Adenauer for the office of chancellor, sounded encouraging. Armed with the reformed people's party concept that freed the Social Democrats of their traditional workers' party image, forty-seven-year-old Brandt optimistically started out to imitate the boyish John F. Kennedy; he pitted his widely acclaimed charm and youth against Adenauer's old-age dourness.

Brandt's conversion into a hatless, informal "smiling Willy" by the SPD's enthusiastic election commission members was an easy one. They had made a thorough study of Kennedy's stylish campaign down to the shape and size of the last campaign button. Brandt projected the perfect picture of an efficient, with-it politician. He was articulate and in full control of his emotions; he even had a touch of folksy humor. He looked tanned—rumor had it that Willy devoted daily sessions to a trusty sun lamp—and vigorous, and while he did not strike his audience as a handsome man, he was considered good looking by the ladies, who were utterly charmed by his dimpled smile.

The party, impressed by the one-man show that led to Kennedy's victory, had put all its hopes and money on their in-house beau. Brandt raced up and down the countryside, making twenty to thirty speeches a day, shaking hands, signing autographs, kissing babies and even unpretty women, all in the line of duty.

Novelist John Gunther described him as a "dangerous opponent to the ruling party." He praised his ready wit and his natural charm.

THE SPD'S NEW LOOK

In accordance with the *Godesberg Program,* the confining Marxist-Leninist theories of class struggle and planned economy were cast overboard for Professor Schiller's "Competition as far as possible—planning as far as necessary." Later on, Brandt amended this view by stating that the economy constitutes by no means a "wild life sanctuary for the upper ten thousand." Drumming up trade and sympathy for Berlin during his world travels that year and as a member of a different committee, Brandt "wasn't able to work on it very much."

The Godesberg reform program was the product of painstaking teamwork. Herbert Wehner, Fritz Erler, Adolf Arndt, Willi Eichler and Gustav Heinemann—the new man in the party in 1959, who above all effected a reconciliation between the party and the church and a better understanding between church and state—were the prime movers, in Willy Brandt's opinion.

Wehner's highly controversial Germany Plan was cast off and forgotten like an old, ill-fitting shoe.

As a shrewd judge of political climes, Brandt had greeted Wehner's reunification plan, launched as a test balloon in answer to the CDU government's passive stance, with due restraint. Wehner envisioned a demilitarized "tensionless zone," consisting of East and

West Germany, Poland, Czechoslovakia and Hungary, a thinning out of foreign troops on German soil, and the renunciation of NATO and Warsaw Pact membership by these states. Their safety would be guaranteed by a European security agreement. Berlin's status quo was to be maintained until the signing of the peace treaty. In conjunction, preparations for an all-German conference, economic institutions, and the establishment of an all-German parliament, responsible for drawing up an election law to be approved by referendum, were planned.

Unfortunately, Wehner's federation plan differed little from Polish Foreign Minister Adam Rapacki's proposal made in 1957. "Here the gate to the West is opened for the Communists," Heinrich Krone, the CDU's parliamentary floor leader commented in his diary in March 1959. Krone need not have worried. Wehner's plan offended Khrushchev even more. By coldly informing a delegation of Social Democrat leaders that no foreign power, including the Soviets, was interested in Germany's reunification—no matter under what terms—the Soviet Premier had closed the subject, once and for all.

In August, when Krushchev visited America, Krone deduced: "The U.S. cities compete to have the dictator. A new era of coexistence begins. The danger of illusions dawns. . . . The world wants to arrange itself. Moscow and Washington are the two poles. We must not stand aside. Together with the West we must start talks."

Wehner's criticism that, thanks to CDU inactivity, the subject of reunification was no longer topical, overlooked the CDU conclusion that the discussion about "Berlin has to be built into an all-German discussion." Brandt, it will be remembered, had expressed precisely the same position on the eve of Khrushchev's Berlin ultimatum in 1958.

Despite Adenauer's insistence that a common foreign policy with the Social Democrats could only be conducted at the expense of hard and necessary politics, and the weakening of the German position, there seemed to be a genuine rapprochement in the foreign policy concepts of the two parties, even though they stemmed from differing thought patterns.

Krone, on January 1, 1960: "Dulles is dead. Coexistence is the catchword. The great temptation! Poor Germany. Our fellow countrymen behind the Iron Curtain."

And on January 12: "In England and in the United States one does not especially agree with the Chancellor's [Adenauer's] Berlin speech; it is too hard line for them and not in alignment with their coexistence politics. Brandt is the coming man in Bonn too. We cannot take the rise of Berlin's governing mayor seriously enough. It will not do that we just display Konrad Adenauer next year during the election; people want to know from us who comes after him."

When Wehner abandoned his Germany Plan that summer and proposed a common foreign policy, Krone was delighted. "Great debate in the Bundestag. A masterful achievement by Wehner. Wehner has the power in his party. He would govern when Brandt should become chancellor. . . . Wehner's speech is a sensation. The SPD gives in."

If Krone's diary notes reveal anything, it is that the Christian Democrats were having second thoughts about their rigidly executed Westpolitik, crowned by the reconciliation with France and membership in the European Economic Community as well as, since 1955, NATO. Adenauer's attempts to combine East and West politics in the changing political atmosphere of the superpowers' rapprochement found expression in the secret Globke Plan of 1959. It was a complicated structure aiming at a referendum on unification of the two parts of Germany after a five-year interim period devoted to the improvement of inter-German relations under the protection of the four powers, by special arrangement with the United Nations.

The fact that the grand old party saw a viable and even dangerous candidate in young Brandt should have given him additional heart and courage. But somehow the campaign was not going well. The troublesome old stories of Brandt's radical past bubbled up again. CSU Vice-President Richard Jaeger compared the change of names from Frahm to Brandt to that of Hitler, whose family name was Schicklgruber.

Brandt's proposal for holding a mammoth international peace conference on the German question, to be attended by all of the fifty-two nations which took part in the war against Nazi Germany, found little resonance. Neither his demands for the preparation of an all-German peace treaty by the four powers, including the right of the Berliners to have a voice in the discussions concerning Berlin, nor the plea for a common response of government and opposition to Khrushchev's repeated threats from Vienna, struck the voters' fancy. Adenauer duly ignored Brandt's challenging suggestions for TV debates. Brandt's presumptuous sounding assurances that he wanted to cooperate with the CDU government and was willing to travel with Adenauer to Washington and to Moscow to help the cause of the German people were flatly turned down.

The Kennedy influence

Germany's voters did not know what to make of Brandt's breezy campaign style with its colorful balloons, gadgets, racy 16,000 mark luxury Mercedes convertible upholstered in gleaming red leather, and the personalized slogan: "Ahead with Willy Brandt." The Germans, accustomed to crusty, crotchety old Adenauer, were not ready for a Kennedy cardboard copy of their own, even though they admired the popular, attractive millionaire who inspired America's youth with the kind of idealism they nowadays detect only in their dusty old philosophy books.

Besides, no matter how many smiling Brandt-Kennedy photos—a result of Brandt's visit to Washington in March 1961—appeared in the papers, Brandt was no Kennedy. He lacked the easy grace, the light touch and beguiling nonchalance, surefire identification marks of the well-bred rich, that obscure the hard-as-nails toughness of the profound understatement or the casual quest for the gentleman's C.

Adenauer promised continued security, stability and prosperity. Germany's economy was booming. Brandt's appeal for more social justice and a more constructive foreign policy, above all the improvement of relations with the Soviet Union and the East bloc, did not make much of an impression on a prospering middle class.

The voters' attitude was not changed by the events of August 13, 1961, when East Germany's rulers, under cover of Soviet tanks, sealed off Soviet-dominated East Berlin from West Berlin with concrete barriers and barbed wire fences. Simultaneously, all means of communication between the East and West sectors of the city were severed. The legal barriers which the Communists had tried to impose on West Berlin over the protests of the Western powers during recent years had now been ensured by a concrete wall. The hole in the Iron Curtain through which some 2.5 million refugees from the East had escaped was finally plugged.

Khrushchev had vowed before he met President Kennedy at their disharmonious Vienna summit meeting in June to "eradicate this splinter from the heart of Europe." He had talked about stabilizing the Eastern frontier and hoped to add new luster to the sovereignty the USSR had bestowed single-handedly on the East German regime. As in 1958 and at the Paris summit conference in 1960, Khrushchev pressed for a peace treaty in Vienna, and pressed hard. He argued that formal ending of World War II and the recognition of the existence of two German states that would automatically set an end to the Allied occupation rights and all its concomitants were long overdue. If the Allies were not ready to sign such a treaty or treaties, the Soviets would go ahead and sign one with East Germany alone and turn over their rights to its access links to the outside world on land, water and air across East German territory to the sovereign German Democratic Republic. West Berlin was to become a free city. Why does America want to stay there, he had asked?

Kennedy played it cool. He knew after the Bay of Pigs fiasco that he could not afford empty gestures. If America was to relinquish its rights in Berlin after a presence of fifteen years in that city, the result would be an irreparable loss of confidence. America's commitments and pledges would be regarded "as mere scraps of paper," White House advisor Theodore C. Sorensen reasoned matter of factly in *Kennedy.*

"The President's first and most basic decision was that the preservation of Western rights in West Berlin was an objective for which the United States was required to incur any cost, including the risk of nuclear war," Mr. Sorensen observed in his recollections about the Berlin crisis. Aware that Khrushchev believed America would never risk responding with a nuclear attack should he move to cut off West Berlin, surrounded entirely by East German territory, Kennedy decided on a quiet but quick military buildup of its combat troops. After six weeks of intensive meetings, the plans for a counteroffensive, including an additional military budget request of $3.2 billion, stand-by authority to call up the reserves and guidelines for economic sanctions were outlined by July 19. This was almost a month before the wall went up in East Berlin.

The Berlin Wall

Now Khrushchev had swallowed half the city. In flagrant violation of Berlin's four power status, he had incorporated the Soviet sector into the territory of the GDR. In effect, he had expelled the three Western powers from the Soviet sector of the city. The halfway advance was meant as a compromise and test of Kennedy's intentions toward honoring his commitment.

While the Berlin wall was considered "illegal, immoral and inhumane" in Washington, it did not rate as a cause for war. Kennedy dispatched a contingent of fifteen hundred American troops riding in armored vehicles down the Autobahn. He was counting on the psychological impact of such a show of force, however symbolic, on the worried West Berliners. He was certain that the Soviets would get the message and recognize the troops as "our hostage to that intent," Sorensen quotes Kennedy.

"It was his first anxious moment during the prolonged crisis, his first order of American military units into a potential confrontation with the Soviets." Sorensen reports that Kennedy stayed at the White House during that crucial weekend keeping in constant touch with the convoy's commander. "When the first group of sixty trucks turned unimpeded into West Berlin, he felt that a turning point in the crisis had been reached."

The crisis brought Brandt's campaign to a virtual standstill. Once more, Berlin had become the center of attention. The spotlights of the world were directed on its saddest sightseeing attraction, the abominable wall. The mayor, who had come under heavy criticism for his continuous absences from the city he represented, took full charge. "For me there is no election campaign anymore; for me there is only the battle for Berlin . . ." he announced somberly. "At most I will reserve one day a week for an election rally, and it will be devoted to Berlin, or better yet, the German destiny."

During a party rally in Nuremberg, Brandt launched into a sharp attack against Chancellor Konrad Adenauer by accusing him of masking the seriousness of the crisis in order to be reelected. Calling Adenauer's policy during his twelve years in office on the problems of divided Germany and Berlin completely negative and nearly militaristic, Brandt demanded codecision of the people by plebiscite. He could not know, of course, that the CDU's Globke Plan prepared for American consumption in 1959 had aimed precisely at the same objective. The neutral Swiss *Neue Zürcher Zeitung* took note of a "belligerent" and "polemical" tone in Brandt's demands for a common foreign policy. Its somber conclusion was that the SPD's only chance was that worsening developments in the Berlin situation would sway Adenauer to invite the party to partake in a "national government" in the fall.

Brandt's moment of glory was at the moving mass demonstration in front of city hall, three days after the erection of the wall. Two hundred and fifty thousand worried and highly agitated Berliners waited for a word of encouragement, for assurance by the Allies that Berlin was neither forgotten nor abandoned. Brandt had no comfort to give. He had written a letter to President Kennedy asking for immediate action but had not received an answer yet.

As a matter of fact, a written answer would never be forthcoming. Reportedly, Kennedy was angered by the confidential tone of the letter—in which Brandt referred to the American president as a "friend"—and the clumsy attempt to make use of his prestige in the election campaign. Upset by "that bastard in Berlin" who tries to "involve me in the upcoming elections," Kennedy confided to his advisers that he did "not trust that man at all."

Walking onto the open staircase to address the tense crowd, Brandt's great composure in a crisis and his superb instinct for the prevailing mood saved a fairly hopeless situation. Once again, he found the right words to alleviate the feeling of blind desperation. "This city wishes peace, but it will not capitulate," he said in a firm voice to the applause of his grateful listeners. Brandt had expressed exactly what they thought and felt. He was the voice of the people.

What will become of Berlin, they asked? How far will the Western powers go? Understandably, the Berliners who had hoped for a show of force by the Americans, perhaps even an attempt to tear down the wall, were disappointed. They realized that the Americans would defend free access to the city by air. To hope and dread at the same time that the *Amis* will risk war over Berlin was a psychologically draining experience.

The crowd cheered when Brandt criticized the Allies for not insisting on their rights in *all* of Berlin, namely East and West. They cheered when he said that the events of August 13 constituted no direct threat to West Berlin because the Soviets were too clever to endanger the peace of the world by an outright attack. His emotional admonition to stay away from East Germany's famed Leipzig trade fair—"Who wants to make money at the fair might as well stay there"—earned him even greater waves of applause.

Again he had vented the shored-up anger with a cue for action. The helpless Berliners suddenly felt they could do something: they could boycott the fair.

Not much of an innovator when it came to the formulation of abstract ideas and philosophical concepts, his activist's mind was turned on by the mood of the masses. His speech sparkled with creative rhetorical nuances. "The morale of the world will be worth as much as Berlin's morale is worth. . . . All of us will have to behave in such manner that our enemies will not be happy and our fellow countrymen will not despair. . . . We have the sobriety, determination, and the firm will to stand up for all of Germany, for unity and justice and freedom. . . ."

An unvarnished analysis of the situation was revealed by Brandt in an interview with *Die Zeit.*

"In East Berlin and in the zone, hate and stark desperation prevail. For the West Berliner, the reality of life has fundamentally changed from one day to the next. These people have lived with only one hope —one day we will be the capital again—and now. . . . Why don't we appeal to the United Nations? Why do we always talk around the problem the world must face? . . . What happened to avert the crisis? Nothing! And what happens now? Nothing, again!"

Brandt's spirit and the spirits of the West Berliners brightened instantly when the news of Vice-President Lyndon B. Johnson's visit and the return of General Lucius Clay, the well-remembered hero of the 1948–49 blockade as city commander of the U.S. forces, broke a few days later.

The letter to Washington

The appearance of the two distinguished Americans was deftly interpreted by Brandt as Kennedy's first answer to his "personal" letter.

In Bonn, a slightly different version was circulated. The Johnson visit was certainly not credited to Brandt's "embarrassing" letter, written against all rules of protocol and without consultation. How the confidential letter to Kennedy, ostensibly not meant for the eyes of the German public or the Soviets, found its way into the columns of the *Frankfurter Allgemeine Zeitung* was never determined.

Brandt was furious about the breach of confidence. Only two copies of the letter existed: one went to Chancellor Adenauer, who claimed to have found out about it only through Washington, and the other to Foreign Minister Heinrich von Brentano. Despite a criminal investigation instituted by Brandt, accusations as to who was to blame for the leak flew back and forth. Both political rivals had an interest in making its contents known to the public: Adenauer to embarrass Brandt, and Brandt to show on how confidential a footing he was with Kennedy.

The *Zürcher Zeitung* aptly remarked that Brandt's "letter action" went directly against the agreement that Berlin was to be represented by the federal government in foreign affairs. Krone was of the same opinion: "Berlin makes its own foreign policy. Brandt bypasses [Mayor] Amrehn and Berlin's CDU," reads his diary entry for September 9, 1961. "There are forces in Washington who want Brandt as chancellor. Those don't want the 'old one' [Adenauer], he is too hard for them. One looks for an understanding with Moscow; Germany is in the way. Dulles is dead. Adenauer may go. I don't know how strong these forces are. . . ."

Brandt's wordy document, condemned by Adenauer for its "enormous arrogance" and "arm-twisting method," was full of advice. It warned that U.S. inactivity and a purely defensive posture could lead to a crisis of confidence and too much self-confidence on the part of the East German regime. It urged the reinstatement of four power responsibility for all Berlin while a three power status for West Berlin was being proclaimed and a guarantee of Allied presence until the time of reunification was re-issued by the Western powers.

It was typical of Brandt that he wanted it both ways. The Christian Democrats were aghast: A three-power status for West Berlin amounted to a legal acceptance of the Soviet coup. Furthermore, Brandt expected a "clear word" on the viability of the German question and insistence on a peace treaty, corresponding to the German people's right to self-determination and the security interests of all participants.

The chancellor and his opponent were agreed on two points: Both opposed plans for making Berlin a "free city," and both suspected that the Americans had withheld knowledge of the plan for building the Berlin wall. Actually, the White House was aware that something was up since former Secretary of State Dean Acheson's interim report on Berlin in April 1961 warned of an imminent crisis. The erection of the wall was a joint decision made by Khrushchev and

East Germany's Ulbricht about that time. Therefore it is not unlikely that Washington had intelligence about the nature of the project.

Ulbricht in effect gave away the show in June when he said to the *Frankfurter Rundschau:* "I take your question to mean that there are people in West Germany who want us to mobilize the builders in the capital of the GDR to erect a wall. . . . I am not aware of any such intention."

East Germany's General Hoffmann proudly observed ten years after building the "Anti-Fascist Protective Wall," that "the enemy" was taken "completely by surprise." Sorensen noted that it "shocked the free world" but failed to register surprise.

Adenauer was not above intimating that "everything that had happened since August 13 was meant by Khrushchev as aid to the election campaign of the SPD." Yet it was the hard-line anti-Communist CDU chancellor who won the elections. The wall had proved to the majority of the voters that the "old fox" was right, but the SPD had climbed from its meager 31.8 percent to 36.3. While the CDU/CSU still shored up 45.2 percent, it had lost 5 percent and the absolute majority since the 1957 elections. At the same time, the free-wheeling Free Democrats, coalition partners for all parties, established themselves as a third force to be reckoned with; they had jumped from 8 to 12 percent.

Following a strange yet familiar pattern, Willy Brandt had not reached his goal in the first round. As a positive result of the elections, he was firmly established as Mr. Berlin, a notable public figure whose name had become a household word around the world. He had met just about every major world leader and would see to it that they did not forget Berlin, the German question, or Willy Brandt.

"Willy Brandt is the brave and courageous leader of this encircled, anxious city," Cassandra of the *Daily Mirror* cabled back to London in the hot summer of 1961. "If we do not support him, and if we give way on Berlin, it will supersede that other German city, Munich, as a symbol of fatal weakness inevitably leading to war."

The atmosphere of confrontation had changed into one of tough bargaining and settlement talks when Kennedy finally came to the troubled city in June 1963 to be seen and to conquer the jubilant Berliners with his open smile and the immortal: "All free men, wherever they may live, are citizens of Berlin, and, therefore, as a free man, I take pride in the words, *Ich bin ein Berliner.*"

It was a magic phrase. Partially framed to accommodate his pronunciation difficulties with foreign languages, it became a slogan the Germans are still joyously reciting today with a gleam of admiration in their eyes and a hint of nostalgia in their voices.

After the Cuban missile crisis and the nuclear test ban treaty, Khrushchev had taken measure of the young American president who, despite his easy charm, proved to be no pushover. "I think [the Communists] realize," said President Kennedy, "that West Berlin is a vital interest to us . . . and that we are going to stay there," Sorensen recorded. When Kennedy took his stand, warning Fidel Castro and Khrushchev that the U.S. would not tolerate Soviet missiles in Cuba and was not willing to accept a change in the status quo, he mentioned Berlin twice in the same speech.

Along with heads of state, the governing mayor of Berlin had been informed of the emergency and he signaled full support for the course chosen—for the sake of freedom and peace—to Washington. Brandt saw in the Cuban crisis a "turning point in international developments." Like his opponent in the Kremlin, Kennedy "had gazed into the abyss and had not shuddered."

In *Meeting with Kennedy,* Brandt affectionately described his visits and discussions with the American president, who according to his Boswell, Ted Sorensen, "was particularly fond of Britain's Hugh Gaitskell and West Germany's Willy Brandt." Kennedy's unforgettable triumph in West Berlin, his confrontation with the reality of the wall and "the imprisoned men and women, standing there by the hundreds, offering a silent greeting under the eyes of their guards and jailers," on the East German side of Checkpoint Charlie, as well as the adulation, the "unending jubilation, handkerchiefs waving" of the West Berliners, transformed into a sea of enthralled humanity shouting, "Kenne-dy, Kenne-dy" had become Berlin's great day also. It is a fair guess that there are probably more squares, bridges and boulevards named after Kennedy in West Berlin than in any other city.

As the proud host, Brandt was glowing in the reflected glory of those hours when a "river of enthusiasm and gratitude" flowed through the embattled city. The Berliners had been carried away by Kennedy; Kennedy, in turn, was hooked on Berlin. "We'll never have another day like this one, as long as we live," Kennedy said to Sorensen as Air Force One flew them to Ireland that evening.

Kennedy's assassination on November 25, 1963, came as a deep shock to Berliners. They fully shared the grief of the American people. To Berlin's governing mayor, Kennedy's death was a severe political loss. He had counted on Kennedy support in the next elections—and most likely would have received it this time. After Brandt had paid his respects to Jacqueline Kennedy following the funeral, Bobby Kennedy escorted Brandt to his car. "He loved Berlin," the president's brother said in parting.

Shortly thereafter, in December, another death occurred that had impact on Brandt's life: that of the Social Democrat's longtime chairman, Erich Ollenhauer. At the extraordinary Godesberg party convention, Brandt took another giant step upward on the ladder of success with his election as party chairman. Wehner, of course, remains as omnipotent vice-chairman. The Social Democrats were willing to take their chances again with Willy in the 1965 elections. Only this time they would build him up with a strong supporting team, instead of campaign gimmicks.

End of Adenauer era

Meanwhile, the political scene had drastically changed in the Federal Republic. The aged Dr. Adenauer, Brandt's formidable opponent in 1961, had been outmaneuvered and forced to resign as the result of an intricate play for power by the ebullient CSU chairman, Franz Josef Strauss, and the strengthened FDP. Strauss promised to throw his weight behind Adenauer's deputy, Economics Minister Ludwig Erhard. The engineer of Germany's economic miracle became chancellor in October 1963.

The Adenauer era had come to an unnoticed end in 1961 at the Berlin wall. The CDU premise was to achieve security through Western integration and rearmament, including the switch to tactical nuclear weapons in 1956 as an essential step toward reunification. This was violently opposed by the majority of the Social Democrats. Schumacher and his SPD gave priority to reunification. The politics through strength concept had been radically altered by the nuclear stalemate between the superpowers.

When the American government asked for Bonn's initiative in matters of the German Question, the SPD followed suit with its proposal, first broached during the 1961 campaign, for a joint review of foreign policy in the light of current unprecedented international developments. Its insistence on an all-party government was ignored as opportunistic because of its timing. Considering the nuclear stalemate and the ambivalence of American policy makers, "vacillating between deterrent and détente" as Strauss put it, it was clear that new alternatives concerning reunification had to be developed by the Germans themselves.

Brandt visualized a long-range policy of tension-easing rapprochement that would eventually unify all of Europe, as well as Germany. He was convinced that a conscious cooperative effort at peaceful coexistence was bound to grow in strength and loosen the rigid power blocs over the years. In his opinion, the nonproliferation and test ban treaties were the first steps on the painfully long road to reconciliation. To reduce the perilous confrontation in Europe, the development of mutual trust and confidence by means of measures for arms limitations, balanced disarmament followed by renunciation of force and, finally, a collective security system that included Warsaw Pact and NATO states were listed as essential items in Brandt's complex peace order catalog.

The policy of "little steps" to political but not ideological coexistence was seconded by Egon Bahr's famous speech at the Evangelic Academy in Tutzing in 1963, which advanced the concept "change through rapprochement." The German question can be solved, so proclaimed Bahr, Brandt's closest adviser and press officer, only in the framework of a long process of rapprochement between East and West. The improvement of relations with Ulbricht and the effort to improve living conditions in East Germany by expanded trade and communication would have a positive effect. The normalization of relations between Bonn and Moscow, East bloc countries, and the German Democratic Republic was in essence what came to be known as Ostpolitik.

The only other imaginative reunification and foreign policy program relating to international changes was expounded by Franz Josef Strauss. However, Strauss had been badly disgraced by his dubious role in the *Spiegel* affair, which had robbed Adenauer's weakening government of much of its luster. The *Spiegel* incident brought Strauss' blossoming career to an abrupt halt in 1962 and provoked a major government crisis. The allegations of treason, the search of the publishing house, and the unorthodox handling of the arrest of *Spiegel* editors were startling events that reminded many a German of bygone police state methods. Adenauer's FDP cabinet members resigned in protest and demanded the ouster of dynamic Defense Minister Strauss. Despite his comeback as finance minister during the Grand Coalition, Strauss never quite recovered from his fall.

With time on his hands for thinking, CSU Chairman Strauss began to talk and write about the Europeanization of the German Question so that it would not be treated as a national concern but one of common West European interest. Strauss distrusted political concepts involving goodwill. His faith in power politics remained unshaken. He saw Western Europe as a third world power. Gradually it would develop its own nuclear weapons system, while a cooperative partnership with the U.S. would be simultaneously maintained. Such a strong independent "Union of free European countries," he argued, could be expected to have an enormous magnetism and fascination for the East bloc countries. They would be attracted, as to a center of gravity, until their "national striving for self-determination flows into the wish for a political unity of all of Europe," his *Challenge and Response* optimistically maintained.

In defense of their thesis Bahr and Brandt revealed that "change through rapprochement" was a concept taken from Kennedy's "strategy for peace." This, and the warning that all-German politics must not shuttle back and forth between "all-or-nothing" propositions, calmed down the comrades. The CDU remained suspicious. If it was true that Brandt wanted to open an office for German-German relations dealing with the questions "of both German states," then his plan was nothing but another version of the confederation plans of Ulbricht, it charged, and in effect represented recognition of the GDR.

The argument was interrupted when Brandt left on a tour of Africa—to woo seven nations, all UN members, in the name of Berlin. He also made headlines in London, Paris and Washington. When he returned there was an extra bonus!

After difficult negotiations, East Berlin unexpectedly lifted the restrictions for the issuance of travel permits for West Berliners during the Christmas holiday season. By the end of the eighteen-day period, 1.2 million West Berliners had visited their relatives in East Berlin.

The SED party paper *Neues Deutschland,* stating that it was the wish of the GDR government to continue "a policy of understanding," rejected Bonn's prodding as "intervention." It stressed that questions concerning West Berlin be discussed with East Berlin's government only. Bonn's questions regarding German affairs, on the other hand, should be addressed directly to Pankow, seat of East Germany's government. The agreement on travel permits was a political matter, the SED paper informed its fellow Germans in the West, and not a "humanitarian" move.

All lecturing aside, Willy Brandt had scored the first convincing point in the battle of his policy "of small steps."

Brandt had not made it easy for the GDR rulers. The population was confused about the existence and the "character of the two Germanys and West Berlin as a special political entity, and the relationship between them," according to a poll. Worse, Honecker and Ulbricht differed in their reaction to the embrace of the West German policy. In connection with Brandt's candidacy for the chancellorship [1965], Ulbricht urged investigation of what "effects West Germany's possible orientation on the Swedish [Socialist] model might have on prospects for closer understanding between the two Germanys," Heinz Lippmann wrote in *Honecker.* Ulbricht thought, in fact, that some "interesting points" for discussion might be produced. Honecker, on the other hand, maintained that the liberalization trend had gone far enough and that the struggle for the "extensive development of Socialism and the solution of the national question in Germany" waged under complicated conditions, warranted equally complicated measures. Honecker apparently was of the opinion that the ideological vigil could not be relaxed before the German Democratic Republic was sufficiently strengthened and secure.

Top campaign form

Willy Brandt threw himself into the campaign of 1965 with all the energy and self-confidence anybody could ask of a candidate. After all, with the eminent father figure Adenauer in retirement, this was a battle that could be won. The CDU's economic miracle man Ludwig Erhard was hardly a charismatic figure. His campaign slogan, "no experiments," suited his conservative, slightly cumbersome professorial demeanor. It exuded comfort but no electrifying sparks or inspiration.

Supported by the cast of the SPD's most outstanding minds, Brandt was confident of winning his second round. The efficient Herbert Wehner, genius of strategy and organization, masterminded the overall concept. The telegenic economics professor Karl Schiller and the fast-talking Helmut Schmidt would pinch-hit where needed. Dr. Gustav Heinemann and the eloquent Professor Carlo Schmid lent a touch of sartorial dignity to the campaign crew of about a dozen "Sozi" personalities. For the first time in German history, intellectuals and celebrated artists had come out of their attics and mansions to plug a political cause.

The candidate's statement: "We have developed the new style forward-looking people's party. . . . In order to get people moving we must keep on the move ourselves," had attracted writers like Günter Grass, who crisscrossed the country making almost as many election speeches as Brandt, playwright Rolf Hochhuth, Martin Walser and others. Hans Werner Richter, of the famous literary Group 47, even edited a book entitled *A Plea for a New Government.*

They heartily agreed with Brandt that twenty years of CDU/CSU government were enough. "Enough divisiveness, enough resignation, enough looking back. The German nation has not forgotten the grim lesson of its history. But it looks ahead—to a future which must offer the same rights as it offers other peoples." After all those uninterrupted years of government by one party, the intellectuals and many of the middle-class Germans felt it was time for a change, time to establish that democracy really worked in Germany.

Let the Sozis have their chance this time, many of the liberals argued. A change was a matter of principle for them. It was of little consequence who headed the party that had never held power in the Federal Republic, so long as their objective was achieved: to prove that Germany's undemocratic authoritarian past had been overcome. For this group the credibility of the democratic system was the ultimate challenge in this election. This attitude, of course, was by no means to be construed as an unkind reflection on Adenauer's laissez faire era.

Willy Brandt was in top form. He was calmer, more self-assured, better briefed, and in the process of finding his own style. The thin breezy Kennedy veneer had given away to the image of a thoughtful political leader at home in the space flight age, the media, the international arena. Opposite the burly cigar-smoking, 68-year-old Erhard, he represented youthful vigor, the future. The stately Brandt cut an elegant figure yet, retaining a certain awkwardness, he affected the public as a simple, folksy man.

He was indefatigable. His campaign managers had laid out a brutal schedule, including 550 speeches and countless side tours to factories, socials, press conferences and block parties to charm the voters, especially the female ones, who had decided the last elections with their vote for the CDU. As before, personal attacks focused on his emigré past. These were fought with headline-making court actions and injunctions against slanderous brochures by the still overreacting candidate. Rut had to appear in court to testify that Willy, wearing a Norwegian soldier's uniform, never pulled the trigger against his German countrymen during the war. She denied that she had even discussed that point in her interview with the Danish magazine, *Alt for Damerne.*

Posters with the legend, "We will not vote for the traitor to our country," were superseded by headlines about Willy's son Peter. Like his father before him, 16-year-old Peter was a member of the SPD's "Falcons." Peter, who had objected to West Berlin as "frontier city of the cold war" because it was a nonsensical posture in this age of peaceful coexistence, had joined the protesters against "U.S. military intervention in Vietnam."

Since father Brandt had just assured President Johnson of his full moral support in Vietnam, Peter's conduct caused a great deal of needless embarrassment. The overblown incident was dramatically revived by the press when Peter withdrew his signature from the leaflet sponsored by the Socialist [Communist] Unity party attacking American action in Vietnam. Intriguingly, his dissociation from the Communist "Committee for Peace, National and International Understanding" was accompanied by an announcement that he still stood by tne contents of the resolution.

In order to keep the boy out of mischief, Brandt took his independent son on his campaign trip. Young Brandt showed that he was just as inventive as his father by turning out a campaign report that was dutifully printed in the SPD's official paper, *Berliner Stimme.* Brandt's party friends shook their heads. His detractors wondered openly about the difference between fatherly tolerance and irresponsible indulgence.

The exemplary whistle-stop tour through towns and out of the way villages was by special train. The accompanying press dubbed the strenuous campaign marathon a "tour of tribulation."

Brandt, the activist who worked best under pressure or in an intense situation of acute danger, was a natural campaigner. He seemed much more at home in front of a crowd, nailing down complex issues in simple language, than behind a desk or conference table, facing the burdensome task of making decisions. Everything appeared to go right in this campaign; still, something was amiss.

In the effort to become a respectable people's party, the SPD had drawn closer to the middle. As a consequence, the party found itself without rousing issues and attractive alternatives to bolster its image. Talking about a "better way to prosperity" in a society already prosperous evoked no excitement among listeners. Erhard, in office a relatively brief period, could hardly be held responsible for the "immobilism" of Adenauer's "Germany policy." In the end, the voters decided that the SPD did not differ sufficiently from the CDU to merit a change, even for change's sake. At least they were not willing to exchange a functioning known quality for an unknown one.

It was possible that Wehner, the clever strategist, knew all the time if the campaign was lost, as it was—the CDU's vote had leaped to 47.6 percent, the SPD's was 39.3 percent, and the FDP's 11.4 percent—then at least it had established the prelude, the perfect precondition for a grand coalition.

The candidate and all his vigor had not been of much help. When the name *Willy Brandt* was used in word association tests, the public thought of folksy things like "garden restaurant, lightning, tar, or baby carriage." Only 39 percent thought of him as "ideal chancellor." Less than a third of the group tested believed that he had served "Germany well." A study by the Ima Institute revealed that the negative picture resulted not from his controversial past, but from a feeling that Brandt "lacked substance" and had been "built up too much."

This opinion was widely shared by the party's leaders. Most of them preferred the substantial thinker Fritz Erler, though wanting in features that were visually pleasing to crowd and camera, as their chancellor candidate to the all too flexible and adjustable cover boy. If Brandt was more than a rubber lion and showman, they argued, he would have shucked the limelight of Berlin for the immeasurably more demanding position as opposition leader in the Bundestag to prove his capabilities. The impression that Brandt was a self-important blowhard, likely to back down when it came to delivering the goods, dated back to 1959 and 1963 when he failed to meet Nikita Khrushchev in East Berlin. Although his party comrades and even Chancellor Adenauer urged him to accept the Soviet premier's invitation, he wavered back and forth before arriving at his negative decision, which puzzled everybody. Berlin's CDU coalition partners, opposed to Brandt's acceptance of the Soviet bid, threatened to blow up the coalition. It fell apart anyway, which made Brandt's retreat even more pointless.

"The difficulties which the welcome invitation caused at home do not challenge but paralyze him," Hermann Schreiber commented in *Spiegel.* Brandt's SPD friends feared a pattern in his indecisive reactions to genuine challenges that could not be solved by juggling or compromise.

The public opinion polls, showing that the SPD was leading by a nose, were mistaken. The defeat came as a mortal blow to the totally exhausted Brandt, who had believed the optimistic prognostications of his advisers. The tremendous disappointment and its ramifications triggered a deep new depression.

"I will not talk around the matter," *Spiegel* quoted Brandt, "the SPD has not reached its election goal." Brandt had lost his second campaign. Could there be a comeback for a two-time loser, his friends wondered? Like Nixon after one of his famous crises, Brandt complained to the press of being deeply hurt by the "dirty election campaign."

He went about with the dazed look of a sleepwalker. Surrounded by an aura of petulance and doom, he cut himself off from present surroundings, from the world that rejected him, by retreating into himself. No, "they" would not have Brandt to kick around any more. Rumors of his resignation as party chairman flourished in Bonn and Berlin. In the corridors of the SPD headquarters, the name of Fritz Erler dominated in the quick exchanges among the dispirited functionaries. But Erler's health was not good; he died within the next year.

Brandt returned to Berlin prepared for a new letdown. However, the sturdy Berliners still loved him. When he entered the House of Representatives, the governing mayor received a full round of applause.

Still there was the ominous announcement: "The office of candidate for chancellor has ceased to exist in the SPD. I shall serve my party best by giving up my candidacy for 1969."

As in any Horatio Alger story, it is always darkest before dawn.

The comeback

When Brandt returned, tanned and rested from a vacation, it was clear that the restive, 51-year-old politician was fully determined to fight for his political life. He hoped to regain lost momentum by trying to revive the issue of the exchange of speakers between the SPD and the East German SED. Brandt, Wehner and Erler were supposed to speak at public meetings in Karl-Marx-Stadt, formerly Chemnitz, while three SED functionaries were to address the West German population in Hanover. Ulbricht had been friendly toward the idea in the beginning but as time went by got cold feet and pressed for a postponement.

Honecker, in charge of security at home and abroad, had taken a different tack. While agreeing that it was the SED's main goal to strengthen its influence on "the peace-loving people in West Germany," he nevertheless engaged in exhortative demands. Either the working people of the two Germanys reach an understanding, he stated, or the solution of the German question is impossible.

The position that a reunification of Germany is only possible with a socialistic-communistic government in the West, incidentally, is still held by the government of the German Democratic Republic today. It is interesting to note that *Pravda,* the official organ of the Soviet government, printed an article in March 1975 in which the West German Social Democrats were encouraged to warm up to the "popular front" idea and to foment a coalition with the Communists.

In emphasizing that any kind of "infiltration into the German workers' and peasants' state is over forever," and that they intended to protect humanity from the "blood-stained imperialist system," Honecker had given a different signal. Nothing came of the proposed exchange of speakers. It was quietly buried during the "safe conduct law" discussions, designed to suspend a West German law calling for the arrest of GDR officials in any way responsible for shots fired at the Berlin Wall.

The turbulent party convention in Dortmund in the summer of 1966 provided Brandt with an unexpected chance to prove his conciliatory mediating qualities. The lost election had filled the membership with lethargy and discontent. The critical left vehemently attacked the "bourgeois tendencies" of the party for its approval of the emergency laws. A representative of the trade union openly warned of a breakaway of the unions if these conservative tendencies persisted.

From East Germany, the chief of propaganda of the Politbureau, Albert Norden, attacked the SPD leadership for turning the party into a "branch of the capitalistic" CDU, and for the betrayal of the cause of the workers. Brandt, who had not delivered a very memorable formal speech before, stepped up to the microphones once more. This time, talking freely without the iron corset of a prefabricated manuscript, he convinced the critics that this was not the time to weaken the party by internal strife and dissent. His stern call for solidarity and full endorsement of the Godesberg Program turned the tide. It calmed the defiant functionaries and prompted a wave of wild emotional applause for the chairman, who was reelected by 324 out of 326 votes. It was a ballot, Bolesch-Leicht exuberate, such as even the legendary August Bebel had never achieved.

Bolstered by the overwhelming vote of confidence, Brandt threw himself into the regional election battle of Nordhein-Westphalia. Aided by a slight recession, which resulted in the closing of some of the region's coal mines, and by rising unemployment in West Germany's most populous state, Brandt carried the Social Democrats to their first shining victory after the demoralizing defeat in the general elections. A turning point had at long last been reached.

"We cannot yet do everything we wish," said a beaming Willy Brandt, "but the others can no longer do as they wish."

As Germany's strongest single party—the Social Democrats had captured 661 of 1349 seats in the 11 state governments—the SPD issued a statement in which it announced its claim for the nomination of the federal president from its own ranks. Meanwhile, Brandt enhanced his mounting prestige with a spectacular five-hour meeting with Pyotr Abrasimov, Soviet ambassador to the GDR. The highly publicized rendezvous on October 12, a conference on normalization of relations, attended by the photogenic Rut, overshadowed an event of much greater importance for the SPD: the active pursuit of a Grand Coalition. Wehner had put his feelers out before in that direction. Erhard's increasing economic difficulties provided the

SPD with a genuine chance to push ahead with this marriage of political convenience.

PUSH FOR A GRAND COALITION

Early in September, when it became obvious that Erhard had lost his grip on the unfolding economic minirecession, Brandt tested the grand coalition waters by declaring: "Those who suspect us of trying to squeeze into a position of mere co-rulership just because our strength has grown are mistaken." Grandiloquently, Wehner seconded that notion by virtually asking for Erhard's resignation: "We are not pushing ourselves onto the wobbly ship of government. It would have to be rebuilt from scratch and have a different crew."

By the time the FDP ministers left Erhard's cabinet on October 27 over the irreconcilable disagreement on the balancing of the budget and the increase in taxes, the coalition negotiations between Wehner and the CSU's Baron von und zu Guttenberg, on the one hand, and Erhard's prospective successor, Kurt Georg Kiesinger and Brandt, on the other, had reached a feverish pitch. Insiders confirmed that Brandt's unwillingness to enter into a grand coalition with the conservatives, and especially with an ex-Nazi like the Prime Minister of Baden-Württemberg, was a myth.

Spiegel reported on September 15, 1969, that Brandt rejected the Grand Coalition initiated by Wehner. Then, when confronted with the party's fait accompli on November 24, 1966, Brandt supposedly rejoined, "Well, then go ahead, but without me." This was unequivocally contradicted by Klaus Sönksen, Brandt's personal assistant and close associate from 1964 to 1970. Sönksen confirmed that Brandt would have preferred a coalition with the Free Democrats had the combined votes sufficed to make it feasible. He insisted, however, that Brandt had nothing against a coalition with the CDU/CSU or working with Kiesinger, whom he knew and respected from committee meetings in the Bundestag since the 1950s. As prime minister of Baden-Württemberg, Kiesinger was assuredly not held responsible by Brandt for Bonn's blunders.

"They always had a good relationship," Sönksen commented, "and it is absolute nonsense to think that Wehner directed the coalition negotiations by himself. As chairman of the party, Brandt was actively involved in laying the groundwork. It was nothing but accidental that Brandt was too late for the leadership vote on the CDU coalition issue. Because of a ground fog no planes were leaving Berlin. We had to drive to Hannover and take the plane from there."

Chancellor Erhard had resigned under pressure and his successor was trying to form a cabinet to lead the "limited-term partnership." Brandt's announcement of his party's participation in the new government of November 26, after the deadlock over the distribution of eleven ministries for the CDU and nine for the SPD was broken, resulted in violent protests from the Social Democrats. The Bundeshaus was flooded with letters and cables urging the SPD representatives not to join the Christian Democrats. While the public reacted rather favorably to the Grand Coalition as a means of solving the current economic crisis, thirty idealistic Social Democrats marched on Bonn to warn their comrades of the dangers in making common cause with the conservatives in an oppositionless one-party government.

During the party leaders' meeting—which lasted until 4 A.M.—one of the deputies said: "If the Social Democrats join a German government after a break of 36 years, we must make sure that there is no crash landing." Many of the party members had fallen for their own party's propaganda line depicting the CDU/CSU as a restoration party, hawkish, antiprogressive, pro big business, antisocial, reactionary, and made up of politicians who try to capture the vote by willfully attempting to instill insecurity and ignorance in the voting public.

In the end, after three ballots, the pragmatic coalitionists, patiently arguing that only participation in government could remove from the public mind the well-ingrained stigma that the Social Democrats were not fit to govern, won out over the integrity of the purists who abhorred compromises with the "enemy" and predicted the ruination of the party. The uncompromising SPD veteran Franz Neumann, old, unbent and righteous foe of Willy Brandt, was among them. Once more he demonstrated his independence by refusing to give his vote to ex-Nazi Chancellor Kiesinger. Pointedly charging Brandt with ruthlessly depriving him of his Berlin mandate as a member of the Bundestag, the formidable "storm bell of Berlin" died a bitter, forgotten hero and a badly disappointed man two days after his seventieth birthday in 1974.

The anxiously awaited oppositionless Grand Coalition, headed by

Chancellor Kiesinger and Vice-Chancellor Brandt as foreign minister, was born on December 1, 1966. Born with it, like a Siamese twin, was the extraparliamentary opposition composed of young militant leftist Social Democrats, the Jusos, and the radical student left. When Brandt heard of protest meetings in Berlin and elsewhere, he declared he had expected a strong reaction from a party of 720,000 active members, never known as a club of "yes" men. "I know my son Peter," he joked at a press conference. "He will be there." He was there, among thousands of young people, intellectuals and artists who had supported the SPD and felt betrayed. In a letter of protest, Günter Grass appealed to Kiesinger not to burden the country with his chancellorship.

It was an auspicious start.

"This is, of course, no great leap forward in the country's political development," Brandt insisted, "and no great leap into government authority for us Social Democrats. But it remains to be seen whether this 'grand solution' may not be a big step if it is carried out with integrity. That would at least be something."

If the 1965 campaign was the precondition to the Grand Coalition, the Grand Coalition was the prelude to the SPD's move into power. After storming the bastion on the Rhine two times and failing, Brandt finally had entered by way of a conspicuous detour. The liberal, pro-Brandt press made much of his remark that he reached power after he had given up all "personal ambition." The ambition was no longer to "be someone" but to "do something."

This was difficult to believe, especially in view of the publication of a book of his selected writings, *Draussen,* gleaned from his journalistic output in exile. The stringent samples of Brandt's political credo, screened and edited by twenty-six-year-old Günter Struve, were supposed to give proof of his nonradical, non-Marxist past and to establish him as an unassailable democrat. These fragments, amended by letters and current introductions, which furnished a great deal more pertinent and open information about the author's political engagement and unquestionable Socialist heritage than the streamlined Brandt-Lania memoirs, represented an "important historical document" to his fans. His real friends, however, wished he had made available the original texts of his major writings to avoid the impression of offering "doctored" material.

Brandt liked to strike a philosophical pose in the wake of his defeats. A brief illness suffered during the week before the anxiously anticipated downfall of Erhard's government, a frightening gastrocardiac attack, possibly of psychosomatic origin, causing shortness of breath, suffocation and heart attack symptoms, led to the dramatic shedding of exterior trimmings.

"Since I have looked death in the eye," Brandt gravely told his friends from the press, "I see things under the aspect of the irrevocable." Such an experience makes relative all other insights and observations. "Now I see the world with different eyes, in a new perspective."

13 Building an Image

Whether it was this mysterious illness or the new, important office of vice-chancellor, near fulfillment of his high-flown dreams, Brandt had indeed changed.

He was less uptight, more composed. The anxiety to please at any price, mark of the eternal candidate, had disappeared. The new foreign minister was less restive than Berlin's governing mayor, more relaxed and dignified but also more aloof. As the first postwar Sozi vice-chancellor, he certainly was not welcomed with open arms by the conservative, striped pants set, but soon earned its respect by working late hours and quickly familiarizing himself with organization charts and the issues. He also gained the reputation of being able to quickly grasp the essentials of complex international problems and examine possible solutions.

The young officials who worked directly with him thought him one of the most considerate, correct and fair of chiefs. They praised his ability to listen and to digest rapidly the bulky background material they stuffed into his briefcase. They admired his proficiency in languages—besides the Scandinavian tongues, he was fluent in English and conversant with French and Spanish—his wide acquaintance with world leaders on a personal level, and his unfailing memory for historic developments and events.

Brandt, the internationalist, felt comfortably at home in his new job. For the first time in his life, the years of emigration, the thorough knowledge he had gained of other societies and their differing mentalities, even his foreign-born wife, had become professional assets rather than political handicaps to himself and his party. The warm reception the certified anti-Nazi received abroad as representative of the "other Germany" spread its reflected glow over the whole staid old officialdom.

If he lacked the talent for sociable small talk—protocol officers remember nightmarish state dinners with the foreign minister as silent dinner partner to frustrated ladies from all over the world, including India's Prime Minister Indira Gandhi—he nevertheless, at the drop of a hat, could deliver an official toast with arcane grace. Above all, he was willing to act, to meet, to travel, to initiate instead of procrastinating.

Before his disenchantment with Ospolitik set in, historian Golo Mann rated Brandt as one of the foremost foreign ministers in German history. Mann stood not alone in his positive judgment. For Brandt, the three years spent in the Foreign Office count as the most satisfactory in his entire life. After the fall, his confidants were eager to convey the message that the SPD chairman would not mind being recruited for that office again.

For Rut Brandt, the transition from Berlin to Bonn was a considerably more painful process. As Berlin's elegant First Lady she had found a secure place among the broad-minded Berliners. With her husband away most of the time, whether in Bonn or Timbuktu, building goodwill for the divided city, she had created her own circle of loyal friends who accepted her and her individualistic lifestyle. Early on, she had insisted on a degree of privacy by putting her family life ahead of representational duties connected with the mayor's office. She had not clamored for publicity by visiting orphanages or homes for unwed mothers.

The Berliners were even generous enough to forget and forgive her ill-conceived literary excursion, *Rut Brandt Tells Her Life Story,* which appeared as part of Willy's first election campaign. These "exclusive reports" in Berlin's most sensational boulevard gazette *BZ* in 1960 were designed to clear up the past. The series became the target of unmerciful derision because of its simplistic, true-confessions style, and the detailed description of her labor pains during the birth of her first son.

The small formal town on the Rhine frightened her. She would like to keep her villa in Berlin when she moved to Bonn, Rut told reporters. She would make use of this escape hatch for a long time. After nine years, Berlin was home to her. Three sons had grown into genuine Berliners, talking in the unmistakable vernacular of the city. How would the uppity wives of the state department's officials receive the pretty Norwegian worker's daughter, whose German, enchanting though it was to gentlemen and to members of the press, was anything but perfect? She did not relish her prospective life in a fish bowl, or the necessity of assembling a new circle of confidants. Actually, there were friends who knew that Rut, like son Peter who stayed on in Berlin, had opposed going to Bonn and only relented out of a sense of duty to her husband's career.

Of course, Rut need not have worried. The vivacious woman charmed the Bonners almost as much as the Berliners. Those who refused to be charmed by her unsophisticated friendliness reminded each other of the importance of her husband's position. Only the press, having hoped that Rut Brandt might be the person to create a Bonn salon where artists and literati would gather for spirited exchanges with the reigning politicians and thinkers of the land, was badly disappointed at the discovery that Rut had neither the educational and cultural attributes for becoming the country's Madame Récamier, nor the ambition and social background for creating a glittering jet-set Camelot as Jackie Kennedy had done. The intellectual ladies of the press visibly winced when Rut innocently singled out *Valley of the Dolls* as her favorite American novel, absolutely unaware of the revealing nature of her remark.

Bonn never became Rut's oyster, not even as the reigning chancellor's wife. Bravely accentuating the positive, she adjusted to its ways and it adjusted as best it could to Rut, who maintained that "one sleeps better in Bonn." The remark, no doubt, was made after she had discovered the proximity of Cologne, Hamburg, Munich and other places. Shunning ladies' teas and enjoying cocktail party small talk, Rut resolutely went about christening ships, looking for a tailor who would come to the house, being photographed in "dirndl" dresses, and admitting to being lazy, sleeping late, and having breakfast in bed.

Willy Dreams Politics

While she did not give interviews, she sometimes revealed her loneliness in informal "talks" with reporters over a drink or a cup of tea. "It is good that there is a radio, my husband never tells me anything," she inadvertently confessed. She proclaimed to be without ambition, not the kind of pushy woman who seeks self-fulfillment by driving her husband to success, and freely attested to the fact that her political influence with Willy was zero. "Sometimes I believe he dreams politics," she complained with an amused shrug.

As the years went by, her tone became more desperate and more sarcastic. Asked in 1970 if her husband was feeling better after a severe attack of the flu, she snapped back: "Maybe—the other day on television he looked pretty bad." Bonn may have grown accustomed to Brandt's continuous absences, Rut did not. She had no feeling for power, the woman whose ambition had been to run a high-class hairdressing salon told the *Frankfurter Neue Presse.* When Brandt had to decide if they would remain in Norway or go to Germany, she told him she could not give advice in such a matter. "You will have to decide this yourself. I will follow you. In professional things, I don't interfere."

In spite of her inherent robustness and assertiveness, Rut was not a liberated woman. In attempting to act the chancellor's wife, she had her portrait painted by Bonn's society painter, Baroness Maria Josepha von Fürstenberg. Rut posed in the aristocratic artist's studio three times and loathed the resulting likeness. One of her husband's officials diplomatically described her reaction this way: "She felt like all people who stand in front of their own portraits. She was a little nonplussed. She surely will not hang the picture in her room. But it could be that she will give it to one of her sons. . . ."

As Rut learned to cope with life in Bonn, her celebrated gay laughter on the dance floor was heard less often. Substituting for her husband at concerts, dining at the swankier restaurants with the wife of former *Spiegel* editor and later government spokesman Conrad Ahlers, visiting art shows, and answering letters from the public, some thirty a day, made her long for the good old days in Berlin. Henry Kissinger and Brezhnev as dinner partners were no substitutes for "only a few minutes of marriage a day." If Willy came home early, which was seldom enough, he went up to his attic room to work and she looked at television, she told the papers.

Her metallic turquoise BMW was seen dashing all over Bonn and Cologne. At the annual press balls, Rut still enjoyed the attention of a great star, dancing and laughing until the wee hours. The gossip sheets neither forgot to mention her new curly, streaked hairdo nor the lucky partner who got to dance most frequently with Brandt's wife.

In the end, feeling sorry for lonely, outgoing Rut, the press reported that she lived withdrawn "like a recluse" in her villa on Venusberg. Reportedly, she fled to see old friends in Norway and Berlin at ever shorter intervals.

According to the hostile *Bild,* Rut did not know of her husband's decision to resign from the chancellor's office. It is hard to believe that a man would make such a momentous move without consulting his wife.

The much maligned Grand Coalition was better than its reputation. Wehner's ingenious adjustment strategy, which featured the dramatic divestment of predominant Marxian traces at Bad Godesberg in 1959 and the disastrous Wehner Plan of the summer of 1960 in favor of an auspicious alignment with the conservative parties' Atlantic Alliance and West European policies, introduced the necessary climate for the Grand Coalition. It in turn was to change and revise the profile of the SPD into that of a responsible democratic burgher's party in the image of Western democracies.

As an activist junior partner of the CDU/CSU, the Sozis were given a chance to prove to the public that they, too, were able to govern. Known to the suspicious German voters as a negative force, they at long last were in a position to demonstrate their ability to help their country climb out of the recession quagmire and move ahead.

Wehner's calculations proved correct. After three years of Grand Coalition, the efficient SPD team had enhanced its prestige to such a degree that in 1969 it presented itself to the voters as a credible alternative capable of taking over and leading the next government.

The Sozis charged into the political arena like a starved bunch of understudies, knocking themselves out to show off their talents in the dress rehearsal, one eye firmly fixed on the dazzled audience, waiting for applause, the fateful signal that they were ready to take over the main parts. The weary old officials in Bonn's ministries were speechless. Never had they witnessed such tempo, such energy, such eagerness to get things done. The Social Democrats knew, of course, that they did not have a minute to waste. The choice was simple. Either they saw to it that this coalition was a success or they would be relegated to the chorus line on the opposition benches. So they furiously set to work to bring off the experiment, the first of its kind in German history and subject to misgivings from all sides of the political spectrum.

The three pillars supporting the Social Democrats' winning strategy in 1969 were economic, social and peace policy issues. Economics Minister Karl Schiller managed to turn the recessional tide. His policy mix of government steering and free enterprise, brought about by the "concerted action" of government, management and unions, resulted in the stability of "controlled growth." His intention of curbing imported inflation by the revaluation of the mark, fiercely resisted by CSU Finance Minister Franz Josef Strauss, becomes Chancellor Kiesinger's foremost target in the 1969 election campaign.

Attorney General Gustav Heinemann, assisted by Horst Ehmke, proposed a major reform of the criminal law, the first in fifty years to focus on rehabilitation rather than punishment. Under Helmut Schmidt's guidance, a bill that provided pay for sick workers, patterned after the provisions made for employees, is passed. Bills providing for tax reforms and long-term financial planning were also enacted. So many reform bills accumulated in the hopper—the most important dealt with codetermination, profit-sharing and prohibition of land speculation—that only the experts could sort them out.

Activating Ostpolitik

It was Brandt, however—aided by Wehner as Minister for all-German Questions—who stole the thunder by his impressive performance as foreign minister. Promising to shift from the confrontation over "reunification in peace," an issue with the Christian Democratic Unions, to a continuum of the general line of German foreign policy practiced since Adenauer in 1951—integration into the military alliance of the West with its orientation toward Washington and Western Europe—Brandt proposed to explore the possibilities of normalization of relations with the East. He was hardly confirmed in office when he explained to the French, during a NATO Council of Ministers' meeting in Paris, his concept of détente and peace policy, dovetailed into the prevailing rapprochement strategy in Washington.

The French press praised the "new beginning" and Denmark's Social Democratic Prime Minister Krag, an old friend of Brandt's, commented that only a German anti-Nazi could have made such a convincing speech. After establishing good rapport with the grand Charles de Gaulle—a prerogative the conservatives thought reserved for Adenauer and Erhard's Foreign Minister Schröder—Brandt was off to open diplomatic relations with Romania and to resume the bogged-down talks with Yugoslavia's Tito which had been broken off earlier because his recognition of the GDR violated the Federal Republic's Hallstein Doctrine. Brandt did not abandon the traditional Hallstein Doctrine all at once but applied it only to nations friendly to the West German government. Following his theory of "small steps," he got rid of it in piecemeal fashion by insisting on "pragmatic" considerations and finally arguing that the doctrine in effect left it to the East Germans to decide where the Federal Republic's flags were hoisted. His economic scouts swarm into Bucharest, Belgrade, Warsaw and East Berlin as well as Prague, to establish and strengthen relations with Bonn.

While Chancellor Kiesinger and his CDU/CSU were in agreement with the impatient foreign minister on a policy of reconciliation with Germany's neighbors in the East, including the German Democratic Republic, as well as mutual renunciation of force, a policy of little steps to ease the lot of seventeen million East Germans, and talks about disarmament and security, the mounting tactical differences caused continuous friction. Kiesinger was the first federal chancellor even to accept and answer the hand-delivered letters from the government of the GDR. Its premier, Willi Stoph, made use of the occasion for repeating his and the Soviets' old demands: recognition of the existing borders, especially the border between the two German states, renunciation of nuclear weapons, and disarmament in both states.

It was the old quest for recognition of their statehood, pushed before and after Khrushchev by the Soviets, to consolidate their power vis-à-vis the built-up NATO forces in the West. More importantly, it was a move to force the West Germans to deal with Moscow on the question of reunification, thereby diminishing the U.S. influence in central Europe. Full sovereignty for the GDR would shift the balance of power in Europe to benefit Moscow, the Americans thought. Recognition of the German Democratic Republic was the last thing they wanted to endorse, even in the name of détente. They held out until 1974. For similar reasons, the State Department never showed any eagerness to advance the Soviet's pet idea of multilateral talks in the framework of a Conference on Security and Cooperation in Europe (CSCE), definitely supported by Brandt.

Former Assistant Secretary of State George Ball, reviewing the situation in 1971, voiced his reservations toward Brandt's Ostpolitik by pointing out that the American government could not be expected to be maneuvered into "the impossible situation" of talking the Germans out of initiatives which in their view eased the fate of the East German population.

Ball did not think mutual Soviet-German assurances of renunciation of force a solid enough basis for a German foreign policy. Showing concern over Bonn's hurried approach, which he thought rendered it unable to coax concessions out of the Soviets—in the Berlin negotiations, for example—Ball reiterated President Nixon's warning that there was no quick solution to the European East-West conflict.

Nixon insisted on making headway in matters of substance instead of atmospheric conditions. Sharply attacking as "illusionistic" the "differentiated relaxation of tension" limited by the USSR to certain allies in the West, Nixon called for a finely attuned Allied policy complementing the combined efforts on behalf of détente. Individual contacts, he subtly hinted, could only lead to the embarrassing situation of having to choose between national interest and European obligation.

Secret Diplomacy

Kiesinger's contacts with Soviet Ambassador Zarapkin in Bonn were probably as cordial as those enjoyed by Brandt. Yet it soon became apparent that the CDU chancellor wanted to tread slowly when it came to the execution of Ostpolitik, whereas his SPD foreign minister wanted to plunge ahead.

Brandt used his excellent contacts, Sweden's Prime Minister Tage Erlander, Foreign Minister Torsten Nilsson, Finland's Prime Minister Kekkonen and his old political friends in Norway, to open the channels of communication to the Soviet government. Using the same indirect method, he approached Poland's government through intermediaries in Ankara and The Hague.

But not all contacts were made this way. Kiesinger was furious upon learning that his foreign minister and Egon Bahr had instituted rounds of top secret talks with Italian Communist leaders. These preliminary discussions had been conducted by the SPD's Egon Franke, Friedrich Wesemann, and ex-Communist functionary Leo Bauer, Brandt's special confidant and ghostwriter until his death in 1972.

Bauer, a swashbuckling Gordon Liddy type fond of adventure, women and referring to himself as the "grand soigné conspirative," was one of the most controversial figures of Brandt's inner circle. Also known as Rudolf Katz when in exile, he fled to Paris after being arrested by the Nazis as a member of the Communist party and became Wehner's friend in the Popular Front days. His life story has all the elements of a great thriller: top Communist functionary in Spain; Secretary to the High Commissioner of the League of Nations in charge of conducting the exodus of German political refugees from Prague; alleged contact man for the Comintern and OSS; imprisoned in Switzerland; Communist representative in Hesse's state parliament after the war in 1946; thereafter chief editor for an SED-directed radio network in East Germany; sentenced to death in Moscow in 1952 as "Titoist" but more likely for his connection to double-agent Noel Field; released after a few years in a Siberian labor camp; East expert for *Stern* magazine in West Germany, through Wehner's intervention; after 1968, chief editor of the SPD intellectual magazine, *Neue Gesellschaft.*

When the sensational news broke, fanning suspicions of a "sell-out" to the Communists, the conflicting comments from SPD spokesmen ranged from summary dismissal as defamatory rumors to the claim that Kiesinger had had knowledge of the secret meetings. When asked about the incident in 1975, Klaus Sönksen had a perfectly reasonable explanation. The talks with the Communists, initiated to test the general negotiation climate, were strictly party business and conducted as such with the approval of the SPD executive committee. A report to Chancellor Kiesinger was not necessary because the talks were not held under the auspices of Foreign Minister Brandt but of Party Chairman Brandt, Sönksen maintained.

In a talk with me, exspeechwriter Klaus Harpprecht, however, insisted that Bauer's missions were undertaken on a strictly private basis and that Kiesinger was unofficially informed of them.

Once more, one of the ugliest rumors about the new SPD Foreign

Minister's radical leftist past, nurtured by a front page article in Sweden's liberal *Aftonbladet* on December 14, 1966, began to make the rounds. *Aftonbladet* reported that Brandt's new position must have come as "somewhat of a shock" to the Swedish Security Police: "In its secret files voluminous material about Willy Brandt can be found. He is said to be under suspicion of East espionage."

While most of the documents dated back to World War II when Swedish security exchanged information with the Gestapo, *Aftonbladet* thought it significant that material on Brandt, listed as Frahm, was still being collected in 1966 under the entry, "östblocket" espionage. True to the motto that where there is smoke there also must be fire, the fact that the sensational item—it was learned that Swedish security kept approximately 300,000 such files in its vaults—did not surface in the German press until years later, unfortunately served as source material for even wilder speculations.

Another flap resulted from a reproach voiced by SED chairman Ulbricht at a Communist party convention in Warsaw in 1968. Ulbricht charged that the SPD had not kept its promise to recognize the GDR by "partial" agreement. When the right-wing press speculated that Brandt's emissary Egon Bahr had jumped the recognition gun in secret talks with East German Communist leaders, Ulbricht's words were immediately interpreted as false or vile attacks on Bahr, originating in the GDR. West German papers printing these defamations were only aiding Ulbricht, so the SPD line went. Suddenly everybody—from shocked Kiesinger to defensive Brandt and silent Bahr—wanted an investigation.

At a press conference, Brandt tried to soothe the excited public and the press with the surprising news that Bahr had indeed "conducted many talks of which the public knows nothing." Since these talks had been blessed with his approval, there was no occasion for alarm. Somehow, Brandt never answered the specific question. In "the interest of the state" he preferred not to comment on Bahr's meetings. The press was not happy. "The Foreign Minister should have put his cards on the table," a Cologne paper charged. "He has spread a protective veil over Bahr."

For a time, the Grand Coalition hung by a thin thread. But neither the conservatives nor the Sozis felt like facing the voters as the party responsible for the breakdown of the political mismarriage.

Although Brandt and Soviet ambassador Zarapkin had worked

out a fourteen-point program in 1967, which ranged from cultural exchanges, trade and troop reductions, to the question of German partition, nothing was heard from the Kremlin until it wanted to discuss Berlin in 1968. Lashing out at Brandt's naiveté, Kiesinger mockingly observed that the Soviets were only fooling Bonn by keeping it on their "renunciation of force string." In Brandt's willingness to sign the nuclear nonproliferation treaty, Kiesinger saw but another instance of a "capitulation that comes much too soon."

Meanwhile, the climate of détente had drastically changed. Brandt's progress in Ostpolitik was seriously stunted by the Soviets' brutal military intervention in Prague. On August 21, 1968, Soviet, Hungarian, Bulgarian and East German troops and tanks of the Warsaw Pact forces marched into Czechoslovakia to crush the liberalizing trend that had begun to blossom under Alexander Dubçek's brief reign.

"We will not permit the central principle of our ideology to be watered down," East Germany's Honecker warned. At the Ninth Plenary Session of the Central Committee he spoke of the "antisocialist development in the Czechoslovakian Soviet of Socialist Republics" and decried the "revisionist, counterrevolutionary trend" that could no longer be stopped by political measures. Turning on the West German SPD in general and Brandt in particular, Honecker unequivocally rejected the "building of bridges," the "change through rapprochement," the "seduction of Eastern Europe," along with the "new Ostpolitik" and modish "convergence theories."

Unflappable Brandt, though distraught at Honecker's abuse, was by no means discouraged enough to write off his Ostpolitik as an impossible dream. He kept aloof. "What matters is to safeguard one's own interests. One must couch what one wants in interests shared by a good many others. . . . What matters is sensing that we cannot march wildly through the landscape but must make the attempt to figure out how, after horrible impressions, new positions can be built up again which will not lead to more destructive reactions."

In an article *German Foreign Policy after August 21st* he submitted conclusive evidence that his intrinsic tenacity was still intact: "I believe it is part of the fundamental principle of acting in foreign politics to consistently continue a policy recognized as correct over long terms. . . ." The future of the middle and smaller powers depends on their community of spirit and action. The superpowers will respect that as time goes on—if they are interested in securing peace, he concluded confidently.

Changing climate

The year 1968, marked by intellectual unrest and student uprisings all over the world, was a disappointment to the Social Democrats. Since the party had taken the grand coalition vow, it had lost five out of six regional elections. Ironically, its worst losses were charted up in liberal Bremen, where the Sozis had ruled supreme for twelve years. In Baden-Württemberg, the SPD's vote had slipped surprisingly from 37.3 to an all-time low of 29 percent. Even in their very own fortress, Berlin, 5 percent of previous SPD voters had turned against them and, so pollsters and political scientists said, against the Grand Coalition.

The dispirited SPD triumvirate—Brandt, Wehner, Schmidt—hardly spoke to each other. Wehner blamed the fiasco on the desertion of the unions. Schmidt tried to praise Brandt into the genteel retirement of the federal presidency. Brandt did not believe the computers. When he did, he felt like resigning from the cabinet to stitch together the fraying party machine. Schiller sensibly demanded better and more publicity focusing on the successful legislation of their team.

The worst of the facts was that the right-wing "Neonazis," the National Democratic party of Germany, whose membership had swollen to 50,000 (the FDP had 80,000) since its inception in 1964, had harvested 10 percent of the Baden-Württemberg vote and 5.2 percent in Lower Saxony. Indirectly, the SPD and its one-party coalition was held responsible even for that scary phenomenon. The Neonazis had emerged as a counterforce to the leftist students and radicalized youth who had assumed the role of the extraparliamentary opposition, registering criticism by protests in the streets. The rebellious New Left—crusading against the immobile establishment, bureaucracy, authoritarianism, and a good many other things—had badly upset the law-abiding German burgher.

Student uprisings were primarily responsible for a cabinet crisis in Paris, the reshuffling of the administration in Prague, and a shakeup of West Berlin's city government. As Marx had taught them, the leftists tried to create from the critique of the old world the foundation for a new society. They protested against the war in Vietnam, the Greek junta, and Bonn's "emergency laws" which could provide a political strongman with the tools for totalitarianism. They showered the Shah of Iran with eggs and tomatoes, protesting his dictatorship, and intended to bombard Hubert H. Humphrey with plastic bags filled with pudding which were confiscated by the embarrassed police as "explosive material." They demonstrated for codetermination of the workers, reforms of the outdated educational system, and recognition of the GDR and the Oder-Neisse border line. They wanted a "ruler free-society," a radical democracy they called it.

There was violence and bloodshed and a potential for terror that survived the movement in the Baader-Meinhof group, the shooting of Berlin's chief justice, Günter von Drenkmann, and the kidnapping of CDU mayor candidate Peter Lorenz in 1975. The movement had its own martyrs. In June 1967, Benno Ohnesorg, a twenty-six-year-old student of literature, was shot dead in cold blood by a police officer during the Berlin demonstrations against the Shah. Nine months later, Rudi Dutschke was struck down by a bullet. The attempted assassination of Red Rudi, perhaps the most prominent student leader, prompted the outbreak of riots all over the country.

Resentment mounted sharply on both sides. The Germans reacted against the violence by voting for law and order.

Rebellion brewed in the ranks of the Jusos. At the 1968 SPD convention in Nuremberg, they would no longer reverently listen to their elders. The march through the institutions meant also a march on the party hierarchy. They heckled the august speakers and would not be silenced by admonishing lectures on the meaning of solidarity. To their unending surprise, Herbert Wehner, Carlo Schmid and Willy Brandt were vilified and even physically attacked by the angry youths, who demanded a stronger voice at the decision-making level.

According to Norman Crossland of the *Guardian,* Brandt responded to the question if the blow over the head with an umbrella had hurt, with a quickwitted: "No, the man rather hit me out of principle." It had become accepted practice for politicians on both sides of the spectrum to ridicule the rebels or to demand ousters from their respective parties.

Klaus Schütz, Brandt's long-time assistant and hand-picked successor as governing mayor of Berlin since 1967 did not ingratiate himself with Berlin's student population by sniffing, "Look at those characters!" Strauss fully justified his reputation as the New Left's bogeyman by snapping, "Look at the appearance of those people! Protesting students belong in the penitentiary."

Brandt—perhaps in memory of his own radical background and in sympathy with the youths—played it cool. "We cannot regard what presently happens in our country as a children's disease that, like measles, will go away. Nobody can claim to be in possession of ultimate wisdom." On another occasion he struck an equally conciliatory note: "We need the challenge of the young generation, otherwise our feet will fall asleep. . . ."

Chairman Brandt would have to live with this challenge, which threatened to tear asunder the moral underpinnings of the party and presented the danger of a party within the party, time and again, for years to come. The emergence of the Jusos as a self-determining entity, more radical and more outspoken than the rank and file and therefore more suspect in the eyes of the public—which was not always able to distinguish between Juso rhetoric and party program—became an irreversible irritant in party politics. Brandt would have to muster all his talents for integration and studied indifference, commonly mistaken for tolerance, to cope with this new problem.

What bothered Brandt before the elections of 1969 rolled around was the tactical necessity of defending the Grand Coalition as the glorious chance to "make out of this state what we imagined, what corresponds with our program . . . the chance to test and build up the leading role of German social democracy in this process. Negatively stated, this means: if we don't succeed, the SPD will also be credited with the weaknesses and shortcomings of this government. Nobody will be able to get around this. . . . Either the SPD succeeds in carrying this state ahead rapidly, in changing it with sufficient thoroughness, or the SPD will have to pay for the failure. . . ."

Convinced that the Free Democrats, whose profile had visibly been turned to the left under the leadership of their new chairman Walter Scheel, would make the more compatible coalition partner, Brandt put out feelers in that direction. Brandt and Scheel did not only see eye to eye on Ostpolitik—the FDP was the first party that had dared to recognize the Oder-Neisse line and had boldly drafted a general treaty in 1968 between the "two" German states—but concurred that some reforms and the strengthening of civil rights were also areas for agreement. The great test of the FDP's willingness to swing its light but decisive weight behind the SPD came during the election of the federal president. Instead of voting for the CDU's ex–foreign minister Gerhard Schröder as a successor to the unfortunate Heinrich Lübke, the FDP helped elect the SPD's Gustav Heinemann on the third ballot with 512 to 506 votes. Straws were in the wind.

Challenging Kiesinger

It was a lackluster election campaign that unfolded toward the end of August. Chancellor candidates Kiesinger and Brandt were hardly in a position to attack each other on policies they had shaped and executed together. Neither dared to anger the FDP, whose vote could tip the scale one way or another. And the cocky FDP, which had been eating humble pie outside the governmental fleshpots for three long years, was careful to offend no one.

In spite of the SPD's catchy slogan, "It's the voter who counts," voter influence in shaping his government had its obvious limitations. Before the elections, none of the parties felt obliged to inform the public with whom they would or would not form a coalition. Any combination was possible. As things stood, the conservative CDU/CSU voter, favoring foreign policy along Adenauer lines and a "social market policy" as espoused by Ludwig Erhard, might be settled with Brandt's Ostpolitik of rapprochement (a policy of wishful thinking, according to Kiesinger) and Schiller's progressive economics, caustically tagged as "planned economy" by CDU/CSU experts. The SPD voter on the other hand, casting his ballot for codetermination and Ostpolitik also could have a rude awakening.

Not until the evening before the elections was the cat let out of the bag. During a televised panel discussion with party leaders Kiesinger, Brandt and Strauss, Scheel surprised panelists and viewers by advocating a change of government for change's sake. In view of its past alliance with the CDU/CSU, only the informed voter was able to grasp that the veiled offer was intended for the Social Democrats.

The campaign developed into a slow-motion escalation of animosity between the partners of the Grand Coalition. Genuine differences and personal resentments stored up during the past three years were no longer rigidly repressed. In the process, so many damaging things were said and done that a continuation of the partnership became more than questionable.

From the very beginning, both parties displayed distinct campaign styles. With the slogan, "It's the Chancellor who counts," the CDU/CSU geared its whole vast machinery to Kiesinger's gentlemanly father-image. His country squire smile beamed from some three million posters. "Kiesinger, the widow's comfort," irreverent students shouted. His promise of "security and stability" was aimed at the 21.1 million women of voting age, a significant 3.6 million more than men. The candidate who could best woo the women would be the winner. In that contest, the forecasters correctly predicted, silver-haired Kiesinger ranged far ahead of Brandt.

Much to the chagrin of the SPD, which in 1919 championed the cause of votes for women as it championed the legalization of early abortions in 1974—repealed by the Supreme Court in 1975—West German women had helped to elect the Conservatives four times since 1953.

Without a fatherly type among its foremost politicians, the SPD took a different tack. Instead of an individual, a star, they sold the whole team. Whenever Brandt graced a poster, the other half pictured the attractive, youthful looking Professor Schiller guaranteeing "economic stability" and "job security." Other posters exhibited the handsome features of Helmut Schmidt, designated as minister of defense, or the little-known faces of Attorney General Horst Ehmke, Transport Minister Georg Leber and others.

Not missing a trick, the SPD also engaged in an extensive "sympathy" campaign. In sizable advertisements, actors, writers, journalists, professors and doctors explained to the country's newspaper readers just why they had "confidence" in the SPD. Once more, Günter Grass toured the country with his literary sideshow. This time, he recruited celebrities from the intellectual set for the "Social Democratic Voter's Initiative." Famed novelist Heinrich Böll composed an often cited "Open letter to a German Catholic woman" in which he levelled the charge that women "mark ballots on the wrong spot from sheer habit."

It should be noted that the women's heretofore admired politicians generally took a dim view of women's political activities. "I cannot make up my mind in favor of more women in politics," commented Strauss. Kiesinger, in the spirit of philosopher Immanuel Kant, advised women "to stay in the background" with regard to politics.

The greatest difference in style, however, was exhibited by the chancellorship candidates themselves. Following Kiesinger on the campaign trail, one was stunned by the old-fashioned rhetoric, the kind of philosophizing which in the Germany of the past generation was widely esteemed and revered as the product of a "humanistic education." The dapper Kiesinger, dressed in well-tailored grey flannel and citing de Tocqueville, Goethe, Spengler and the Romans—in Latin, of course—was an educated man. Yet many a young voter wondered what a "modern Germany" might be like when shaped by a politician who praised the "revolutionary achievements" of Konrad Adenauer and boasted of rapping the knuckles of his foreign minister in a fatherly fashion behind closed doors.

Echoing Strauss, Kiesinger charged that the Federal Republic and Europe had been relegated by the superpowers to a role of watching world politics instead of having a part in shaping them. While conjecturing a likely reconciliation between Russia and China, he urged the mobilization of Europe's "world-shaping will." If J. J. Servan-Schreiber hoped to activate and unite European forces against the infiltration of the American dollar, management, and technology, Kiesinger envisioned organizing a united Europe as a counterforce to the "yellow danger." "The signals indicate storm," he shouted 330 times into microphones. "I only say, China! China!" The picture of massive Communist forces in China, Moscow or wherever they may be, evoked a strange, not quite definable, instinctive fear in the West German citizen who had seen the Berlin wall and witnessed the events in Czechoslovakia.

Kiesinger's outbursts were aimed at Brandt's new flexible policy toward the East. "If there should be a change in government, the world's confidence in Germany will be shattered," he announced gravely.

Brandt's statement that West Germany's relationship with Moscow had "nearly normalized" in comparison with the 1950s is attacked by the chancellor as "wishful thinking." Kiesinger made it perfectly clear that he would go to Moscow only if "a sign is given" that the Soviets were willing to "give justice to 17 million East Germans living in Communist imprisonment."

"Moscow plays with the Social Democrats," jeered a CDU advertisement. That Brandt was "subservient to Moscow" could be heard in both camps of the union parties. Chafing under these attacks, Brandt made the public announcement that he could not assume the office of foreign minister under Kiesinger again. "I cannot take on that responsibility," he explained. In a private talk one evening, Brandt gave even more startling reasons. "You know how violently my willingness to negotiate with Moscow has been assailed. Yet Kiesinger himself sent two of his trusted people on secret missions to Moscow. The sad part is that he did not think it necessary to inform me or my office of these ventures. I found out about them from Soviet ambassadors abroad."

The constant accusations from the conservatives forced Brandt to a headline-making, grandstand performance such as had proved successful at previous elections. One week before election day, the foreign minister turned up in New York to repair the damage. The German voter had to be reassured that his proposed "normalization of relations with the East" did not interfere or impair the Federal Republic's friendship with the U.S. Moreover, the voters had to be made aware again of the foreign minister's decisive part in "reducing the world's mistrust" of the *Bundesrepublik.* Lastly, it had to be demonstrated that Ostpolitik was not based on wishful thinking but real possibilities. Therefore, a talk with Soviet Foreign Minister Gromyko was scheduled as a clincher. "That just so happened," Brandt told me with a zany wink.

Brandt sincerely believed that his "policy of little steps, even of advancement by the inch," was without "reasonable alternative."

Again and again he hammered in his main point at some two hundred campaign speeches: The division of Europe and Germany can only be overcome by a peace policy! Renunciation of force, reduction of troops in East and West Europe, renunciation of production of nuclear weapons—one of Brandt's first actions as chancellor was the signing of the nuclear nonproliferation treaty on November 11, 1969. Strauss, who had rigidly opposed such a "policy of renunciation," was instructed that one "cannot renounce what one does not own." Not Strauss's concept of a European atomic power, but a European peace order, would lead to security for the Germans. Brandt expressed both *skepsis* and hope. Despite recognizing the ideological schism as a fact, he nevertheless insisted on taking into consideration the rapid changes of our times and their effect on communism, which after all "is no *canon* cast in iron."

In his book, *A Peace Policy for Europe,* he rendered a sober assessment of the chances of success for such a policy.

"German foreign politics today does not only carry the burden of the second lost war, not only the burden of the Hitler regime, it carries another burden: the mistrust of wide circles abroad over whether our will for negotiation is genuine and if the Democrats in this country are able to succeed with their will for negotiation."

The New Brandt

As one of the journalists traveling with Willy Brandt through the German countryside, one got to know the best, the most impressive facet of the politician's personality. Brandt the activist took to the frantic pace of the campaign like a fish to water. It was impossible to tell if the constant movement from the climaxes of applause and cheers expanded his introverted personality on those occasions; if it was the indefinable chemistry between the expectant crowd and its mystic communion with the speaker that carried him beyond himself; or if the sound of his own strong, cracked voice booming over the loud speakers inspired him to total concentration and total rapture. There was no doubt that crowds turned him on, stripped him of his reticence and stilled his restlessness. Like all the best politicians, he was a master when it came to portraying feelings and was thrilled by the predictable responses of the masses, which conveyed that magnificent illusion of ultimate power.

In this state of mental intoxication, Brandt managed to come out of his shell of privacy. The man who tended to become paralyzed in social situations and instinctively shrank from social contacts inevitably sought the company of the accompanying journalists. He charmed them with political jokes, spirited banter, avid listening and all-round sociableness. Brandt, liberated from the remote and distant person who scarcely takes an interest in other people, never broke up a good party, never turned down another drink or another cigarillo. Only toward morning, when the stimulating effects of the mass encounters had worn thin, would he sit lost in thought, falling back into the apathetic posture that had become an integral part of his rigidly controlled self.

Brandt had developed into a highly polished public speaker. No matter whether he talked in a public park, at a student rally, or an official city hall meeting, he always impressed his audience with his sincerity. He made no promises and posed no threats but analyzed the situation as he wanted it to be understood. His soft-sell seldom drove his audiences into frenzied cheering. Yet there were sympathetic vibrations enveloping a crowd by chain reaction.

When Brandt spoke into the microphones, his whole body was involved. Occasionally a clenched fist wandered into the pocket of his jacket. Sometimes he twisted his fingers hard enough to make his knuckles turn white. His heels incessantly beat the floor, moving with the intense rhythm of his sentences. His powerful torso, reservoir of enormous energies, rose and stretched in transferring its penned-up force into the spoken words.

Brandt had matured. His lost campaigns no longer bothered him. He was no longer haunted by the past. His face had the "lived-in" look of a man who knew how to enjoy life and had lost no time in so doing. His gestures were sparse. He never screamed, never indulged in sarcasm. Unperturbed, he answered the most impertinent questions. Sometimes with a wry touch of humor.

Impressed with the new Brandt style, one of the foreign journalists who had not seen the candidate since the 1965 elections wanted to know if the smooth performances were, perhaps, the result of elocution lessons. No, he was informed by one of Brandt's aides, the candidate had simply gained a lot of self-confidence during his years as foreign minister.

In word association tests, the name Brandt now evokes thoughts of "home movies, bicycle, and margarine." *Spiegel* seems inclined to evaluate this as progress.

But it was the voter who had the last word. Election night, September 27, fully made up for the excitement lacking in the campaign. It was the night when losers were dramatically turned into winners. Due to the peculiarities of the West German electoral system, a combination of relative majority voting and proportional representation, winners can be losers if the coalition battle is bungled. The SPD did not bungle.

While President Nixon dispatched a telegram of congratulations to Chancellor Kiesinger upon learning that the CDU/CSU had received 46.1 percent of the vote to the SPD's 42.7 percent, Brandt did some last-minute bargaining with Scheel's badly battered FDP. The Free Democrats, winning a meager 5.8 percent, had barely cleared the 5 percent hurdle required for a party to be seated in the Bundestag. With Wehner keeping the coalition channels to the CDU/CSU open—just in case—Brandt did some behind-the-scenes bartering with the ambitious Walter Scheel. By nimbly forming a coalition with the undisputed loser of the elections, whose much heralded liberalization under the guidance of Chairman Scheel had produced the disastrous shrinkage from 9.5 percent in 1965, the SPD had indeed managed to transform defeat into a tenuous victory.

Germany's oldest party dating back to the days of the publication of the Communist Manifesto in 1848, had ceased to play second fiddle. After twenty years, it was to take the initiative in the capital on the Rhine. Its ascent to power gave renewed credence to the proper functioning of German parliamentary democracy. The overdue change of the governing parties itself was irrefutable testimony that German democracy had passed the acid test. The Social Democrats' brass assembled in the party's "temporary" headquarters, properly called the "barracks," was ecstatic with joy. Few of them could remember the last SPD chancellor: The luckless Hermann Müller was toppled along with the Weimar Republic thirty-nine years before.

What did it matter how they finally had wrested the power from the Conservatives! Who cared about the percentage so long as Wehner's calculations to attain respectability in the eyes of the middle-class, white-collar voters by way of the Grand Coalition turned out to be correct.

When Willy Brandt stepped in front of the TV cameras shortly before midnight to announce the victorious minicoalition, nobody in that overcrowded room overheated by too many bodies and overcharged by too many emotions would have disagreed with his subjective exercise in relativity in reading the figures.

"The SPD is the biggest party; the SPD is the strongest party; the CDU has not won but lost; the distance between CDU and SPD has been well halved. This is the result. . . ."

It was a curious way of dealing with the given facts. One felt a little like Alice in Wonderland. No accentuating of the positive could gloss over the fact that the grand old winner really was the CDU/CSU with its solid 46.1 percent.

At the CSU headquarters, Herr Brandt's "leftist" minicoalition was given at best a year and a half, maybe even two years. It lasted two and a half years, till it was stalemated in April 1972. It was clear to Strauss that Brandt was certain to run into trouble with his signing of the nonproliferation treaty and Schiller's procyclic economic policy. The floating of the mark to "find its own level" was not regarded as a proper instrument for curbing the overheated economy.

Strauss's disciples comforted each other with the thought that only a swing of seven votes was required for a vote of no confidence.

Willy Brandt had indeed acquired a formidable opposition in the bargain.

At the inauguration ceremonies, Federal President Heinemann, fully savoring the importance of that historic moment, stated solemnly: "This is a caesura in the history of Germany."

On October 28, 1969, Chancellor Brandt set his goals in his first policy statement.

"The politics of this government will be developed under the sign of continuity and under the aspect of renewal." He wanted to "dare more democracy" and assured the citizens of the opportunity of participating "in the reforms of state and society." Twenty years after the founding of the Federal Republic of Germany and the GDR, the danger of widening the gap in the German nation must be checked by trying to substitute a regulated "next to each other" for a "with each other."

In order to achieve the objectives of his intra-German policy, a complex interdependent structure of renunciation of force treaties with the Soviet Union, the People's Republic of Poland, and the Quadripartite Agreement on Berlin precede the Traffic Treaty, the Basic Treaty, and other agreements with the German Democratic Republic.

As guiding principles which cannot be renounced, Brandt listed: the right of self-determination; the striving for national unity and freedom within the framework of a European peace agreement; the Federal Republic's ties with West Berlin without impairing the Four Powers' responsibility for the whole of Berlin; and the rights of the three powers as regards Germany as a whole.

To find a modus vivendi with the GDR, Brandt is the first West German chancellor who is willing to relinquish the previous German federal government's cherished claim "to speak for all of Germany [East and West] as the representative of the German people in international affairs" as the only free and legitimately established government. The position that the East German regime is illegitimate, inasmuch as it had come into existence without free expression of the will of the people, was affirmed by the three Western powers at the New York Conference of Foreign Ministers in 1950. Its abandonment equals recognition of the GDR as a sovereign state.

The Brandt era had begun.

14

The Chairman

"Are you sure you are not a spy?" Rheinhard Wilke, former chief of Chancellor Brandt's office, now the SPD chairman's trusted assistant and confidant, greets me with an attempt at humor as I step into the humble suite of offices Chairman Brandt occupies in the Bundeshaus in the summer after the fall, in 1974. Wilke, once a typical specimen of a slightly stuffy German official with his immaculate navy blue suits and stiff formal demeanor, has substituted a beige turtleneck for his starched, white shirts. His once neatly clipped hair hangs long and shaggy about the collar. His face looks gaunt and still bears an expression of faint bewilderment at the quick change in his life from powerful adviser to the head of state to a mere party aide. His half-empty cubicle of an office, furnished in modest department store "modern," sports neither a visitor's chair nor his name on the door.

Still protective of his boss, Wilke cuts short inquiries into the Guillaume affair. He sees no sense in talking about it while the investigating committee is in session.

"Surely, you must be interested in telling your side of it to avoid distortions of the truth," I venture.

"Ah, the truth will come out," Wilke retorts without much conviction. His fingers nervously fidget with an unopened folder on his desk.

Remembering that the investigations into the Steiner-Wienand scandal involving corruption had come to nothing, nobody in his right mind in Bonn is expecting any startling results from the Bundestag's hearings on the celebrated spy affair. (They were right: the lengthy report of the commission for "preventive secret protection" issued in November 1974 excelled in intricate legalistic footwork and inconclusiveness.)

Wilke is glad that I ask about Brandt's activities as party chairman to counteract the SPD's heavy chronic losses in the regional elections.

"Brandt is less involved in the politics of the day than in fundamental matters concerning the party. Willy Brandt will take care of the pressing need to find a formal consensus. Now we have a consensus on the contents of the program. What we need are opinion-orienting discussions to determine a common point of departure."

Wilke only vaguely alludes to the differences in the party between the young left-wing anticapitalistic, anti-NATO Jusos and the regular rank and file membership sticking with the conservative interpretation of the Godesberg Program.

"Above all, Brandt will relieve Helmut Schmidt of the burden of dealing with intraparty problems which reflect the tensions in our society. Schmidt doesn't want to do this and is not equipped to do this. On the other hand, Brandt has accepted this task. Just as everybody in the party has accepted the new tandem Schmidt-Brandt."

Traditionally, the office of chancellor and party chairman are tied together in one and the same person in the SPD and the other parties. Wilke neither confirms nor denies rumors that Brandt kept the office of party chairman primarily because of Schmidt's and Wehner's insistance that he do "his duty." He is convinced, however, that Brandt's leadership of Europe's largest party—990,000 members—is bound to influence European developments, even though the chairman no longer occupies the office of chancellor.

"The influence of the party will be felt in Western and Eastern Europe. What the chairman does with it, what it emanates, will carry weight," he predicts.

As if Wilke wanted to give me a hint about Brandt's real long-range goal, he reminds me of a statement made by the chairman in Strasbourg: "We will be able to create a [united] Europe."

For the time being, Chairman Brandt tries to knit together the unravelling SPD and spruce up its battered image as a divided party, too much occupied with its own ideological quarrels to care about the actual worries of the people and obviously not in control of its leftist faction of wild-eyed Socialist visionaries.

To this end, fifteen working conferences around the country, at the grass roots, with the SPD's 10,000 precinct functionaries, have been scheduled throughout the summer.

After his ascent to foreign minister in 1966, Chairman Brandt had become a frequent visitor in Washington, Moscow, Scandinavia, the South of France and other exotic places, but little was seen of him by the loyal party workers in North Hesse, the Eifel or Eschborn in the Taunus.

The Juso Problem

It was no accident that the disenchanted voters turned to the conservative CDU/CSU, the pollsters told the SPD. The influence of the uncompromising Socialist Jusos, who constituted a third of the party's membership in 1974, had a disastrous impact on the voters. The SPD drift to the left that turned off the bourgeoisie and blue-collar workers alike also made itself felt in the composition of the party's thirty-six member executive committee. While only a decade earlier no left-wingers were represented there, now the count was up to sixteen.

A party embroiled in a discussion of redistribution of property and wealth, nationalization of banks, and state control of investments, when the man on the street worries about inflation and threatening unemployment should not be surprised by its loss of votes, the experts said. Advocating unfeasible reforms creates a pressure of expectations that the government cannot fulfill, Ursula Feist, director of the *infas-election* research institute, concluded. High-flown visions of the future inhibit realistic reform strategy. At the same time, they block the public's perception of the government's actual accomplishments, and discontent grows despite increasing achievements.

Feist was no less leery of the Jusos' steady provocation of the voters' political engagement. Excessive consciousness-raising causes public apathy rather than commitment, Feist asserted.

Such a cool, critical analysis of the situation was not accepted by the Juso leadership, who preferred to seek in the opponent's camp the causes for their party's defeats. Juso chairman, Heidemarie Wieszorek-Zeul blamed rather the "ignorance of wide parts of the public" and the "CDU and CSU and their backers from industry for consciously inciting . . . fear and insecurity" among the masses.

It was up to the chairman to straighten things out, to strike a delicate balance between the pragmatists and the radical Socialist reformers. But it was no easy job to bring the loud, obstinate Jusos with their resurrected Marxist vocabulary of class struggle and socio-economic theories back into the party's anxiously maintained middle-of-the-road fold without crushing their proselytizing spirit that had created the unprecedented political awareness among the electorate from which nobody had benefitted more than the Social Democrats. Only Brandt, the mediator, who confessed in a 1961 interview with the Yugoslovian Communist youth weekly *Mladost* to having been and still being "what one calls a leftist Socialist," was thought capable of performing this touchy reconciliation. To many, the "as well as" man, whose heart was undoubtedly going out to the Jusos while his practical, flexible mind stuck to the modifications that had led the party to victory, symbolized the state of the party. Among them were quite a few who blamed the chairman's lackadaisical attitude toward the overbearing Jusos for their party's dilemma.

Brandt had not forgotten that the self-appointed young watchdogs had given the Social Democrats their first break by shocking the German burgher out of his economic miracle dreams in 1969 into a new political participatory role. Their demands for democratization of society on all levels and for a realistic East policy, including recognition of the GDR and the Oder-Neisse border, brought these vital issues into the homes of every citizen. Even if they were thoroughly annoyed with the young leftists' outbursts, demonstrations and marches, the Germans could not help but become acquainted with the topical arguments and counterarguments. In Bonn's one-party Grand Coalition atmosphere, the leftist students and Jusos, and other groups, had evolved into a political ferment. By their suspicious examination of each piece of legislation for possible authoritarian or antisocial content, they had unwittingly become the unorthodox teachers of due democratic process.

They resembled the enterprising McGovern kids in many ways.

They were well educated, from middle- or upper-class families. They were full of idealism and convinced that they were capable of changing society, even the world, with their missionary fervor. It never occurred to the self-assured children of the affluent society, who formed an intellectual dialectical debating elite, that the society they had found wanting did not care to be changed. A democratic system where politics and money were wedded seemed outright immoral to the Jusos. Young, pure, romantic and uncompromising, they had no tolerance for so-called "tactical" delays and detours practiced by the experienced party hacks. So the Jusos set out to raise the public's political consciousness to their level. It was as simple as that . . . they thought.

It was the crash landing of McGovern's crusade in Miami all over again. This time German style: filled to the brim with ideological reflections and frustrated brooding.

Last but not least, the Jusos had to be credited with taking the wind out of the sails of the newly founded (in 1968) German Communist party (DKP) that had replaced the outlawed Communist party of Germany (KPD) after twelve years. But unless the energies of the young fanatics who had found a home among the Jusos could be harnessed, the party's zealous young helpers were about to become its wrecking crew.

Had Brandt played with fire by allowing them too much leeway?

"Our party does not need verbal radical excesses. And it is at any rate no asylum for opponents of democratic socialism," Willy Brandt stated during the working conference in Eschborn.

"What our party does not need either is provincial narrowness and fear of necessary renewal. Hostility to reforms leads to growing tensions and radicalization. Who wishes to safeguard what has been proven to be of benefit must be ready—in the framework of given possibilities—for continuous renewal." And to leave no one in doubt that his stern ten-point declaration laid down in April to force the Jusos to adhere to the party line was meant in earnest, the chairman added: "Our party is proud of its tradition, but it needs no flight into the dusty [Marxist] concepts of the last century."

Was the SPD indeed in danger of ceasing to function as the traditional democratic bulwark against communism?

Cultivating Grass Roots Support

Chairman Brandt, looking tanned as usual, rested and serene as though he just ducked in from a picnic instead of a fall, is determined to block radical infiltration.

"Who supports another party or makes common cause with Communist groups does not belong in the SPD. Who leaves the foundation of the Godesberg Program by propagandizing or practicing violence against our constitution and law is in the wrong place in the SPD . . ." he tells the informally dressed, shirts-and-jeans crowd of some 600 provincial party functionaries. Unimpressed, the younger, more restive delegates keep milling through the vast city hall between the long rows of tables laden with beer bottles. It is not a disrespectful crowd that breaks the pattern of the chairman's speech—a little praise here and a little scolding there, justly meted out to the Conservatives and Jusos in about equal proportions—with brief rounds of applause, but it is an inattentive one. In contrast to American political town hall gatherings of that sort, the congregation assembled on this fine June Sunday had only a sprinkling of women among its relatively young and active-looking comrades.

Chairman Brandt speaks slowly, gravely almost. His voice is deep and raspy. He smokes again, cigarets, but mostly he occupies himself with keeping his pipe in working condition. He smoothly glides over the efficiently handled change of government—never mentioning the spy scandal—in almost self-congratulatory fashion. His decision to resign the chancellorship was made after a "thorough self-examination" but he does not feel like resignation. After the applause dies down, he assures his listeners that he intends to continue to make his contribution to foreign and, especially, European politics. He will stand prepared for reelection as chairman of the party, not in competition with the chancellor but as the continuum of five years of reform work.

Describing a series of circles with his hands the chairman talks about an "expectation gap," a "gap of fear" and a "harmony gap" as being responsible for the party's bad fortunes in the regional elections. The dramatic voter losses are basically put at the doorstep of the Jusos, who hurt the party's image, the hostile conservative press, and the energy crisis. The population reacted with fear to the latter because it could not figure out the underlying complexities of world economics. It looked to the government for solutions and expected much more than Bonn was able to give.

As he warms up to his topic, Brandt's voice, like that of a skilled evangelist, alternates loud accentuations and softly modulated phrases when he tackles the sticky Juso problem. While reassuring his audience that the Jusos are not a party within the party, and rejecting authoritarian socialism on principle, the chairman stresses that without appealing and adhering to the middle, democratic socialism will not be able to win a majority. New forces have to be drawn into the party. Attention has to be paid to the danger of the party's organizational superiority being lost in bureaucratic idling and overlapping work projects.

By conceding to the comrades: "Our picture of the CDU does not correspond with the realities," the chairman refers to the shocking but undeniable fact that the young voters have been turning away from the SPD. By lowering the voting age from twenty-one to eighteen years in 1970, SPD strategists hoped to make vast inroads into the untouched voter reservoir. The development was no more encouraging among the students. In 1974, 30 percent of the male students had surprisingly joined fraternities, hardly refuges for flaming liberals.

The morale-lifting words of Chairman Brandt about "hard work," "pulling oneself up by one's bootstraps," a periodically revised "consensus," "inner unity," and "new strength" were rewarded with measured but heartfelt applause. Yet the wild cheering or the loving ovations with which the Berliners honored their chairman were missing.

If the ensuing discussion period had been as salty as the large portions of ham and potato salad served during the noon intermission, the working conference might have been more useful in pinpointing the precise trouble spots. As it was, Brandt, sitting in isolation among the comrades at the table on stage center soon began to look like the incarnation of utter apathy. To be sure, the ward leaders had a lot of petty gripes which they unabashedly aired for the benefit of their illustrious comrade from Bonn, using the familiar "Du" as was the custom among comrades.

But even the informal, intimate form of address failed to bring the absorbed chairman out of his remoteness. Still, he responded with astonishing alertness to complaints that the functionaries at the grass roots received their information by way of mass media instead of from the SPD's headquarters in Bonn. They wanted to have their say in the annual decision-making discussions; they wanted to know what was going on in Bonn.

A blue-shirted worker from Oberursel criticized the presentation of the profit-sharing concept as misleading; a woman with an exceptionally sturdy voice called the way the SPD handled the abortion legislation a "tragedy"; somebody wanted a definition of the "new middle"; and somebody else charged that new members were criminally neglected by the party. A young, shy girl was literally pushed by a bunch of supportive comrades before one of the mikes distributed around the large hall to tell the benignly smiling chairman that there are not enough women in leading positions in the party. Women should not just be members but coworkers, she insisted. A bespectacled youth vented his frustration about always talking to the same people and the difficulties of activating new and more members.

Several comrades aired their discontent over the avalanche of paper that poured into their offices from Bonn. There was so much printed material that even the good stuff went into the wastebasket unread and often unopened, an angry functionary shouted. Someone had a brainstorm: The SPD slogan "Solidarity *Now*" should be replaced with "Solidarity *Always!*" A Juso in rumpled corduroys argued against the personality cult in the party. His "persons should be interchangeable" drew a round of applause from the younger crew.

The auditorium was anything but quiet. The blue-eyed girls with bleached blond hair, tight sweaters and high platform shoes, sexy and very conscious of their sexiness, used the discussion period for visiting old friends and making new ones. Groups of men rambled up and down the aisles, beer bottles in hand, hardly lowering their cheerfully bantering voices.

The chairman, looking pensive and/or bored, somehow managed to retain his air of isolation, not an easy thing to accomplish considering that he was surrounded by party luminaries at both elbows. Ostentatiously, he stared into space way above the heads of the crowd, as if he were seeing things that would reveal themselves only to him. Was that studied posture of loneliness part of the Brandt charisma? Or was the Nobel Prize recipient really bored by all this bickering among his followers? One of them had the unmitigated gall to support his complaint that the party expected them to follow its not necessarily sagacious directives to the letter with a quote from Schmidt, who once speculated that party resolutions are not "necessarily the last word in wisdom."

For all his show of absentmindedness, the chairman, lumbering to his feet after the last question, had listened closely enough. Thanking the comrades for their many splendid suggestions, he nimbly covered the field from price stability to "what is workable," along with the bread-and-butter issues of party organization and the ethical values shared by Marx and the Sermon on the Mount as ideational sources of the Godesberg Program that must be developed further.

In his effort to wind up this conference with a harmonious finale, he acted much like the conductor of a huge symphony. Emphasizing accord and downplaying discord, highlighting single voices of reason and giving full amplification to the middle section, he performed the miracle of blending the whole range of opinions into an agreeable orchestration with the sound of unity.

The conference was a success inasmuch as the comrades were able to let off steam in front of the powers that could do something about it. They had been heard. They will remember, perhaps forever, that the great Willy Brandt, who had hobnobbed with the world's most important people from Kennedy to Brezhnev, that their Willy, with whom they have gone through defeats and victories for a decade, had shared their point of view. Clearly, if anybody could put the out-of-kilter party together again, it would be Willy, they told each other.

Their hearts went out to the lonely man on the rostrum.

The press conference which followed was hardly conducted in a chummy atmosphere. Some twenty local journalists, mostly under the age of thirty, showed up with a lot of candid questions up their sleeves about Brandt's attitude toward the Jusos' "anticapitalistic structural reforms" and other socialistic alternatives. Brandt, obviously tired from the three-hour trip that morning and the five-hour meeting in the smoke-filled city auditorium, was in a noncommunicative mood. The Nobel Prize winner, who rated standing ovations from the journalistic fraternity's most distinguished and polite members at Washington's National Press Club and other glamorous places around the world, did not relish being treated like a small-town politician taken to task by the hometown press. These young people insisted on clear language. Fancifully worded "no comment" answers stimulated verbal exchanges that made Brandt cringe. When he intimated that he was not interested in pursuing a certain subject any longer, one of his young interlocutors snapped: "Well, the fact that you are not interested is in itself interesting!"

Brandt's face froze into a slit-eyed mask. The irreverence of the shirtsleeved reporter had visibly shaken him. It had been a direct assault on his dignity, and dignity is important to the man who had fought long and hard to come by this elusive commodity that relates to moral relativity.

He had no verbal comeback.

I knew that this was not the moment to ask the chairman about his role in the development of a socialistic Europe. Although the theme had been loosely struck at the party's convention in Hanover in 1973 and was firmly anchored in the Jusos' anticapitalistic Europe policy, which recognizes the development of a socialism in the Federal Republic and Western Europe—resulting in a common socialist strategy—as a precondition for a European security and peace policy, Brandt for good reasons has been known to be allergic to the discussion of this highly controversial topic.

Evading the Socialist issue, he stiffly lectured me on the merits of "social democracy," a term replaced by that of "democratic socialism" within the party years ago. "If it does not function, then Europe will not function." Brandt talked about the need for extending and updating the fundamentals of the Godesberg Program according to economic and social progress and cooperation with other socialistic parties in Austria, England and Scandinavia. In contrast to the Jusos, who don't exclude cooperation with selected Communist organizations to achieve the object of a Socialist breakthrough in Western Europe, Brandt rejects working with the Communists.

No "Historical Compromise"

When Chairman Brandt and his wife, Rut, travelled to Portugal after the fall of its dictatorship in October 1974, at the invitation of Socialist Foreign Minister Mario Soares and his Marxist Partido Socialistica Portugues, he expressly stressed the linkage of the SPD and PSP but rejected the whole "popular front" concept of a coalition with the Communists. Brandt was not always as specific as in Lisbon. Asked the vital 64-dollar question on another occasion, the chairman gave one of his typical "as well as" comments. Yes, the sharp dividing line toward the Communists was to be maintained. At the same time, he did not seem to close the door altogether. He pointed out the vast differences and variable forms between the Communist parties in Western Europe, notably in Finland and Yugoslavia, and remarked that their development merited close attention.

A "historical compromise" was advocated by Italy's Communist leader, Enrico Berlinguer, who with Luigi Longo had helped Brandt's SPD establish its first contacts with the Soviets and their bloc in the 1960s. In order to get out of the thirty-year-old ghetto of the opposition, Berlinguer had thrown a good share of Communist doctrine overboard before he boldly advocated a coalition with the conservative Christian Democrats. Among those not trusting the siren song of the Italian Communists is Dr. Henry Kissinger, who fears that such a coalition would provide the Communists with a chance to wrest the power from the CDs and establish a dictatorship in Italy.

Frowning on "tactics," the Jusos, known for their absolute honesty and integrity, have spelled it out that they are aiming for the dissolution of the NATO and Warsaw military blocs and the exit of U.S. troops from the Federal Republic because of their tendency to "endanger" the socialistic transformation process. Instead of NATO, which the Jusos view as an expression of "supranational capital interests," they envision a collective security system after the creation of a tension-free European zone and the withdrawal of foreign troops. They regard the realization of their demands as prerequisite for progressing with the development of European socialism.

In a way, all this is vaguely reminiscent of the buried Wehner Plan. How much the party's direction is subject to the influence of its vocal advance guard, represented in the Bundestag by about sixty left-wingers, seems to vary from issue to issue and therefore is open to question.

Undoubtedly the assumption expressed in 1972 by the Soviet's urbane ambassador to Bonn, Valentin Falin, that West Berlin one day will become part of the GDR, and Erich Honecker's 1975 prediction that in the revolutionary world process "socialism will not make a detour around the Federal Republic" were generated by the Jusos' "democratization of industry program." The socialization of key industries, credit banks and multinationals, based on the Juso premise that "the planning of social processes inevitably calls for the limitation of private economic power" and that "everything else is an illusion," was aimed to erase the dividing line that separates the capitalistic Federal Republic, integrated into the "imperialist system," according to Honecker, from the socialist GDR.

The GDR's distinguished writer, Stefan Heym, who likens the quarter-century-old struggle between the capitalist and socialist republics as a fight for Germany's soul, arrives at similar conclusions by inversion. "Let there be two or three million unemployed in the capitalist part of Germany and Erich Honecker, first secretary of the Socialist Unity (Communist) party, can safely lease the Wall to the government in Bonn," he predicted in his *Letter from East Germany,* published in the *New York Times* in March, 1975, when unemployment in West Germany had passed the million mark.

Pravda's recommendation in the spring of 1975 that the SPD should seriously begin to entertain popular front ideas is ostensibly meant to reflect on the attitude of the Marxist Jusos. They in turn submit, however, that they are not in agreement with the understanding of the GDR's idea of the state as a centralized, party-controlled apparatus. They rather favor a federal structure than the monopolistic state capitalism carried by the Communist party. This disagreement, however, does not mean that the Jusos, for example, would not fight for control of the multinationals side by side with Western Communists emancipated from Moscow, Juso leader Klaus-Detlef Funke explained to me in the summer of 1974.

Much apprehension is felt in France about Bonn's attempts to speed up the process of European unification under the aspect of socialism. The European Economic Community, equipped with the maximum characteristics of a free market economy and minimum means for state intervention, is not generally regarded by the French as a suitable nucleus or starting point for a European Union.

"Therefore it is entirely absurd," Hans Joachim Weseloh, distinguished diplomatic correspondent for the *Frankfurter Allgemeine Zeitung* concludes, "to try to transform the European institutions into a platform for a socialist Europe. From an official French point of view, this argument is especially applicable to the political development of Europe. A liberal economic and political system does not mesh with a centralized organization; a European state socialism could only exist under an authoritarian government. De Gaulle once had said, in a similar vein, for a European federation a 'federator' is required, who, as things stand, could only come from the Eastern direction."

Instead of a European Federal Union, in which national interests would be subordinated to European necessities, the French would concede to a community with a council of the nine heads of state who would get together—as often as possible—for "cabinet meetings." The loose arrangement would at best resemble a "union of states," Weseloh suggests in his article, "The council of nine heads of government as [an] executive body," February 26, 1974.

In other words: Socialists need not apply. In sharp contrast to the official French thinking, the Jusos Munich resolution on "Anticapitalistic Work in Europe," confirms that they anticipate reaching their goals in cooperation with the West European workers' organizations. On the basis of an analysis of the international capitalistic developments, they pursue the following strategy: "The Young Socialists will formulate the demands of a European social program in which it will be made clear as a principle that the best system and the highest standards have to be enforced in the EEC for the workers and employees."

If the Jusos' so-called "double strategy"—a twofold action program concentrating on work in the party, often in terms of dialectical contributions, and the mobilization of the masses by way of political consciousness-raising sessions—mystified the public, the different readings, supposedly all neatly tied together by the Godesberg package, confused the SPD's membership.

OR '85

To clarify and to imbue the party's sociopolitical criteria with greater concreteness, the Social Democrats commissioned work on a "long-range program" at their 1970 party convention in Saarbrücken. The position paper, based on the marvelously elastic tenets of Godesberg, was not to replace that good old serviceable theoretical standby, but to amend it. Under the guidance of a reluctant Helmut Schmidt, who took a dim view of long-range theoretical perspectives in a world full of unexpected and uncontrollable economic developments, his confident disciple Hans Apel, eventually elevated to finance minister by Schmidt in 1974, and "red" Juso-supporting Jochen Steffen, Schleswig-Holstein's SPD chairman, a first draft was submitted. Already obsolete because of its quantifications, it was revised and edited in 1975 into a 245-page document that became known as OR '85. The Orientation Framework 1985, put together with much sweat of the brow and tons of research material, was compiled by a committee of thirty chaired by Peter von Oertzen, Horst Ehmke and Herbert Ehrenberg. It attempted an ambitious in-depth analysis of global and regional social, economic and political developments from the point of view of democratic socialism. From this were to be deduced the necessary guidelines of future social democratic policies founded on the principal values of freedom, justice and solidarity, which were to be enhanced.

The hoped-for result was more inner solidarity. OR '85 was to provide clarification of the goals, priorities, instruments and methods of a democratic socialism that was striving for a "better order of society in the interest of the people, above all working people." Isms which disregard the interdependence of the three principal values—as liberalism and conservatism do—endanger all of them, we learn from the introduction to the twenty-five point catalogue.

Practical recommendations range from the "role of the state" as active influence in the guidance of economic and social developments and the Federal Republic's "tie-up with world politics and world economics" to the problems the SPD's reform policy encounters in the "resistance of the privileged" as well as those groups the reforms are designed to aid. Their resistance is traced to the Conservatives who turned them against the beneficial measures.

Chairman Brandt saw to it that the launching of OR '85 became a gala news event, graced by a fairly noncommittal Chancellor Helmut Schmidt in a display of solidarity. In his judgment, the section dealing with free "market and planned economy" is of major interest. Brandt stresses that OR '85 goes beyond Godesberg in its interpretation of "public responsibility." He anticipated the most heated discussions about the degree of indirect economic controls and the possibilities of direct government influence on the economy.

Global inflation, limited economic growth, and the concentration of multinational corporations as power centers, to be counteracted by international "political control mechanisms," are isolated as special pertinent problems of industrial societies. Successful social reforms are not possible "without constant, qualitatively sensible economic growth, modernization of industry through long-range structural policies, and efficient democratic control over the economic managing power." Rephrased in Schmidt's pragmatic language this means: reforms cost money. As a greatly sobered member of the planning commission, Hans Apel, noted as early as February 1971, the financing of the reforms presented a genuine problem. "It becomes clearer all the time that we cannot pay for all the things the experts envision in their fields by 1985. Holger Börner has calculated that the traffic sector alone requires 530 billion marks by 1985 to fulfill all wishes and pleas for highway construction, railroads, building of canals, and air traffic. . . . A painful but beneficial process of disillusionment lies before us."

The role of the state is seen neither as a free-floating "jury" between interest groups as the conservative bourgeois knows it, nor as an agent of a state monopolistic capitalism. The state is not defined as caretaker but as an institution carried by its society and responsible to it. "The state's ability to influence and steer the economic and social development in the interest of common welfare has to be improved, especially there, where the market is unable to regulate economic and social problems. A better coordination is required and a greater refinement of the already existing instruments of steering."

As was to be expected, the mammoth work, read with great care by the conservative opposition, met with criticism from all directions. While the CDU's potential chancellor candidate, Gerhard Stoltenberg, discovered neo-Marxist tendencies in reference to the description of the Federal Republic as a "class society" and his colleague, chancellor candidate Helmut Kohl, worried about the SPD's interpretation of freedom as a collective rather than an individual category, the CDU's in-house intellectual, Professor Biedenkopf, recognized a drift toward the middle that often approached the conservatives' position.

All of them, however, regretted that the Social Democrats were not able to free themselves of past ideological fixations concerning the "fundamental contradictions of our time," the contradiction of the capitalistic order of society and the democratic state from which the SPD derives almost all "problems of our society." Biedenkopf points to other causes for modern society's ills. None of them trust the SPD's basic affirmation of a free market economy, qualified as it is by demands of a "democratization of the economy" or undefined "democratic controls."

Brandt, who is fond of projections that get away from the daily business and had emerged as a strong backer of the study, thinks one of the most useful by-products is that the Social Democrats now no longer ask for what is desirable but that they also ask: What does it cost? Still, his friend and avid supporter Jens Feddersen, editor of the *Neue Rhein-Zeitung,* was not alone in the assessment that the public, barely coping with current problems, could not be expected to be intrigued by Sozi thinking games for 1985.

Only time will tell if OR '85 will become the SPD's most costly and time-consuming white elephant or a useful political instrument for blunting the existing alienation inside and outside the party.

"I'd rather see the Jusos in a discussion than in the streets," Brandt tells me during a visit to his office in the Bundeshaus. "But I will not draw the line regarding the radical wing to please the CDU."

Brandt is in an agitated mood. His face looks red and puffy. It is an open secret in Bonn that the relationship between Chancellor Schmidt and his party chairman resembles nothing more than a tenuous truce. Schmidt and Brandt, this is the only combination to keep the party together and keep it moving. Brandt is the best salesman of the policy that Wehner designs and Schmidt enacts, a functionary confided. He also intimated that Schmidt, much more popular than his party, according to opinion polls in 1975, does not mind having Brandt around to bear with him the brunt of possible further defeats.

"Schmidt talks about Brandt," Udo Bergdoll of the pro-Brandt *Süddeutsche Zeitung* reported in February 1975, "mostly by looking back, in appreciation of his 'historical achievement' of having extended Germany's ability to act in the nick of time with his Ostpolitik. The current Brandt is an elliptic topic for Schmidt."

A Friendly Picture of Germany

Brandt still does not want to be reminded of his recent or early past.

"I don't want to comment on myself," he declares. "Therefore, I am not writing a conventional book of memoirs but reminiscences about my experiences in foreign politics."

No, he has no intentions of writing on August Bebel, the hero of his youth, and he would just as soon not talk about his so-called models, Julius Leber and Ernst Reuter, with whom the press always wants to identify him, because that really bores him, Brandt says.

Why is he so uncomfortable talking about the two men who had instilled in him "decisive political impulses" as they paved part of his road to success? He used to build the glorious names of the two antifascists into the colorful mosaic of his own life for added luster. Now that he stands on his own renown, had he tired of feeding the myths of the ambivalent relationships? In a foreword to Leber's reissued writings, Brandt credited him mainly for teaching the young rebellious boy "how to resist."

Brandt knew, he says visibly irritated, that I would bring up Schumacher's name. "Kurt Schumacher! Those were different times! We had a totally different world of experiences. Schumacher was a good European all right, but characterized by a strong national component. Whatever there was between us, it was mostly a difference in temperament. When you are young you might possibly orient yourself on others. But in the end you only orient yourself by your own experiences."

As he talks of the uncomfortable subject, one feels he is as intent on convincing himself of the validity of his statement as he is his listener.

Enveloping himself in the clouds of smoke from his ever-present pipe, Brandt changes the topic by complaining about the abominable treatment he has received from the German media. He does not seem to remember that it was the lavish praise of the liberal press, the organs of the influential intellectuals, that originally propelled the unknown antifascist into national limelight, eventually putting him on a high pedestal, together with Bismarck and Adenauer, as a national hero.

No, he remembers much more clearly the papers which tried to stop him, ruin his image, defame his party, and downgrade his government's accomplishments with their constant unjust criticism. No, and it was not only the hostile Springer press that persecuted him from the beginning, even *Spiegel* turned against him. Brandt sounds bitter and a little paranoid and a lot like Richard Nixon when he lets off steam about the mass media. The most objective reporting was done by TV, he asserts. Television and radio, of course, are public broadcasting companies in the Federal Republic. Their management is controlled to a large degree by the states and the reigning party.

Is he content with the outcome of his Ostpolitik?

Brandt tries to evade an answer. It is really too early to tell. However, he has a "friendly picture of Germany and its social renewal."

"I have never said that the way of Ostpolitik would be easy." He seems defensive. "We will be facing further hard ordeals."

Historic Mission

In his March 1975 speech before the American Council of Germany in New York, Brandt gives a thoroughly realistic resumé:

> Our so-called Ostpolitik has only disappointed those who had illusions. Who knows himself to be free of illusions might have thought possible more convincing results in one sector or the other. It is also certain that weighty improvements have been achieved. Aside from everything else: The new Ostpolitik which in reality always was a West Ostpolitik, has provided the Federal Republic with a larger freedom for action. Starting from the realities left to us by World War II, we have freed ourselves from the prison of wishful thinking and unfulfillable demands.

The policy of tension relaxation clears the way not only for West European unity but also for the overall cooperation between East and West Europe.

Conscious of his key role in this historical process, Brandt stresses how much it was promoted and helped by the détente between America and the Soviet Union.

Brandt has discharged what his friends tend to characterize as his "historical mission." It is almost impossible to imagine that any other politician or any other method than Brandt's "little steps" could have eased the German public into acceptance of the painful realities of Hitler's heritage, the losses of the Eastern provinces and the fact of two ideologically hostile, competitive Germanys instead of one *Vaterland.* Still, it would be preposterous to assume that Brandt, the statesman, determined the course of Ostpolitik unaided. The process of détente with Moscow was started by Charles de Gaulle and adopted by the astute Kennedy. Once the historical forces that made détente the irreversible alternative to nuclear war were set in motion, the global actors who affected it became virtually interchangeable regardless of the unforgotten contributions of Richard Nixon or Willy Brandt, who unsentimentally sacrificed Adenauer's cherished but unattainable German reunification for the prospect of a future unification.

Betting on the imperative of interdependence, Brandt remains an incurable optimist.

Once the mission was accomplished—without the formal consent of the Christian Democrats, who on the whole decided to abstain from voting on Brandt's East treaties which they nevertheless vowed to respect—a spy from East Germany was discovered in the chancellor's office. Whether the timing was significant—in France the crucial race between Socialist Mitterand and Giscard d'Estaing was in its last stretch—or not, and what would have happened had Günter Guillaume been discovered at a different time, sooner or later, are questions to be answered at some future time when the secret records are made public. If there is reason to believe, as the *Washington Post*'s Kremlinologist Victor Zorza does, that "Guillaume was controlled by the KGB's spy masters in Moscow and not by the smaller fry in East Berlin" the extraordinary spy affair may well remain a closed case.

As fulltime chairman of Europe's largest party, Brandt wants it understood that he intends to be more than an ornamental figurehead, he still could wield considerable influence as a go-between for the capitalistic and socialistic parts of the world. The crafty, seasoned, unsinkable politician has proven keenly attuned to the rapid political shifts and changes of our time. During the last four decades of his stormy career he has relied heavily on his well-developed political sensibilities, his antennae for future straws in the wind. As a politician who travels freely between the superpower capitals, lecturing students in Nashville, Tennessee, listening to President Gerald Ford one week and visiting with Brezhnev and young Soviet workers in a factory outside Moscow the next, Brandt, who understands the art of survival on a personal and collective level, may have a very specific role to play.

"My problem in life often has been that I understood both sides too well. That I was able to sympathize with the pros and cons. I have repeatedly been caught up in situations where I was for and against a cause or a program at the same time. It's caused me much trouble," he philosophizes during our visit in Washington.

Precisely, it would seem, the objectivity which paralyzed his decision-making capabilities while he was chancellor. But precisely the impartiality that would be the foremost prerequisite of a persuasive mediator.

As Henry Kissinger's celebrated nineteenth-century balance of military power concept ran aground on the way to Vietnam, Cyprus and Chile, as well as in the Middle East, in Portugal and in the oil fields of Arabia, the idea of global economic and social interdependence deserves undivided attention. To be sure, the Kremlin-inspired conference on European Security and Cooperation, much pushed by Brandt and distrusted by Kissinger, could hardly be termed a rousing success. A similar gathering, designed to establish a collective security system, was promoted by Khrushchev since July 1955 "as the only way to unite Germany." The resulting Helsinki summit of July 1975 and its ambiguous declaration have been deplored by its critics, among them the *New York Times*, as a "regrettable unilateral gain for the Soviet Union without any corresponding advantage for the United States," because of its tacit affirmation of Moscow's hegemony in the Socialist bloc which, in the eyes of the Soviet Union, qualifies as a surrogate peace treaty.

Yet the thirty-five-nation conference served as an impetus for the beginning of a period of adjustment between East and West that might well present itself as the only genuine alternative for survival in the finite, physical life-sustaining world of tomorrow.

Brandt's optimism does not just pertain to Ostpolitik but to social and economic changes in modern society as well. Reforms are a risky business in tradition-bound Germany, where the explosive tempers of pragmatists and theoreticians readily prepare the ground for first-rate polarizations.

It remains to be seen if the party chairman will be able—as he thinks he was in the spring of 1975—to mediate a reconciliation between the Jusos and the party membership. Only if the SPD succeeds in integrating its radical fringe can it concentrate its energies on exploration of its vital goal to find out whether the synthesis of freedom and socialism into democratic socialism is indeed a workable proposition or a political mirage. History has no reassuring examples to date. The freedom of the individual is dependent on the social order of society. Political scientists argue that reconciliation of freedom and socialism inevitably changes society and, therefore, the properties of individual freedom.

Still, the SPD's experiment merits careful observation. In view of the fact that neither capitalism nor communism exists in its pure form anywhere in this world, the test tube policy-mix could be just the shot in the arm the weary old Western democracies need in their search for a viable compromise solution for survival. What we need least, of course, is a liberal centralized authoritarianism that resembles the Kremlin's hierarchial public administration.

"We are convinced that democratic socialism is strong enough to throw back the reactionary forces of the capitalistic world, to inhibit a new rise of fascistic forces and to unite all those who want to overcome communism and find the way to a social democratic order for the world. Social democracy or technocratic totalitarianism, these are the alternatives of our time." (From the official SPD declaration framed as an explanation of the principles of Godesberg.)

Brandt who had expressed grave doubts about the future of the parliamentary system, has hardly been a creative politician. Neither the Godesberg Program nor the Grand Coalition was his idea. His Ostpolitik has no claim to originality.

However, when an idea needs dissemination, when a cause needs proselytizing, then Willy Brandt takes first place as public interpreter and spokesman. This is his gift, his ingenious, unmatched contribution to German politics and international relations. This is the actual thread that gives continuity to his eventful, inconsistent political life as a dyed-in-the-wool Socialist whose narrow functionary's understanding has widened and expanded over the decades into the evolutionary visions of a devoted pragmatist.

"The balance of terror must not calm us down. We need additional security. We need the logical results from the recognition that world peace has become a condition of life in our technological age," Brandt stated at the Storkyrkan in Stockholm in December 1971 as the proud recipient of the Nobel Peace Prize.

At sixty-two, Brandt is still an attractive public figure. Heavier than ever due, he admits, to more red wine and more time spent behind a desk, he entices capacity crowds to listen to him at Washington's National Press Club and bedazzles even the more cynical journalists with his aging film star's charm and boyishness. Although he exudes merely low voltage sparks now, much of his charisma has remained intact. The prickly aggressiveness and strident urgency have been insulated by generous layers of warmth and mellowness.

What was bound to happen to Kennedy, and to Nixon especially, is also Brandt's happy lot: Their stars have not tarnished as rapidly abroad as they have dimmed to the more scrutinizing eyes at home. Brandt will probably be able to draw new strength from the reservoir of goodwill and credit he has been able to build up abroad for as long as he is in need of it.

"Do you love power?" I asked him a few years ago over a cognac.

"Not anymore. Not since I was so sick a couple of years ago that I thought I would die. Since then I have a new perspective. Now I only love life."

All things considered, perhaps the best qualification for any politician.

Bibliography

Adenauer, Konrad. *Erinnerungen I-IV.* Stuttgart: 1965–68.

Adenauer, *Studien.* Edited by Rudolf Morsey and Konrad Repgen, Band III. *Untersuchungen und Dokumente zur Ostpolitik und Biographie,* Mainz: 1974.

Apel, Hans. *Bonn, den . . . Tagebuch eines Bundestagsabgeordneten.* Cologne: 1972.

Appel, Reinhard. *gefragt: Herbert Wehner.* Bonn: 1966.

Bergmann, Uwe; Dutschke Rudi; Lefevre Wolfgang; Rabehl, Bernd. *Rebellion der Studenten oder Die neue Opposition.* Hamburg: 1968.

Bericht der Kommission "Vorbeugender Geheimschutz" über die Prüfung von Sicherheitsfragen im Zusammenhang mit dem Fall Guillaume. Bonn: November 1974.

Berkandt, Jan Peter. *Willy Brandt.* Hanover: 1961.

Bolesch, Otto; Leicht, Hans Dieter. *Der lange Marsch des Willy Brandt.* Tübingen/Basel: 1970.

Brandt, Willy. *Ein Jahr Krieg und Revolution in Spanien.* Amsterdam: 1937.

———. *Forbrytere og andre tyksere.* Oslo: 1946.

———. *Weitergeführte Demokratie. Der Monat,* February 1949.

———. *My Road to Berlin;* as told to Leo Lania. London: 1960.

———. *Begegnungen mit Kennedy.* Munich: 1974.

———. *Draussen.* Edited by Günter Struve. Munich: 1966. (*In Exile*. London: 1971)

———. *Reden und Interviews 1968–1969.* Bonn: 1970.

———. *A Peace Policy for Europe.* New York: 1969.

———. *Reden und Interviews.* Foreword by Rüdiger von Wechmar. Hamburg: 1973.

———. *Der Wille zum Frieden.* Foreword by Golo Mann. Hamburg: 1972.
———. *Über den Tag hinaus.* Hamburg: 1974.
CSU—Landesleitung. *Rotbuch.* Munich: 1973.
Dollinger, Hans. *Willy! Willy!* Munich: 1970.
Dornberg, J. *Deutschlands andere Hälfte, Profil und Charakter der DDR.* Munich: 1970.
Drath, Viola Herms. "Two Germans," *Commentary.* New York: June 1969.——— *Was wollen die Deutschen?* New York: 1970.
Dulles, Eleanor Lansing. *Berlin: The Wall is Not Forever,* Chapel Hill: 1967.
Fest, Joachim. *Hitler.* New York: 1974.
Frederik, Hans. *gezeichnet vom zwielicht seiner zeit.* Munich: 1969.
Gaus, Günter. *Zur Person: Willy Brandt.* Bonn: 1964. *Zur Person: Helmut Schmidt.* Bonn: 1966.
Hacke, Christian. *Aussenpolitik und Oppositionspartei, Eine Analyse der Strategie und Zielsetzung der Parlamentarischen Opposition des 6. Bundestages im Bereich der Ost-und Deutschlandpolitik.* Inaugural-Dissertation, Clausenhof: 1974.
Harpprecht, Klaus. *Willy Brandt. Porträt und Selbstporträt.* Munich: 1970.
Ihlefeld, Heli. *Anekdoten um Willy Brandt.* Munich: 1968.
Kahn, Helmut Wolfgang. *Helmut Schmidt—Fallstudie über einen Populären.* Hamburg: 1973.
Kennan, George F. *Realities of American Foreign Policy.* London: 1954.
Kiep, Walther Leisler. *Good Bye Amerika—Was dann?* Stuttgart: 1972.
Kleist, Peter. *Wer ist Willy Brandt? Eine Antwort in Selbstbezeugnissen.* Rosenheim: 1973.
Krag, Jens Otto. *Dagbog.* Denmark: 1973.
Kreisky, Bruno. *Aspekte des demokratischen Sozialismus.* Munich: 1974.
Kirkpatrick, Evron M. *Target: the World, Communist Propaganda Activities in 1955.* New York: 1956.
Kürschners Volkshandbuch. *Deutscher Bundestag.* Bad Honnef/Darmstadt: 1954–74.
Lendvai, Paul; Ritschel, Karl Heinz. *Kreisky.* Vienna: 1972.
Lippmann, Heinz. *Honecker.* New York: 1972.
Ludz, Peter Christian. *The German Democratic Republic from the Sixties to the Seventies.* Harvard: 1970.
Mander, John. *Berlin Hostage for the West.* Baltimore: 1962.
Mee, Charles L., *Meeting at Potsdam,* New York: 1975.
Mewis, Karl. *Im Auftrag der Partei.* East Berlin: 1971.
Mortensen, Claire (Susanne Sievers). *. . . da war auch ein Mädchen.* Munich-Inning: 1961.
Prittie, Terence. *Willy Brandt.* Frankfurt: 1973.
Rowse, A. L. *All Souls and Appeasement.* London: 1961.
Schiller, Karl. *Berliner Wirtschaft und deutsche Politik.* Stuttgart: 1964.
Schmidt, Helmut. *Strategie des Gleichgewichts.* Stuttgart: 1970.
Schoenbaum, David. *The Spiegel Affair.* New York: 1968.
Sorensen, Theodore C. *Kennedy.* New York: 1965.

SPD; *Handbuch sozialdemokratischer Politik,* Bonn: 1953.
———*Die Alternativen unserer Zeit,* Bonn: 1960.
Strauss, Franz Josef. *Herausforderung und Antwort.* Stuttgart: 1968.
verlag politisches archiv; *Guillaume . . . der Spion.* Landshut: 1974.
Windelen, Heinrich. *SOS für Europa.* Stuttgart: 1972.

Index